Argumentation and the
Social Grounds of Knowledge

Argumentation

AND THE

Social Grounds of Knowledge

Charles Arthur Willard

The University of Alabama Press

Permission to quote copyrighted material is
gratefully acknowledged as follows:
Lines from "The Red Wheelbarrow" from *Collected
Earlier Poems of William Carlos Williams*. Copyright
© 1938 by New Directions Publishing Corporation.
Reprinted by permission of New Directions.
Lines from "The Man With the Blue Guitar" by
Wallace Stevens, from *The Collected Poems of Wallace
Stevens*. Copyright © 1954 by Alfred A. Knopf.

Library of Congress Cataloging in Publication Data

Willard, Charles Arthur.
Argumentation and the social grounds of knowledge.

  Bibliography: p.
Includes index.
1. Reasoning—Addresses, essays, lectures.
2. Knowledge, Theory of—Addresses, essays, lectures.
3. Knowledge, Sociology of—Addresses, essays, lectures.
I. Title.
BC177.W54   121'.3   81-16199
ISBN 0-8173-0096-1   AACR2

To Joseph W. Wenzel

Contents

Preface

The ideas in this book have been stewing and simmering for many years. Embryonic and piecemeal versions of some of them have appeared in essays and convention papers, and I have greatly benefited from the replies and critiques they stimulated. Essays by Brant Burleson, Bill Balthrop, J. Robert Cox, Thomas Farrell, G. Thomas Goodnight, Bruce Gronbeck, Dale Hample, Charles Kneupper, Ray McKerrow, Daniel O'Keefe, Richard Parker, Robert Rowland, Malcolm Sillars, Joseph Wenzel, and David Zarefsky have helped me sharpen my thinking and clarify my aims. I owe them a great debt.

I argue here that arguments are social comparison processes which undergird knowledge—a claim which is certainly a correct description of the development of my own thinking. I have benefited in estimable ways from ongoing dialogue with Barbara O'Keefe, Daniel O'Keefe, Joseph Wenzel, Sally Jackson, Scott Jacobs, and Thomas Goodnight. They have profoundly affected me in the course of countless arguments and chitchats. Our relationship has been, if not a movable feast, a movable argument. Their voices continually intermingle with my own in this book (for instance, most of the objections I pause to consider along the way are theirs). While they will doubtless object to many of my conclusions (and certainly should not be blamed for them), they are in many ways responsible for much of what is good in my arguments.

Several people have given freely of their time and efforts to help me improve these essays. Daniel O'Keefe, who is gradually teaching me to write, has helped me on many projects, and his assistance with this work is greatly appreciated. I have benefited as well from helpful criticisms from Joseph Wenzel, Trevor Melia, E. Culpepper Clark, Sally Jackson, Scott Jacobs, and J. Robert Cox. I also owe a considerable debt to Marcia Brubeck of the Guilford Group for her editing and to my wife, Amy R. Willard, for her important contributions to the editing, typing, and preparation of the manuscript.

Perhaps the greatest respect one pays a scholar is to be preoccupied with his work. If this is true, I owe a substantial and still accumulating debt to Stephen Toulmin. Though I have diverged from his thinking and objected to his agenda, my thinking has in most cases spun off from his. His work caused me to rethink the importance and bases of argumentation and to consider whether it might yield insights into epistemic questions. In deliberating the strengths of his arguments, I found that they illuminated the breadth and complexity of the problems I set for myself. Toulmin's writings, in sum, proved to be sure and dependable markers for the row one has to hoe in considering the place of argument in a sociology of knowledge.

Finally, I thank David Thomas, editor of the *Journal of the American Forensic Association,* for giving me permission to use certain fragments of essays I have published in that journal. In a few cases, I have used these fragments intact; in other cases, I have changed their content to accommodate to criticisms. I have also used many arguments from my essay "Some Questions about Toulmin's View of Argument Fields" (1980a) in the third chapter of this book. While the thrust of my criticisms is retained here, many particular arguments have undergone refinement, new ones have been added, and some have been either deleted or changed so substantially that they bear only a rough resemblance to their earlier drafts.

Perhaps the worst fate this book could suffer would be to be thought of as a "system" or a fully accomplished point of view. Judged by that standard, it is wholly unworthy. Our predecessors often saw themselves designing grand systems, fully self-contained and capable of "plodding through time intact" (I have forgotten whose phrase that is). My intentions here are entirely different. My aim is to present a sustained argument favoring a particular line of thinking, analysis, and research. My assumption is that this project has attractive prospects. I do not believe (for instance) that in arguing that knowledge is balkanized into argument fields I am describing once and for all what knowledge *is*. Knowledge *is* anything we are capable of making of it; and only shortsightedness could permit us the comfortable conceit that we now have all of our options in view. Thus the field theory on which most of my arguments are based is nothing more than a checkpoint along a road whose end we cannot see. I advance this field theory in the spirit of making empirical claims about our present epistemic situation and in the belief that careful field studies may yield insights that will eventually relegate the field theory to the past. Field theory— as I understand it—describes an imperfection in our social arrangements. It is a fault we must either learn to live with or find ways of transcending. The way we now live with this balkanization of knowledge is through argument, and it is entirely possible that argumentation can devise the resources for transcending field divisions as well. The only thing I am sure of is that most argumentation theorists are embarked upon projects which will prove unsatisfactory in solving the problems field theory exposes. These theorists see themselves as trying to improve upon the projects established by their predecessors. So proceeding, they will leave an unnecessarily modest legacy to their successors. While the present project may turn out just as badly, I see nothing wrong with proceeding as if the idea of argument as a process of social interaction is a seminal one—a useful way of construing our present situation as well as a promising way of assessing our prospects for the future.

University of Pittsburgh
Pittsburgh, Pennsylvania   CHARLES ARTHUR WILLARD
November 1981

Argumentation and the
Social Grounds of Knowledge

Introduction

> And new philosophy calls all in doubt,
> The element of fire is quite put out;
> The sun is lost, and th'earth, and no
>   mans wit
> Can well direct him where to looke for it.
> ....
> 'Tis all in peeces, all cohaerence gone;
> All just supply, and all relation.
> —John Donne, "An Anatomie of the
> World: The First Anniversary"

So Donne greeted the Copernican world view. The tenor of his argument is a familiar one. We have Yeats's lament that "things fall apart, the center does not hold" and Holmes's affectionate nod to Watson as "a fixed point in a changing universe." Such sentiments are common enough in Western thought to constitute a genuine "fixed point" themselves. The fixed point is the belief that relativisms are pernicious doctrines with unbearable consequences. Relativisms paint a desolate landscape of chaos, opacity, and irrationality that belittles human accomplishments and mocks the ambition to say clear and determinate things about ourselves and our world. Relativisms *must* not be true.

There are (roughly) two broad stances toward this fixed point. There are the ists and isms saying that relativity is a formidable problem only because humans have not yet *discovered* the order of things; and there are the ists and isms saying that we have not yet *contrived* a successful universal system. The first view assumes that a search for universals is a grand ontological program and that a universal once gotten is immutable and axiomatic. The second either brackets ontology or rejects it for the more modest aim of studying man-made systems—these systems being temporary approximations, working hypotheses which are continually subject to revision. The first view assumes that relativity is only an appearance and (thus) that relativism cannot be sustained; the second assumes that relativity is true but that relativism is not its inevitable outcome.

Both lines of thinking arose coincidentally with the demise of absolutism. Since Aristotle, absolutists had abstracted selected aspects of science as guarantors of knowledge; these successive candidates were undone either by skeptical challenges or by developments within science. Euclidean niceties gave way to projective geometries; Newtonian space and time, which had muzzled the skeptics for a time, surrendered to the Copenhagen Interpretation, Heisenberg's Indeterminacy Principle, Bohr's Principle of Complementarity, and the Second Law of Thermodynamics—all of which serve to question our ability to know and predict physical processes. Mathematics, which since the time of the Pythagoreans had been the rationalist's paradigm case of certainty, surrendered its claims to certainty to Gödel's Incompleteness Theorem; and reductionist views of language such as the picture theory in Wittgenstein's *Tractatus* withered in the face of the attacks in Wittgenstein's *Investigations*.

Both versions of the fixed point concede that the case for relativity is very powerful; the first stance regards relativity as a temporary setback that will eventually be subsumed by a sufficiently elaborate system; the second stance regards the case for relativity as being virtually conclusive. Thus while both stances see themselves as doing battle with a formidable opponent, they confront two different opponents. The ontologists do battle with relativity, while proponents of the second view accept relativity and do battle with relativism.

Both stances share an abiding concern for justificationism. Weimer (1979) suggests that despite vast differences, the different ists and isms are all variations of one and the same metatheory: "The traditional distinctions between philosophies are largely epiphenomenal; they are surface level differences between essentially similar positions that share a common deep conceptual structure" (1979, p. 2). They are all different postures toward *justification*. The "neojustificationist" (Weimer, 1979) view does not depend on ontology, but the strategic aims are the same—avoid relativism by creating universal guarantors of knowledge such as impartial standpoints of rationality (Toulmin, 1964, 1972) or ideal speech situations (Habermas, 1970a, 1970b, 1973, 1975, 1979). The difference between such neojustificationist views and ontological schemes is exemplified in Toulmin's (1964) criticisms of the preoccupation with *validity* and the cult of the system. The deeper unity between the two stances is that they share a focus on justification—the first being concerned with validity and certainty, the second being preoccupied with "warranted" beliefs. In this respect both stances present a united front to relativism.

A peculiar circularity arises. Relativism has disastrous consequences because it destroys the grounds of justification; but the raison d'être of justification is to avoid the consequences of relativism. Just as it makes no sense to raise an army unless one has an enemy, so absolutism, probabilism, or any form of justificationism make no sense unless the evils of relativism are taken for granted. Relativism is thus a precondition of justificationism. But this fact *justifies* relativism in two respects, namely, logically, as the precondition of justification, and psychologically, as a set of implications that can turn out to contain the seeds of their own destruction. Relativism and justification, then, are different pieces of the same pie. Just as every justificational scheme courts infinite regress and contradiction, so—as Pascal said—no one can be a skeptic all the time: the act of arguing for relativism contradicts relativism; were one thoroughly skeptical and exhaustively a relativist, one could not live.

As things stand now, the relativists are winning—and not for a good reason. Skepticism has always been parasitic to the systems it questions (that is, it uses the implications and procedures of the systems and takes its force from the strength of the claims made on behalf of the systems). It is thus a peculiar strength of the relativist's position that logic can be used as a weapon while it is held in disdain. Regress and contradiction arguments draw blood from those who believe in them. The relativist thus comes equipped with a weapon that cannot be turned upon him.

The fixed point and its enemy have been at loggerheads since Plato assaulted the Sophists. Our intellectual history has been a succession of knowledge claims beset by skeptical and relativistic attacks. While contemporary arguments are more complex than their predecessors, they seem to be just as inconclusive. Nowadays it is not as if men propose theories and Nature shouts *no* (Lakatos, 1968); rather, men propose guarantors of knowledge, and skeptics shout, "there are critical exceptions," "it needs terms from without," or "infinite regress!" The relativists are winning, in sum, because they have fought the justificationists to a standstill. The dispute between them is itself a fixed point.

A Reformulation of the Problem

In these investigations I want to chase a grandiose thesis with modest weapons. The thesis is that the disputes between justificationists and relativists have been conducted on unproductive grounds, namely, the assumption that there is a clear, knowable difference between "genuine" and "conventional" knowledge and that this difference stems from the equally clear difference between ontology and sociology. It is possible to opt out of such grand disputes without despairing of finding guarantors of knowledge. That is, the search for dependable guarantors can proceed by setting aside ontological schemes and justificationism, aiming instead at an empirically accurate sociology of knowledge.

Viewed one way, this thesis is innocuous and uninteresting: it is a plea for descriptive work aimed at understanding social consensus—something which, as far as I know, no one would object to. Viewed another way, the thesis is an immodest promissary note: it invites us to consider whether a sociology of knowledge might contain resources for defining epistemic guarantors which cross particular social boundaries. From a justificationist point of view, this immodest promise cannot be redeemed; but this is not necessarily a weakness if the justificationist perspective proves to be seriously deficient.

I want to play the hunch that justification and relativity are not best seen as the regnant constructs they have been historically. They are at most middle-level theoretical terms subsumed (given meaning) by higher-order constructs which describe more fundamental matters. The highest-order construct for epistemic purposes is "communication," and its immediate subordinate notion is "perspectivity." These ideas, I shall urge, give meaning to certain sociological terms—in particular the terms associated with "communities of discourse," "groups," or—in the guise they are given here—"argument fields." Disputes between justificationists and relativists are social arguments about conflicting perspectives. The facts of communication and perspectivity give these disputes their character; and it is thus to communication and its attendant concepts that we must look to understand what it means to guarantee a knowledge claim.

In considering the nature of justification and relativity, we are inquiring into distinctively human activities, ways of proceeding in the social world. We are not examining Nature as something over and against consciousness; and we are (thus) jettisoning the assumption that a guarantor of knowledge cannot (by definition) be a product of social-psychological processes. We are assuming that, if epistemic guarantors are impersonal, they have this status because they are residua of traditions of human practices. By the old view, Russell and Whitehead doubtless thought they were storming the gates of heaven in the *Principia Mathematica*. By the present view, they were merely knocking on the door of a stuffy British club.

Appending matters of justification and relativism to the concepts of communication and perspectivity has far-reaching consequences. It requires, for instance, that the antagonistic polar opposites which fueled the traditional dispute be seen as interdependent: subjectivity is the precondition of objectivity, doubt the precondition of certainty, fixity the precondition of change, and so on. It requires that we reconsider the reasons why epistemic guarantors are thought to be impersonal and transubjective, that is, what the sociological conditions are which enforce this requirement. It implies as well that the disputes between justificationists and relativists are more interesting per se than any particular arguments they have made. The fact that people believe in and strive for certainty (by our view) is more interesting than any particular claims which have been advanced in pursuit of this aim. As a descriptive matter, we shall want to say that epistemic guarantors are social practices, the standards and procedures people use to check their thinking. For reasons that will soon be clear, I pluralize guarantors to flag the fact that there are many of them; they differ in nontrivial ways across social domains—some being flatly incommensurable, others being so ambiguously related as to defy comparison. In every case (I shall say), "knowing" is something that people do—often together. While traditional theories often focus upon the solitary thinker, I want to focus upon knowing as a process of social comparison (Festinger, 1954). The only thing wrong with the solitary thinker view is that it sometimes is taken to be an exhaustive epistemic picture. Here I shall be concerned with placing the solitary thinker in his social habitat, namely, the fields of discourse in which he moves, the people on whom he tries out his ideas through argument processes. While giving the solitary thinker his due, I shall argue that "knowledge" is most often an interpretation that is trusted because of the social comparisons that countenance it.

The thesis is an attempt to refocus the interdisciplinary enterprise of "epistemics" (Toulmin, 1972) around descriptive rather than normative aims. By "epistemics" I mean a field of study concerned with knowledge claims, judgmental and veridical standards, and their social roots. It is a sort of sociology of knowledge, although the communication and argumentation concepts I shall use are common to only a few variants of that tradition. The present view differs from many sociologies of knowledge in that it presupposes no deterministic relation between social structures or relations and individuals. It supposes instead that social domains are constituted by the defining activities of their actors, by the communication practices which define and accomplish the daily business which given groups take to be their organizing concerns. To understand the place of epistemic assumptions in such ongoing projects is to understand what situated actors take their knowledge claims to mean; and to understand what people take their epistemic claims and situations to mean is to understand the presuppositions behind these claims and situations. Thus the central activity of epistemics is "criticism"—which I understand to mean the study of the effects of presuppositions upon arguments and claims. In speaking of "argument criticism," I shall be referring to rhetorical criticism of a particular sort, namely that concerned with the social (that is to say, "rhetorical") grounds of knowledge. And by the phrase "critical epistemology" I intend to point to the unity between argument criticism and epistemics—that is to say, epistemics is best seen as a critical tradition, a body of knowledge which argument criticism is capable of producing. I do not intend the label "critical epistemology" to convey Marxist or Frankfort School ambitions. The present program does not contradict these traditions; but its aims are different enough that I prefer to insist upon a distinction. "Critical" shall mean—here at least—a particular kind of rhetorical criticism.

Even though the justificationists and relativists have fought to a standstill, epistemics does not need to sit by passively waiting for the battle to be won. Nor does it need to enter the fray. It can—as it were—abandon the contested ground and move to more peaceful surroundings. Moreover, epistemics can accomplish this freeing move without the simpleminded assumption that the grand battle will never be won. The only assumption necessary to this move is that, despite the grand stalemate, there is still fertile ground to be plowed.

Let us proceed with a worst case scenario. Let us assume that an extreme relativistic thesis is correct. There are no successful universals to vouch for our knowledge claims and no ideal entities to authorize our moral judgments. Only man-made orders guarantee knowledge and justify our values; and these communities of discourse are themselves rooted in faith and irrational commitment. The conventions and orthodoxies which bind these communities together are the verities we shall have to respect. Since different communities hold manifestly different beliefs and values (and confront the phenomena which concern them with markedly different epistemic and moral stances), the belief that any particular community's beliefs and procedures are superior to another community's can only be an arbitrary social convention. While we are not surprised when communities which venerate their elders condemn the practices of communities which allow the elderly to die, we are no less surprised to discover that the former cannot justify condemning the latter except by virtue of arguments special to the former's field of discourse. While we intuitively believe that Nazi genocide was evil incarnate, we cannot prove it by any of the means traditionally thought to guarantee our knowledge and rationality. While we somehow believe that evil on the Nazi scale ought to be answered by the cosmos itself, not by mere human voices, we have no apparatus to vouch for this belief. "Legitimation" has replaced "justification"; and in the absence of convincing arguments (arguments, that is, which meet our own veridical standards), we have to say that Hitler was legitimized by the Germans and answered by some societies which disagreed with him.

Provisionally granting this worst case scenario, we nonetheless want to ask how man knows and evaluates. We want to confront the obvious fact that people, in the course of their routine activities, make the worst case scenario pragmatically untrue (or, at least, they so relegate it to the background that it becomes a paradigm case of an academic question). Except for a few existentialists, most people do not wallow in angst (at least not in public or in the daylight hours). Quite the contrary: they arrange their social lives, veridical procedures, and political institutions in ways that seem appropriate to the problems that confront them. They muddle through. They often stop to consider whether their knowledge is trustworthy; they temporize their way across events (Kelly, 1955), sometimes knowing full well that their concepts are merely provisional guesses. Other times, of course, people proceed blindly, trusting to a naive faith in their concepts because (presumably) too much doubt is not to be borne.

Traditionally, the standard epistemological question has been, "how is it that man knows that he knows?" This has obscured an equally important question, namely, "how is it that man *doubts* that he knows, and what are the consequences of such doubt?" Our provisional acceptance of the worst case scenario permits the inference that a sociology of knowledge is a necessary precondition of successfully answering these questions. It implies that the social practices of actors in different domains of discourse are interesting in themselves. If we take them on their own terms, we may define many epistemic issues in interesting new ways. The possibility of such new definitions challenges the old view that social practices are mere happenstances, desiderata, layers of misconception waiting to be peeled away to discover the verities. Many ists and isms reflect this denigration of the social— perhaps Russell's theory of descriptions and Ryle's view of the aims of analysis are exemplars. But reductionism is not a precondition of denigrating the social: most justificationists hew to some version of it—witness the ongoing dispute within the philosophy of science between the "sociologists" and the "rationalists" (Laudan, 1977).

Epistemics does not have to be a "justificationist" enterprise in order for us to study the justificational practices of particular communities of discourse. In their daily practices, people proceed on assumptions that seem remarkably similar to the assumptions of formal epistemology. They aim to objectify their thinking by checking it against trusted communal standards. They weigh the value and dependability of judgmental and veridical standards; they trust different standards to different degrees and for different reasons; they act conventionally, in orthodox ways, not because they are mindless sheep, but because more often than not it is the sensible thing to do. They trust authorities and make arguments-from-authority—again, not because they are mindless followers or true believers (though they sometimes are), but because trusting authorities is oftentimes the surest and least doubtful way to deal with decisions. Reflectively and in the natural attitude (Schutz, 1962), they do the work justificationists have traditionally done.

I want to discard the pointless dichotomy between social practices and formal epistemology and to jettison the a priori assumption that social practices are inferior. Plato's influence has been strong: situated actors are thought to grapple with shadows, while academics deal with the verities. The result of this dichotomy is that social practices do not get carefully studied (for epistemic purposes). Social practices are sometimes dragged into philosophic disputes by the heels to support or refute grand theories; but rarely are they thought to be philosophically important in themselves. For reasons that will soon be clear, this prejudice distorts our thinking about social life. It justifies pointless (and unprovable) claims of the sort "the fact that belief X is sociologically legitimate has no bearing upon whether belief X is justified." Our worst case scenario forces us to start with the admission that we cannot presently prove such a claim in any way that is pragmatically useful.

It will do no harm if we turn out to be mistaken. If someone eventually defeats the *tu quoque*,[1] avoids infinite regress, solves the problem of induction, or produces a noncircular universal standard of knowledge, rationality, or value, the empirical work necessary for dealing with the implications of such successes will have been done. Our empirical program might countenance the sorts of contrasts between social practices and "genuine" worthiness that have hitherto been taken for granted.

It might be objected that a worst case scenario that does no harm if it turns out to be mistaken is (in effect) innocuous. Thus, the objection might run, all the worst case scenario yields is a justification of the sociology of knowledge—a task Mannheim's successors long ago completed. While we must acknowledge that this objection might turn out to be true, it is not a prima facie objection to the present scenario. Our scenario leaves no room for the comfortable ambiguity sociologists of knowledge have usually tolerated respecting the relationship of a sociology of knowledge and formal epistemology. The conventional wisdom has been that sociology and formal epistemology differ in kind and (thus) need not account to one another. Sociologists felt no obligation to refute universalist's views of justification and epistemics because they so defined their subject matter that justification, truth tests, and the general concerns of logic were matters to be left to the philosophers. The worst case scenario, as conceived here, does not allow this comfortable division. It proposes the possibility that a sociology of knowledge may turn out to be the whole epistemic story. At bare minimum it requires a reconsideration of the breadth and scope of the claims sociologists of knowledge must make.

The present scenario enforces these requirements because it aims to do justice to the two broad constructs to which (as I have said) any theory of knowledge must accommodate: communication and perspectivity. The assumption is that the communicational arrangements and practices which hold discourse communities together are the central processes by which men come to believe that they know or come to doubt that they know. The "facts of communication" are thus the raw materials out of which epistemic generalizations must be fashioned. This—I claim—is a nontrivial starting point even if universal projects eventually succeed. It suggests, at the outset at least, that the focal concern of epistemics must be with the ordinary practices by which situated actors pass judgment on knowledge claims. The preliminary assumption is that knowing is a process of symbolic interaction, social comparison, trying ideas on for size. Knowing is thus a communication process bound up with a pragmatic need to ameliorate doubt and to overcome relativity. Relativity, let us say, is the organizing problematic of daily life in three distinguishable but related senses.

The most obvious kind of relativity inheres in subjectivity, the knower's boundedness to a subjective and idiosyncratic horizon and field of attention. The doctrine which takes this boundedness to be the final arbiter of knowledge is "subjectivism," the most extreme versions of which make perspectivity a unidimensional concept—rather as if we use Mead's "I" without the "Me." There is a parallel between the arguments of philosophers against subjectivism and the ordinary practices of situated actors. For instance, most people most of the time prefer to avoid subjectivism (Outhwaite, 1975). They coorient themselves to other people in order to transcend their doubts about their idiosyncratic interpretations (Bannister and Fransella, 1971; Cicourel,

1970, 1974; Douglas, 1970a; Delia and O'Keefe, 1979; Farrell, 1976; Friedrichs, 1970). They check their thinking against communal standards (Willard, 1979a).

The second—more complex—sense of relativity inheres in differences between the ways aggregations of people pass muster on knowledge. This is a more elaborate sense of relativity than the broad (and proportionately crude) notion of "sociocultural relativity" that unraveled the absolutist's systems. Differences between cultures are less important for epistemic purposes than are differences within societies and cultures. Every society is balkanized into "communities of discourse" (McKerrow, 1980a, 1980b), "rhetorical communities" (Farrell, 1976), "domains of objectivity" (Foucalt, 1972), "social relationships" (G. J. McCall et al., 1970), "speech communities" (Hymes, 1972), "disciplines or rational enterprises" (Toulmin, 1972), "social frameworks" (Goffman, 1963, 1967, 1969, 1971, 1974), and—to use traditional sociological labels—"organizations," "reference groups," "collective mentalities," and "shared frameworks of assumptions" (Filmer et al., 1973; Turner, 1974). These rubrics draw distinctions that cut rather differently, focus upon different phenomena, and propose different particulars as defining characteristics of social divisions. They reflect in different ways concepts drawn from the sociology of knowledge, social psychology, rhetoric and communication, sociolinguistics and ethnography, and ordinary language philosophy. They prove that one can draw distinctions among human activities for many different purposes. In this respect, they embody Kelly's (1955) principle of constructive alternativism, namely, that all phenomena are capable of being alternatively construed. While this sort of relativity is important, we require a way of distinguishing among human activities that does justice to epistemic relativity and minimal violence to the best features of the other distinctions.

A reformed version of Toulmin's (1958) notion of argument fields may prove equal to this task.[2] It may do justice to the distinctions drawn by the other rubrics while explaining substantive and procedural differences in the ways social aggregations pass muster on knowledge. Most of these rubrics deal with a sociological dimension. Let us stipulate that argument fields are real social entities, thus making the notion overarch the more familiar terms such as "group," "organization," "social framework," "social relationship," and the like. In speaking of argument fields, then, we refer to real gatherings of flesh-and-blood people engaged in situated activity.[3]

Think of a field as a constellation of practices organized around one or a few dominant assumptions. If we discern enough recurring themes in a group of social practices to permit the inference that they constitute a tradition of activity, we have a field. Some such distinctions will prove more straightforward than others: we may proceed with ease vis-à-vis atomic physics, microbiology, and structural engineering but may encounter considerable complexities in defining more diffuse and ordinary communal organizations, for example, the "proabortion movement" versus "liberal Democrats." I hope to prove, however, that by succeeding with the more difficult distinctions we shall have gone far toward explaining epistemic relativity in a precise way. We shall say that the most fundamental sense of relativity inheres in differences among human practices; incommensurable standards of judgment and verification will be our paradigm case. This statement yields a relativistic thesis of a particularly blunt and combative sort: fields disagree in nontrivial ways about nontrivial things; fields are in some respects autonomous epistemic enterprises; this means (1) we do not possess theoretic resources for distinguishing convention and orthodoxy from "genuine" worthiness, and (2) cases of interfield disputes are insoluble, that is, we cannot say that field X's judgmental and veridical standards are in any sense superior to field Y's unless "field theory" yields plausible judgmental principles.

I propose to prove that this thesis is a powerful one, that it poses problems for justificationist schemes and any variants of criticism that defend evaluation. I aim to do so by showing that field theory describes relationships between ideas and activities that cannot be ignored or trivialized in accounts of knowledge and knowing. If this notion proves plausible, I shall conclude that the relativity depicted by field theory cannot be "solved"—in any number of senses—by traditional justificationist schemes. In particular, it is pointless to try to subsume interfield differences with some overarching, regnant, universal standard that succeeds in ways acceptable to all fields in resolving differences. I take just this goal to be characteristic of most ists and isms in contemporary epistemics. My claim is that this goal cannot be unmuddled unless field theory is trivialized; given the case for field theory, this is an unlikely result. My intention is to replace such traditional solutions with ways of thinking about interfield differences drawn from traditional communication theory.

The third sense of relativity requires mention here because a failure to distinguish it from the other senses often yields confusion. I refer to the differences in situations embodied in the "situationalist" doctrine. This line of thinking derives one of its strong relativistic theses by stipulating that all situations "possess" obdurate characteristics apart from the psychological perspectives of the actors "in" them; they are, as it were, canisters or preexisting shapes into which actors fit themselves and their developing lines of action. Objections to this thesis are raised along similar lines, that is, there are commonalities across situations that vitiate the relativistic thesis—these commonalities being properties of the situation, not the perspectives of the actors.

Quite apart from the difficulties of proving that situations possess characteristics independent of the perspectives of their actors is the seemingly insoluble problem of making the relativistic or absolutist interpretations of situationalism coherent. Kelly (1955) argues that "experience" consists of the sense a person makes of events, the recurring themes he derives from them. The relativist side of situationalism either has to say that there are *no* recurring themes across situations or that there are some; the former option is counterintuitive, and the latter requires that the actors' perspectives be considered. Similarly, the absolutist may either claim that actors' perspectives are utterly irrelevant or that they fit in some nontrivial way into a situation's characteristics; the former is counterintuitive and the latter muddles the main advantages of being an absolutist. The dispute is more trouble than it is worth, since in both cases, the disputants collapse in the face of arguments to some variant of what should be the starting point of the study of situations, namely, the definition of the situation (Ball, 1972; Znaniecki, 1955; Willard, 1978a; Schwartz and Jacobs, 1979; McHugh, 1968; Gusdorf, 1965).

Taking the definition of the situation to be a seminal concept, we may say that situational relativity is a particular kind of subjectivity—the first sort of relativity discussed above. Situational definitions are thus the starting points for analysts who wish to attribute meaning to situated utterance. Field theory buttresses such programs by explaining the genesis of definitions. Subjectivism and situationalism are problems, obstacles to proceeding confidently for ordinary folk and philosophers alike; fields are reference points, communal traditions which actors enter to objectify their personal interpretations and to make particular situations predictable epiphenomena of general rules. To study argument fields is thus to consider the ways situated actors wrestle with relativity and doubt, this occupation being the core subject matter of epistemics.

Argumentation as Guarantor of Knowledge

Having presented a grand thesis and a special view of the problem of relativity, I turn now to the modest program that might secure the thesis. I want to say that argument fields are bound together by their members' communication practices—especially *argument*. Actors objectify their thinking by testing it against others' views through the most explicit public means available to them. Their arguments reveal the judgmental and veridical standards they trust—this trust stemming from, inter alia, the pragmatic results of arguments. Argument studies thus may be plausibly said to be fruitful ways of understanding the similarities and differences across the fields (Willard, 1980a, 1980b, 1981a, 1982). I shall briefly introduce the boundaries of this thinking by considering the claim that argumentation—the scholarly field devoted to the study of argument practices—might play a pivotal role in epistemics.

The Field of Argumentation

It is often said, with gloom or glee, that particular disciplines are "on the brink" or "at an abyss." Argumentation is nonetheless unique because it now stands upon several brinks and abysses. Nor do these crucibles present a united front: argument scholars are girding their collective loins to travel several divergent paths at once—some far less promising than others.

Among the most promising paths, argumentation is ready to lay claim to an especially useful conception of *rationality*. By plugging communication concepts into an account of reason and rationality, we stand to produce an empirically grounded view of rational practices and the cognitive processes that make them possible. We thereby avoid some familiar difficulties. If human nature is said to consist most basically in the communication processes by which people learn and act (if humans are said to exist by and through communication) we shall want to say that rationality is—whatever else it is—a precondition of communication. So proceeding, we need not see rationality as an incidental by-product or tautologous implication of "reasoning" processes. Nor must we locate rationality in *systems* as opposed to people; systems may symptomize rationality, but this does not entail the conclusion that rationality is a property of systems.

Rationality has been a persistent preoccupation of Western thought, although philosophers have not united around any particular sense of the term. More often than not, it has been defined by virtue of contrasts rather than by positive characteristics, for example, as contrasted with emotion or experience. Its enduring core seems to be as a name for the highest aspirations of particular philosophic systems. It most often crops up when theorists seek definitive statements about human nature. This tendency is exemplified by Aristotle's distinction between animal and human soul. While Aristotle's successors have disputed the particulars of rationality, they have shared the value judgment behind the term. Santayana would have called this judgment an *animal faith*, and I suspect that we all share it: there must be some feature of human nature and practices that is unique among the animals. Whatever this definitive characteristic is taken to be, "rationality" is usually the name given it.

But rationality has been more a piety than an accomplishment. The main uses of the word make it in every case redundant to some other term except, as a loose adjective, when it names the value placed upon the results of the other concept. If "Reason" is thought to be a faculty to be contrasted with, say, Passion and Will, "rationality" merely gives value to someone's relying on Reason. If reason is a process (as in the usual senses of "reasoning," "ratiocination," or thought), "rationality" specifies those procedures of which a particular theorist approves. One might equate rationality with certain reasoning (for example, Blanshard [1962] defines reason as a faculty and function of grasping necessary connections) or with balancing one's options (as in, say, a utilitarian calculus). In every case, "rationality" is a valuing of some other concept—the other concept being a better name for what is being said to be important. Respecting these examples, which comprise a hefty part of the concept's history, the concepts undergirding rationality proved unattractive or needlessly restrictive. The faculty view shared the fate of faculty psychology. The reasoning process view encountered difficulties in defining what could count as reasoning. The restriction of rationality to necessary reasoning, while internally lucid, ruled too many intuitively "rational" processes out of the concept, while the broad utilitarian view let virtually anything into the process. These traditional uses of rationality, then, did not use the concept in such a way that it did useful work.

More recent approaches have shared this fault as well as the additional distinction of making the rationality construct trivial and uninteresting. We have theories which equate rationality with reason giving, giving good reasons, having an ordered set of preferences, and being consistent. Rationality is in each case redundant to other terms that better describe what is being advocated; and, for reasons soon to be clear, all of these uses except the good reasons tradition trivialize the concept. The good reasons view, while nontrivial, is beset by the usual skeptical challenges and by the far deadlier implications of field theory.

I propose to discard these senses of rationality on the grounds that they are unsalvageable and counterproductive—unsalvageable because they cannot survive the combined offensive of a skeptical critique and field theory, counterproductive because they do more harm than good; we spend more energy trying to salvage them than their prospects plausibly justify. If we succeed with a universal of rationality, it will be so abstract as to be substantively trivial; it will not perform the decisive judgments we ordinarily expect of universals. I shall argue that a reformed view of the idea of "presumption" (tied to Mead's notions of reflexiveness and role taking) is a universal of rationality. It speaks not to the correctness or goodness of particulars but to the communication practices by which actors objectify their thinking. It coheres with Habermas's (1979) felicity conditions of discourse; it warrants "warranting" as a general rule, but it does not speak to the rightness of particular warrants.

This universal sense of rationality coheres with the empirical program advocated here, the study of why actors need an idea like rationality. My claim is that the various formulations of rationality are less interesting than the reasons people have had for producing them. The struggle to describe rationality has been an attempt to secure a distinctive human nature and a search for dependable standards of judgment. Faced with ambiguities and disputations, philosophers and ordinary folk alike want to say without reservations that this or that is good or true. Their key terms have been "validity," "authority," and "proof" (as contrasted with, say, convention and orthodoxy). I propose to assess the prospects for seeing these distinctions and practices as social norms. Whether or not an argument is valid is less interesting for these purposes than the reasons actors in a particular field think it valid. Particular theories of rationality are less interesting than the historical struggle itself.

We might gloss the present argument to say similar things about knowledge and moral claims. Respecting both, people act as if their thinking were guaranteed by something and differ sharply about the things needing guarantors and the things that can be guarantors. When their standards are challenged, they often act as if the facts of the world are at stake. They have their terms of art to assess or describe moral and epistemic rightness. These terms of art are sometimes treated as verities; they become part of a field's taken-for-granted, not-to-be-questioned framework.

The consequence of this situation is that sociological conventions are worthy of study in themselves. They may illuminate grander schemes, provide bases for them, or demolish them. And this is one of argumentation's brinks: we are in serious danger of becoming important; other lines of inquiry may have to take account of our work. If, for example, we find practices that do not square with grander schemes, we shall not blithely assume that the practices are at fault; our main assumption shall be that social practices cannot easily be brushed aside as happenstances or unimportant social accidents.

While this may be a pleasing pass for the field, some abysses need to be looked at. They are not trivial matters. They are capable of retrenching argumentation from its advances. Like most abysses, they are dangerous because they are tempting: they seem easier, more efficient, more consistent with traditional views.

The first abyss looms large if we stay in the normative justification business. We owe this temptation to our history: argumentation was traditionally seen as an applied logic; we let logicians hand us legitimizing concepts and defined our work as being evaluative, that is, saying how far ordinary arguments fell short of ideals. While simpleminded followership of logic is no longer accepted, it has produced a successor view that is the abyss I am concerned about. I refer to the practice of flirting with relativity as long as it serves one's purposes in attacking absolutistic claims (utilizing the full argumentative resources of a relativ*ism* while on the attack) and then, returning with the left hand what one has grasped with the right, producing some vaguely reworded version of traditional evaluative principles. This practice is remarkably common. Argumentation theorists and critics, having used field theory to reject absolutism, have retained the belief that evaluative work is justified and that interfield disputes can be *settled*. This is a relativism for absolutists: we can talk like absolutists while ignoring the burden of proof.

What sticks in the craw is that when one takes relativity seriously, one's evaluative standards are called increasingly into question. Veatch (1962) and Toulmin (1972) thus object to relativ*ism* because it makes evaluation impossible. I shall attempt to prove that they are unsuccessful with this argument; but their efforts are interesting here because, as far as I can see, they suggest that the core objection to relativisms is not that they are not true but that they get evaluative schemes into trouble. Evaluation is an implicit standard by which relativisms are judged. One can dabble in relativity as long as one does not abandon the right to make clear and determinate judgments. This fact makes relativity "true but innocuous." We take it to be true when convenient; but when it threatens our justifications for doing criticism, we holler "thief." An ontological argument is thus held hostage to social preferences and favored practices.

T. S. Eliot (1960) argued that evaluation is at best a pleasant avocation of critics, their main business being explication. The implication is that critics must earn the right to evaluate and must convincingly prove that they have done so. I shall later argue that argument critics lack the theoretic resources for discharging this burden. I will tie a reformed sense of criticism into the special sense of rationality defended here in a manner not unlike Weimer's (1979) "comprehensively critical rationalism." I proceed this way on the grounds that evalua-

tion is a central villain in Western thought: it creates insoluble problems and (despite its importance) has received little careful attention.
The necessity of evaluation has been largely taken for granted.
Toulmin exemplifies this tendency as he steers a middle course between absolutism and relativism in a search for an impartial standpoint of rationality. He makes no case for the impartial standpoint
except as a way of answering certain facistic claims. In this he resembles Veatch, who wants to refute relativisms in order to answer the
facist's claim that logic can justify horrible actions. Here, an ontological argument is held hostage to political concerns.

Argumentation and epistemics are fields whose ideas must be carefully looked after. Taking evaluation for granted is thus in principle
doubtful. It is surely plausible to proceed as if anyone's claim of a right
to evaluate others needs justifying. The "need" to evaluate denies
nothing of the relativist's claims: relativisms may have disastrous
consequences (though they need not), but the claim that these disastrous results are embodied in the self-evident values of evaluation is
nothing but a prejudice.

A consequence of taking evaluation for granted is that argument
critics believe they have no work to do if they lack evaluative standards; they see themselves doing "normative" work by virtue of a duty
to evaluate claims. They therefore wrench standards from anything
that can be made to yield them. They make their speculations about
relativity fit these preferences. After tumbling the granite fortresses of
the absolutists, argument theorists have been passively handing back
their hard-won turf by using jerry-rigged normative systems that
succumb to the same criticisms that did absolutism in. My organizing
example will be the theorists who embrace field theory but speak of
individual fields in the same terms the grand systematizers used to
talk about the universe.

To avoid misunderstanding, the present claim is intended to call
evaluation into question in two senses: (1) as the organizing model of
criticism, and (2) as the field-defining posture of argumentation. I
replace these concerns with description and explication as the pivotal
procedures of our field. In the practices of other fields, we shall doubtless find that actors proceed as if evaluation were a perfectly legitimate enterprise even when they do not regard their standards as
absolutes. My aim is not to protest but to study this approach. There is
no dodging the consequence that relativity calls evaluation into question, but field actors grapple with this problem in ways worthy of
study. The precondition of evaluating their practices would be a
critic's proof that events have been correctly explicated and that particular judgmental standards are appropriate. Field theory makes

both requirements problematic. Whether they are in principle possible depends upon empirical findings.

There is another abyss which stems from a distrust of one's own subject matter. In argumentation this takes two forms: one tries to look as much as possible like an analytic philosopher or (alternatively) like a "hard" scientist. On the philosophic side, this entails rehashing particular schemes regardless of their appropriateness to ordinary discourse, seeing argumentation as an applied logic, and judging the adequacy of our concepts by analytic standards. On the social science side, a brutish behaviorism is adopted with the aim of dragging the field kicking and screaming into the 1950s world of behavioral science. Like scavenger fish, we trail after the seminal movements of other disciplines, eating their leavings and having no higher ambitions.

Both paths require abandoning the theoretic resources that are so promising. I am pleading not for disciplinary purity but for a reassessment of which ideas are most appropriate to argument studies. Foci on social interaction, communication, and the public evolution and uses of meanings are resources yet to be used effectively to yield insights into knowledge, discourse standards, and field conceptions of rationality. For instance, it is not trivial or innocuous to claim that *argument is a form of communication.* Taken seriously, this claim forces readjustment respecting most issues in argumentation. It makes the artful practices of social life our core research concern; it permits the inference that arguments are social comparison processes (Willard, 1979a, 1979b, 1980b); and it requires that the species display some of the characteristics of the genus. Argument being a communication process, we must assume that the things we say about communication apply to argument and that arguers use the communication modalities available to communicators generally. As a result we are compelled to the conclusion that if argument scholars respect their own concepts, they are not studying the same phenomenon that philosophers do.

It might seem that I am so framing the dispute that I can snipe at philosophers while denying them rejoinder: "we are not doing philosophy as it is usually defined" thus helps me avoid certain criticisms. This objection would seem to be reinforced by the fact that some logicians are uninterested in disputing whether logic illuminates empirical instances. Other logicians would disagree, however, and therein lies an important distinction. Whether a theorist of any discipline finds the arguments that follow interesting depends upon how he defines his work, how he defines the range of phenomena appropriate to his work. Let us say that every theoretical construct has a focus and range of convenience (Kelly, 1955). A construct's focus of convenience consists of the events it *best* explains or interprets; its range of convenience consists of the events it can be made to explain. So viewed, formal logic has a relatively narrow range of convenience and an extremely narrow focus. Whether ordinary discourse fits into its range of convenience has been at issue for decades. But if there are other constructs whose *foci* of convenience fit ordinary discourse, they may prove superior to attempts to expand logic's *range*.

In the investigations to follow, I hope to prove that communication concepts are more appropriate to argumentation than are logical ones. Their foci of convenience are more appropriate to ordinary discourse than are the ranges of convenience of many of the concepts we have been prone to borrow. This is a vital concern because it is plausible to believe that the things which pass muster as knowledge do so because of argument practices; every field's design characteristics for what shall count as knowledge stem from its explicit or implicit theory of argumentation. If the case for these claims proves plausible, argumentation's concepts will be foundational to most or all senses of "knowledge," and its empirical work will embody "the facts to be reckoned with" for every epistemic scheme.

I can perhaps clarify this claim with an example. I propose that without communication concepts, we are ill equipped to discuss any claim of the following sort: "social practices are irrelevant to genuine worthiness; convention and orthodoxy symptomize human frailties, not virtues; field practices for passing muster on knowledge claims are as apt to be accidents of history as they are to be traditions adopted for good reasons; there is thus a plausible and perfectly obvious opposition between a sociology of knowledge and projects which display genuine knowledge." This sort of argument is rather standard in many disciplines. Because it has often been assumed to be true, ordinary social practices have received little careful attention, and the sociological bases of the "nonsociological theories," for example, the "rationalists" in the philosophy of science or the "formalists" in philosophy, have been assumed to be innocuous. Thus grand disputes about claims of this sort tend to be fruitless. Notice, for example, that contemporary variants of such disputes seem remarkably like Plato's disputes with the Sophists. If you say that a formal system proves worthiness, while no social tradition ever could, I will demand that your prove your claim. I predict that you can do so only on grounds that deny me a reply (for example, your proof would use arguments that rule empirical claims out of the dispute; if I confront you with empirical cases contradicting your universal, you might accuse me of muddling ought with is).

Situated actors grapple with relativity more often than philosophers do. It is nothing but a prejudice that their efforts are always inferior. At minimum, this assumption is an unacceptable starting point for a social science. If we find out that particular efforts are inferior to, say, formalist procedures—and can lucidly say why—we shall have secured some concepts that now are taken on faith. Moreover, I want to play the hunch that this sort of result would stem from our finding that formal philosophers and scientists use sociological practices that are more conducive to fruitful result than are those of ordinary folk. It is more likely, however, that our empirical programs will not secure global and grandiose vindications of whole projects; they will tell us instead that particular ways of knowing are differentially appropriate to different phenomena. Either result will force the conclusion that the *sociological versus rational* dispute has been premature.

The claim to be considered, then, is that all knowledge has social roots. The organizing problem is to specify "social roots." The two exemplars of this idea to be weighed here are (1) the situated actor engaged in social comparison processes and (2) the "domains of objectivity"—the argument fields—to which actors refer for purposes of objectifying their interpretations. The organizing assumption is that both exemplars exist by and through communication and that they are animated by the process of perspective taking.

So my grandiose scheme is to redesign the field of argumentation from the ground up. This will be nothing but pompous posturing if the preceding claims prove to be trivial. The exceptional promise of the field of argumentation is that it studies the most explicit kind of communication. "Arguers" lay out publicly more total information about their assumptions and thinking processes than other interactants (Willard, 1980b). Situated arguments are ambiguous, context embedded, and enthymematic (implicit); but they are less so than other utterances. If we want to study how actors grapple with knowledge, how they pass muster on claims and use standards of verification and judgment, their public arguments are especially fruitful sources of information.

The Agenda for Argumentation

My project is, as I said, more modest than my aims. I want to suggest more productive ways of understanding some of the key issues in argument theory. This program is thus a companion piece to my "Theory of Argumentation" (1980d), and I shall have to take for granted here some of the claims made there. The most important of these is that the most precise and useful sense of the term "argument" is as a form of social interaction, *a kind of interaction in which two or more people maintain what they construe to be incompatible positions* (Willard, 1978a).[4] It is a "social relationship" (M. McCall, 1970; Scheff, 1970) built from a coorientation in which actors mutually attribute argumentative intentions to each other, that is, a definition of situation which makes the actors define themselves as arguers, "we are having an argument." A second sense of "argument" concerns *utterances*. I refer to the sorts of claims present when someone says "that is my argument" or "he made this argument." Argument scholars often use the term "product" (as opposed to "process") to denote this sense of argument; but "product" implies *thingness* in the old sense of serial prediction or propositional logic. "Utterance" seems more precise than "product" to specify the sorts of claims present when "we are having an argument." We might well decide to buttress this second sense of argument by saying that it is the result of a communicative act (in the Searle-Austin sense), that is, in the sense that a "promise" ensues from the act of "promising." D. J. O'Keefe (1982) has thus suggested that argument utterances (to use my terms, not his) result from "making" arguments. I am inclined, however, to say that we may secure a clear sense of argument utterances by looking at argument interactions and seeing what sorts of utterances appear. The organizing claim, then, is that arguments are social interactions, having many of the characteristics of social interaction in general (these characteristics being detailed in Willard [1978a, 1980b]). I deployed this thinking to attack traditional uses of logic and recent uses of Toulmin's layout of argument to analyze situated discourse, that is, saying that they are inappropriate to situated utterance. Ordinary utterance is intended toward, given meaning by, the definition of the situation; it is context embedded. To understand a particular argument is to understand the intentional defining activities of the speakers.

The investigations that follow extend this thinking and specify its implications for argumentation's self-definition as a scholarly field and its empirical agenda. I shall aim my arguments at theorists, researchers, and critics within the discipline, but my aim is to prove that argument studies are fundamental to other lines of inquiry as well. If when all is said and done my claims are arcane, and argumentation's importance for other domains is not clear and plausible, I shall have failed utterly. Argumentation should be the study of how actors pass muster on ideas. So viewed, it proceeds not from ontology but from communication theory. Its core question is not "what shall be the guarantors of our knowledge?" but "how do circumstanced actors objectify their thinking?" The difference is nontrivial: the present view takes conventions and orthodoxies as being interesting in themselves and problematic (because we cannot prove that they are inferior to formal schemes). Notice I do not say that ordinary routines are superior to formal ones: the whole point of leaving the justification business behind is that such questions are fruitless. The minimum expectation is that the sociological argument will have nontrivial implications for every sort of knowledge claim.

Passing muster is a social comparison process. To prove this, I shall take an analogy with cognitive development rather literally. "Learning" is a process of successive comparisons, a communication enterprise in which a person checks private interpretations against communal standards; arguing is one important way in which this is done, because a field's standards are not (except for a few instances of scientific measurements) "things"; people speak for them, describe them, and detail their implications and probative value. Thus when people consult argument fields, they do so by dealing with other people. My basic model here is the person trying ideas on for size, testing their "fit" to events (Kelly, 1955). Kelly's man-as-scientist metaphor (which is ambiguous in that the man as scientist might be a Humean, a Vienna Circle positivist, or a Kuhnian) suggests that human action is calculative, forward-looking, and strategic rather than merely "responsive." I shall thus insist upon a three-way analogy between cognitive development, an actor's integration into a field, and participant observation. According to the constructivist account, a child is socialized into a world of prearranged meanings by virtue of successive interactions with other people (Delia and O'Keefe, 1979); the child constructs his environment by a meaning-constitutive process of construing the recurring themes in events. Integration into particular social domains is merely a somewhat more complex version of these processes; and participant observation is a body of procedures by which the researcher enters a field. In a way consistent with this analogy, I shall say that fields are psychological perspectives that actors take from time to time for particular reasons; field theory thus becomes a way of fleshing out Mead's "generalized other."

Entering an argument field usually amounts to a decision to use a particular set of judgmental and veridical standards and to abide by the consequences. So the organizing question with respect to any field is why its actors trust its standards. This is a different question from the one Toulmin poses, namely, what is the source of authority for our concepts? Following constructivist thinking, we shall have to say that the person in interpreting events decides that something confers authority on an idea. Thus it is more appropriate to ask why people come to have faith in particular sources of authority: the glue that binds fields together is this faith in authorities and authoritative standards, not the authorities and standards themselves. The things we think we know and the ways we trust to help us know them are our own creations; so the authority of a belief is not a thing but a feature of the way we look at it. The ideas that countenance other ideas do so because we use them that way. We thus require the sort of explanation common to coherentist theories (Lehrer, 1974; Rescher, 1973, 1976, 1977a), although in every case we shall want to make our account square with Kelly's (1955) account of how personal construct systems yield interpretations.

Most argumentation theorists believe that phenomena like faith and trust have no place in accounts of rationality. They might admit that such "states" are *results* of rational considerations; but they would likely never grant that faith might be a precondition of rational belief. I propose to prove that the field theory elaborated below undermines dichotomies of this sort by proving that the surest thing to be said of rationality is that it is a rhetorical phenomenon, a term fields sometimes use to name orthodox ways, an orientation toward proceeding in "not obviously lunatic" fashion. If this thesis proves plausible, it is oversimple to dichotomize faith and rationality: an actor's decision to enter a domain of objectivity entails in a nontrivial sense a *credo ut intelligam*. One believes in a field as a precondition of understanding. We have some familiar arguments to buttress this notion, namely, the now-fashionable claim that theories of rationality are always rooted in an irrational faith and the claim that scientific method cannot itself be justified by scientific method. The matter of importance is not that one or the other account is the better one but that such disputes are not very important. Field theory requires that we account for faith and rationality as pieces of a larger conceptual puzzle.

I propose to elaborate this larger puzzle by fitting together a plausible stance toward it. My aim is to define the recurring issues of argumentation in ways conducive to productive research, to assemble a conceptual framework that argumentation critics, analysts, and researchers might find useful. At every stage I shall try to do justice to the notion that a theory of argumentation is—whatever else it is—a theory of communication.

The unifying thread is the notion of perspective taking, understood as a social interpretive accomplishment; and I shall trade on the ambiguities among several senses of perspective taking, namely, perspective taking as a personal psychological act, as an entrance into a social domain, as an acceptance of a starting point (buttressed by a willingness to work through and abide by its implications), and as an analytic decision someone makes.

I want to point to weaknesses of familiar ways of conceptualizing argument, rationality, and critical judgment and to consider the ways field theory might recast these notions. My aim is to present the field theory in sufficient particularity to defend its consequences. With these moves I hope to justify a particular set of questions and a point of view toward them upon which we might redesign the field of argumentation. Assuming a modicum of success with these tasks, the result will be a sociology of knowledge founded on the concept of argument.

The twofold nature of this project will gradually become clear. Having set forth the task of designing a "field," I shall preoccupy myself with ordering and defining its organizing concepts and practices. So proceeding, I shall be simultaneously describing the "field devoted to the study of fields" and presenting a paradigm case of any field description whatever. In making field-defining claims, I shall have to succeed with the topoi and proprieties expected of any actor in any field who makes such claims. This agenda embodies the same checkpoints one would necessarily pass through in describing any field. The investigations to follow thus coalesce to produce a "field study" of a peculiar sort: I shall tie all of argumentation's organizing concepts to the notion of argument fields; argumentation thus becomes a metatheoretical framework for understanding fields in general; argumentation's paradigm in turn becomes a reflective version of itself.

1 The Nature of Argumentation

The problem of defining argumentation's relation to epistemics takes two forms. There is a theoretical problem of devising a fit between particular views of argument and conceptions of knowledge, and there is an empirical problem of deciding upon the range of human activities to which the theoretic stance must be appropriate. The former is often translated into the question of whether it is the theory of argument that yields a picture of knowledge or the reverse. In pointing to paradigm cases of knowledge, philosophers have usually pictured them in terms of the systems that produce knowledge. Knowledge has thus been said to be geometric, syllogistic, mathematical, and logical. The latter problem is often translated into two hitherto unrelated questions, namely, whether epistemics is inevitably empirical and how narrow the range of things that count as knowledge can be. The great formal systems were irrelevant to most empirical processes, so the degree to which empirical claims might bear upon their probity became a matter of considerable torment. One could hold a system together by successively narrowing the range of things counting as knowledge, or one could admit empirical considerations but insist that only particular social practices, for example, science, could enter epistemic equations.

The seemingly straightforward claim that *argument is epistemic* thus presupposes that some exceedingly complex theoretical and empirical decisions have been made. A satisfactory description of arguments has been produced, and a detailed picture of what argument outcomes look like has been drawn. These schemes have been made to yield design specifications for what may count as knowledge; and the fit of the epistemic package to the empirical world has been exhaustively considered and defended. These minimum accomplishments have been given broader meaning by virtue of their fit into a regnant theoretical framework that either accounts for or justifies the exclusion of the facts of communication, social life, and psychology.

Each step of this agenda opens certain doors and closes others. Each entails theoretical moves which coalesce to justify traveling a particular path rather than others. In this sense every theory can be seen as standing in a "figure-ground" relation to its precursors. The history of every domain is a mosaic not of accumulated truths but of the experience of seeing particular systems of ideas through to their implications. A domain's historical backdrop thus enables new theories to travel new roads with the knowledge of where the better-traveled roads lead.

The claim that argument is epistemic might well lead one to travel in very deep ruts. If "argument" is understood to be serial predication, one follows the great systematizers from Aristotle through Russell who equated knowledge with things that can be rationally known. One seeks a universal system of entailments as a guarantor of knowledge claims. The logic of these entailments would be one's paradigm case of argument and of knowledge. So proceeding, one would be taking the terms with which epistemology has been historically preoccupied as the necessary checkpoints along the way: the most fundamental organizing problematic would be a question of the sort "what is the nature of knowledge?"

If one takes such a question to be but a piece of a larger puzzle, some less-traveled roads suggest themselves. If one believes, for example, that the great systems have been done in by the skeptical critique and by particular tu quoque arguments, one would want to accommodate to the facts of relativity. Thus Toulmin (1972) has defined the problem of human understanding as the problem of recognizing the basis of intellectual authority. This view closes the door on the "cult of the system" and organizes epistemics around the search for recurring themes in the practices by which scholars and ordinary folk seek to guarantee their knowledge. The aim is to infer from the different ways people handle conceptual change an epistemic "self-portrait" that provides a useful explanation of our epistemic situation and yields the "proper canons of rational criticism."

If one believes that such tasks are subsidiary to more basic problems (and thus are prematurely or imprecisely posed), one strikes out upon still another path. Three particular beliefs might justify doing so, namely, (1) that previous theories have used tenuous views of argument, (2) that communication concepts are promising resources for reconciling sociological, psychological, and ideal accounts, and (3) that most attempts to divorce epistemic questions from matters of communication have been founded upon value judgments that cannot survive skeptical scrutiny. The first belief suggests the need for a conception of argument that owes no debts to serial predication and closes the door on the assumption that a theory of argument must be made to fit epistemic ideals. The second implies that the new view of argument might provide new ways of seeing some old dichotomies, for example, *subjectivity versus objectivity, person versus society,* and *belief versus knowledge.* The third belief implies that the traditional terms of epistemology are least useful when couched impersonally. If any sense of an impersonal guarantor of knowledge is to be retained, it must be derived from the practices of field actors as they check their thinking against trusted standards.

The soundness of the claim that argument is epistemic thus depends upon a complex series of interlocked moves. Narrow views of argument require narrow senses of knowledge. Communication-based views of argument entail epistemic propositions that cohere with the facts of communication. The place to start toward a communication-based view is with a consideration of the nature, function, and scope of the term "argument."

Paradigm Cases

My first aim is to present paradigm cases of two senses of the term "argument" and to consider their implications for a theory of argumentation. These implications are capsulized in the claim that the argument-as-interaction view (Willard, 1978a) is a promising way of organizing our thinking and that views of argument utterance ought to square with this organizing principle. It is necessary, then, to take seriously the notion that argument is a form of communication by emphasizing that coorientations, mutual definitions of situation, give meaning to utterance. If a successful paradigm case of argument interaction can be assembled, we need only look at the utterances in that exchange to derive a paradigm case of argument utterance.

Thus I start with a plea for holism. We distinguish the two senses of argument to emphasize relationships between dissensual coorientations and utterances, but it is plausible to expect that both senses be unified by overarching principles—in this case, the notions of communication and perspectivity. It is less plausible to assume that interactions and utterances can be analyzed with tools that bear no relation to one another or are flatly incompatible. Explanations of interaction and of utterance should be cut from the same cloth and should be interwoven in the fabric of a unified and lucid epistemological package. Empirical research into the two senses should be complementary by virtue of its coherent fit into a broader framework. There should not be a "schizophrenic" division between the interaction and utterance senses. They should be of a piece—two sides of the same coin. Thus paradigm cases of the senses of argument should bear clear resemblances and display coherent fits with one another. Having *defined* argument as a kind of interaction in which two or more people maintain what they construe to be incompatible positions (Willard, 1978a, 1980b), and having spelled out the appropriateness of this definition to "constructivist/interactionist" thinking, I want to approach the problem of argument from the different direction implied by the giving of paradigm cases.

Designs for the Paradigm Cases

Here are my designs for a paradigm case. You do not need to agree with them to follow my arguments; clarity is what is needed. There are, to be sure, contending senses of what paradigm cases should be and doubts about their value. But the present task is not to settle these disputes but to consider the foci and ranges of convenience of several views of paradigm cases and to weigh their utility for our purposes. I shall not, strictly speaking, be making a "paradigm case argument." I want to elaborate a definition of argument, not to replace it, and to do this in every case by holding the paradigm case accountable to an outside standard, namely, its fit into a holistic account.

One sense of paradigm cases is that they are norms or ideals, broad aims toward which people should strive. Thus Greco-Roman pedagogy focused upon Great Men, while its mythology centered on heroes worthy of emulation. This sense of paradigm cases is obviously of fundamental importance to field studies. To know a field is to know its cardinal virtues, its paradigm cases of excellence, and its minimum standards of competency. To describe a field is to survey not merely its attainments but its dreams and ambitions as well. But this particular reading of paradigm cases is not well suited to argumentation's attempts to describe its own subject matter. While *verstehen* thinking obliges us to respect a field's normative paradigm cases for purposes of understanding it, most of the more contentious disputes have arisen when a particular field's ideals are mistaken for universals. Argumentation requires a general sense of "argument" that does justice to the particular features of field-dependent exemplars and the differences among them and which serves as well the particular analytic and critical aims appropriate to our organizing questions. Our paradigm case of argument must serve these functions while squaring with our second-order constructs for describing differences among field theories.

Another sense of paradigm cases is something on the order of Plato's ideas, Kant's synthetic a priori ideas, or the categories defended by nativists. All instances are species of some genus. This is a poor exemplar of argument because it blurs context embeddedness, definitions of situation, and notions of social comparison. It likewise does not fit our metatheoretical aims of taking account of differences and similarities across fields. We are not trying to build a "city of truth" (Toulmin, 1976) which yields evaluations of other fields. Taking sides in interfield disputes is just what should be ruled out of criticism.

Another sense of paradigm cases is the "ideal type." There are variations on this theme, but the root idea is that one can look at typifying instances to gain a knowledge of classes. One seeks typical Germans, blacks, or blue-collar workers. Weber's grand vision failed because rich variations appeared within his groupings. Ideal type accounts tended to confuse averageness with a group's exemplar of excellence. Worse, ideal types were sometimes confounded not with the group's ideals but with the analysts'—causing more confusion than the concept was worth.

Another (more congenial) sense of paradigm case is the "clear-cut case." There are several variations, and it will pay to be careful. We might mean (1) the simplest case, (2) the statistically average case, or (3) the numerically most common case. I can accept (2) but prefer (3). All three, however, pose difficulties. Variations (2) and (3) presuppose that we have a plausible sense of the phenomenon being averaged or counted. This is not a minor problem, but (1) is far worse.

The simplest case reasoning is familiar. A warhorse example will suffice (see Black, 1970). If a visitor from outer space, knowing nothing of our world, asks what a table is, we would not show him some exotic or oddly styled one (say, a French Provincial with nineteen legs and a television built in). We would look instead for a simple four-legged table, something unambiguously a table, about which there would be wide agreement. By mastering the simplest case, the visitor could elaborate the idea "table" to more ambiguous and exotic cases. The central assumption is that a straightforward, unambiguous paradigm case of X is the clearest basis for understanding borderline or fringe cases of X.

This reasoning poses a peculiar paradox. On one hand, the simplest case reasoning loads the dice in favor of propositional logic. "All men are mortal, and so forth" fits its specifications best if we seek the most straightforward case of what everyone would call argument utterance. If we take logicians at their word, however, we ordinarily think of logical reasoning as an exotic attainment, a phenomenon rarely encountered in daily life. Propositional and syllogistic serializations are unusual accomplishments, rarefied attainments, specialized refinements of ordinary thought and speech—related to ordinary logic in the same way the nineteen-legged French Provincial table is related to ordinary tables. If we make them paradigm cases, the visitor from space will be misled in the same way argument theorists have been led astray by logic. Ordinary talk would be seen as an elaboration on logical forms rather than the reverse, leading to a misunderstanding of both. Propositional and syllogistic logics are the clearest outcomes of the simplest case reasoning but—paradoxically—not simplest cases. Schemes that make particular logics first forms of reasoning do not escape this paradox; rather, they crush it under the weight of their systems.

It is also worth asking whether simple examples best represent complex abstractions. The table example is a suspiciously congenial one to the simplest case scenario, but what would a simplest case of (say) justice, Freudianism, hatred, the good, or some such look like? The simplest case of justice might be atypical of the activities and outcomes we ordinarily associate with the term, as might the simplest case of any of the others. It is not implausible to expect that the simplest case of justice might turn out to be revenge—an eye for an eye being more clear-cut than other complex and presumptively more attractive schemes.

Simplest case reasoning inevitably makes conceptions of utterance prematurely normative. Instances of utterance may be intuitively straightforward by virtue of their fit into a system, likely a logic. This "fit" requires bracketing the empirical question of how ordinary speakers in fact argue. I shall consider in a moment the elided, enthymematic, implicit, and intuitive character of ordinary speech. For now it may suffice to reiterate the importance of the context embeddedness of utterance. Propositional serials which serve equally well in any context are proportionately different from circumstanced speech. Something that makes sense apart from contexts hardly seems adequate to the task of exemplifying situated utterance.

Consider as well the requirements of holism in the simplest case view. If propositionalizing is a paradigm case of utterance, what paradigm case of interaction is implied? Presumably there must be a forum which produces essentially propositional claims, either writing or formal debating. These are straightforward and unambiguous instances of contexts that produce propositionalizing. But this statement courts contradiction for advocates of the simplest case. Debates are formal rituals—hardly straightforward unexceptional instances of interaction. Written discourse is a kind of interaction, if we stretch things somewhat; but by the simplest case account, would we want to say that written discourse is the simplest instance of interaction, the most straightforward and unexceptional case? Such an assertion does violence to our intuitions about what ordinary interactions are like and blurs the fact that arguments may be embedded in larger conversational structures.[1]

Thus the simplest case scenario is incapable of yielding a plausible paradigm case of interaction. One might, of course, defend the schism between views of utterance and interaction and refuse to be bound by the requirements of holism. In this case, we would no longer be arguing organizing examples but far broader theoretical issues. Thus a larger aim of this chapter is to close this option off by making a plausible case for holism and an equally plausible case against the schism. If, on the other hand, one refuses to defend the schism, one assumes the burden of proving that a plausible paradigm case of interaction might result from the simplest case of utterance.[2]

It is worth considering the values of the statistical average, and numerically most common cases are superior paradigm cases when wedded to the sort of definition defended here. Having objected to the simplest case reasoning on empirical grounds, especially that it obscures or rules out "borderline" cases and thus does violence to the practices of ordinary language users, we are left with the implication that a broader conception of argument "must capture all the ambiguity, imprecision, and difficulty in application that natural categories possess" (Jacobs and Jackson, 1981, p. 119). The simplest case reasoning proposes (possibly) artificial categories, bearing the advantages of clear-cut boundaries and reliable defining characteristics and the disadvantages of obscuring or ruling out the characteristics we intuitively assign to ordinary speech.

But these two alternatives to the simplest case reasoning cannot stand apart from the broad theoretical framework being developed here. Frequency measures, after all, often blur salience; we might well find that field actors take as their organizing examples cases which are not the most frequent but instead are "the best" or "the most typical" (in the manner of the idealistic sense of paradigm cases). An example (owed, I believe, to Eleanor Rosch) is that robins are prototypical "birds" for the people asked to select them, even though they are not the most common. A penguin might be the archetypal "bird" for people in certain locales and a fringe case for people in other areas. The *salient* example may well be the field-defining one.

The frequency-measure paradigm cases thus cannot stand alone. Having said as much, however, we should not automatically infer that salience and frequency are utterly unassociated (for example, the unicorn may be everyone's paradigm case of the ideal animal while hardly their paradigm case of the typical animal). Robins are not the most plentiful birds, but they are plentiful enough to invite notice. Thus in some cases it may be that what people take to be the "clearest cut" cases are so taken because they are relatively plentiful.

The most prudent course is to see the frequency-based paradigm cases of argument as companion pieces to our empirical program dealing with ordinary utterance. The principles of generating a paradigm case are thus not abstract analytic rules by empirical generalizations about ordinary practices. Frequency is a necessary but not uniformly sufficient condition of a good example. To defend a frequency measure, our broader theoretical and empirical program will have to prove that the thing being said to be frequent is *plausible*.

The most plausible paradigm case of both senses of argument must exemplify *situated* speech. It seems specious to say anything else, since people are never circumstance free. Utterance which can be given meaning apart from a speaker's intentions is by definition unusual (in the sense that we might see a speech text as a literary work of art—which makes it something different from a "record" of situated utterance).

The *definition of situation,* then, is the cognitive act that endows utterance with meaning; humans define and interpret events rather than responding to them (Blumer, 1969; Schutz, 1945, 1953, 1962). It is a rhetorical process "in the sense that actors 'construct'... the referents of judgment as well as the interrelationships of these objects, events, and valuations. Such an interpretive process gives order or coherence to actors' perceptual cues and, as a consequence, justifies conclusions such persons may reach in 'this' situation" (Cox, 1980, p. 5). A definition of situation is an interpretive scheme built out of an actor's "self-indications," his naming of social objects, and his accommodations to the assessed perspectives of others (Cox, 1980). This thinking dovetails into the universal of rationality as perspective taking, about which I elaborate in the next chapter. It also coheres with the definition of argument as a form of social interaction—it makes the same interpretations of the importance of coorientations, episodic and dispositional attributions, and specific definitions of situation.

I do not know who invented this thinking; but Znaniecki (1934) had inklings of it in his focus upon the *humanistic coefficient* in sociology—which meant that data are "always somebody's, never nobody's, data." He concluded that, if a social scientist ignored personal interpretations and definitions of situation, "if he attempted to study the cultural system as he studies a natural system, i.e., as if it existed independently of human experience and activity, the system would disappear and in its stead he would find a disjointed mass of natural things and processes, without any similarity to the reality he started to investigate" (1934, pp. 36–37). Znaniecki (1940) gave social scientists the task of explaining "the experience of men who are dealing with them [the data] actively" (1940, p. 5). This line of thought was an expansion on themes established in the classic study of Polish peasants (Thomas and Znaniecki, 1958) and was extended in Znaniecki's (1952) study of primitive behavior.

A vast literature has accumulated dealing with the definition of situation (Cicourel, 1970, Berger and Kellner, 1970; Emerson, 1970a, 1970b; Bernstein, 1958, 1964a, 1964b); and elegant arguments about indexicality of expressions have been made (Bar-Hillel, 1954; Garfinkle, 1967). Waller's (1970) description captures this thinking:

> Strictly speaking, the definition of situation is a process...in which the individual explores the behavior possibilities of a situation, marking out particularly the limitations which the situation imposes upon his behavior, with the final result that the individual forms an attitude toward the situation...in the situation.... Actually, the definition of situation is a process by which the individual explores and feels out through behavior and thought the behavior possibilities of a situation, is a process most intimately subjective, and one that must be worked out anew in the mind of every human being. [P. 162]

This view fits with Kelly's (1955) man-as-scientist metaphor (Willard, 1978a, 1979a, 1979b, 1980b) and in particular with the idea that behavior is experimental. Waller's thinking is a bridge linking constructivist and interactionist thinking with our developing notion of argument fields. He claims that group life creates and sustains broad ranges of permissible definitions: "From their experience has arisen a consensus concerning what is and what is not thinkable in those situations" (1970, p. 162). Groups display the residua of the past definitions that form their histories; they may be defined as configurational fields built upon communal definitions. So defined, they are argument fields.

This thinking requires that we not equate argument fields with physical entities or natural systems and that we not traffic in metaphors imported from the natural sciences. We want to say that fields are social arrangements—balkanized variations on Mead's "generalized other." They are broad and variously loose frameworks used by their actors to guide situated activities. This notion compels us to redefine some traditional sociological notions about groups. Roles, for example, should be seen as constructive accomplishments; role taking becomes the process by which a person accommodates to his interpretation of the expectations of others; and "epistemic progress" becomes an offshoot of situated activities rather than the product of impersonal conceptual ecologies. We can explain convention and innovation and stability and change by studying the ways field actors balance these considerations in making particular decisions. To equate "field" with "structure" is to obscure these social and processual features of knowing and progress.

Where does this reasoning lead us? We have arrived at the minimum conditions of a useful paradigm case of argument interaction, namely, (1) its enabling condition is dissensus, the arguers' beliefs that their positions are incompatible; (2) it is a coorientation based upon mutual attributions of argumentative intent, "we are having an argument"; (3) it is a social comparison process regardless of the motives of the arguers, that is, an argument need not be a disinterested dialogue in order to serve epistemic functions; (4) its purposes and meanings cannot for descriptive purposes be abstracted from the perspectives of the arguers; and (5) definitions of situation inform the procedures and outcomes of the interaction and endow utterances with meaning.

It might be objected that one cannot have an argument without making arguments (see Brockriede, 1977). Statements of a specifiable order which are by some criterion nameable as arguments must be present before we have a paradigm case of argument interaction. This objection presupposes that dependable criteria are readily at hand for identifying argument utterances. I shall shortly turn to criticisms of the criteria often defended for these purposes, for example, the view that an argument utterance is a claim linked to an explicit reason. But two objections must be raised here. First, "I love you for sentimental reasons" becomes an argument by such criteria. One often finds claims and support in interactions that intuitively do not count as arguments. Second, speech is inherently ambiguous and dependent upon the speaker's intentions. A claim such as "Reagan ought to be supported" might or might not be an invitation to argument, depending upon the speaker's intentions. Almost any statement can be viewed from alternative standpoints, depending upon attributions to the speaker. "I love you" is possibly a factual claim, demand, plea, explanation, or justification—some of these constructions being straightforward invitations to argument, others not. This objection thus does not endanger the paradigm case; it asks us to ignore the essential ambiguity of speech. Since no claims are unarguably innocuous (excepting, perhaps, some expressive utterances), we have no choice but to say that whether or not an utterance is an argument depends on our attributions to the speaker, not to it.

Some utterances are doubtless straightforward. Their speakers mean what the things they say mean; there are no surprises lurking beneath the surface:

1. "You're too fat." "I am not."
2. "Reagan should be re-elected." "No, he shouldn't."
3. "This is a clear case of X." "This is a clear case of Y, not X."

And so on. These seem to be clear-cut cases of dissensus, although it is always possible that such adjacency pairs have some arcane meaning; they might be code phrases bearing arbitrary correspondences and may thus be impenetrable to us unless we have the key. Nonetheless, such clear-cut cases appear often enough in ordinary discourse that we are passably safe in saying that they exemplify dissensus of a particular sort. So we might well study texts of these exchanges without bothering to investigate the circumstances of their utterance.

But there are equally common occasions for which codes are normal devices. There are situations for which we confidently assume that statements bear not just any among their possible conventional meanings but particular, arcane meanings. It is a taken-for-granted part of social life that some things are kept ambiguous, equivocal, and unclear enough to avoid conflict, for example, "do you like my new dress?" and "isn't my sister pretty?" sometimes demand quick footwork for appropriate replies.

It is a standard device in labor, diplomatic, and contract negotiations to keep the degree of difference between the parties submerged in great piles of talk. This practice has the advantage of blurring rather than sharpening differences, thus enhancing the possibilities for rapprochement. I shall return to examples of this sort in discussing Goffman's views of facades below.

Consider another example which is as ordinary and unremarkable as examples 1 through 3:

4. "Busing is a simple issue of local autonomy. It is a question of local rights versus federal control."

This statement illustrates something rather ordinary in political life. The speaker asserts a claim about busing based upon data and/or a warrant he would rather not publicly articulate. Plausible surrogates are thus substituted. The audience understands that the politician cannot say, "keep white neighborhoods white" and grants the speaker considerable latitude in conjuring up substitute data and warrants that will pass public inspection. The politician and listener agree that busing must be opposed in order that nonwhite children may be kept out of the "good" schools; both agree that the speaker must speak in code in order to accommodate to certain public proprieties. There is nothing "in the talk" in example 4 that expresses this agreement we are reading into it.

A text of example 4 would serve no more complex a function than as a code bearer to be translated by attributions made to the speakers. Moreover, we want to do something more than merely identify arguments. We want to be able to describe them and to say what they are about. Thus while texts may be straightforward in some cases (and while texts are indispensable resources for some kinds of studies of argument fields), there are plausible cases for which texts are undependable.

We have, in sum, plausible working specifications for a paradigm case of the two senses of argument. At least some of the objections that might be raised to it have been considered; and we will shortly have the occasion to consider some others as well. But we are well enough provisioned to proceed with the project of exemplifying what we mean by argument interaction and argument utterance.

The Paradigm Cases and a Loose Paradigm Case Argument

We need a paradigm case that buttresses our definition of argument as a kind of social interaction. Yet that definition combined with our assessment of the importance of ambiguity in ordinary utterance suggests that no single argument can display all the possibilities. An array of particular features has been imputed to interactions based on dissensus, to speakers' intentions, and to discourse. It is unrealistic to expect that a single example can display them all in a satisfactory way. Several are needed—which means that in dealing with paradigm cases, I am departing in important respects from the traditional procedures of philosophers who accept the "paradigm case argument." I intend to present several exemplary arguments whose cumulative implications comprise the paradigm case.

Example I

"Abortion's murder, man."
"Shit. Where'd you get that crap? Abortion's just taking out a piece of dead meat."
"It's not dead meat. They got pictures. They look just as human as you do."
"What they look like doesn't mean shit. They can't think. They don't have feelings."

"They do, too. There's studies showing feelings."
"That's just the nervous system."
"I don't give a shit what it is. It's still murder when you kill it."
"Why, if it's not human?"
"Killing's killing."
"Ohhhhh, and I guess you don't hunt deer."
"That's not the same. Deer's not human."
"What, are they [fetuses] human?"
"They're human. They look just like humans."
"Looks don't mean shit. Looks don't."
"It's not looks. They got brains, hearts, everything."
"So do deer."
"Deer's not human."
"Deer's got more value than anything's not born yet."

This text seems straightforward enough. It suggests several conclusions about the nature of argumentation. Notice, for example, that forcing either speaker's arguments into a syllogistic mold would distort them. "Abortion's murder" can easily fit onto a syllogism, but it gradually becomes apparent that a syllogism would not reflect what the speaker means. Neither all or even most killing is murder (the killing of deer brings this out)—only acts which lead to certain feelings are "murders." No syllogism can represent the sort of connection the speaker is making between his intuitions and his claims.

Neither participant seems especially tentative; they are not engaging in dialogue and disinterestedly inquiring. Questioned afterward, both arguers reported a concern for "setting the other guy's facts straight." The encounter was not a game in which strategic decisions could be made for purposes of winning. Trained debaters could read this sample and could note several points at which argumentative ground might be gained by granting certain arguments to turn them against one's opponent. Our arguers were not completely innocent of these possibilities, but they were "bound by the facts." This was presumably not a reflective attitude so much as a naive realistic conception of the "facts" and the need to correct the other's errors.

Example I also illustrates one way verbal constructs are subsumed by regnant nondiscursive ones. The *murder versus hunting* dimension is elaborated as things progress, and it becomes apparent that the "murder" pole is subsumed by an affective and relatively inarticulate nondiscursive dimension. This fits Kelly's (1955) view of cognitive organization, which assumes an interdependency of nondiscursive and verbally labeled constructs. When nondiscursive constructs are regnant in a cognitive system, they often pass for intuition; they become the background assumptions of the verbal constructs and operate in much the way our arguer "just knows" murder when he sees it. The argument thus becomes heated, and the positions appear irreconcilable as at least one disputant equates his background assumption with the facts of the world.

Nevertheless, epistemic functions are served by the argument. First, there is a movement from the initial crude equation of "physical" and "human" characteristics toward a religious orientation (witness the reference to souls). The arguer's assumptions are brought out into the open in a way unlikely to occur in other sorts of interaction. Second, comparisons are drawn with other sorts of killing, thus elaborating certain implications of the claims each arguer makes. Third, the breadth of the construct "abortion" is expanded: it is shown to subsume certain other constructs and itself to be subsumed by others.

The text of I is a more or less dependable record of the interaction, although we depend upon subsequent interviews to justify this claim. The knowledge that the first speaker is a Catholic "and I work at it," while the second thinks "Catholics are full of shit on that stuff," augments our initial guesses about the assumptions underlying their particular claims. Thus we use this text to attribute cognitive processes to the speakers.

Example I does not, however, justify the conclusion that all arguments are similarly straightforward. Consider, for example, an argument that compares with I in the same way that example 4 in the previous section compared with the first three:

Example II

P: "Queers are always jumping you in the john."

T: "That's only a tiny percentage. There's more hetero rape by far."

P: "That's just because they haven't studied it enough."

T: "There's lots of stuff done on gay life-styles; most of them couldn't care less about jumping straights in johns."

This text seems to show an argument about national trends. There is nothing in the talk to suggest otherwise. Some theorists might regard the first statement as a claim and might search for the relevant backing, data, and warrant. While the statement *can* be treated this way, nothing of the sort is happening here. *P* is expressing fears about his college roommate who has "come out of the closet" and is being reassured by *T* that his fears are groundless. Though the argument proceeds in global, impersonal terms, both arguers understand that they are talking about *X*, not national trends; in every case they mean something other than what they say. Consider this interview result:

P: "Well [smiles; long pause] we were *really* talking about *X*."

W: "Why did you couch everything in national or statistical terms?"

P: "It seemed kinda gross to talk about a good friend that way. I'm not sure any of that stuff applies to him."

Thus the text of II cannot stand as a record of the arguments made. It displays arguments, but they are not the same arguments the speakers were making, and nothing in the talk reveals that this is so. The arguers are using a code implicitly agreed upon in order to observe a rather ordinary social propriety (others were present in the room). Sample II is a paradigm case of argument interaction, though the arguer's motives differ greatly from the arguer's motives in I: *T* is reassuring *P;* it is his main motive for arguing; two close friends may part ways unless *P* can think through his views of *X.* Sample II is also a paradigm case of utterance in that it typifies ordinary utterance. Goffman's conception of public codes and masks, to which I shall turn in a moment, exemplifies this aspect. The arguers are trying to keep matters from becoming too explicit; their statements are intentionally ambiguous and would mislead anyone overhearing them. In this, they resemble:

Example III

K: "You see, we aren't gonna get anything done around here without first dealing with our problems."

C: "Yeah, I wonder what he'll say when he hears that..."

Superficially this exchange makes no sense unless "problems" and "he" mean the same thing. Sample III typifies a convention observed by a group in which I have participant-observed. The vague locution "problems" is routinely used, across many contexts, as a surrogate for a person's name. III is one of the few instances in which this convention is apparent in the talk. In the majority of exchanges in this group, the equation is carefully concealed.

I shall augment these examples with several additional ones as the discussion proceeds. But examples I through III have implications that coalesce to a degree that warrants a specific discussion of their consequences.

The Implications of the Paradigm Cases

Our three examples combined with two additional ones to be considered immediately have nontrivial implications for our views of (1) the focus and range of convenience of propositional logic; (2) several leading criteria for defining argument utterances; and (3) the truth conditions of claims.

Propositional Logic and the Enthymeme

Our paradigm cases yield a far less restrictive view of argument utterance than traditional accounts. Vis-à-vis ordinary speech, our paradigm cases imply that propositional logic works best for the most mundane and uninteresting cases, that is, that situated speakers do not routinely use propositional serials in ways that make them analyzable apart from the speakers' perspectives. Propositional logic requires consistent conventional meanings for its terms; probability calculi, for example, assume a strict stability in certain values. But situations rarely admit of this degree of stability in meanings.

Positive and analytic philosophers are misleading guides for present purposes. They would have us make ordinary speech fit into particular analytic frameworks. But we learn nothing about situated utterance in doing so. The proof of the claim inheres in two demonstrable conclusions: (1) the sterility and otherworldly quality of the grand systems and (2) the lack of useful data generated from logic-based theory and research in the social sphere. The case for (1) has been made by others (for example, Toulmin, 1964, 1972) and requires no elaboration here.

I have elsewhere (Willard, 1980a, 1980c, 1980d) critiqued the research traditions that use syllogistic and propositional logics as models of cognitive processes (for example, Abelson, 1959; Abelson and Rosenberg, 1958; McGuire, 1960). I concluded that while this research proves that subjects can be made to work with syllogisms, certain ambiguous, contradictory, and equivocal findings suggest that the subjects are being asked to reason in ways alien to them. The "atmosphere" and "conversion" effects are the most obvious manifestations (Woodworth and Sells, 1935; Sells, 1936; Sells and Koob, 1937; Chapman and Chapman, 1959; Henle, 1962; Simpson and Johnson, 1966; Wason and Johnson-Laird, 1972). There are subtler ones as well (Willard, 1980c). While researchers have often berated their subjects for refusing to proceed logically, they have overlooked the possibility that their views of logic presume forms unfamiliar to their subjects. It is taken for granted that the subject's logic is "inferior" to syllogistic logic. There is thus much talk of "contamination"; the syllogism is the basic form of thought but is contaminated by such nonlogical elements as "wishful thinking" (McGuire, 1960). These accounts cannot admit that such "contaminants" might be fundamental aspects of reasoning and that the failure of subjects to work syllogistic problems "successfully" is more a comment on the otherworldly nature of logic than of the failings of the subjects.

When argument scholars concern themselves with the traditional topoi of analysis (validity, probity, probability, soundness, and truth), they commit themselves to a particular vision of utterance that coheres with these notions. They make the empirical phenomena fit their frameworks and ignore the seminal conceptions of their own field. They obscure the context-embeddedness of utterance, the pivotal importance of the definition of the situation, and the facts of communication. They produce trivial research as a result. They can only lament their subjects' failures to succeed with particular logical procedures. Their subjects, socialized into a logic of lived experience (working logics, the logics of situations, multivalued social logics), work poorly with syllogisms because syllogisms have nothing to do with ordinary thought. Kelly's (1955) definition of thought as movement along and through pathways created by networks of constructs comes far closer to the sort of logic most people work with most of the time. This reasoning makes taking communication seriously a precondition of useful and interesting research. It implies that the various logics ordinarily employed by philosophers are poor paradigm cases of argument.

Propositional logics are sometimes muddled with "expansions on the enthymeme," that is, with filling in the missing parts of an enthymeme and then proceeding with a full-dress logical analysis. If we work from a propositional logic, however, we of necessity assume something we cannot prove, namely, that the missing elements of enthymemes are always, routinely, or ordinarily propositions. If our aim is to do logical analysis, we make the missing elements of the enthymeme into propositions whether they are or not. Syllogisms become expanded enthymemes. Most of the researchers who use syllogistic models of inference agree that although the enthymeme is the form of all natural argument, the "whole syllogism is there." They assume that people pass over premises so rapidly that they attend to only a few links in a chain of reasoning.

This is a breathtaking leap of faith. The research that proves subjects can be taught to work with syllogisms hardly countenances the conclusion that enthymemes—understood as elided syllogisms—are the basic form of all naturally occurring reasoning and utterance. The research merely proves that our reasoning about enthymemes has been elastic and loose enough to permit virtually anything to be fitted onto the logical model. Aristotle neatly partitioned his world so that the unstated premises (even of pathetic appeals) had to be propositions; the enthymeme was nothing more than the communicated version of the practical syllogism. Subsequent commentators disputed many aspects of the enthymeme but did not consider the nature of that which is elided. Researchers similarly assumed that whatever is missing in an enthymeme is something that fits traditional analytic molds.

This assumption passed as innocuous because subjects in fact can be taught to work logical procedures.

I intend not to rule syllogisms and propositional serials out of argument but to specify their fit more plausibly. They are rarefied, refined versions of ordinary thought. They do not necessarily tell us much about ordinary logic. Most theorists who want to make the syllogism the model of thought, and thus the implicit backdrop for the enthymeme, often confuse the forms they think arguments should take with descriptive statements about how people in fact argue. But if some of the logics do not appear in situated discourse and decision making, their priority as normative ideals is doubtful and their usefulness as judgmental criteria downright destroyed.

The importation of propositional logic into descriptive studies is thus tenuous. The missing elements of enthymemes may be intuitions, emotions, or manifolds of these and linguistic elements. It bears repeating that Kelly's view of cognitive organization requires that discursive and nondiscursive elements be seen as interdependent. Kelly also distinguishes between personal constructs and concepts. Constructs have their truth conditions in the cognitive systems that give them meaning while concepts are supposed to have truth conditions in the external data to which they refer.

Moreover, it is plausible to assume that interpersonal attributions— our imputations of internal states and processes to other people—are a legitimate instance of knowledge. They have been omitted from many epistemologies because they depend for their truth conditions upon subjective processes, while such things as the law of gravity presumably do not. Since scientific laws are more amenable to traditional lines of analysis, attribution processes have been ruled out of knowledge. These are not trivial matters since they constitute most of ordinary life; life-and-death questions often turn on them; our successes and failures in person-perception directly affect our life prospects, far more so in fact than most of the standard scientific instances of knowledge. They have been ruled out of epistemics not in a considered way but because they are harder to operationalize than most instances of knowledge. Ideas like love, respect, fear, honor, justice, and equity are oftentimes bound up in our most important decisions; but since they cannot be objectified in ways consistent with traditional thinking about objectivity, they are cast into the waste can of "the irretrievably subjective." Here we are developing a case for abandoning the dichotomy of *subjective versus objective*—which makes personal knowledge of other persons a legitimate instance of knowledge which poses special problems of interest to epistemics in general.

A paradigm case of argument requires at least some examples for which the truth conditions of claims are not structural features of language. People often make claims that are not grounded in some specifiable body of data apart from their psychological perspectives. In the philosophic sense, such statements could not be said to have truth conditions. There is likely a psychological counterpart of truth conditions, but it could hardly be satisfactory to traditional logicians. A statement such as "I believe you" often serves important regulative functions in an argument interaction; it specifies the ground which is undisputed and urges the conversation forward toward disputed ground. Indeed, such statements are sometimes used as data for subsequent arguments (especially by skilled arguers). For expositional ease, let us call such statements "perspective-rooted statements" (PRSs).

PRSs occur because arguments often turn upon personal characteristics and actions. It is a serious failing in argumentation that it has historically focused exclusively upon legal and political arguments while ignoring the more common variety of arguments in which people argue about each other. The result is disregard of the central epistemic functions of social interactions as social comparison processes in which arguers submit their constructions of events to the test of others' opinions. It is common in the interpersonal communication literature to claim that actors make attributions of other people. These attributions often become the foci of disputes and thus constitute an important genre of argument.

This is a subject with respect to which argumentation can make substantive contributions to interpersonal communication theory and research. Arguments share many generic characteristics of interaction, but they also have unique characteristics; and the study of the causes, effects, and procedural implications of these unique interactional effects should yield important substantive contributions to the interpersonal domain of theory and research. I can possibly illustrate this claim with the following hand-recorded exchange:

Example IV

W: "You drink too much."
P: [smiles, outraged voice] "I do not."
W: "You're always. I don't think. Everytime I see you you're drinking."
P: "That don't mean nothing. I hold it OK. I don't get drunk that much."
W: "All the time."
P: "Not drunk."
W: "Then you got a funny definition of drunk."
P: "People don't think. I don't drink too much; no problems."
W: "Just haven't been arrested for DWI [driving while intoxicated] yet."
P: "How much you drink, you know…, how many beers a day, doesn't

> mean nothing; guys drink a lot, doesn't cause problems; drunks can
> drink just a little and have problems; look at those boozer commer-
> cials on the box."

Only one of *P*'s claims has "truth conditions" outside his personal
perspective, namely, that television advertising by the Alcoholics
Anonymous organization links problem drinking to problems caused
by drinking any amount. His core claim appears to be "I do not drink
enough to cause problems; I am seldom drunk by my lights; I drink an
appropriate amount for me." The exchange, then, turns upon PRSs.

PRSs also occur in the context of broader arguments about politics
and other "external" matters. A lengthy argument, involving six people at different times (several came in and out of the room and partici-
pated once in a while), concerned whether Nazi war criminals should
be pursued and punished. Most of the argument turned upon questions
of how many criminals were still at large and whether the German
government is adequately pursuing the remaining criminals. In the
midst of this *W* (who had defended pursuit and punishment) is attacked personally:

Example V

> *W:* "I still think the guards themselves, guys who hold rifles on Jews as
> they go into the gas chambers, need killing."
> *C:* "Well, you're just a vindictive bastard; it does no good; you just
> impose religious...an eye for an eye, on the legal system."
> *W:* "Religion has nothing to do with it."
> *C:* "An eye for an eye; except how do you do an eye for an eye when a guy
> kills thousands of people; you'll probably want to torture them for the
> number of days of the people they killed."
> *W:* " 'Eye for an eye' doesn't mean religion; but, I hate to sound like '*X*,'
> but there's a whole generation of young people growing up who think
> evil isn't punished in this world; 'eye for an eye' corrects the failure of
> a social system to protect citizens who depended on it for protection."
> *C:* "So, 'eye for an eye' is like social contract?"
> *W:* "Yes."
> *C:* "For the social contract, you exact revenge on millions of people?"

To call *C*'s argument "ad hominem" is not to say anything interesting
about it. In truth, *C* is attempting to draw into the open a better
presentation of *W*'s construct system. He elicits an equation of revenge
with social contract theory; the argument proceeds to resurvey its
previous ground in light of the newly emergent assumptions. PRSs
thus serve clarifying functions even in the guise of ad hominem

attacks. It arguably makes no difference what the motives for the attack were, since it pragmatically forced *W* to clarify his view of revenge and to clarify other issues as well.

What is interesting about this sample is that the truth conditions of the claims reside in the cognitive system of the arguers rather than in events of the outside world. A core epistemic function of argument is revealed as *C* accomplishes at least two things: he learns more about *W*'s views per se and broadens his own conception of the implications of revenge arguments. Propositional logic would have the analyst searching for the empirical truth or falsity of the arguer's statements. If consensual theories of truth and value hold true, this is an endless and fruitless search. What is at issue in this argument (and of fundamental importance to the student of situated discourse) is that claims are being made and attacked that bear only upon a single person's views—a characteristic I claim to be paradigmatic of ordinary discourse. So viewed, ordinary talk is in at least some respects beyond the bounds of propositional logic.

The force of these claims is apparent if the reader grants that one often finds exchanges such that one would have to know the speakers to know what the words mean. Knowing the conventional meanings of the recorded speech act would not do. I shall divide ordinary argument fields into several categories, and one of them can be mentioned here—the *relational field*. My example is that of spouses who evolve specialized conventions over time that permit them to argue in elliptical and uniquely coded ways that would be completely inaccessible to someone who did not know them well. Nine years ago, my wife and I moved into a new apartment; and for one day our typewriter sat on a section of the kitchen counter. For some reason we called that the "typewriter table," to stand for the counter space to the immediate right of the stove. We have since moved twice and have never again set the typewriter in a kitchen. Yet the space to the immediate right of the stove is still the typewriter table. We often say "put it on the typewriter table" and know full well what we mean.

The special understandings which spouses build up over time perfectly represent what we mean when we think of argument fields— they are fields of background awarenesses that give meaning to data, warrants, and claims; the "logic" of their speech acts is not merely a species of conventional speech act logic. Family units are unique universes of discourse and merit our attention as much as broader social divisions—especially since it is likely that broader social divisions are similar in kind, that they have similarly arcane languages that we cannot understand without knowing the speakers. This

statement in a nutshell sets forth the research project for understanding argument fields—a posture we shall gradually flesh out in the
essays to follow.

Does this mean that PRSs are unresearchable? They are uniquely
subjective and obviously outside the range of conventional logic (or of
research based on logic). The role repertory grid techniques spawned
by Kelly's views aim at tapping a person's implicit theories by chi-
squaring the relationships that the individual believes obtain. Behind
every judgment an individual makes lie implicit theories about the
realm of events on which the judgment bears—theories of love, personality, honesty, argumentation, politics, and knowledge. Role repertory
grids reveal the content and form of these theories by finding out, for
example, that X believes people with cold eyes are mean with their
money or that people who believe in capitalism are always dishonest
or any other imaginable relationship. Fransella and Bannister (1977,
p. 2) say: "In using the metaphor of 'theory' we are not arguing that
such theories are formal and articulated. They may be verbal or nonverbal or preverbal, they may be tightly structured or loosely structured, they may be easily testable or almost too tangled to test, they
may be idiosyncratic or commonly held. But they *are* theories in the
sense of being networks of meaning through which persons see and
handle the universe of situations through which they move." Two
matters are noteworthy here: first, constructs are not to be confused
with verbal labels; constructs are discriminations rather than verbal
labels and are thus not necessarily tappable by propositional logics;
and, second, role repertory grids do in fact display the meanings of
PRSs.

In a way, completing a grid is merely a procedure for structuring an
interview. The grid, Fransella and Bannister say, formalizes the interview and allows the interviewer to assign values to a person's beliefs
about relationship. Thus data about a single person's system can be
treated to statistical analyses usually reserved for groups, for example,
cluster analyses, t-tests, correlational consistency measures, coefficients of concordance, and the like, and all possible ways of looking at
an individual's cognitive system. The grid thus arguably exposes the
truth conditions of PRSs and displays the operative working logic of
an individual. Toulmin and others believe that introducing psychological terms into logic makes the notion of logical form "impenetrably
obscure." The successes of role repertory grid techniques belie that
claim. They arguably prove the opposite, that is, that imposing logical
form on the processes of individuals makes psychologic impenetrably
obscure. Psychologic always fails if judged by absolutist logical standards. If these logical standards are suddenly construed to be useless

and otherworldly, psychologic can be examined in an entirely new light. "All forms of grid technique are sorting tasks which enable the person to tell us something of the way in which he sees and orders his world. We need not rely on normative data for an understanding of the construct patterning revealed. There is no fixed content and no one particular form that is the only right one for a particular context" (Fransella and Bannister, 1977). We need to discover not how an individual should construe events but how he in fact does, to define the pathways along which he is free to move.

I can perhaps recapitulate the present argument and exemplify its main implications by taking notice of an essential ambiguity in an idea that contemporary philosophers take rather at face value. I am referring to the argument springing from critiques of Kantian and neo-Kantian transcendental idealism which says that *knowledge does not affect the known*. The autonomy of the known serves as the keystone to many philosophic edifices nowadays, and it is an underlying assumption of traditional propositional logics when they are used to undergird epistemological accounts. The argument, which found one of its earliest and most eloquent statements in Hartmann's critiques of the neo-Kantians, is based upon assumptions about physical entities, that is, that knowledge of them does not change their character.

There are sound arguments drawing solely from the natural sciences against this position; but we need not deal with them here. Our claim is far more decisive: *social reality does depend upon the knower—but in an ambiguous way.* Since this ambiguity needs excising, we had best spend a moment considering it. Put simply, it is this: any attribution made by a social actor can simultaneously be described in physicalist and in constructivist terms. "She loves me" is thus construable two ways: whether or not I decide that she loves me, she either does or does not (that is, her cognitive processes do not depend upon mine), *yet* whether or not she loves me may very well depend upon what she attributes to me, and her attributions may be affected by my communications (which spring from my cognitive system).

This argument does not preclude the possibility of error. I can decide that she loves me not, when in fact she does. I can be at one moment correct and later incorrect if she loves me on Monday but does not on Tuesday. But the self-fulfilling prophecy is a core metaphor in social theory: whether she loves me or not may depend upon my social communications—and my communications depend upon whether I think she loves me. If I so define a situation that I am among hostile people, I may behave so that people who were indeed not hostile end up being hostile.

This is partly what symbolic interactionists mean by the phrase

"situations defined as real are real in their consequences." Constructions of events *are* the events. Thus the apparent ambiguity stems from
using physicalist notions to underpin our views of social processes.
Kelly, in saying that every individual is a unique locus of process and
thus of causation, ends up with a view that does not need physicalist
concepts at all. The villain here is a presumed parallelism between
physicalist notions and social accounts. Once we abandon the parallelism, the ambiguity goes away. The twin notions of social comparison
and constructivism mean that my thoughts affect my communications
which affect other social actors: the known is thus neither fixed nor
autonomous. The known in the natural sciences presumably does not
make attributions and behave toward the knower; the known in social
processes does both. We thus have Hawthorne effects (and countless
variants thereof) in social research, because a research act is itself a
form of communication with identifiable effects of its own. Because
social life entails the mutual interplay of actors, alternative taking of
influence, the claim that knowledge does not affect the known does not
hold.

To recapitulate, argument interactions—like all interactions—employ the full arsenal of communication modalities. The working logics
of ordinary argument thus partake of the same materials, discursive
and nondiscursive, that all conversation does. Language is not the sum
context of cognitive processes, and—as a consequence—utterance
takes meaning from the full cognitive context of meaning. The job of
criticism is to make this full context explicable. Propositional logic
fails us when it inappropriately reduces argument products to exclusively linguistic formulations, ignoring, for example, nonverbal
communication. It also assumes a narrow conception of "truth conditions" that is ill suited to ordinary communication analysis.

Criteria for Defining Argument Utterance

There are two popular ways of defining particular utterances as
arguments. Neither depends upon attributions to speakers. For different reasons both are ruled out by our paradigm cases. The two accounts are that an utterance counts as an argument if and only if (1) a
claim and explicit reasons for the claim are given or (2) a claim is given
and we are able to imagine reasons for the claim. These accounts are
related variously to the "reason-giving" theories of rationality in ways
that will become clear in the next chapter.

Theory (1) is lucid, though arbitrary. It makes the restrictive stipulation that an utterance is not an argument unless at least one reason is
explicitly linked to it by the speaker. Strictly speaking, this criterion

does not square with any of our examples. Rarely do the arguers explicitly state reasons. Either taking them for granted or waiting until they are called upon, the speakers observe what Grice (1975) calls the "quantity maxim" (to gloss, be as informative as necessary but not more than necessary). Reasons sometimes gradually emerge in our samples; but this is a symptom of the inquisitorial character of the interactions, and the reasons are not linked to the claims from the outset.

Criterion (1) yields a peculiar and otherworldly stance toward two common phenomena, namely, (1) that people often give reasons when they do not see themselves as arguers and in contexts that we would not ordinarily term "argumentative" and (2) that people seeing themselves as arguers often make solitary claims and series of claims unlinked to explicit reasons. Ordinary talk—of most sorts—is ambiguous and implicit; the implicit assumptions that do not need saying are often the framework endowing utterance with meaning. Thus explicit reason giving is moderately rare except in academic settings. Our paradigm cases do not rule reason giving out of argument; they imply that it is not the necessary condition of something's being an argument. Arguers often give reasons; but reason giving is a product, a symptom, rather than a necessary condition. The defining characteristic of argument utterance is that someone intends toward it as a claim upon attention and belief. Since virtually any statement can be so viewed, our paradigm cases do not use the presence of particular sorts of claims to define argument interaction. The paradigm cases suggest that argument utterances are the communication modes and devices employed by speakers who are dissensually oriented.

Line (2), that something is an argument if we can conjure up a reason, is too vague and muddled to be of much use. It is sometimes substituted for (1) because (1) is too narrow—the aim being to do justice to the elided, ambiguous, and enthymematic character of situated utterance. Since it is intuitively the case that arguers often leave reasons unstated, taken for granted, in the background of their overt claims, line (2) seems attractive because it does justice to this possibility.

But this view has no defining capacity without a very narrow concept of what may count as a "reason." It must rule out personal preferences and emotive alignments to avoid the implication that virtually any statement can be an argument. If someone has claimed that we should "stay drunk for a month" and, when pressed, avers that "it would feel good," line (2) dares not admit that this is a reason. If statements of this sort (for example, "because I want to," "I like it," "I prefer it") are said to be reasons, there are no limits upon the notion of argument. But we naturally ask on what principle line (2) rules such preferences out. We surely will not accept the justification of a restrictive sense of "reason," basically because line (2) will not succeed without it. But answers of this sort are usually what proponents of (2) have in mind. This occurs often in reason-giving accounts of rationality, to which I shall turn in the next chapter. By this account, proponents of (2) cannot defeat the tu quoque augmented by field theory, that is, cannot defend particular narrow definitions of what can count as a reason. Thus, (2) is either muddled or arbitrary.

Both lines (1) and (2) are inferior to holistic paradigm cases. If the examples are plausible, a conception of argument interaction may be the conceptual lens for understanding particular utterances. Explanations of both should be of a piece, that is, unified within a coherent theoretical framework—an accomplishment of the present paradigm cases but not of the reason-giving definitions. The use of particular orders of utterance to define argument requires a lucid connection to a view of interaction—which lines (1) and (2) lack. Both visions, for different reasons, are so at odds with our commonsense expectations of what ordinary talk is like that the present paradigm cases are prima facie superior.

The Linguistic Primacy Argument

Using one's paradigm case of argument interaction to define argument utterance broadens the utterance notion considerably. It implies that the full range of communication modalities comes into play in arguments, including kinesic, paralinguistic, and proxemic cues; it requires that we cease thinking of arguments exclusively as strings of propositions. The assumption is that a paradigm case of social interaction which had interactants exchanging nothing but propositions (that is, which ruled nonverbal communications out) would be implausible; hence a paradigm case of argument interaction will display communications in a variety of modalities. Taken seriously, the claim that argument is a form of communication requires that we not arbitrarily rule out of argument the characteristics we routinely and commonsensically impute to interpersonal communication in general. While arguments *have* special features (Willard, 1978a, 1980b), these are not arbitrary demarcations based upon a preference for working with propositional utterance.

The claim that argument may legitimately be viewed as a form of social interaction has proved remarkably uncontroversial. But the claim that the interactional view entails a broad conception of utterance has provoked an array of objections (Kneupper, 1978, 1979; Burleson, 1979a, 1979b, 1980a; D. J. O'Keefe, 1980, 1982; Balthrop, 1980; Gronbeck, 1980; McKerrow, 1980a, 1980b; Zarefsky, 1980). This result is odd, since I do not see how one can take the interaction view seriously and nonetheless maintain that arguments are basically linguistic (propositional) communications. In some cases, I think, the interactional view has been granted but has been thought to be innocuous. In other cases, a schism is defended between the body of theory and research undergirding the interactional view versus particular preferences for dealing with propositional utterance (for example, propositional logic, validity schemes, probabilistic systems, analytic programs, and language studies). This schism yields the peculiar result that the explanations and methods appropriate to the two senses of argument either bear no relation to one another or are flatly incompatible—reasoning that in turn leads to trivialities such as the recent disputes about whether one can utter arguments without being in an argument interaction or whether one can be in such an interaction without uttering arguments. I cannot see that it much matters how such disputes turn out; but the fact that they are even discussed proves that the schism between the two senses of argument is operating.

The strongest criticisms of the broad conception of utterance have stemmed from claims not that it is implausible or untrue but that it would vitiate traditional research and criticism. Critics are best able to judge propositional utterance; the broad definition casts the critic's bona fides for making flat declarative evaluations of reasoning into doubt. In the third chapter I shall claim that this objection is correct but that the critics who make this charge assume rather than defend the value of critical evaluation. I shall claim that these are tenuous and that evaluation (as traditionally conceived) has no place in useful criticism. For now, notice that this criticism of the broad sense of utterance does not deny its truth but merely protests its consequences.

A recurring criticism of the broad sense of utterance is that it blurs the most straightforward uncontroversial cases of argument, namely, propositional serials. This claim benefits from the simplest case reasoning vis-à-vis paradigm cases. Propositions become by this view the core of our sense of argument, while other kinds of communication fall into the penumbra of the definition. Consider, for example, Balthrop's (1980) claim:

> Until the beast is better known, I would urge that investigations of argument center upon those items which are clearly identifiable as providing support or justification for claims advanced. It may in truth turn out that argument can acquire presentational form or that nonverbal behavior can provide justification or representation. But to concentrate energies on phenomena which are intuitively borderline is to

run the risk that characteristics may be included as belonging to the
giving of reasons in specific situations which are not essential to such
activity....[P. 203]

But if the beast is not well known, how could any of its features be
clearly identifiable except by caprice? Logic is admittedly easier than
the empirical program required by the broader view of utterance; but
this does not legitimate logic as an analytic paradigm for understanding talk. Balthrop seems to claim that we should concentrate our
efforts on the things we do best, but the brief for a broad view of
utterance is a broadside against these procedures. The kicker comes
with Balthrop's reference to "phenomena which are intuitively borderline." Our paradigm cases suggest that syllogistic and propositional logics are borderline, rare, and exotic practices—the specialized
rites of natives in alien fields. In the next section, I shall turn to
particular claims about ordinary utterance that taken together say
that utterance for which propositional arrangements are the whole
story is itself intuitively borderline. Balthrop is thus expressing a
preference for the niceties of traditional analysis rather than defending them.

I propose to deal in paradigm cases because they are the first line of
evidence against such practices. The fact that propositional analysis is
more easily done and more consonant with traditional thinking proves
nothing unless ease and orthodoxy are equated with descriptive accuracy. More to the point, restricting one's sense of argument utterance
to propositional utterance rules a considerable array of intuitively
important phenomena out of argumentation. I have in mind clear
coorientations based on dissensus that proceed by virtue of messages
which are either nonpropositional or which entail juxtapositions of
discursive and nondiscursive elements. These interactions are "arguments" in that they involve someone making claims on another person's attention and belief (Toulmin, 1958, 1964); they sometimes
display reason giving (if the notion of "reason" is broadly construed);
and they serve the epistemic functions we want to ascribe to
arguments.

We have, for example, *nonverbal arguments*—exchanges in which
interactants acknowledge dissensus and deal with it in ways that
enhance their understandings of the events at hand. A variety of filmed
interactions of this sort has emerged in the nonverbal communication
literature. One such example (owed, I believe, to Birdwhistle) pictures
a woman seated alone at a library table, none of the other tables in the
large room being occupied. A man enters and seats himself next to the
woman. A battle ensues. The woman stares coldly at the man, sniffs
loudly, and by a variety of other actions makes clear claims upon his

attention and belief. The man eventually yields and moves to another table. No words are exchanged (before, during, or after the interaction). Obviously a coorientation of considerable complexity has been sustained: the rules of library seating have been violated; disapproval has been expressed; and the proprieties have been protected.

I recently observed an exchange in which a shabbily dressed man made as if to enter the lobby of a luxury hotel. The man caught the eye of a policeman standing nearby (as if to ask permission). The policeman's posture stiffened. The shabbily dressed man made shivering motions. The policeman continued to stare at the man. Finally, the man moved away. This involved, I think, a dissensual coorientation based upon background awarenesses of some complexity. It involved as well *explicit* reason giving (the shivering motion) as well implicit reason giving (the man and the policeman seemed to share an understanding that it was the policeman's job to keep bums out of hotel lobbies).

Consider as well television commercials which seek to create favorable associations between pleasant aesthetic experiences and the viewers' interpretations of product uses. Beer and wine, for instance, are sold by association with pleasant social occasions—propositional descriptions and claims being of minor importance in some commercials and even nonexistent in others. Films of happy people motoring through exciting countryside, with dramatic shots of the car reacting to the road, are claims upon our attention aimed at affecting our beliefs about the car and our uses of it. They are arguments (given our special assumptions), but they are couched less in words than in clever camera work, staging effects, and music.

Also, I have observed a variety of encounters in which one person uses words while his interlocutor uses no words at all. A typical example is this one:

Child: I didn't take your rings, Mommy.
Mother's posture stiffens; fixed stare, arms folded.
Child: I didn't!
Mother purses lips.
Child: I wasn't even in there!
Mother abruptly turns away from the child; returns to dishwashing as if to dismiss the child.
Child: I'm sorry. I'll try to find 'em.

Now, I do not want to claim that nonverbal arguments of the sorts mentioned here can stand alone as paradigm cases of arguments. Completely nonverbal exchanges are plausibly rarer than instances of the last sort, in which only one interactant uses no words. It bears repeating that I am not (strictly speaking) making "the paradigm case argument." I am elaborating a definition with a series of examples which defend the breadth of the conception of argument the definition implies. While I do not think nonverbal argument is a central aspect of daily interaction, I want to argue that it is common enough to merit our attention and (as well) typical enough of daily discourse that it merits inclusion in a definition of argumentation.

We also have *combinatory arguments*—arguments which combine propositional and nondiscursive content. These, I think, compose a far larger proportion of daily talk; and were we making (strictly speaking) *the* paradigm case argument, utterances in which discursive and non-discursive symbolism function interdependently to convey someone's meaning would be the sorts of examples we might most easily defend.

To start with, we have the standard arguments of nonverbal communications researchers to the effect that paralinguistic, proxemic, and kinesic cues often augment or contradict verbal utterances (see the various essays in Weitz, 1966). Sarcasm and irony, for instance, are possible only by virtue of these nonverbal resources. Of central importance is the fact that interlocutors respond, not to their opponent's words but to his intentions (for instance, in the sense that we respond to someone's sarcasm, not to his words). My claim is not that the words are unimportant: sarcasm and irony, after all, could not succeed as communications without the words. What is important is that sarcasm and irony could not succeed by words alone; they are made possible by the interdependencies of discursive and nondiscursive elements.

Nor are combinatory arguments exclusive to dyadic communication. The Nixon campaign of 1968 used film clips of war scenes overlaid with taped passages from Nixon's acceptance address; the words behind the pictures said something like "never in our history have so many lives been lost, so much money been spent, to so little effect as in Vietnam; I promise an honorable end to the war in Vietnam" (not verbatim). Doves perceived this as a dovish message and hawks heard it as hawkish. It was not the words alone that gave meaning to Nixon's message but their juxtaposition with nondiscursive elements.

Combinatory arguments also result from staged political events in which the speaker addresses a wildly enthusiastic audience of supporters. It is plausible to regard these events as staged performances for the benefit of television cameras—the cheering audience as much as the speaker being the "source" of the message. The audience's enthusiastic confirmation of particular claims of the speaker are as much a message to onlookers as anything the speaker says.

Perhaps *fear appeals* are the best examples of combinatory arguments. We know that strong fear appeals often backfire because the listener is roused to such a state of anxiety that he resists the message. We know that milder fear appeals combined with a stress upon solutions secure optimum opinion change and that the higher the credibility of the source, the greater the opinion change with such appeals. This fact permits the inference that fear gives meaning and direction to thought in important ways, that it can so organize one's thinking that certain claims are ignored, while others are accepted. Fear thus directly affects what will be seen as a good reason for something; or, conversely, it can lead someone to start rehearsing arguments against the message or to block the message out. Since arguments often occur in contexts (or about matters) involving fear and anxiety, we do not go far wrong in assuming that such emotions give meaning and scope to propositions. To describe a fear appeal is thus to describe a nondiscursive component of argument.

It might be objected that these are not arguments—merely instances of persuasion. But persuasive messages contain arguments, that is, specific claims upon attention and belief, and it is common to equate "making arguments" with the invention of persuasive messages. The complex forms—nonverbal and combinatory arguments—are attempts to impose form on the cognitive processes of hearers, to establish particular formal relationships. It is this characteristic that most theories which relate argument to reasoning try to capture. In the most precise sense, enthymemes are attempts to impose form on the hearers' thoughts. Nondiscursive and discursive messages similarly do the same. Attractive action sequences in car commercials are arguments about what it is like to use the car. They establish formal relationships in someone's mind in ways that square with our usual conceptions of argument's relations to cognition. Persuaders, let us say, use nonverbal and combinatory arguments when they seem more appropriate to the task at hand than propositional assertions.

To recapitulate, the paradigm cases augur for a broad view of messages. A conception of interaction may thus be a conceptual lens for understanding utterance. It is not the presence of a particular sort of claim that makes an interaction an argument; it is the coorientation of the speakers. Most of the claims for narrowing the notion of argument utterance to propositional serials are based more upon research and analytic preferences than upon considered claims that propositional serials are the best paradigm cases. Propositionalizing is the "simplest case" and by far the most accessible to traditional research and analytic procedures; but these considerations do not in themselves justify the simplest case reasoning. If the examples here are nontrivial, we have a prima facie case for broadening our view of what may count as an argument utterance. We are led to the conclusion that propositional models have unduly narrow foci of convenience. It remains to be seen whether nondiscursive symbolism falls within their ranges of convenience, that is, whether we understand nondiscursive messages exclusively by translating them into propositions—a question to which I now turn.

Theoretical Holism

The paradigm case argument that has preoccupied us till now presupposes the value of theoretical holism.[3] The explanatory constructs and research methods appropriate to argument interactions and utterances should fit together in a consonant arrangement under the umbrella of a communication theory that explains their relationships. Research findings about each should coalesce in ways predicted by (and which buttress) the organizing theory. The psychology and sociology of communication should be two sides of the same coin—different levels of generalization about phenomena that fit together in a unified, integrated, and coherent theoretical framework. Argumentation should fit into this framework as a communication theory of a special kind, that is, that concerned with interactions based upon perceptions of dissensus and the special importance these bear for epistemics. Such internal coherence is the minimal precondition of a good theory, and strictly speaking it is a metatheoretical case for holism.

These metatheoretical concerns are augmented by commonsense expectations about ordinary interaction and speech. It is plausible to expect that a person's behavior is of a piece with the ways he organizes his thinking and that his social behavior will stem from his interpretations of situations. This holism of cognitive processes and action lends plausibility to holistic views of social life; it implies that people in groups are still people; things said of their group behavior must square with things said of individual behavior unless exceptions can be proved. People demonstrably do different things in groups but, as the discussion of argument fields will show, group accounts have worked least well when group actions were said to differ *in kind* from individual actions. Field theory is a group theory of a particular sort which equates group life with perspective taking (a specialized version of Mead's "Me"). There are no good reasons to suppose that a person's cognitive processes differ in kind when he enters group life; thus explanations of communal action must stem from and cohere with cognitive accounts. Objectivity, I shall argue, is always a subjective accomplishment—a claim which makes sense when cognition and action are viewed holistically.

Epistemic investigations often start with the most basic sense of the term "field," namely, a person's field of attention or phenomenal field. Posed in the Cartesian manner, one must first know that one knows before questioning the possibility of knowledge; one must have at least the intuition that one knows in order to ask how one knows. The phenomenal field, then, has often been thought to be the starting place for studies which yield insight into the conditions of knowledge. This focus is appropriate for many reasons and is utterly essential to a sociological account. The paradigm cases must square with this basic sense of "field" in order to ensure that the sociological account of argument fields does not flatly contradict the psychological one. These two senses of "field," then, must be two sides of the same coin.

Argument fields are real social entities taking their existence from the defining activities of actors. They are points of reference, objectified stances people take to check particular interpretations against communally trusted standards. Viewed another way, fields are the distinctions we draw between the ways different communal traditions objectify their thinking. I shall essay in the third chapter to consider the breadth and overlap of the various distinctions theorists have chosen to draw among human activities. Both of these views of fields, however, imply that argument fields have something of the character of the recurring cognitive processes that animate them.

The paradigm cases of argument should by all odds link the psychological and sociological senses of "field" together. Communication coordinates individual viewpoints, making social life possible. Argument interactions are important versions of this continual accommodation of the psychological to the sociological (and the reverse). Conceptions of argument thus need to square with psychological and sociological accounts. Entering a field is a cognitive accomplishment, a form of perspective taking in some respects synonymous with "coming to know." Arguments are rather common social comparison processes by which this perspective taking occurs. They are intended toward by virtue of a person's interpretive schemes—the definition of situation being of paramount importance—and they have social effects, that is, they are important aspects of the ongoing accommodational acts that make up argument fields. The psychological and sociological senses of "field" are thus *perspectives*, and arguments are the *processes* by which these perspectives are brought together. A holistic theory will explain all three in the same terms.

The "constructivist/interactionist" framework can serve this holistic aim (see Willard, 1978a, 1978b, 1979a, 1979b, 1980b). It involves a merger of Kelly's (1955) personal construct theory (Adams-Weber, 1979; Bannister, 1962, 1966, 1970; Bannister and Bott, 1973; Bannister and Fransella, 1971; Bannister and Mair, 1968; Fransella and Bannister,

1977) with selected aspects of Chicago School symbolic interactionism (Blumer, 1969; Denzin, 1970). One effects this merger by virtue of higher-order assumptions about communication and its place in cognitive development and social interaction (Delia, 1976a, 1976b, 1977a, 1977b, 1978; Delia and O'Keefe, 1979; Delia, O'Keefe, and O'Keefe, 1982). One focuses upon the meaning-constitutive processes by which actors place interpretations upon events and arrange their constructs into hierarchical systems. Thinking is defined as movement along pathways among networks of constructs. The man-as-scientist metaphor ties this concept together: a person's behavior is experimental—a trying of constructs on for size. Social life is one manifestation of this process. It is premised upon the person's ability to take the perspectives of others and to accommodate a developing line of action to others' expectations. Field theory is a specific way of talking about Mead's "generalized other." Fields are, inter alia, traditions of practice, of expectations; they are points of view a person may take.

My aim has been to build a conception of argument interactions and utterances from this theoretical framework. This effort yielded the claim that argument utterances are implicit, elided, and enthymematic—reflecting the cognitive processes that produce them; their meanings cannot, strictly speaking, be reduced to simple "propositionalizing" in all cases; nonverbal arguments are important though rare, and combinatory arguments are as important as propositional ones. And propositional serials rarely stand alone—a matter I shall address in a moment.

Linguistic Determinism

The present framework is not the only way of holisitically linking views of psychology, sociology, and argument. At least one variant of the "linguistic turn" (Rorty, 1967) would have it that language determines thought, utterance, and (therefore) social life. Argument utterances would be seen as exhaustively linguistic formulations—these obeying the same laws, that is, the structural imperatives of a language system, that inform all thought. Social *structures* would be inferred from distinctions in the language; they would be seen as offshoots of the language. This view looks mightily like the old Sapir-Whorf hypothesis—or, more probably, like Russell's theory of logical types. Both accounts would holistically link argument, psychological fields, and sociological fields, together in terms of the determining force of language.

The criticisms of linguistic determinism are familiar and require no rehashing here. The constructivist/interactionist scheme can be presented alongside the deterministic view, and certain comparative arguments can be made. Among them, I shall claim that deterministic accounts blur intuition and nondiscursive symbolism into language—which is untenable—or they ignore these things because they do not square with a strictly put deterministic thesis. For another thing, I shall urge that deterministic accounts have not yielded the useful research one might expect from a plausible theory. If the present framework produces useful and interesting research, all the while assuming that language is not the sole or even the most basic mode of cognitive and social organization, we may be pardoned for bypassing linguistic determinism in much the same manner that people bypass seedy taverns.

There is another reason for avoiding a specific critique of determinism. I want to object to particular ways of thinking about rationality and evaluation in criticism. I proceed on the assumption that a reader who stays with me while I do so is interested in such matters in themselves. Determinism trivializes rationality by making it a feature of a language structure, not of people; the subject of rationality and its attendant issues could not envisionably be interesting if the deterministic thesis is accepted. This argument does not refute determinism; it justifies our avoiding getting bogged down in the arguments that do. Evaluation in criticism likewise could not be interesting on the deterministic account: if the structure of language determines cognitive organization, *choices* are features of the structure of language and evaluations of choices the worked-out implications of that structure. If a critic believes that language in any nontrivial sense determines thought, then attributions of good and evil, right or wrong, justice and injustice must be to the language structure, not to the person—which makes evaluation banal. Again, this argument does not refute determinism; it validates our decision to ignore it on the grounds that the issues which interest us do not fit deterministic thinking. If our speculations ultimately guide useful research, we shall have added the coup de grace to the case against linguistic determinism.

The Schism Revisited

Till now, the value of holistic accounts of interaction and utterance has been taken for granted. The main justification for it has been that the account integrates the psychological and sociological senses of "field." But the grounds on which someone might reject the holism of interaction and utterance need to be considered. Let us imagine an interlocutor who is not in the least impressed with the case for holism and who is not a determinist—in this case, does not believe that language is the sole or even the most fundamental mode of cognitive organization. The interlocutor seeks to pursue an ordinary language program which brackets psychology, regards arguments as serial predications, and studies the outcomes of particular linguistic arrangements. He might thus insist upon the schism by virtue of a linguistic focus.

The study of language systems is manifestly valuable and of foundational importance to many pursuits. If languages, understood as systematic arrangements of rules and equivalences, contain important possibilities and constraints, we surely need to know them. Studies of languages qua systems thus owe no apologies to us. Since language is of pivotal importance to communication, linguistic studies may augment the present program.

Difficulties arise if our interlocutor makes somewhat broader claims, for example, that studying languages qua systems will yield a complete account of situated meaning. Some argument theorists make equations of this sort (for example, Kneupper, 1978, 1979). The schism between interaction and utterance is implicitly defended because the implicatures of linguistic arrangements are thought to account for meanings comprehensively. I have elsewhere critiqued this thinking (Willard, 1981b) on the grounds that it assimilates all features of nondiscursive symbolism to language—a theoretical move not countenanced by the literature. I shall resurrect some of these claims in a moment. Hence I want to consider whether such broad claims collapse argument criticism to literary criticism of the sort championed by Derrida and the Yale deconstructionists.

The belief that one can look at a literary work in itself, apart from its creator, is a rather standard one. It is owed to Eliot, Ransom, Brooks, and the New Criticism as well as to Gadamer and the hermeneutic tradition. The guiding assumption of this thinking—which is of foundational importance to my own views—is that an author's linguistic arrangements have implications of their own which might or might not cohere with the author's intentions. This assumption seems intuitively sound. Linguistic formulations are amenable to various alternative interpretations; every language system contains possibilities far broader than any particular person's intentions are likely to be. The implicatures in a language system are such that we always risk saying more than we mean and sometimes something different from what we mean. So the author's intentions for a literary work have long been seen as merely one line of interpretation among many for purposes of understanding literature.

This thinking vivifies the differences between literary and argumentation criticism. Argument critics are centrally interested not in works of art but in what speakers mean; they seek to understand situated action, the effects of arguments upon occasioned activity. The range of possibilities in an utterance is a part of this project (and a precondition of explanations of misunderstandings); but the broader aims of argument criticism require that attention be paid to what an arguer *means*. To study the epistemic functions of argument, one must see how arguers function; we could not know how someone takes something to be knowledge without knowing how he takes things *period*. Similarly, to study the social grounds of knowledge, one must study the ways individuals accommodate their intended-toward actions with the developing lines of others. The minimum expectation of such projects is that we understand not all of the possible implications of an utterance but the particular intentions operating in the situation. Thus while literary critics can for certain purposes bracket the author, argument critics cannot.

Derrida takes many of the traditional assumptions of the New Criticism and animates them with particular methodological preferences for spieling out all of the possible implications of a literary work. In this he resembles the hermeneutic tradition. The difference becomes clear when we consider the breadth of his claims. Deconstruction, that is, proceeds in a perfectly respectable and sensible way until one realizes that Derrida *rules out* rather than brackets the author. He does so by virtue of a thoroughgoing linguistic determinism meshed together with a particularly narrow view of structural linguistics. The author is uninteresting to Derrida because authors in general are *possessed* by language, that is, bound by its implicatures. Criticism is thus that branch of linguistics that studies implicatures in literary works.

Pinned to determinism, such studies cannot be interesting. If the author cannot be a background element of a literary work, then how can the efforts of critics be important? If authors are seized by particular logics of the language system, so are critics. Some deconstructionists see themselves as spieling out the range of a language's implicatures but by a breathtaking leap deny this autonomy and insight to authors. Moreover, criticism could do no good: since the logic of the language will play itself out regardless of authorial intentions, it will do so regardless of critical intentions. If, as Derrida insists, "there is only language," criticism is impotent and an illusion; critics become possessed by particular implicatures and, in a manner not unlike the practice of mediums who let the dead speak through them, they present not their own work but that of the language system. This implies that criticism is indistinguishable from literary creation; critics are no different from authors; their best work would be the writing of more literature and poetry. Presumably they would not sign their articles.

In ancient Greece, men were possessed by the gods; in the Middle Ages they were possessed by demons and angels; in later times they were possessed by vapors and bile; nowadays, since it is faddish to make language man's most fundamental attribute, we say that man is possessed by language. The importance of language (which is not in dispute here) rules out holistic accounts only if determinism is postulated. The insistence upon linguistic determinism creates rather pointless disputes. Sans determinism, the methods of the deconstructionists fit into a variety of projects, including the present one. Authors, critics, and situated social actors are alike concerned with the problem of saying what they mean or with concealing their intentions for tactical reasons; they alike consider as best they can the range of implications of expressions—these considerations composing what rhetorical theorists call "invention." Deconstructive methods are appropriate and indispensable to studies of invention as long as determinism is not insisted upon. Insist upon determinism, and the deconstruction becomes the whole—uninteresting—story. Back to Sapir-Whorf.

I prefer Kelly's (1955) view of freedom and determinism. Higher-order constructs determine the meanings of subordinate ones (and therefore are free of the subordinate constructs). Every unexamined assumption, Kelly says, is a hostage one gives to fortune; theories are attempts to explain phenomena and are thus "the thinking of men seeking freedom amidst swirling events." Reflective thinking about one's presuppositions frees one from them. By this account, one is enslaved by language insofar as one is unreflective about its effects; one becomes free of language by considering it reflectively. This removes the unproductive dichotomy of author and critic which deconstructionist accounts often entail. It implies that there are virtually no limits to the implicatures humans can dream up—these innovative implicatures being avenues to freedom from the effects of older ones. Thus in arguing about language we are not talking ontology. We are considering traditions of practices—these bearing (I shall argue) the full breadth of human symbolic accomplishment.

If argument critics take up Derrida's deterministic account—which I want to distinguish from deconstructionist methods—they will have nothing interesting to say about situated talk. If they defend the schism of utterance and interaction on the grounds that a person's intentions are shaped by language, they will by definition preoccupy themselves with texts at the expense of situation action. Since this account requires that choices be seen as implications of linguistic structures, argument critics will become structural linguists; they will be uninterested in particular strategic choices arguers make. If language informs all thought, then it is a language system that is responsible for good and evil, truth and falsity; it is the language system that produces choices.

If language informs all thought, argument fields will be distinguished by virtue of structural elements in a language. This eventuality would be something like using a theory of types (à la Russell or Ayer) to define social organizations. I shall not repeat my arguments against this view (see Willard, 1981a) other than to point out that this reasoning flies in the face of overlaps and shared concepts among fields. If "psychology" is a field because psychologists speak of "psychology" and its special words, no field using the same words and concepts would be distinguishable from psychology. Yet many obviously different traditions use the terms "attitude," "belief," "ego," or "persuasion." The imported concept is in fact a remarkably common feature of fields (Willard, 1982). Fields do use arcane vocabularies, but the vocabularies overlap enough to make this aspect unreliable as a criterion for distinguishing fields. The facts of language are symptoms, not causes, of field divisions, and a successful field theory based on this assumption will not merely call the deterministic view of deconstruction into doubt but will arguably discredit it.

We started with an interlocutor who presupposed no determinism, and we found little to dispute in his position. He maintains the schism between utterance and interaction for particular—and entirely respectable—purposes that do not contradict our own. So viewed, the focus of the New Critics, the hermeneutic tradition, and the deconstructionists on the alternative constructions that can be placed upon texts can be a useful adjunct to argument criticism. Deconstructive methods may indeed play a pivotal role in studies of nondiscursive symbolism. By this account language studies are important elements of a far larger and more complex puzzle. And for purposes of argument criticism, holism remains the preferred theoretical posture. The three ranges of concepts—the phenomenal field, argumentation, and the sociological field—are linked together not by a single unifying (and determining) thread such as language but by a complex of symbolic forms that are either interdependent (as in the case of nondiscursive symbols) or independent (as in the case of intuition) of language.

The Nondiscursiveness Thesis

People intend toward utterance. They try to say things to people by so arranging their utterances that the things they say mean roughly

what they want them to mean. They define their communication
problems in situations and try to accomplish by speech what they
intend to accomplish. For many reasons they often err: they say less, or
more, or something different from what they mean to say. Excepting
the most mundane cases of referential communications, people who
want to say what they mean are forced to select among a variety of
options—all of which can be made to say things other than what the
speaker intends. Like deconstructed literary texts, situated utterances
can mean any number of things, depending upon the interpretive line
someone takes toward them.

Explanations of how speakers try to make the things they say mean
what they want them to mean have recently turned upon the notion of
indexicality (Bar-Hillel, 1964, 1970; Garfinkle, 1967). Indexical expressions are often contrasted with "objective" ones when they are
equated with (say) Russell's egocentric particulars or Reichenbach's
"token-reflexive words." Their ideal, of course, was to purge ideal
languages of all such words for analytic purposes. Thus social scientists who focus upon indexicality see it as a particularized feature of
talk, the occasioned nature of speech. In Garfinkle's words, "Accounts
are reflexively and essentially tied for their rational features to the
socially organized occasions of their use for they are *features* of the
socially organized occasion of their use" (1967, p. 4). Intending toward
utterance is of a piece with intending toward occasions—which we
may roughly gloss to say that the definition of situation guides speakers in making the things they say mean what they want them to mean.
Cicourel (1974) has captured this sense of indexicality in a way to my
liking:

> Language itself is the most artificial and "the most human of all human
> constructions...." But it does not follow...that only the expressible is
> thinkable, and that if this is true, only the thinkable is expressible. The
> thinkable is expressible only through indexical expressions. Our reflex-
> ive use of the particulars of the setting (the intonation of language use, the
> social and physical ecology, the biography of the speakers, the social
> significance of the occasion, etc.) and our kinaesthetic, somaesthetic,
> perceptual, and linguistic memory, to mention some of the apparently
> central ingredients, all contribute to the irreparable indexicality of com-
> munication. [P. 140]

Situated speech thus presupposes competence with the rule structure
of the language and an interplay between this competence and situated performances. This reasoning leads to an ethnomethodological
view that sees meaning as "situated, self-organizing and reflexive

interaction between the organization of memory, practical reasoning, and talk. Linguistic rules are seen as normative constructions divorced from the cognitive reflection and ethnographic settings in which speech is produced and understood" (Cicourel, 1974, p. 100). Language is merely one part of this scheme: "Our human experiences continually outstrip our ability to express them in speech acts. We must assume that a number of tacit properties are operative or plausible when we code, recode and then use information to communicate..." (1974, p. 111). Cicourel stresses that many features of cognitive and communicative processes proceed nonverbally, including aspects of language chunking, visual information processing, and intuitive organizations of experience. There is a holism of cognitive processes—whose products may be looked at from any number of analytic perspectives, including syntactic-formalism—in which verbal expressions are bound up and interdependent with partially verbal and utterly nonverbal elements.

This view squares with personal construct theory's (Kelly, 1955) account of mind. Constructs are discriminations. Some are verbally labeled; some are not. They are hierarchically arranged in systems, regnant constructs giving meaning to subordinate ones. This means that discursive and nondiscursive symbols are interdependent—each endowing the other with meaning. Kelly (1955) stresses that it is not possible for a person to express all of the elements of a system because some of the discriminations cannot be clearly represented verbally. Thus people do not always mean what they say and often mean considerably more (or less) than what they say:

> It may be impossible for one to express certain constructs in such a way that others can subsume them within their own systems without mispredicting him. They "take him at his word," but he does not mean by his word what they think he means. It therefore appears that he does not mean what he says. Sometimes a person's verbal experession represents such a contamination of constructs that he himself, when he hears a transcription of his remarks against a different background of circumstances, may be amazed at what seems to be an important part of his verbal behavior. [P. 111]

Cognitive processes are much richer than the linguistic code—which means that communication is always a struggle toward expression. Verbal and nonverbal elements are interdependent—which means that cognitive activities are often preoccupied with giving verbal handles to nondiscursive elements and with making verbal discriminations square with nondiscursive orientations.

This view has far-reaching consequences for views of argument utterance, some of which are captured in the shorthand phrase "nondiscursiveness thesis" (see Willard, 1981b). The nondiscursiveness thesis (NDT) stands inter alia for these ideas: (1) argument is a species of communication, sharing most if not all of the generic characteristics; (2) the things we say of people "having an argument" should square with the things we say about interactants generally; (3) arguers and all interactants employ from time to time, in varying degrees, all communication modalities; (4) personal and communicated constructs are not exhaustively linguistic, so meanings are not exhaustively linguistic; (5) discursive symbols are not the sole or consistently the most fundamental mode of cognitive organization; and, therefore, (6) views of argument utterance best reflect this complexity when not restricted to propositionalizing. The intuitive idea is that traditional views of utterance have been unrealistically narrow; arguers use the full range of verbal, kinesic, paralinguistic, and proxemic codes to make the things they say mean what they want them to mean. Nondiscursive symbolism is often an integral part of what someone means by an expression.

The term "nondiscursive" derives from Langer's (1957) distinction between language and the rich array of nonlinguistic symbolic forms composing cognitive life. While her broad communication theory is incompatible with the present formulation,[4] her distinction between discursive and nondiscursive symbolism is congenial. She stresses that many of the most fundamental sources of disagreement, especially values, are not reducible to language. Many aspects of our sensuous, mental, and emotional life—"our felt life," as James had it— cannot be expressed in words: "The symbolic presentation of subjective reality for contemplation is not only tentatively beyond the reach of language—that is, not merely beyond the words we have; it is impossible in the essential frame of language" (Langer, 1957, p. 24). Thus, for example, when personal construct theorists speak of implicit theories (of personality, causality, or argument), they are not saying that such theories are articulated or formal; they may be nonverbal. Nor do they mean that experiences are always verbally labeled. We cannot reduce to words aesthetic experiences of (say) combinatory or nonverbal arguments; we cannot verbalize a C major chord superimposed on an A minor trill. The language bound arts, poetry and fiction, express some of their most profound insights only by indirection: they hint and suggest in an attempt to so juxtapose form and ideational content as to call up in the reader feelngs that cannot be directly expressed. Consider, for example, Williams's classic:

so much depends
upon

a red wheel
barrow

glazed with rain
water

beside the white
chickens[5]

The term "nondiscursive" may subsume a variety of common but less clear dichotomies, for example, *verbal versus nonverbal, affective versus cognitive, emotional versus logical, conceptual versus preconceptual,* and *language versus la parole.* These are themselves broad distinctions; they are often confusing because they cut in different ways. *Discursive versus nondiscursive* is broad enough to subsume most of the conceptual baggage carried by these dichotomies, and this breadth allows us to explain some of the incompatibilities among the distinctions in elegant ways. Notice, for example, that *emotional versus logical* fits poorly into the present scheme. Theorists who defend the primacy of language often equate rationality with language and irrationality with the nondiscursive; the breadth of the NDT makes this view irrelevant for our purposes (although it remains interesting as a social belief).

Like Cassirer, Langer stresses a parallelism between the discursive and nondiscursive realms; unlike Cassirer, she is willing to assert the primacy of the nondiscursive. There is thus no *rational versus irrational* dichotomy in her thinking, since both realms partake of both elements. Distinctions such as *conceptual versus preconceptual, affective versus cognitive,* or *intuitive versus rational* are not especially meaningful, since they turn upon the more basic *linguistic versus nonlinguistic* dimension. This fact suggests the need for a broader conception of rationality.

Rationality and Nondiscursive Symbolism

The present view is that rationality needs to be understood holistically, in terms of the intuitions, passions, values, and situational adaptations that give meaning to words. This thinking is elaborated and defended in the next chapter. It is appropriate here to consider the implications of the NDT for rationality. Since rationality historically has been operationalized in terms of propositional and syllogistic logic, that is, verbal formulations of whatever sort, the NDT bears far-reaching consequences for such operationalizations.

It is the nondiscursive endowment that gives humans many of the characteristics we are prone to praise and blame: senses of justice and fairness, rightness and evil, propriety and appropriateness, and—in general—the cognitive arrangements that undergird valuing. Language is far too impoverished to express these intuitions and "senses," but it would be fatuous to conclude that they are unimportant or that they do not measurably affect the outcomes of private and social projects. Modesty leads women to ignore the "sound arguments" for having Pap smears; this disregard often kills them. Fear often changes the course of decision making—as Aristotle advised that it should for men of practical wisdom. Love and hate alter the meanings of many symbols; patriotism, ideology, ethnocentrism, and prejudice are powerful influences upon arguments (in both senses). Faith, hope, and charity (and whatever other platitudinous virtues we can conjure up) are far more complex symbolic structures than the words we have to describe them. In every case these virtues constitute the bases for valuing—which I take to be the foundation for a successful account of rationality.

The positivists make propositional expressibility the necessary condition of rationality. This ignores the intuitive grounds of, say, my sense of justice, fair play, and fitness: rational arguments could consist of nothing but propositions about justice. Since it is often difficult and sometimes impossible to articulate intuitions in propositional form, they are thus fiated out of rationality. Values are reduced to the things that can be said of them and passions are reduced to being synonymous with the things said about them. Two points are noteworthy: (1) proponents of primacy have not accomplished this view of rationality by virtue of rigorous arguments; the warrants for their claims are virtually indistinguishable from their data, since they only proclaim that propositional utterance is the necessary condition of rationality; and (2) this perspective ignores the fact that most moral theorists, even those loath to accept the intuitionist line, have seen a need to grapple with the idea of intuition; it is certainly arguable that no conception of justice can stand completely apart from assumptions about intuition—and surely the idea of justice typifies the sort of thing that rationality is supposed to be about.

Western philosophers have usually distinguished intuition from inference on the (circular) grounds that intuition cannot be inferential. Two major philosophic senses of "intuition" have emerged, distinguished according to their epistemic status: (1) intuition that cannot be propositionally expressed, that is, A knows X; A cannot advance reasons for knowing X and does not know how he came to know X; and (2) intuition that can be propositionally justified post facto, even though it is not attained that way, that is, A knows X, does not know how he came to know X, but can formulate serial predications that justify X not as an immediate apprehension but as an entailment. It is this second sense of intuition that moral philosophers have grappled with; the common attitude toward this sense has been that "intuition is not itself inferential; but it is a real and important phenomenon which clearly bears upon human cognitive life; it is clearly the source of values, moral judgments, and a host of other conceptions; although it differs in kind from discursive utterance, it likely gives meaning to many propositions, especially statements about the good; and, since the existence of intuition is uncontroversial, its interactions with inference cannot be ignored." Philosophers more inclined to the first sense of intuition have usually agreed with these assumptions but have argued that there are features of intuition that can never be linguistically cast which are nonetheless fundamental to ideas like rationality and justice. Bergson typifies this school. Thus despite myriad disputes about its nature, function, and expressibility, moral philosophers have consistently seen the need to address the issue of intuitionism. Positivists, thanks to the predefining nature of their linguistic assumptions, merely fiat intuition out of the picture.

Two psychological senses of intuition can be added to the philosophic ones: (1) nonpropositional knowledge, that is, knowledge of phenomena which are themselves not capable of being linguistically expressed—perhaps Bergson's conception of time is an exemplar of this view; and (2) immediate knowledge, that is, the direct experiencing of some phenomenon's essential character without the ability to state propositionally what that essence is; an offshoot of this thinking is the group of perceptual theories which define lived experience, the ongoing stream of perception, as the organism's intuitive orientation to events. So viewed, intuitions are uncontestedly real phenomena which exert psychologically interesting effects. At issue is the operationalizability of the idea of intuition. Positivists have lamented the "mystical" quality of intuitionist accounts and the inability of social scientists to research the subject successfully. Psychologists of other stripes have been contesting a variety of alternative research designs and theoretic formulations.

To these four senses of intuition can be added a conception of ordinary parlance, that is, "hunches," intimations, gut feelings. Philosophers and social scientists have regarded the existence of hunches as uncontroversial; philosophers have been uninterested in them because they defy the second sense of intuition—they are completely unexpressible—and psychologists have regarded hunches as being of great interest but essentially unresearchable. The loose idea of hunches interacts with some of the senses of intuition mentioned above; and it is difficult to distinguish between, say, a "sense of justice" and a "hunch" in all circumstances. Thus there is nothing wrong with saying that a "hunch" can be a "rational bet," to use Rawls's fortunate locution. Moreover, it is not unarguably wrong to believe that hunches reflect one's past constructions of experience. So viewed, hunches cannot be ruled out of a conception of rationality.

The unifying notion undergirding all five senses of intuition is that an intuition is something that people treat as knowledge and which is not preceded by inference. It passes muster for knowledge, although it is not produced by a process of inference. None of these senses needs to mean that inference is completely independent and distinct from intuition, although they are sometimes construed that way. Some intuitionists are so called because they seek to explain the *interactions* between intuition and inference. They have united, even with their critics, around the idea that inference and intuition differ in kind but interact. This thinking must be dealt with.

I have elsewhere (1978d, 1979a) detailed the ways personal construct theory can undergird a rigorous and researchable conception of intuition. I located intuition not in some mystical *sensus communis* or faculty but in the effects of regnant constructs upon the subordinate discriminations in the systems they rule. These in part form the background awarenesses underlying daily life (Cicourel, 1970, 1974); they are the taken-for-granted, not-to-be-questioned presuppositions that inform particular constructive processes in situations. This definition dovetails with the senses of "freedom" and "determinism" embraced here—especially with the notion that one may be enslaved by unexamined assumptions. However free or determined someone is, intentions toward utterance are derived from construct systems—these often being intuitively arranged by virtue of long-forgotten constructive accomplishments.

One can stipulate that a statement cannot be rational unless the suppositions behind it are propositions; but this requirement is arbitrary. First, rationality theories that include it fall victim to the tu quoque in the form *justification that the belief that* p *is rationally held either infinitely regresses or collapses to irrational commitment to a particular rationality theory.* I elaborate this point in the next chapter. Second, restricting rationality to things that can be said divorces rational claims from just the things rationality should explain: justice and fairness, rightness and evil, love and hate, faith and trust, hope and optimism, and charity and empathy.

One can stipulate that reasoning must be logical to be rational. But doing so means that rationality has no specifiable results. Logic, that is, can justify almost any evil, silly, or outrageous conclusion. Perfectly logical humans, sans values—without their nondiscursive endowments—are brutes. Their kind of rationality can write *Principia Mathematica* and design Buchenwald; it can reason its way to Kant's antinomies and plan the clearing of the Warsaw Ghetto. It is values, not logic, that cry out against the worst of human practices. Consider, for example:

> Programs to eliminate evil races are good things.
> Auschwitz was a program to eliminate an evil race.
> Auschwitz was a good thing.

Or:

> Races that oppress our race are evil.
> The Jews oppress our race.
> The Jews are evil.

We might need to clean up these syllogisms, but their terms are properly arranged. Logic does not test these premises; experience and our orientations to it are the tests.

To recapitulate, most accounts use "rationality" to name things distinctively human; they proceed too narrowly when they equate rationality with language or with things expressible in language. The result is a useless opposition between intuition and rationality which needlessly rules out nondiscursive endowments of rationality. We require a view of rationality that avoids these limitations and coheres with the facts of communication and perspective taking upon which the sociological view of fields is based.

Argumentation originally cut itself off from the broader communication discipline by virtue of the *conviction versus persuasion* duality. Logic and emotion were discrete matters; the persuasion theorists were in charge of ethos and pathos, argumentation theorists took proprietary interest in logos. This thinking is an historical embarrassment because the faculty psychology undergirding it had been taken for granted. The stipulation that nothing can count as argument (or as being rational) unless propositionally couched amounts to nothing but the conviction-persuasion duality masquerading as philosophy of language. Taken as an exhaustive account, its prospects are just as dim.

Problems of Criticism

Granting the nondiscursiveness thesis, the problem of criticism is to make explicit that which is implicit in talk. The traditional continuity of the field of argument criticism must be founded upon the ongoing expansion of critical instruments, including the language of criticism. Every critical act must both illuminate its object and enrich the language of criticism, each critical act thus hermeneutically expanding the possibilities both of the objects of criticism and of criticism itself. This statement implies that the field of criticism can secure "progress" in the usual sense of that term—an argument taken up below.

The strict equation of arguments with propositionalizing confuses the standard mode of critical communication with the nature of the objects of criticism. It does so whether or not one recognizes that one is translating nondiscursive into discursive forms—whether or not, that is, one is mindful of the pitfalls of translation. Language, Bergson said, inevitably carves up and hypostatizes the unitary flow of lived experience; on its horizon, everything is translatable to language whether it fits or not. The danger, as Russell said, is that one can easily forget or overlook the effects of language: rather as if we carve a chicken into pieces and then assume that chickens by nature come in the pieces we have carved.

Critics who proceed as if all utterance were reducible to propositions thus make their objects fit into molds that may be inappropriate to them. The practice forces them to limit argument studies to speech texts and to consign nondiscursive elements to the realm of the "mystical." The result is unnecessarily restrictive senses of rationality and—since our view of knowledge is as broad as our view of what produces it—of knowledge.

Argument as Communication

The argument is partly made that the things we say about arguers should not be markedly at odds with the things we say of interactants. While arguments are distinctive interactions by virtue of the dissensual coorientations that produce them, there are no reasons to suppose that all of the ground rules change when people see themselves arguing. Arguers are more explicit, and it is socially acceptable to demand reasons; but the argument process does not differ in *kind* from other interactions.

To claim, as some do, that arguers differ from other speakers in that they use propositional logic is intuitively doubtful and contrary to empirical examples. If these examples are successful paradigm cases, we must turn to some form of psychologic to explain their meanings. Conventional meanings become by this view variously loose threads of commonality crossing individual contexts. The nondiscursiveness thesis, so viewed, is merely a request for a less restrictive sense of "linguistic context."

Yet we are not quite ready to flesh out our argument fully. A distinction needs to be introduced that at first blush does not seem to bear upon the present claim. Still, I hope to show that it clears away some troublesome underbrush. The distinction is this: there is a difference between "translation" and "explication." Hermeneutic scholars will be prone to ignore my development here on grounds that it is painfully obvious; yet argumentation scholars have lately gotten themselves into some conceptual cul-de-sacs because they ignore it. Put simply, the nondiscursiveness thesis says that one cannot "translate" nondiscursive symbolism into discursive forms. The two differ in kind, and while translators can work with different languages to arrive at rough and ready translations, it is not clear that analysts can do this with nondiscursive symbolism.

Translators, even in relatively straightforward cases, often have to bracket important doubts as they render the terms of one language to another. They proceed as if an equals sign were operating, although they actually mean "despite difficulties and doubts, and despite differences which make an equals sign inapplicable, the best I can do is say that *pour soi* and *en soi* = 'for itself' and 'in itself.'" They are able to bracket their doubts in part because they work with materials similar *in kind*.

The NDT proposes that nondiscursive symbols are inexpressible within the essential frame of language—which is to say that nondiscursive symbols differ in kind from discursive ones, that they are not translatable into discursive forms. But this does not mean that situated speakers do not try to translate their feelings into words; nor does it mean that nondiscursive elements are unanalyzable or unresearchable. The NDT is not a counsel of despair (or tautology) of the sort one finds at the end of Wittgenstein's *Tractatus* (about those things of which one cannot speak, there is only silence). The NDT is a claim about translation, not about explication. Thus the claim that nondiscursive symbols are untranslatable does not entail the conclusion that they are inexplicable or that they are beyond the purview of research and criticism.

Anxiety is untranslatable (see Kelly, 1955), but it sometimes serves as a regnant construct, giving meaning to many verbal discriminations and lending force and support to verbal claims. So, too, fear, hatred, envy, and one's sense of justice are untranslatable but sometimes of decisive importance to the meanings of beliefs and claims. But the fact that these affects are untranslatable does not require that they be inexplicable. Just as a therapist can elicit information about anxiety and the other affective states (see Kelly, 1955), so the analyst and critic can triangulate (by the language of indirection we have described) toward understandings of the interdependencies of anxiety and the verbal dimensions it rules.

Perhaps the best proof of the interdependency of symbolic forms is the commonplace nature of the struggle to express internal states. We oftentimes cannot easily express what we mean—which is to say we cannot translate our feelings into precise verbal forms. We sometimes adopt a language of indirection as well as a redundancy of expression in order to come as close as we can to saying what we mean. Thus a critic who seeks to make sense of such utterances will impute intentions to us; he will dig below the conventional meanings of what we say to attempt a description of what we mean *in this case.*

Thus the NDT is not intended to imply the nondiscursive symbolism cannot be talked about. Such an interpretation would imply that people cannot express themselves at all. Langer, after all, has devised a language of indirection for discussing nondiscursive symbolism; ballet expresses forms which are untranslatable but which commentators have had some success in describing. Commentators on the presentational arts are forced to invent circumlocutions and specialized vocabularies to call up in their readers something akin to the aesthetic experiences the arts produce. Bergson wrote about intuition, although he believed that nothing about it was directly expressible in language (a point his British critics often overlooked).

As far as I know, every example of nondiscursive symbolism discussed here has been written about at length by someone. The fact that love and hate are not equivalent to the things we can say about them has not prevented insightful analyses of these inchoate passions. Thus the claim that nondiscursive symbols are not translatable does not mean that they are inexplicable. In one important sense, it is the job of criticism to expand its expressive resources continually, to enhance the complexity and fidelity of its vocabulary and modes of expression so as to take in a widening circle of phenomena. An assumption here is that, although a person cannot express the same things as, for example, hatred, with effort, he becomes better and better at it. Actors are thus able, through practice, to expand the range of their replicative efforts. So, too, critics can add to the language of criticism so as to embrace the nondiscursive phenomena which give meaning to situated utterance. The thrust of the nondiscursiveness thesis, then, is to advocate this order or expansion. Obviously, we aim at making phenomena explicable. Some phenomena are more resistant than others. Propositional logic makes our job deceptively easy because it requires no translation and the explication only of conventional—and securely fixed—meanings. This is why it leads us so badly.

Bearing in mind this distinction between translation and explication, we are now ready to complete our argument that arguers do many of the same things that interactants of all sorts do and that, if there are differences, they should not be patently inconsistent with our explanations of discourse in general. Propositional logic is vulnerable here precisely because it leads us to say that arguers speak purely conventionally and with fixed referents, while social interactants do not. No research that I know of countenances such a distinction.

Birdwhistle's (1968) view of infracommunicational modes implies that discursive and nondiscursive elements would be *interdependent*. His claim is that "the spoken and the body-motion languages...are *infra*communicational systems that are *interdependently merged* with each other and with other comparable codes that utilize other channels; they are operationally communicative.... It is unproductively tautologous to argue from the fact that language is characteristic of humans to the position that language is the central or the most important communicative code utilized by humans. All infracommunicational channels are equally necessary to the whole of which they are dependent subsystems" (1968, pp. 379–80). Birdwhistle believes that we do not possess a sufficiently elaborate empirical picture of communication to attempt to weigh the relative importance of discursive and nondiscursive symbols to a cultural community. Doing so would be, he says, akin to arguing whether sex or food is more important. We need not love his analogy to grasp the point.

In a similar spirit, Beldoch has explicitly embraced Langer's distinction between discursive and nondiscursive symbolism and proposed that it explains the fundamental interdependent and distinct relationship between the two symbolic domains. He focuses upon research into the abilities of subjects to identify emotional states in others and draws from his tests of this ability some conclusions which are useful to us here (Beldoch, 1964):

> Thus, the three tests of ability to identify intended emotions seem to fall within the realm of non-discursive symbols, for they involved expressions of feeling on the basis of formal, or content free properties of each mode of communication. In contrast, the measure of verbal intelligence would seem to involve, according to Langer's view, discursive symbolization. Therefore, the correlations between verbal intelligence and the three measures of ability to identify expression of emotion may reflect a relationship between abilities to deal with symbols both in the discursive and non-discursive modes of communication. If this inter-

pretation is valid, the results suggest that these two kinds of symbolic activity are positively related, but have considerable independent variance, and both kinds of ability may very well be involved in the communication of emotional meanings in everyday, human interaction.

Conceptualizing the ability to identify communication of emotions in terms of a symbolic activity, related to but different from the usual measures of intelligence, may help rescue the concept of "emotional sensitivity" from the mysterious and perhaps unknowable realm of empathy, "third ears," and other notions which have been proposed to account for observed differences in ability to identify communications of feeling. For in terms of this point of view, emotional sensitivity involves symbolic processes which can be investigated empirically, with the aim of discovering the general principles of "emotional intelligence" in perhaps much the same way as psychologists have discovered the principles underlying discursive intellectual functioning. Langer cogently emphasized throughout her work that non-discursive symbolization is governed by a logic, a set of principles, which is different from that of discursive symbolization, but is not theoretically any more mysterious, unknowable, or less open to empirical investigation. [Pp. 39–40]

Beldoch seems innocent of an important implication of these words, that the researchers who have "discovered" the discursive principles of thought have ignored the *interdependence* of discursive and non-discursive symbolism. Granted that discursive and nondiscursive symbolism have considerable independent variance, they are also believed to be interdependent—which means that one research program cannot stand without the other. Beldoch's argument is thus a serious criticism of research in discursive intelligence.

One clear conclusion to be drawn from Beldoch's argument is that no assumptions about "translation" need to be made. Interdependence is a notion that entails two independent but interacting domains—precisely the assumption made by Beldoch and Birdwhistle. If they were straightforwardly translatable into one another, they would be intermeshed rather than interdependent. Oil and water proverbially do not mix—but the oil sits on top of the water and could not burn unless it did.

Thus no assumptions about translation need be made to accept the view that social interaction uses a full interplay of communication modalities. Nor need it be assumed that individuals always translate nonverbal symbols into verbal form in order to assign meaning to them. That would be a profound error. Intuitionist accounts have it that emotional meanings are "sensed" and given meaning by a purely nondiscursive process which differs in kind from the discursive elements. *Reflective thinking* about the emotions is another matter entirely. For this we indeed do try to express our nondiscursive symbols discursively. Situated meaning, however, characteristically proceeds intuitively—the whole point, I think, of Bergson's conception of *la durée*.

Researchers are now dealing with a variety of communication modalities in circumstanced conversation; the NDT forces a consideration of the place of this work in conceptions of argument. We have notions of content-free speech (Davitz and Davitz, 1959), Hall's (1959, 1966) work in proxemics, studies of facial expression (Ekman, 1964; Haggard and Isaacs, 1966), gaze, mutual gaze, and eye contact (Kendon, 1967; Exline, Gray, and Schuette, 1965; Exline and Winters, 1965; Argyle and Dean, 1965), leakage and deception (Ekman and Freisen, 1973; Goffman, 1969), posture (Mehrabian, 1968, 1969), and touch (Argyle, 1970; Scheflen, 1972).

What this literature does *not* countenance is a conclusion that cognitive life is "schizophrenic" or that discursive and nondiscursive symbols are somehow cut utterly apart from one another. That they are interdependent is the far easier conclusion (Adams-Weber, 1979; Argyle, 1964, 1970; Bannister, 1962, 1966, 1970; Bannister and Agnew, 1977; Bannister and Bott, 1973; Bannister and Fransella, 1971; Bannister and Mair, 1968). The "acquisition of pragmatics," the development of communication competencies, is not in itself cut off from nondiscursive symbols (Bates, 1976; Blum and Gumperz, 1972; Brown, 1977; Bruyn, 1966; Cicourel, 1974; Denzin, 1970). Personal construct theorists, following Kelly's (1955) suggestion that constructs may be nonverbal, have articulated this thinking into a useful research program (Duck, 1972, 1973a, 1973b, 1977; Landfield, 1971; Mayo and Crockett, 1964).

This thinking serves to redirect our thinking about linguistic choices. Even if we took the primacy argument at face value, analysts would nonetheless face substantial difficulties in determining which conventional choices a situated speaker had made. The NDT argues that choices are rooted in the assumptions in use by the speaker at any moment, the interpretive schemes he has deemed appropriate to the events at hand. His orientations to events may be intuitive and nondiscursive; he may not be able to articulate them even to his own satisfaction. He researches these nondiscursive elements as he grapples with ways of expressing them (Rowe, 1978; Psathas, 1973). Like us, every speaker sometimes wants to say clear and determinate things about phenomena which do not seem clear and determinate—and it is this struggle that produces adaptations to situations (Schutz and Luckmann, 1973; Stebbins, 1967; Speier, 1973; Szasz, 1961, 1970; cf. C. Taylor, 1964).

As far as I can see, this thinking is consistent with Habermas's (1979) view that "in speech, no matter what the emphasis, grammatical sentences are embedded in relations to reality in such a way that in an acceptable speech action segments of external nature, society, and internal nature always come into appearance together" (1979, p. 68). On this ground, Habermas criticizes information theorists for assuming that communication occurs on a single level, namely, "that of transmitting content" (p. 43). Nothing mystical here: the claim is that communication occurs at every level or modality and that people have orientations to situations that are not communicated verbally—indeed sometimes cannot be. The definition of the situation, then, is prototypical of interpretive schemes as holistic amalgams of discursive and nondiscursive symbols.

We owe mostly to Goffman (1959, 1961a, 1961b, 1963, 1967, 1969, 1971, 1974; Argyle, 1964, 1970; Douglas, 1970a) the special argument that impression management—the intentional maintenance of a public facade—often informs an actor's behavior. His dramaturgic perspective focuses upon the staging problems and concerns for appearances vis-à-vis an audience that guide behavior in social interaction; the intuitive idea is that every person seeks to manage his appearance so as to affect the constructions made by others. Every actor, that is, "performs" just as professional stage actors perform, using certain tried techniques as well as innovating from time to time. Discursive and nondiscursive elements can be parts of these scripts. The importance of both is that they are often intentionally managed in order to sustain (or create from scratch) a predesigned facade. Goffman has produced a body of observational and speculative data bearing on social interaction. He maintains a distinction between the signs a person sends and the signs he *gives off* that roughly corresponds to the present arguments about nondiscursive symbolism. Notice how his reasoning (Goffman, 1974) dovetails with our own on the effects of the knower on the known—but here the focus is on the effects of knowledge on the knower:

> Moreover, what people understand to be the organization of their experience, they buttress, and perforce, self-fulfillingly. They develop a corpus of cautionary tales, games, riddles, experiments, newsy stories, and other scenarios which elegantly confirm a frame-relevant view of the workings of the world.... And the human nature that fits with this view of viewing does so in part because its possessors have learned to comport themselves so as to render this analysis true of them. Indeed, in countless ways and ceaselessly, social life takes up and freezes into itself the understandings we have of it. [P. 563]

This is Goffman's warrant for taking ordinary social life seriously:

actors use concrete, actual, obdurately real activity in order to perpetrate fun, deception, games, experiments, rehearsals, fantasy, ritual activities, analysis, and a host of other experiments.

It is too comfortable, Goffman says, to contrast social masks with "real" internal processes, since people become so engrossed in their performances that these take on a reality of their own that makes such distinctions doubtful or even impossible. Such phenomena would be unanalyzable except for the fact that social actors model their theatrics upon exemplary representations:

> ...In many cases, what the individual does in serious life, he does in relationship to cultural standards established for the doing and for the social role that is built up out of such doings. Some of these standards are addressed to the maximally approved, some to the maximally disapproved. The associated lore itself draws from the moral traditions of the community as found in folk tales, characters in novels, advertisements, myth, movie stars and their famous roles, the *Bible*, and other sources of exemplary representation. So everyday life, real enough in itself, often seems to be a laminated adumbration of a pattern or model that is itself a typification of quite uncertain realm status.... Life may not be an imitation of art, but ordinary conduct, in a sense, is an imitation of the proprieties, a gesture at the exemplary forms, and the primal realization of these ideals belongs more to make-believe than to reality. [P. 562]

But a contrast with "real" characteristics is not what is important; the copies are mere transformations of the original, "and everything uncovered about the organization of fictive scenes can be seen to apply only to copies, not to the actual world," *yet* this would make frame analysis the study of everything but ordinary behavior:

> However, although this approach might be the most congenial, it is not the most profitable. For actual activity is not merely to be contrasted with something obviously unreal,...these activities are not all that fanciful. Furthermore, each of these...is different from the others in a different way. Also, of course, everyday activity itself contains quickly changing frames, many of which generate events which depart considerably from anything that might be called literal. Finally, the variables and elements of organization found in nonliteral realms of being, albeit manifest and utilized in distinctive ways in each of these realms, are also found in the organization of actual experience, again in a version distinctive to it. [P. 563]

There is constant and interdependent interplay between facades and realities, between performances and actual attributions, that make them in some senses indistinguishable. It needs saying that nothing in this scheme smacks of structuralism or determinism: Goffman is not defending any sort of traditional sociological account. People adopt masks for reasons of their own; they execute and sustain masks and performances for their own reasons as well.

Goffman's program is thus to understand the basic units of social life—the ways individuals organize their experience, define situations, and present themselves (that is, manage impressions) in face-to-face encounters. Following Schutz (1945), Goffman wants to speak of provinces of meaning in ordinary life, the frameworks of assumption by which men build social enterprises and inhabit them. A syntax of social occasions is developed in a way consonant with methodologies for dealing with occasionality, especially the dramaturgical model. People are assumed to organize their experience by virtue of roles that have been prepared for them in social life and by adapting to definitions of the situation; social structures are thus, inter alia, recurring ways of defining situations. Convention and intention are holistically bound together every time a person deals with a situation. This view squares with the field theory emerging here for reasons that will shortly be clear.

This empirical project—indeed all of Goffman's thinking—uses a holistic sense of communication that admits no strict distinctions between discursive and nondiscursive elements. One does not write theatrical scripts without a vision of the action. Goffman acknowledges a considerable debt to Merleau-Ponty's sense of holism (Merleau-Ponty, 1973, pp. 133–34). Merleau-Ponty's definition countenances a plea for an expansive sense of context, especially that nondiscursive symbols are fundamental ways of organizing experience and particular frames of action, that is, definitions of situation.

Talk is not ruled out of this scheme; it is juxtaposed with nondiscursive symbolism in just the way Goffman believes it is for actors. The main research assumption is that "what is implicit and concealed can thus be unpacked, unraveled, revealed" (Goffman, 1974, p. 564), that is, dramatistically. One may thus draw upon Grician implicature theory (Grice, 1975), Cicourel's interpretive sociology of language, and the conversation-analytic tradition (Gumperz and Hymes, 1972; Hymes, 1962; Jacobs and Jackson, 1980, 1982) in ways that square with the nondiscursiveness thesis. Goffman's frame analysis is just such an organizing view of talk.

Goffman's work undermines propositional lines as paradigm cases of argument; his examples reinforce the claim that logical serialization is exotic in the way that a French Provincial table with sixteen legs is exotic. Nor can we be satisfied with a weakened propositional logic. It would still do violence to the holism of cognitive processes described by the nondiscursiveness thesis. There is only one way to salvage the linguistic primacy position, but it is fraught with pitfalls. The argument is this: when people think they are "arguing," that is, when their definitions of situation are such that they come to the coorientation "we are arguing," they so constrain their communications that their words are more important than nonverbal cues. An example which might augment (if not support) this claim would be formal debates in which the propositions uttered *are* often of paramount importance. Yet this is perhaps a tad too facile.

For one thing, we have presented plausible arguments earlier that formal debate is a poor exemplar of ordinary argument. For another, no empirical research countenances the interpretation that the listeners to debates focus less upon nondiscursive and more upon discursive communications, that they are unaffected by dress, appearance, facial cues, eye contact, kinesic cues, proxemic cues, paralinguistic cues, and even managerial matters. The nondiscursiveness thesis can consistently contain the empirical finding (assuming that it is found) that interactants when they define themselves as arguers try to use more words than is usual in interaction. That would not be a surprising result: we have already claimed that arguments bring more of a person's assumptions out into public view; and words and propositions are surely important media for this epistemic and social comparative function.

The present claim is that the linguistic primacy position is inconsistent with our understandings of social interactions. As long as it requires the assumption that words and propositions are purely conventional structures to be understood apart from the definitions of the speakers, it will be incompatible. Once it is granted that situated utterance takes meaning from the holistic enterprises that comprise social interaction, a less extreme explanation of the place of language can be defended. The starting place of analysis is with definitions of situation, not with conventions (whether or not these ultimately turn out to be the same for all practical purposes); it is definitions of situation that give structure to social encounters; and we can conclude with Goffman's (1974) conclusion:

> This report is not concerned with aspects of theatre that creep into everyday life. It is concerned with the structure of social encounters—the structure of those entities in social life that come into being whenever persons enter into one another's immediate physical presence. The key factor in this structure is the maintenance of a single definition of situation, this definition having to be expressed, and this expression sustained in the face of a multitude of potential disruptions.
>
> A character staged in a theatre is not in some ways real, nor does it have

the same kind of real consequences as does the thoroughly contrived performance by a confidence man; but the *successful* staging of either of these types of false figures involves use of *real* techniques—the same techniques by which everyday persons sustain their real social situations. [P. 563]

Taken alone, propositional logic would give us plays without stage directions.

Summary

The social grounds of knowledge can be captured by the catch phrase "argument is epistemic." The clarity and usefulness of this phrase and its attendant concepts depend upon (at least) two interlocked moves: developing a view of argument consonant with our accounts of social life in general and developing views of argument interaction and utterance which square with our accounts of communication in general. These moves in turn presuppose that the ways ordinary folk come to believe that they know are of intrinsic interest *whether or not* we ultimately want to defend a distinction between genuine and conventional knowledge. We could not, after all, defend such a distinction without a dependable empirical account of the social processes attendant to knowledge claims. Thus the notion that argument is epistemic cannot illuminate the social grounds of knowledge unless the idea of argument is itself a carefully contoured piece of a larger communication theory.

We have said that argument interactions are created and sustained by virtue of definitions of situation and that argument utterances are the sorts of utterances usually found in such interactions. Since there are no reasons to suppose that arguers change the nature of communication when they enter arguments, it is plausible to think that arguers use the full range of communication modalities.

The claim that argument is epistemic requires empirical examples to make sense. It is not enough to prove that a particular kind of argument might in the abstract produce knowledge; we must prove that people in thus and so circumstances take things as knowledge because they proceed with social comparisons in thus and so ways. This justifies the study of particular cases. The study of particular cases requires that we know not merely what a speaker's claims might be taken to mean but what the speaker intends them to mean and what other interactants take them to mean. While most (or all) utterances admit of a variety of conventional interpretations, people in particular cases intend their utterances to mean particular things. We cannot define the social grounds of knowledge in these particular cases without understanding these intentions. If A *says* X, we want to know what A means by saying X and what A is taken by his hearers to mean. We could not otherwise point to the interaction of A and B (regarding the truthfulness of X) as having epistemic significance. Without attributing intentions to A and B (that is, without making claims about their psychological processes) we could not explain how they come to regard X as knowledge. And if we fail in this proceeding with a particular case, I do not see how we can succeed with an account of knowledge in the abstract.

To accomplish this faithfulness to empirical situations, the idea of the interdependencies of discursive and nondiscursive symbolism has been defended. Our nondiscursiveness thesis is a plea for a holistic view of mind and (consonant with it) a holistic view of interaction and utterance. The assumption undergirding this plea is that A may well say X because X has survived certain social tests; A believes X because of the checks he has made against the views of others. By the end of the third chapter, we shall have further fleshed out this thinking by saying that A might believe X because X is countenanced by the traditions and veridical standards of a group—an argument field. But this will be an empty abstraction unless we can confidently define the notion of fields of discourse in terms of empirical particulars. The best proceeding, then, is to say that a field exists because of the particular cases we can point to as activities which animate the field. The precondition of such success with particulars is our ability to say what A means by saying X in a situation.

We have said that arguments often entail a struggle after expression, for instance, in cases in which what A means by X are nondiscursive. If this is true, a pivotal aspect of A's epistemic situation is his ability to express himself—to himself and to others. Particular expressions, then, are as apt to be successive approximations of A's intentions as they are to be precise renditions. Our working assumption is that this is as serious a problem for the critic as it is for A and his colleagues.

Notice that the traditional distinction between the solitary thinker and the social world is being blurred here. We do not want to place the individual over and against the social world in which he moves except in the restricted sense that social comparison processes place A in a subject-object relation to the ideas of others. We want to emphasize A's ability to shift perspectives, to see himself as an object, and to make meaning-constitutive decisions about the taking of social influence. In saying that we must understand particular people to understand social arrangements, we are not saying that a particular person's psychological idiosyncrasies are the final arbiters of knowledge (even though any particular person might believe this to be true). Our assumption is that, for most people most of the time, the authorities and consensual agreements of social aggregations are taken to be the most dependable tests of knowledge. Our aim is neither to protest or applaud this but to understand how people enter such fields as cognitive accomplishments. Thus our nondiscursiveness thesis requires that explanations of social frameworks of knowledge square with the claims we make about particular activities in particular situations. Our aim is not to *contrast* public and private knowledge but to study how social actors empirically relate the two spheres.

The results of these arguments are several. First, the definition of situation becomes the organizing construct for argumentation theory and criticism. Arguers accommodate their lines of action to social demands by entering institutions of discourse. They take up pre-established lines of action when they enter argument fields—that is to say, to enter an argument field is to adopt a starting point with a willingness to abide (for the moment at least) by its consequences. One enters an argument field in something of the sense that Searle says one enters the institution of promising—the difference being that the argument field gets defined by the ways it is used. Fields, I shall argue, are traditions built out of recurring definitions of situation. Searle defines the institution of promising as an accomplished body of entailments— something that is what it is. We cannot similarly conceptualize argument fields because fields are social entities: their recurring practices are continually readapted, defined, fleshed out, and changed as people use them. Thus we need to think of social organization in terms of situated activity.

Now, the situated activity with which we are centrally concerned is argument. If we take the argument-as-interaction notion seriously, we shall have to accommodate to a view of utterance consistent with the things we say generally of communication. Argument utterance, we shall have to assume, is as ambiguous, elided, and implicit as other kinds of utterance. Logic and propositional logic can serve as models only for a restricted range of arguments in just the sense that the movements of a Nureyev would be a poor paradigm case of ordinary dancing. Moreover, if we cannot say that all particular interactions are carbon copies of general forms—and I read Goffman to say that we cannot—then we cannot say the same of arguments.

We have, in brief, posed the problem of induction in sociological terms and suggested that it is in principle useful to study the ways actors in their daily practices proceed to solve it. We have proposed that the core component of an argument is the relationship among the arguers and the meanings they intend their claims to have. This is tantamount to saying that these relationships and meaning *are* the social grounds of knowledge. Thus equipped, we are ready to proceed with a fuller discussion of a judgmental device for evaluating both components, namely, the notion of rationality.

2 Argumentation and Rationality

The terms of art that help us do philosophy and social science often acquire a dual character. They are sometimes used in a realistic way to name things—this use being roughly captured in Wittgenstein's picture theory view of simples and elementary propositions. They are at other times used as purely theoretical concepts to be stretched, narrowed, and adapted as convenience and preference dictate—this use being roughly captured in weltanschauungen theories and in Kelly's parallels between ordinary behavior and scientific experimentation. At best, these projects are pursued by different theorists (say, realists versus constructivists). At worst, they are muddled together in an ill-considered way by theorists who believe that both lines of thinking will eventually merge when the latter is successfully tested against the former.

No term better exemplifies this duality than "rationality." It is thought to name an obdurate and distinctively human characteristic and (as well) to be a theoretical construct capable of virtually limitless alternative interpretations. No scholarly tradition better exemplifies the muddle of realistic and interpretive accounts than argumentation. Rationality is seen as a real and describable property of inference and utterance and (by implication) as a personal characteristic of social actors. It is also seen as a theoretical construct taking any number of guises—the aim of such theoretical exercises being to bring the construct into line with the facts. This is largely owed to the field's historical preoccupation with criticism and the associated belief that rationality and its kindred terms (reasonableness, justification, and validity) are judgmental criteria by which critics may weigh the people and practices they study.

Such criticism works best when the two senses of rationality are indistinct or ambiguously related. This situation permits the comfortable conceit that critics may study the activities of actors in different fields and proclaim them rational, nonrational, irrational, unreasonable. Taken alone, the constructivist account requires that such terms be coherently fitted into plausible theoretical frameworks and that they work out in empirical research programs guided by the theory. Combined with the field theory gradually emerging here, the constructivist account makes more stringent demands. Criticism (so viewed) is a *field*. Critical judgments are interfield disputes. In this and the following essays I shall argue that interfield disputes are insoluble by traditional justificationist arguments. If criticism is tied to judgment or evaluation, critics are restricted to uttering banalities ("A *rationally* says X because A's field authorizes this judgment") or parading their pieties ("A may have acted rationally by his field's standards, but not by mine").

A field with the pretensions I impute to argument criticism can hardly be founded on an ambiguity. If critics claim to use principles that overarch differences among fields, they assume a burden of proof encompassing the whole of epistemics (and of ontology as well, given the subtle blurring of the two senses of rationality). The standard way of discharging this burden has been to select particular philosophic views (more or less ignoring their success within philosophy) as authoritative grounding for critical procedures. Critics thus justify their work by arguments from authority—a practice they condemn with a vengeance in the people they study.

Intellectual traditions, when they are worth their salt, do not define themselves by the ideas they import from other traditions. Nor do their theorists rest about waiting for another discipline to hand them legitimizing concepts. They organize themselves around insights of sufficient worth to mark them off from other traditions. When they borrow concepts, they transform them in ways special to the character of their practices, traditions, and conceptual ecologies. Failing this, they become indistinguishable from the disciplines they raid or—worse—"applied studies."

Proceeding on the assumption that the notions of communication and perspectivity (and their implications gradually emerging in these essays) are seminal constructs, progress may be made toward defining what argumentation's view of rationality ought to look like. This is a necessary and complex business—necessary because the rationality theories used by argument scholars are untenable for our purposes, and complex because a home-grown view of rationality must square with empirical claims about fields. It must be compatible, that is, with a full-blown sociology of knowledge, justification, and validity.

My claims are these: (1) rationality is a rhetorical construct, and this is the surest thing to be said of it; (2) it is a sociological datum, not a warrant—something field actors believe in and try to live up to; (3) justificationist views of rationality are untenable—the tu quoque is undefeated, infinite regress has not been avoided; (4) a successful universal of rationality will be substantively trivial, so abstract as to say nothing about particulars; consistent with this, a reformed view of "presumption" is a successful universal of rationality; and (5) the grand ontological disputes are irrelevant to argumentation; critics should study the conventions and orthodoxies of rationality in fields and bracket the broader disputes.

These claims do not say what rationality is. If field theory is taken in any but a bland version, rationality is variously manifested—it is just what fields say it is. Justification and validity are thus terms of art describing particular social practices—justification describing a field's procedures and validity describing the characteristics of arguments that meet a field's judgmental and veridical standards. To say that an argument is justified is to bring it into relation with particular field assumptions; to call it valid is to aver that it fits a field's orthodoxies; to say that it is true is to describe its fit into an epistemic framework that so regards it.

These claims by themselves make rationality a rhetorical totem and a field standard but not a human characteristic. This view does not square with our intuitions that rationality is a construct that ought to speak to the human condition and say interesting things about human practices. Aristotle proceeded on the wise assumption that reason was virtually definitive of what it is to be human (and thus irretrievably linked to matters of virtue and vice, belief and knowledge). A view of rationality ought to complement our views of other distinctively human attributes—in this case communication and perspectivity. Rationality, that is, ought to be of a piece with this account. So I shall conclude this essay with (6) perspective taking, which, broadly construed to encompass the reformed sense of presumption, is a precise and usable view of rationality which squares with the facts of fields.

I shall not use the rationality construct as a principle for distinguishing among fields. As many fields share theories of rationality as use incompatible ones.[1] While lurid cases of interfield differences (for example, cost-benefit analysis versus neo-Kantian ethics) need to be understood, we must account as well for cases in which otherwise different discourse domains use views of rationality that are similar. My aim is (rather) to produce a satisfactory statement of how rationality can be seen as a *sociological* phenomenon (the judgment that fields in fact make of their actors) and as a *critical focus* (a way of looking at these sociological practices which does not bog down in attempts to evaluate them).

Rationality as a Rhetorical Concept

Men have labored since antiquity to define rationality, and this fact is more interesting than anything they have ended up saying. Whatever else it may be, rationality is a powerful idea, a prized social value, a totemistic symbol of man's special place in the scheme of things. Taine would have called it *l'idée maîtresse*, making it a focal point of man's flattering self-portrait.

There are remarkable parallels between attempts to define rationality and efforts to understand God. Both concepts require genuflections of a sort; both are used in ways that endow them with brute affective charges; men passionately align themselves with both. This parallel is all the more striking when we consider that rationality has often functioned as a "god term" (Weaver, 1958)—as an ultimate aim of human practices. We do not stretch things too much if we call rationality God's secular counterpart. Thinkers often focus upon it when they despair of describing God, and many claims we make about religions and their rhetorics apply by analogy to the different views of rationality. Bacon is perhaps a paradigm case: we may legitimately see him "changing gods" as he sets about replacing the God of the scholastics with the Reason that was to be the god term of the Enlightenment.

Thus we are on plausible ground in claiming (1) *rationality is a rhetorical concept*. At least two considerations justify our seeing it this way. The first has to do with the rhetorical bases of argument fields and the special place of rationality in them; the second concerns the strongly affective and judgmental character of particular uses of the words "rational" and "irrational."

The Rhetorical Bases of Fields

One basic sense of the term "field" specifies a group of people who share particular substantive beliefs. The full-dress sociological description of these social entities must await the next chapter, but it may suffice here to say that an argument field is a sociological aggregation which people enter because they find it attractive (for any number of reasons) to do so. To explain a group's cohesiveness is thus to explain these attractions, that is, why particular people decide to enter particular fields. The glue which binds fields together must therefore be the faith or trust actors have in the judgmental and veridical standards as well as the experts of particular fields. My use of *faith* and *trust* here flags my view that fields are going concerns *because* people align themselves to the people and ideas of a field. The intuitive idea is that fields are created and sustained by essentially rhetorical means and that—strictly speaking—the other things we want to say about field activities must square with these rhetorical roots (see Farrell, 1976, 1977; Bitzer, 1978; Fisher, 1981; Campbell, 1981).

Consider first that the ticket into any social group is interpersonal dealings with the group's actors. One can consult a group's documents, but one more often than not is likely to consult other people; for example, graduate students adopt the views of their professors, political activists the views of their leaders. A plausible inference is that fields take their legitimacy largely from the ethos of their experts. Stich and Nisbett (1980) thus urge that people do not depend solely upon their subjective interpretations, since "there is a higher court of appeal." An actor can refer to the "reflective equilibrium of his cognitive betters," the people who are recognized as authorities in a given group. "The role of experts and authorities in our cognitive lives has been all but ignored by modern epistemologists. Yet it is the hallmark of an educated and reflective person that he recognizes, consults, and defers to authority on a wide range of topics" (1980, pp. 198–99). Indeed, "it is our suspicion that one of the principle effects of education is to socialize people to defer to cognitive authorities" not merely as an habitual practice but because "it is generally the right thing to do from a normative point of view. The man who persists in believing that his theorem is valid, despite the dissent of leading mathematicians, is a fool" (1980, p. 199).

Deference to authority cannot by itself explain justification because it does not give the "cognitive rebel his due." We do not want to say that cognitive rebels contradict themselves when they reject authority. Stich and Nisbett thus amend their view to say that "an attribution of justification to a rule of inference can be unpacked as a claim that the rule accords with the reflective inductive practice *of the people the speaker takes to be appropriate*" (1980, p. 201). Disagreements between rebels and conservatives in a field are thus disputes about *whose* judgments ought to be heeded for given matters.

Fields are going concerns by virtue of the social interactions that form them. An important product of this social life is the appraisal and followership of particular epistemic authorities—this being a distinctively rhetorical process. People come to believe in a field's judgmental and veridical standards (and its attendant sense of "progress") as a result of these interpersonal relations and authority orientations. The "authority" of particular beliefs thus inheres in their fit into epistemic frameworks that vouch for them—these frameworks being bound together by rules countenanced by particular authorities.

In addition (and largely owing) to these ethos effects is the "animal faith" that actors place in field standards by taking them for granted, making them part of a not-to-be-questioned assumptive framework which serves to guide routine daily activities. The background awarenesses undergirding routine practices (Garfinkle, 1967) and the implicit rules governing talk (Jacobs and Jackson, 1982) exemplify this practice. Views of rationality, deviance, and verification often recede to the background because they seem so obvious as to require no reflection. Thus, to describe an argument field is largely a matter of describing the things its actors take for granted, their self-evident truths.

Every field has implicit and explicit theories of communication and argumentation, these being design specifications for honest communication and sound argument. They often take the form of social norms describing what one must do to behave rationally. This normalcy often reduces to "proceeding in the standard, orthodox way," observing the proprieties, and staying within certain outer boundaries of rational conduct. If, for example, an economist calls a colleague "irrational," he likely means to accuse the offender of deviating from the norms of good economic argument. The rhetorical potency of the criticism depends upon the communal agreement respecting the standard the speaker appeals to (or takes for granted).

Field theory, then, attempts to describe the social grounds of beliefs. The rhetorical bonds which create and sustain group cohesion thus contribute greatly to beliefs in and about particular claims. That a claim was secured rationally is obviously an important part of such judgments: it says that someone has used a rule of inference vouched for by agreeable authorities and that no taken-for-granted assumptions have been violated. This is a rhetorical function—and the first sure proof that rationality can be regarded as a rhetorical phenomenon.

Rationality as Naming

The second justification for seeing rationality as a rhetorical phenomenon is that it is provably an affective, evaluative term. If I call you "irrational," I am not making an impartial claim about the form of your arguments; inter alia I am calling you *deviant*. This naming function is (plausibly) a basic part of what field actors do when they evaluate proposals. Prior to deliberating about them, field actors first decide whether proposals merit serious attention at all. Rationality thus names proposals attained in ways orthodox enough to be prima facie, that is, they merit considered attention. Irrationality names proposals so deviant from field standards that no serious attention is required.

I am ignoring here the standard philosophic term "nonrational" because it seems peculiar to particular schools of philosophy. Philosophers use it to draw distinctions particular to their interests, and it has no counterparts that I can see in other fields. The more usual contrast is *rationality versus irrationality*. The sociological function of this contrast is to point to the orthodox and appropriate ways of proceeding in particular fields—irrationality being the name for ways of proceeding that do not produce proposals meriting serious attention.

Rationality thus serves rhetorical functions, that is, as a name for a field's orthodox ways. It works this way even for fields which deny rhetoric a place in decision making. Consider, for example, Hare's (1975) classic description of philosophic argument:

> Philosophic arguments…have the same sort of objectivity that chess games have. If you are beaten at chess, you are beaten, and it is not to be concealed by any show of words; and in a philosophical discussion of this sort, provided that an unambiguously stated thesis is put forward, objective refutation is possible. Indeed, the whole object of our philosophic training is to teach us to put out theses in a form in which they can be put to this test. Ambiguities and evasions and rhetoric, however uplifting, are regarded as the mark of a philosopher who has not learnt his craft; we prefer professional competence to superficial brilliance. [P. 733]

One might substitute "bombast" for "rhetoric" and do justice to Hare's intentions. A broader sense of "rhetoric" has it that one is rhetorically proceeding when one makes claims on the attention and belief of others—and this Hare is doing. His argument is rhetorical because it enjoins its readers to define philosophic argument a certain way and (presumably) to act accordingly. One might gloss Hare's argument to say "here is what orthodox philosophic arguments look like—do it this way and you are a philosopher; depend on ambiguities, evasions, and superficial brilliance and you are something else." If we think of rhetoric (more broadly), namely, as the use of symbols to induce cooperation, identification, and social unity among people (Burke, 1952), we can construe Hare's appeals as distinctively rhetorical. He is making field-defining arguments—attempts to influence how students see the orthodox ways of philosophy.

Practice versus Sources

Two arguments based upon an emerging field theory have been presented and said to prove that rationality is legitimately construable as a rhetorical phenomenon—a sociological aspect of fields. The organizing claim is that rationality is a secular version of religions and their rhetorics—a concept of considerable rhetorical potency. This line of thinking in no way depends upon a grand ontological view of rationality's *sources*. It does not, that is, depend upon the tu quoque.

Whatever the sources of rationality may be, it is also a sociological concept with which men align themselves much as they do in matters of religion. When they argue about rationality, they usually believe that it very much matters how their arguments turn out; they believe that they are asking about the essential nature of social order and human nature; they are deliberating the verities.

This claim need not raise anyone's hackles regardless of the theories of rationality to which they subscribe: just as one can argue the rhetorical importance of the concept *God* without taking sides in particular theological disputes (that is, one would be making secular arguments), so we can highlight the rhetorical dimensions of the rationality construct without casting aspersions on particular theories (except for some variants of realism). Whatever else rationality is thought to be, it is also an idea around which actors passionately align themselves—a social psychological phenomenon of interest in itself. One can accept this claim if one believes that rationality is a fact of nature like cell division and heartbeats or if one thinks that rationality is nothing but a rhetorical symbol.

The Importance of the Claim

But if my claim is uncontroversial, it is not innocuous. We can see this by thinking through what we shall have to do with the claim if we accept it. Formalists, for example, might say that our claim is innocuous because the desiderata of daily life are mere happenstances, accidents of convention. The existence of orthodoxy is uncontroversial but philosophically uninteresting. Ex hypothesi, the rhetorical view of rationality can do no interesting philosophic work. It will shortly be apparent how untenable this reasoning is and why we need not fear it (Bartley, 1962, 1964, 1968; Weimer, 1979; cf. Ayer, 1956). For now it may suffice to say that if formalists make this claim, the rhetorical view is already doing philosophic work by placing a burden of proof on formalists to mark their speculations off from the social practices they insist on contrasting (in kind) with their work. The rhetorical view has drawn empirical arguments from them, thus (presumably) imposing empirical burdens of proof upon them. As we shall see, this is not a minor matter.

It requires no leaps of faith to say that the rhetorical view is a plausible philosophic claim which prima facie merits attention. In a phrase, it is *the surest thing to be said of rationality*. Other statements we might make about rationality are mired in controversy; the claims of rationalists, idealists, intuitionists, and even the coherentists are—to different degrees—hotly disputed. Given the centuries these disputes have spanned, it is arguably the case that the usual claims about rationality are essentially contested concepts—the standards for settling them being themselves in dispute, making resolutions unlikely. It is not a sure thing to say that rationality is a faculty, or that it is defined by its objects, or that it is an innate formal principle of reason, or that it is the polar opposite of emotion. We court strong objections at every turn. Even the very bland recent views (for example, equating being rational with giving or having reasons, having an ordered set of preferences, being consistent, or some such) are in dispute.

But the claim that rationality is a rhetorical phenomenon is not so easily contested. The formalists who have attacked variations of this claim have not denied it substantively; they grant its truth but say that it draws no blood (for example, Ayer, 1956). They have been more or less forced to make this claim when social practices failed to gel with their grand systems. In something of Frege's manner they have argued that when social instances fail to fit into a broad system (or fail to be illuminated by the grand system), this is the instances', not the systems', fault. If anything, failures in fit were construed to mean that the grand systems were not rigorous enough—the key assumption being that the facts of social life are haphazard (and therefore uninteresting) accidents.

Formalism is in serious trouble if it cannot succeed with this claim. Ontology must be distinguished from practices to avoid the implication that grand systems (the ones said to be invariant universals) must consistently explain and illuminate social particulars. The facilitating notion has been a peculiar (and often implicit) assumption that social events are either less real than universals or (oppositely) epiphenomena of physical processes. Carnap thus insisted that psychology be a species of physics, using an object language permitting operationalization of its concepts. This legitimated the use of a physical model to undergird the social sciences and sustained the view that there is a difference in kind between justificational practices as they occur in practice and universals of justification. Social practices, so viewed, are a chimera we must cut through to reach universals. The spirit is Plato's: we are in the cave looking at shadows.

Despite the importance of this reasoning, no one has ever proved it. On formal grounds, no unassailable standard is available for carving rhetorical "happenstances" out of the "substantive claims" of formal philosophy. The claim one would have to prove would (to gloss) be something like: "There is a universal of rationality beside which social practices are trivialities; this universal is what it is, needing (and using) no rhetorical potency for acceptance; that it might *have* rhetorical effects is uncontroversial but uninteresting, since it is demonstrably true that the justification of the universal does not depend in any way upon its rhetorical potency." At each stage of this argument, we may trot out the tu quoque and the familiar line of skeptical challenges. This would *not* be an instance of the skeptic creating a knowledge standard "so hyperbolic" that it cannot be met (Rescher, 1977a). Our skeptical challenges would take their force and severity from the strength of the claims being made by the formalist. Thus it will not do to fiat the rhetorical account out of epistemics as a triviality. It is presumptively important insofar as the previous arguments about the rhetorical bases of argument fields are plausible. It remains to be seen whether the rhetorical view draws blood from the formalists, and it bears saying that this is not my central interest in making the argument: I am concerned rather with proving that the rhetorical potency of rationality is prima facie interesting to students of knowledge. It should not therefore pass as an innocuous observation that rationality is a rhetorical phenomenon and that its rhetorical effects are uncontroversial.

We are starting an investigation of the subject at the proper place, namely, with the surest, most straightforward feature of rationality. The term crops up in fields as a name for orthodox (conventionally acceptable) procedures. It is a shorthand expression for the correspondence of a claim (and the ways it is gotten) with a community's judgmental, veridical, and procedural standards. This can be largely understood as a weltanschauungen explanation—in which the particular elements of a conceptual framework are understood to be interdependent with a broad paradigm or root metaphor (Pepper, 1942). We thus suppose that observation is not theory free, that one's assumptions affect one's observations (Kuhn, 1970a, 1970b; Toulmin, 1967a, 1967b, 1970, 1972; Feyerabend, 1965a, 1965b, 1969, 1970a, 1970b; Suppe, 1977). A field's sense of rational and irrational procedure will thus be of a piece with the rest of its conceptual ecology. It is thus plausible to look at formalism (or any other *issue field*—a term I shall explain in the next essay) as a school of thought bound together by conventional ways of communicating and arguing. The rhetorical potency of these conventional "folkways" creates the cohesion necessary to sustain the field. We should expect to find interfield differences in the content of procedural and conceptual principles and (thus) that particular actions might stand as "rational" in one field but "irrational" in another. These differences I take to be objects of central concern to students of argumentation and epistemics. But fields of every sort share (at least) the characteristic that they exist because their actors have faith in (and use) their judgmental and veridical standards. The result is that "being rational" is analogous (in a nontrivial way) to "being a good Catholic," a phrase I intend figuratively, although it might be taken literally without doing violence to the present argument.

Setting Universalism Aside

Let me draw a conclusion, the proof of which will accumulate as I proceed. The claim is that we will do our best thinking about rationality if we ignore invariance, universality, impartial standpoints, and such. For now we have as many theories of rationality as there are points of view: there are variants of scientific rationality, utilitarianism, hedonism, reason giving, rule following, and acceptance on faith. All of these lines have conceptual weaknesses stemming not so much from internal difficulties as from attempts to generalize particular views to universal status. Every such attempt smacks into a wall of counterexamples. Laudan (1977) rightly says, "It is relatively easy to show that there are numerous cases in the history of science—cases in which almost everyone would agree intuitively that rational analysis was occurring—which run counter to each of the models of rationality...." (p. 122). This argument extends to every sort of field (as I shall gradually prove)—which plausibly suggests that the wrong sorts of questions are being asked. When we are preoccupied with asking whether some view of rationality is universally valid, we are unlikely to take that view on its own terms, to study it in its natural habitat (as it were). We hold each theory hostage to standards no theory can meet, and in so doing we ignore the standards each in fact does meet. So I want to play the hunch that it will be no great loss if issues of universality and invariance are set aside. We might instead ask about the focus and range of convenience (Kelly, 1955) of a rationality theory, that is, about the phenomena it serves best and those which it might be stretched to serve. This turns our attention to our own thinking, our particular assumptions and purposes, and away from grander aims of saying what rationality immutably *is*. The case for playing this hunch is not conclusive, but the arguments to follow feed it, each in a special way, and I shall take occasion as things progress to point out how this is so.

At this point I claim to have justified viewing rationality as a social judgment field actors make. It is plausible to assume that rationality is a powerful rhetorical device, a pivotal part of the social glue binding fields together. One can view rationality this way regardless of one's broader beliefs about the human condition. I have used the tu quoque only tangentially to argue that the rhetorical view cannot be fiated out of epistemics; I have not depended upon tu quoque arguments to prove that rationality *is* a rhetorical phenomenon. So proceeding, I claim to have proved that the rhetorical view is nontrivial and that it might (in principle) bear upon more grandiose matters.

Rationality as a Sociological Datum

I turn now to the second claim, that rationality is a datum, not a warrant. Remember that our attitude toward this claim is peculiar to our aims: the facts of daily life are not conceptual underbrush needing to be cleared away; we are not (à la Russell) peeling away layers of misconception. Given the rhetorical argument above, there are no ways to make that familiar line coherent. We are bracketing ontology entirely and are interested instead in sociological norms in themselves. For starters at least, we are taking them at face value, on their own terms.

This makes a virtue of necessity. Social norms *are* interesting per se, but it is not as if we can take or leave them. Consensual theories of truth (for example, Habermas, 1979; Burleson, 1979b; Burleson and Kline, 1979) have enjoyed recent success because they appear to be the best available alternatives to absolutist accounts. We lack the conceptual equipment and empirical proof to judge particular theories of rationality or to say that one is better than another. If we could succeed with such comparisons, we would not need the concept of argument fields at all.

Taking Fields Seriously

The claim that argument fields must be taken seriously means that analysis and criticism cannot start with the assumption of a privileged position. The assumption cannot be that the substantive and procedural ecologies of fields are "mere conventions" and that criticism is (provably) equipped to referee interfield disputes (Willard, 1979a, 1980a, 1980b, 1982). Nor can it be assumed that field studies are anthropological comparisons, that is, in the now familiar sense of adopting particular Western views of rationality to see how primitive cultures and practices fit them (for example, Winch, 1958; and the essays in Wilson, 1970). It is more prudent to begin with the assumption that people organize their activities around assumptions and principles that seem *appropriate* to the purposes and tasks that interest them. We should expect to find that views of knowledge and rationality historically evolve in particular fields because of their utility for field practices. We should not be surprised to discover that ideas and procedures are selected by virtue of their foci and ranges of convenience. Instead of defending a particular view of rationality as a universal (that is, as regnant or superior to the views used by fields), we can start by entertaining the possibility that it is fruitful to equate rationality with what people do when they think they are being rational.

In this section I want to prove that a formidable and insoluble battle line exists between those who believe (roughly) that a sociological explanation is the sole epistemic story and those who believe (roughly) that it is not enough to say that ideas are accepted, it is necessary (and possible) to say why ideas are worthy of acceptance. After Laudan (1977), let us call the former "sociologists," or "conventionalists," and the latter "rationalists." Then, after proving that this battle line exists, I want to opt out of it—the deus ex machina being "taking fields seriously."

Toulmin (1972, 1976), whose views are considered in detail in the next chapter, has opted for the "rationalist" side. He sees the conventions and orthodoxies of fields as the preoccupations of philosophy's "anthropological" face—the obstacles to be cleared by philosophy's "critical" face. The facts of fields, taken as the whole story, require a collapse to relativism and skepticism (cf. Rescher, 1977a, 1977b). He critiques Kuhn at length—the nub of the matter being that Kuhn stops at convention and equates justification with sociological authority. Like Kuhn, Toulmin believes that knowledge is balkanized into distinguishable discourse communities. The *"revolution versus evolution"* fray starts (in part) because Toulmin is centrally interested in securing an impartial standpoint of rationality, while Kuhn is not. Toulmin wants to know not merely how progress occurs but how progress worthy of the name (genuine progress) happens. This is not a minor difference: Toulmin brings his scientific account to the service of the broader aim of producing an impartial standpoint of rationality; he produces the evolutionary view to serve that project. His aim is to prove that relativism is not the inevitable outcome of field theory so that the critical face of philosophy can assess *the force of the better argument.*

An important outcome of this thinking has been the development of what best can be called a "flanking movement" rather than a battle line. Some theorists opt out of the *conventionalism versus rationalism* dispute by subordinating rationality to the idea of progress—which avoids using rationality as a core defining construct (for example, Laudan, 1977). Rationality becomes secondary to the coherence of research traditions. This procedure admittedly works. Laudan elegantly avoids *revolution versus evolution* as well as *conventional versus rational* by adopting an "arationality assumption" which functions much as do Mannheim's nonimmanent ideas: the distinction is thus between ideas that need to be sociologically explained and ideas embedded in systems (for example, geometrical proofs). Laudan recognizes that the arationality assumptions (and thus the applicability of a sociology of knowledge to explanations of progress) depends entirely upon which theory of rationality we choose to accept. There are many different models of rationality—many models being buttressed by examples which contradict other models.

The arationality assumption works something like an empiricist's version of the tu quoque. A strength of Laudan's view is that he is willing to live with incompleteness and to accept the interpenetration of rational and sociological factors. He accomplishes this happy compromise by making rationality something akin to problem solving (à la Kuhn). By this view, theorists can grant that sociological factors are preconditions of rational beliefs "yet still legitimately exclude these social factors from the explanation of a certain belief, *provided* we can show that the most crucial and relevant antecedent to the acceptance of the belief was a well-founded reasoning process on the part of the believing agent" (Laudan, 1977, p. 210). The phrase "well-founded reasoning process" does not betray an absolutism in Laudan's view: his aim is historical, that is, to explain either why a social order comes to be or why some particular theory comes to be accepted. Respecting epistemics, his view seems compatible with the field theory emerging here. But he does bracket differences between theories of rationality. Laudan is aware of these differences—indeed his thinking is based on them. But he is not centrally concerned with developing an account of rationality; progress per se is what is of interest. He could go considerably further with his argument if he possessed the sort of field theory we are developing. He would not need to accept the contrast of sociological and "rationalistic" explanation—as he in fact does. He could see the two as interdependent, both in the domain of practice and as abstractions.

It seems better to proceed on the assumption that the *sociological versus rational* battle line depends upon a (presently at least) unprovable dichotomy. If we succeed with the claim that rationality is (nontrivially) a sociological norm, we shall have proved that Mannheim's distinction between immanent and nonimmanent ideas cannot be sustained. Field actors may treat their theories as if they are immanent, but interfield differences between the things said to be immanent prove that this is a rhetorical and sociological phenomenon. To say otherwise is to enter the vicious circles and infinite regresses that did in the absolutists. Consider, for example, what it is to ask whether a belief is justified: community X believes Y; is Y justified? There are at least two levels at which this question can be posed, namely, is Y

universally (independent of any field's standards) justified and is *Y* sociologically justified, that is, given the language of the community *X*, is *Y* based on "well-founded reasoning"? But the former always collapses to the latter in such a way that the two can only arbitrarily be said to be distinct. Arguments favoring *Y*'s universality are never assumption free; one's assumptions come from one's field of discourse. Since there are differences among the things said to be universal, we would infer even if we knew nothing about field dependency that universalists work from different bodies of assumptions. Field theory thus illuminates the peculiar posture universalists must take: *Y* may be sociologically justified, that is, within the setting of *X;* but it is not "genuine" because it does not square with *N*, my standard. If a field actor in *X* replies (tu quoque) that *Y*'s justification is "universal" because *X*'s standards are universals (something field actors in fact often do when their standards, assumptions, and procedures are challenged from outside), our critic has nothing to say.

In the last chapter I shall present examples of such interfield differences. One may prove helpful here, however. Consider the comparison of two distinct fields (serving distinct purposes) which use utterly incompatible theories of rationality and knowledge, namely, *cost-benefit analysis versus neo-Kantian ethics*. Cost-benefit analysis is a school of thought within economics, political science, and practical politics which, inter alia, equates rationality with giving fiscal weights to values, for example, the value of human lives. Its claim is that decision making cannot be rational when values are left vague, intuitive, and unexamined. Value claims should be explicit, that is, rendered in the same language all other costs and benefits of social programs are expressed in. A convenient language is money. Since every social program has both fiscal and value costs and benefits, one cannot compare them unless they are comparably expressed. If lives are saved or lost, then, calculi are needed to make these benefits and costs intelligible. Thus, we might say that a human life is worth $220,000 on the average, although older people are worth less than younger people. A typical instance arises in disaster litigation when the courts parcel out compensation and revenge awards for lost lives. There are sharp disputes within this field about which measures of value are best, though most of the measures turn in some sense on expected or present income. All of the competing theories however, are detailed and consistent views of rational decision making; most of them meet one or another of the standard philosophic accounts of rationality (reason giving, means-end reasoning, consistency, ordered sets of preferences).

Compare the cost-benefit picture of rational deciding to the neo-

Kantian view. If we could impute to Kant a core argument—a complex matter to be sure—it might well be his claim that values cannot be confused with objects. Loosely put, it is a priori unjustified and implausible to confound values and objects. Attempts to express values in the language of quantity are *irrational*—in this sense, demonstrably untenable, fallacious, and even perverse.

We have two issue fields with incompatible views of rationality. No rapprochement is possible, since the theories are mirror opposites. If we think like justificationists, we are tempted to try to referee the disputes between the fields; but what principle might we use to decide which is the superior theory? We doubtless can conjure up principles that can overarch the two fields, but by what principle could we prove that our grand principle takes precedence over the assumptions of each field? In attempting such refereeing, we should surely have to prove that by each field's standards its rationality theories are either defective or at least subordinate to our regnant standard. Otherwise, we would merely be taking sides. The field we side against can, in the face of our criticism, adopt the most powerful epistemic posture available to field actors, namely, the shrug. The actor might trot out the tu quoque and the usual skeptical challenges; but why bother? The outcome of such challenges is a forgone conclusion—the shrug thus being the most parsimonious reply a field can make to outside critics.

There are nonjustificational ways of looking at such confrontations to which I shall turn toward the end of these investigations. For now it may suffice to say that field theory not only exacerbates the justificationist's problem in dealing with interfield differences but suggests as well that assuming this burden is unnecessary. We can proceed on the assumption that different fields adopt their views of rationality and knowledge in order to deal with the tasks that concern them—different theories thus being pinned to specific practices. It is obvious, for example, that the cost-benefit and neo-Kantian views are in some senses linked to different purposes (although we shall not want to take this statement too literally, insofar as moral theorists would not grant that their speculations are irrelevant to advising the polity). Nonetheless, it seems plausible to say that the two fields start out from very different places in pursuit of wildly different aims.

A Research Program

Argumentation theorists want to know a good argument when they see one. They have this aim because they believe that argument is the social process by which we come by knowledge. They also believe that argument is a *good* way of coming to know. They assume that the public process of weighing claims, evaluating evidence, and defending judgments is a rational way of proceeding. The oversimple conclusion from these views is that actors in any field, proceeding by good arguments honestly presented, will produce their "truths" that by some principle can be fitted together. Confronted with profound substantive and procedural differences between social traditions, proponents of the oversimple view usually appeal to an argument on faith, namely, that a universal will be found.

It is just as plausible and no more an argument on faith that no universal will be found. Or, it is just as plausible to say that if a universal is to be found, it will be a product of careful empirical considerations of the foci and ranges of convenience of substantive and procedural standards, their appropriateness, their "fit" to particular purposes and tasks. Our point in raising the notion of argument fields is thus not to add to the skeptic's arsenal. In the abstract, the skeptic hardly needs more weapons. The better aim is to produce a theoretical framework guiding empirical observations of interfield differences, of seeing them on their own terms, of—in a phrase—taking fields seriously.

If A *says* X, we want to know what A means by saying X. If X is an argument utterance or a knowledge claim, we want to know *by virtue of what guarantor* A says X. Our aim is neither praise nor blame. We thus want to know how A decided to say X and why A regards standard N as vouching for X. Our organizing empirical assumption is that A *says* X because A *trusts* N, *which vouches for* X. We thus want to understand A's trust of N as well as the sources of this trust. Our aim is not to bemoan the fact that we cannot separate the ethos of the authorities who defend N, A's belief that his trust of N is confirmed by colleagues, and N's "genuine" worthiness as a guarantor of X. Our aim is (better put) to understand as precisely as possible the interrelationships and interdependencies among these factors.

This purpose requires a studied attention to the facts of fields, to their ways of arguing, and to the claims they take as knowledge. What is insufficiently understood is the fit of these processes into particular field conceptions of rationality. To study this fit is to replace the traditional focus upon objectivity with a concern for "objectifying." The question of whether X is a justified true belief is transformed to "how is A authorized by a community of discourse to justifiably claim X?" The assumption is that argument utterances and interactions are rational because they are countenanced by a field's framework of criteria for saying what is rational. "Justification" is something field actors do; "validity" is a judgment they make, both drawing substance from the facts of a field. Both entail if-then reasoning of this sort: "If starting point N is accepted, one must think through N's implications according to the presuppositional framework attendant to N; if A *says* X and uses N to vouch for X in the standard way, A has justified X; if A proceeds in an orthodox way, A has said X rationally."

To say that rationality is a social norm is not to depend upon the argument that universals collapse to social judgments. It depends upon an argument for putting first things first. Because fields and their facts have not been taken seriously, we know little of the *situated practices* by which people pass muster on knowledge. I propose building a research program with the aim of understanding these practices and letting the ontological chips fall where they may. The grand disputes are simply premature. Our empirical accomplishments are so modest that we would not know a successful universal if we saw one, and doing our empirical homework is surely a precondition of figuring out universals of justified true belief. It seems prudent to make a virtue of necessity and to embark upon an empirical inquiry into the epistemic and rational features of field practices.

The Untenability of Justificational Views

I turn now to (3), justificationist views of rationality are untenable. I hope to prove that the grand systems and good reasons tradition have failed and that more contemporary views are banal. This is well-trod ground (Weimer, 1979; Polanyi, 1958, 1966; Lakatos, 1968, 1970; Kuhn, 1970a, 1970b; Bartley, 1962, 1964; Rescher, 1973, 1977a, 1977b; Davis, 1965; Gurvitch, 1971; Gödel, 1962; Curry, 1980; Bloor, 1976). The familiar skeptical arguments have been extensively considered (Rescher, 1977a, 1977b; Weimer, 1979; Toulmin, 1958, 1972, 1976; Lehrer, 1974). Thus I hope to get away with painting broad strokes to build a particular case against justificationism; that is, I will avoid becoming enmeshed in lists of the isms and their cross-pollinations or bogged down in disputes about what universals are (for example, names versus classes versus physical entities, and so forth).

The Grand Systems as Guarantors of Good Reasons

Historically the various ists (realists, nominalists, idealists, monists, rationalists, and so forth) believed that rationality could be defined vis-à-vis two things: its effects and its internal character. Rationality *did* something (produced good actions, correct statements) and *was* something (a faculty, a system of reasoning). The one did not make sense without the other—what good does it do to talk of a rational faculty unless it produces something special? What good are the special things unless they are linked to some capacity in man?

This thinking works best when rationality is a very narrow concept. Take a narrow system, for example, the syllogism, geometry, mathematics, and so forth, and say "when the form of your arguments meets the tests of the system, you are being rational." So thinking, the ists produced their isms, which proposed certain guarantors of our concepts: the candidates were various formal systems, sometimes combined with God in varied permutations. We can trace the development of this thinking from Aristotle, Aquinas, Bacon, Descartes, and Kant; we can see some of the more grandiose systems in Frege and Russell. Take something as the model of form, see what matches it, and call that "rational."

The problem always was that the first criterion was ignored. This is why there has been a succession of candidates. A perfectly valid syllogism can (demonstrably) produce evil and silly results. We are surely justified in mistrusting logic which (as in our earlier example) validly says, "Auschwitz was a good thing." That is not "demonstrative," because it has probable premises; but if we insist that the premises be empty symbols, then we have so narrowed "rationality" that ordinary thinking of all kinds is ruled out. Demonstrative reasoning is nicely self-contained but too narrow—by definition, most of the important instances of decision making are fiated out of rationality. Loosen the demonstrative requirement, however, and none of the great systems could guarantee results. The same formal procedures could produce *Principia Mathematica* and Buchenwald. Too, the same formal procedures could produce falsity. As things worked out, knowledge and ontology could *not* be indissoluble.

It was obvious to the system builders that if rationality could not be said to produce some specifiable result, it was utterly trivial. In a moment I shall note how contemporary theorists ignore this insight. But the grand theorists knew what the issues were; they tried mightily to produce formal systems that issued in the proper results. The problem always came with skeptical variants of the tu quoque—challenges from *within* the great systems. The reasoning usually went something like (see Weimer, 1979) the following: if you say X and I (in reply) challenge your ability to know X, you must (to be logical) reply, "by virtue of N," that is, a higher-order notion which vouches for X. If I ask how you know N, you say "by virtue of H." And so it goes, infinitely. If you finally stop at a "final guarantor," and I think your stopping place is counterintuitive, I can (justifiably) accuse you of justifying reason by virtue of faith. Rationality thus ends up being irrationally justified. Weimer (1979) and Bartley (1962) call this a "retreat to commitment"—by which they mean that someone *declares* a stopping point to avoid regress on intuitive or passionate grounds. This amounts to hiding from the tu quoque rather than defeating it. I shall put aside for the moment the Weimer/Bartley solution, "comprehensively critical rationalism," on the promise of returning to it below.

So the great systems floundered on the very source of their strength. They were based upon the assumption that rationality had to mean something, to speak to the human condition, and to have specifiable results. But they could not prove by their own standards that rationality *had* acceptable results (that is, without making arbitrary closures or counterintuitive leaps of faith).

Ordinary Adjective Views of Rationality

One solution to infinite regress is to loosen the view of rationality and thereby broaden the range of things which can be rational. The risk is that rationality may have no predictable results or that it might become redundant to other (better) terms. These approaches are standard fare, nowadays: rational actors have (1) ordered sets of preferences (Rawls, 1971), (2) propensities and capacities to follow rules or to take account of them, (3) reasons, and (4) good reasons. Preparatory to considering these accounts, let us take note of how they came about.

Initially, the idea of equating rationality with necessary or axiomatic reasoning was quite narrow (for example, Blanshard, 1962). Pre-Gödel mathematics (Frege's notion of the system) was usually the model. In this century, the scope of necessity has been successively narrowed by three sources of pressures, namely, the Copenhagen Interpretation (Bohr, 1913, 1958, 1963; Heisenberg, 1952, 1958, 1966), mathematical and philosophical interpretations of Gödel's Incompleteness Theorem (Gödel, 1962), and purely philosophic arguments (such as Wittgenstein's) about the tautologous nature of mathematics. The effect of these developments has been to increasingly narrow the scope of necessity (and of rationality when the two are linked).

The second impetus toward the weaker views of rationality came from social theorists. The tie between rationality and necessary reasoning ruled too many intuitively rational activities out, for example, a situated actor choosing among alternatives, an economist weighing evidence and making business cycle forecasts, a judge hearing arguments and making a decision, and—in fact—the processes by which the grand systematizers devised their systems (Aristotle, for example, did not derive his demonstrative syllogism demonstratively). Too many things were "nonrational" by the narrow view.

For purposes of social theory the formalist view was useless. But it was worse than useless: it led to several morasses. The formalists' work was picked up and used by social theorists with breathtaking results. *Morass number one:* the problem of induction (the problem roughly being that induction is not deduction). It is one thing to try to work inductive arguments out demonstratively (for example, Kyburg, 1970) and quite another to tie views of psychology, sociology, argument, and epistemics to Hume's problem (see Willard, 1980d). The syllogism was said to be the basic cognitive model; the practical syllogism was thought to issue in truth conditions of the sort common to inductivism; and *action* was reduced to formal principles without regard for situations and content. Our emerging field theory is a way of looking at the problem of induction, although it does not solve it in any logical sense. It merely proposes that there are social parallels (in every sphere) to Hume's problem—these being solved by the routine activities in fields.

Morass number two: the conviction-persuasion duality. Formalism led social theorists to believe that logic and emotion differed in knowable ways. Even the loosest theories, which often cropped up in the argumentation literature, tied rationality to some variant of "logical thought." The problem of specifying the results of rational thought and action was ignored. So the theories which used the duality were useless and misleading.

Morass number three: criticism was confounded with justification. The assumption was that criticism consisted of weighing particulars against formal principles. The critic's arguments were to be justified by appeal to an a priori (loosely or strictly speaking) system. Set piece warfare ensued. All particulars were found wanting, as they were bound to be; interesting criticism was rare. Argument criticism became an organized tradition of breast beating, since no situated utterance could meet formal standards. It was thought to be important for critics to say whether the actors they studied were rational, presumably on the assumption that rational actors make correct claims, give wise advice, and do good deeds. More often than not, critics either chose acts of which they approved and proclaimed them rational or (oppositely) wrote about acts of which they disapproved and proclaimed them irrational. In any case, purely formal judgments based on the narrow view were inappropriate to such critical aims, since no situated utterance or action could be rational if mathematics remained the exemplar. Thus, critics loosened the notion of rational action in an unreflective way.

Morass number four: "irrationality" lost its meaning. Formalists used "nonrational" as the constrasting pole to "rational" to avoid the unattractive result of saying (for example) that a weather forecaster, reasoning from data to predictions, could count as "irrational" (see

Toulmin, 1976). Even the proponents of narrow views did not want to call forecasting "irrational." This situation left "irrational" floating. Since formalists had ruled loose senses of rationality out, they could not use "irrational" coherently. This theoretical move was peculiar to formalism's aims, although social theorists did not consistently see it as a narrow, field-dependent notion. The narrowest of them borrowed the formal view of rationality and proclaimed it "that toward which" ordinary, situated utterance should aim.

But there *are* legitimate uses of "irrationality," for example, to name utterly random acts and socially dysfunctional acts and to define pedagogical ideals. Humanists often claim that their pedagogical aim is to produce students capable of rational deciding—this aim usually being accomplished by reference to a loose sense of rational and irrational action, namely, conventionally sound versus conventionally unsound practices. Such an account is intuitively plausible: it sees rationality as inhering in reflectively considered norms.

This normative view of rationality may be the one aspect of the concept worth salvaging, whatever happens to the more specialized senses of rational action. We might plausibly assume that fields in part define themselves by the reflectively considered norms for proper conduct they transmit to their novices. "Irrationality" is the considered opposite of each of a field's cardinal virtues. This account would cohere with the more familiar humanist's argument for a pedagogy of rational deciding. In any case, none of this squares with the narrow formalistic view: if rationality has the narrowest possible focus of convenience, the range of the "irrational" becomes so broad as to make the term useless, and the notion of the "nonrational"—while serving particular formal interests—seems to bear no useful service to social theory.

These I take to be the main reasons why theorists in many disciplines started trying out looser and weaker views of rationality. They sought a concept with a far wider focus and range of convenience. Their vision of the work the *rational versus irrational* construct might do were broader than the formalist's narrow view would permit. Let me globally call these loose views "ordinary adjective" senses of rationality. They make rationality an adjective to describe something else. Whether they are successful depends—in part at least—upon what we ask them to do.

Weaknesses of the Ordinary Adjective Views

In ways I shall specify, all of the ordinary adjective views share these defects: (1) they do not specify the outcomes of rationality; (2) they make rationality redundant to some other term, for example, consistency or self-interest; and (3) they trivialize rationality, that is, make it unimportant.

Rawls (1971) equates rationality with having an ordered set of preferences. His POPs (persons in the original position) are rational because they wish to maximize their good and minimize their evil in a sort of hedonistic calculus. But Rawls's use of this thinking proves claims (1), (2), and (3). It is not rationality but the veil of ignorance that Rawls trusts to help his POPs arrive at the principles of justice. Why else defend the original position? The outcomes of rationality are thus presumed to be something less than egalitarian: a *rational* person not behind the veil of ignorance might well adopt a utilitarian solution or (worse) a gambling solution (if the odds seem favorable). What gets the principles of justice is the veil of ignorance, not rationality; rationality is redundant to hedonism (or something like it), that is, it is a form of self-interestedness. Hence, respecting the principles of justice, rationality is not especially important.

Another line of thinking equates rational action with goal-directed behavior (for example, Jarvie and Agassi, 1970), and rational belief with belief based upon some accepted standard. This line can be reformed to fit with the field theory emerging here, but it needs saying that Jarvie and Agassi do not intend to reduce their view to consensualism. The equation of rationality with goal behavior is lucid enough, but it suffers criticism (1) because it cannot specify the goodness or badness of the outcomes of such reasoning. The equation suffers (2) by making rationality redundant to another idea, in this case goal-directed action; hence why do we need the term rationality at all? Thus, the criticism (3) that rationality is trivialized obtains: except for utterly random acts, it is hard to see what actions would not fit it.

Another line of thinking—perhaps the most important for our purposes—ties rationality to the having or giving of reasons (McKerrow, 1973, 1977, 1980c, 1980d; Brockriede, 1975, 1977). I shall subsequently argue that a reformed version of the "presumption" notion better serves this line of thought (because presumption counts in fields as a prohibition against random action). Here I want to argue that the "reasons" tradition suffers serious deficiencies. To start with, this thinking insists that one must have reasons, *whatever they are*, to be rational. Since the whole point of this reasoning is to avoid the heavier burdens of the "good reasons" point of view, evil or silly reasons are presumptively better than no reasons at all. As far as I can see, this makes the results of rational action tangential [proving (1) conclusively]. "I shot the president to impress Jodie Foster," would count as a rational claim.

The only stricture in the reasons tradition is that action cannot come out of the blue. Thus claim (2) obtains: rationality is redundant to the having or giving of reasons—and it is far less precise than the terms usually associated with reason giving. Occam's razor inclines toward "rationality" because the other terms more clearly and accurately describe what the reasons theorists have in mind.

Claim (3) that rationality is made unimportant also applies to these theories. "I mass murdered Jews because I was ordered to" or "as a matter of political expedience" (and most statements of this general sort) shall have to stand as rational accounts. "Rationality" has thus become a neutral term describing the structural relation of claims and reasons—saying nothing about outcomes. It has no necessary connections to good or evil, reasonableness or silliness, plausibility or implausibility; it has lost its basic quality as a term of praise or blame. Thus it is hard to see what work it does, what useful contributions it makes.

With respect to each of these objections, the familiar distinction between "reasons" and "causes" does not help. Across fields of discourse, to call someone's reason a cause is merely to denigrate it (which, of course, was never the intention of the philosophers who have defended the distinction). While the *reason versus cause* distinction may well be adequate for certain mental aberrations, an equally large range of "claims offered up as reasons" will not prove so tractable. I do not see, for example, that the distinction affects the status of any of the examples we are considering here.

Two additional weaknesses plague the reason-giving view of rationality. First, *it courts tautology.* If our conception of "reasons" is sufficiently broad (a matter to which I shall turn in a moment), it is impossible to act sans reasons. Consider, for instance, the standard example that it is irrational to cut one's arm off without a reason. This example is deficient if we ask whether anyone in the world has ever done so. While people in the grip of insanity may do things unintelligible to us, we shall hardly want to pin our view of the rational to contrasts with madmen. If I say, "I cut my arm off for sexual pleasure," proponents of the reasons tradition are less secure in their answer. On what grounds would they argue that my reason is not a reason—that is, on what grounds could they conclusively define my reason as inferior to their own standards for defining reasons? Thus "rationality" becomes a label for prohibitions against things no sane persons do (in any case). This yields the reverse of the very narrow views of rationality: the construct has become so inclusive that virtually nothing is excluded.

The second weakness is this: there is no getting around the broad view of reasons. The reasons tradition has no theoretic resources for carving out certain aspects of a person's cognitive world as being reasons in contrast to other aspects which are not reasons (without, that is, collapsing to the "good reasons" view). Thus hunches, intuitions, values, emotions, desires—indeed, anything to which a person might refer to account for his actions—have to count as reasons. Consider an example of the following sort: "John killed his brother out of love. The brother was terminally ill and suffering; he asked John to kill him as an act of mercy. John weighed his inhibitions against murder and his fears of legal reprisal against his sympathy for his brother's plight." Although a powerful affect is central to John's thinking, the *reason versus cause* distinction is surely inappropriate (partly because we intuitively approve of the motive even if we object to the act). So we have a case that meets several of the criteria for being a rational act. But having opened the door to an emotion of which we approve, have we not also opened the door to emotion per se? If John kills his brother out of malice or greed or envy, the reasons tradition possesses no principled way of ruling the act so motivated out of rationality. Of course, we might argue that the emotions differ in kind (love being a rational affect and hatred being irrational), but this would require a retreat to the good reasons tradition and a proportionate loss of the theoretic advantages of avoiding disputes about the nature and content of reasons. I shall show that this collapse does not salvage anything, but what is at issue here is that the very *bases* of the reason-giving tradition are undermined if we try to argue that love can be a reason and hatred cannot. We cannot rule it out because it is an emotion, because we have entertained other emotions as reasons. The only thing left is to prove that it is a bad emotion, which puts us back into the justification business. This viewpoint *must* use a frighteningly broad view of reasons; that is, there are no principles for narrowing the concept.

So the reasoning-giving tradition suffers from claims (1), (2), and (3) and has the additional defects of either being tautologous or of collapsing into defenses of the content of reasons, that is, justification of specific things as reasons. A variant of this thinking ties rationality to *consistency*. All of the above claims apply to these efforts. Claim (1) applies because consistent thinking can equally produce principles of justice and the Mad Hatter's litanies. Claim (2) applies because "consistency" better says what these theorists mean; "rationality" is dragged in by the back door to give a value judgment that is justified in a circular way. Claim (3) thus also applies: it is consistency, not rationality, that is important.

Another variation on the loose view of rationality ties it to rule following; like the reason-giving tradition, the content of the rules is unimportant; it is even arguable that this tradition amounts to the same thing as the reason-giving tradition. Claim (1) applies because the outcomes of a rule are not at issue; claim (2) applies because "rule following" better describes the matter; and claim (3) obtains because "rules" have to be so loosely construed that no sane person could ever be said not to be following some rule.

There are parallel weaknesses to the ones I added vis-à-vis the reason-giving tradition. First, the rule-following view is either tautologous or incoherent. If one blindly follows a rule, one does automatic routines that do not square with our commonsense expectations about rational action. A common example is that one follows rules in a manner analogous to *the following of grammatical rules*. But this might make rationality something like an instinct (speaking loosely). There are great disputes as to what grammatical development consists of; but a shared idea in many views is that one nonconsciously follows grammatical rules. Take the analogy in a serious way, and the automaton is our model of the rational actor.

It might be argued that rational actors *evaluate* rules before following them (thus abandoning the analogy with grammatical rules). But this is a tautology unless we have something to say if we object to the actor's evaluations. For this we have other words that say more precisely what we mean, namely, "deliberative," "considered action," and the like. Without being able to speak to the character of the rules, we cannot evaluate rule-guided action. Rationality is dragged into this scheme rather than being a foundational part of it. "Rule following" is thus more precise.

These approaches share the weakness that they are merely prohibitions against random action. It is arguably the case that sane people cannot act randomly, so these views amount to saying that we should not do things we cannot do. Claim (1) obtains in each case: rationality has no special or predictable outcomes; (2) applies equally to all: rationality is redundant to concepts which better describe the phenomena of interest; and (3) is fatal: each theory makes rationality unimportant. I shall later argue that "presumption" better serves the aims of these theories.

The Collapse to Good Reasons

One avoids these problems when one stipulates that rational reasons are good ones and that rational rule following is the following of the right rules. But this brings us back to the tu quoque, infinite regress, and circularity. Let me proceed here as if the following propositions are true; I do not mean that they are certainties or that everyone takes them as conclusively proved; but for expositional ease I shall take them to be plausible inferences and good working assumptions.

I. *The grand schemes have not produced successful universals of rationality.* It *is* possible to overstate cultural diversity; but the formalists have vastly understated it. *Field theory* is a far stronger brief for relativism than the gross notion of sociocultural relativism because it says that there are nontrivial differences within cultures. The various ists have thus had nothing useful to say about individuals and instances.

II. *The grand schemes are special cases of ordinary views of rationality.* "Naive social actors," that is, people in the natural attitude (Schutz, 1945, 1953, 1962, 1966, 1967), take things to be universals, and their assumptions look much like those of philosophers: something is a universal if and only if (a) it is a simple, self-evidenced axiom; (b) it requires no appeal to empirical evidence; and (c) instances can be deductively derived from it. These three standards may be interpreted two ways, that is, as in principle analytic standards and as implicit background assumptions of actors in the natural attitude. They have normative and descriptive implications: the universal should say what is the right thing to do in this or that situation and, for descriptive purposes, the universal should illuminate (give meaning to) particular actions in particular situations.

III. *The relation (normative and descriptive) between universals and instances is obscure.* Universals work best when emptiest, when vague and abstract enough to gloss over differences. Deductive schemes have universally failed to illuminate instances; induction (unless Hume's problem is solved) cannot link an instance to a universal; so the best universals are the ones that are impossible to apply to individual cases. This is *our* problem, not the formalists'—Frege's system was self-contained.

IV. *A principle of application would have to be as self-evident and axiomatic as the universal itself.* Infinite regress rears up; we do not now have such a nonempirical principle. Toulmin's impartial standpoint of rationality *might* get such a principle out of his Darwinian metaphor for conceptual ecologies; but this remains to be seen.

V. *A nonempirical universal of rationality is useless (for us).* It would say nothing of value. It would not guide criticism; it would not guide research; and it would not help anyone *be* rational.

VI. *A successful universal of rationality will be substantively trivial.* It will be a principle of cognitive organization rather than a grand archetype. It will not tell us if this or that action is good or bad, sensible or silly, correct or incorrect. To succeed, it will be so abstract that it will countenance no substantive claims.

These claims amount to saying that relativity in one form or another is the "hard fact" to be respected. For social theory, this hard fact takes on a stronger implication than it has for philosophers. All human action, we want to say, is context embedded. Humans adapt to situations, their definitions of situation being the organizing constructs by which they give meaning to their actions and utterances; argument fields are often the psychological perspectives people take to produce adequate definitions of situation.

Definitions of Situation and Ceteris Paribus Qualifications

Theorists of many stripes have considered the definition of situation (Cox, 1980), though we commonly associate the idea with the symbolic interactionists (Blumer, 1969; McHugh, 1968; Stebbins, 1967). The organizing assumption is that definitions of situation are *emergent* and relative to the actor's assumptive framework (Ball, 1972). Our special addition to this statement is the notion that actors may take different general postures, depending upon the fields of discourse to which they refer. Situated actors are thus seen as balancing conventional assumptions and meanings against particular situated intentions. If a critic wishes to analyze a particular instance, *A says X*, the starting point must be *A*'s definition of the situation.

This is a plausible account for two reasons. First, the universalist alternatives to it have proved cumbersome and irrelevant. It has not worked out empirically to try to say that situations are carbon copies of ideal classes or that actors are instances of ideal types. Second, and more to the point, the focus upon situated activity has become increasingly central to explanations of rationality. For reasons to be explained below, the fact that *A says X* by virtue of an *adaptation* to a situation is plausibly a matter of central importance to explaining *A*'s (or *X*'s) rationality. The irremediable indexicality of *saying X* (Blum and McHugh, 1971; Pollner, 1970; Garfinkle, 1967; Bar-Hillel, 1964) requires that making sense of *A says X* depends upon reference to a particular situation as well as upon the field of assumptions or "occasioned corpus" (Zimmerman and Pollner, 1970) *A* uses to define the situation.

The main result is that once we admit that the main job of social theory is to understand situated action, the justificationist model has to be jettisoned. We do not have the conceptual equipment for evaluating an actor's sense of rational action; nor is it especially obvious that such evaluations are valuable to criticism. Rationality is a construct that can do special work for social criticism only insofar as it is not tied to matters of praise or blame, that is, as long as it is not a *judgment*. If field theory proves nontrivial, no critic can *justify* condemning an action in a field. The field's traditions and assumptions authorize the actor's shrug in the face of critical objections.

I shall return to this matter when I consider claim 6, that a reformed view of role taking—coherent with a reformed view of presumption—might succeed as a universal of rationality. I mention it here to introduce another sort of rules-based rationality theory. My main claim about this theory is that it *collapses* to a role-taking view—that is, it ends up saying that the definition of situation is what is important.

Neilsen (1974) tries to develop abstract principles of rationality, benefiting from a ceteris paribus qualification along lines analogous to the reasoning behind prima facie duties. Such rules are not exceptionless; they are "absolute" in the way prima facie duties are absolute (Neilsen, 1974, p. 60). We construe them as constraints on actions, but this does not mean that they always must be obeyed. We may take this statement in the same way we take Searle's (1969) claim that promise keeping is a generic constraint upon anyone working within the institution of promise keeping. So viewed, principles of rationality are generally constraining but not exceptionless. Neilsen thus proposes fifteen principles which inter alia say that we must be objective, we must not ignore relevant evidence; our beliefs should not be contradictory and should have good grounds; we should choose the most effective and efficient means to our ends; and so on. Several other principles sound like Kelly's "constructive alternativism"; they say that a rational belief is always open to evaluation, criticism, and revision. Bartley (1964) and Weimer (1979) might well accept this view into their vision of "comprehensively critical rationalism."

While we might debate the merits of Neilsen's principles, they are less important than the philosophic work done by the ceteris paribus clause. His principles are studded with ceteris paribus qualifications to avoid "obviously unacceptable" results, namely, *ignoring contexts*. I have no objections to this thinking broadly construed. But I want to point to some ambiguities in Neilsen's thinking. For starters, one acceptable way of understanding Neilsen's scheme is to say that the ceteris paribus clause, *not the rules*, embodies the most precise sense of rationality. This notion would mean that the whole system might collapse to the reformed view of role taking below.

The first ambiguity turns upon an unclear sense of what is being called rational. Is it the rules themselves or the following of them? Unless I badly misunderstand Neilsen, we can eliminate both possibilities. There are scarcely any reasons to believe that the rules themselves embody rationality. Neilsen (1974, p. 61) says that his liberal use of the ceteris paribus "flags my beliefs concerning their indeterminacy and my convictions about the importance of contextualism. Only if we could get priority rules—*à la* Rawls—a strict lexical ordering, could this indeterminacy be avoided. But we cannot have such rules with such *ceteris paribus* qualifications...." Without the ceteris paribus, we are back to the absolutism of (say) Frege. It is this qualification that differentiates contextualism (of Neilsen's kind) from, for example, Kant's synthetic a priori ideas. We risk everything by arguing that the rules themselves embody rationality.

Let me put aside the familiar argument that if the rules do not themselves embody rationality (if we cannot defend them as exceptionless or as a priori), we cannot justify the following of them at all. We could use conventionalism or consensualism to answer—and social theorists might be happy with the result. But this consideration is irrelevant to the present matter. I am trying to prove that Neilsen's principles of rationality are not self-contained; they are principles of rationality because of something outside themselves, namely, the ceteris paribus.

If it is not the rules themselves Neilsen has in mind, could it be the following of them? This is unlikely, since Neilsen expresses agreement with most of the previous arguments that demolish such a view. Either exceptionless rule following is automatic and routinized, and thus counter to our intuitive views of what rationality must be, or the whole enterprise collapses to the content of the rules. There are complex arguments about this result, and heroic attempts have been made to rescue followership accounts. But we will not go far by reviewing these matters here: the staunchest of the followership advocates will grant that the case for that view is not unambiguous, and even a little ambiguity is for our purposes fatal.

If Neilsen means neither the rules themselves nor the following of them, he likely means "taking account of rules," an idea that has lately enjoyed considerable attention. Taking account of a rule means that one considers its constraining force, not that one must follow it. Neilsen does not say so, but this is the likeliest candidate. I have belabored the ambiguity only to close off escape routes if we decide that this interpretation is also in trouble.

It will pay to be careful here: by "in trouble" I do not mean that taking account as a descriptive matter is in peril. Taking account may be close indeed to what fields take rationality to be. If we make Neilsen's scheme out to be a social psychological statement about the empirical processes of argument fields, it will prove compatible with the arguments below about perspective taking, reflexiveness, and the reformed version of presumption. The trouble may come only when Neilsen's views are made out to be abstract universals. But this is just his intention.

The problem is that it is deucedly hard to make sense of the notion of "implicit rules" when talking of rationality. I am not rejecting this thinking vis-à-vis every aspect of the rules tradition; but vis-à-vis *rationality*, the idea of implicit rule following or "taking account of" implicit rules seems difficult if not perverse.

Neilsen (1974, p. 61) explicitly eschews the "absurd claim" that rational people can always *state* the rules they follow. His reasons are familiar ones, and there are no obvious reasons for rejecting them. On every front, rules theorists have avoided saying that actors explicitly refer to rules, and some have avoided saying that actors can clearly state rules (to do otherwise would automatically trivialize each of the approaches discussed above). So "implicitness" becomes the organizing assumption.

Neilsen (1974) uses, as many rules theorists do, a linguistic analogy similar to the one mentioned above: "Rational people show by their behavior that they reason and act in accordance with those principles analogously to the way we show by our linguistic behavior that we speak in accordance with linguistic rules many of us cannot state" (p. 61). "Taking account of" rules of rationality is thus something like "taking account of" the rules of language.

Before proving that this is fraught with complications, let me say that this is no minor analogy that Neilsen (or any rules theorist) can jettison if blood is drawn. *His position is nonsense without it.* We have here a view that is mystical when stated baldly: "People follow rules that they are unaware of and cannot state." But there has to be some sense in which they can be said to follow or take account of the things they are unaware of and cannot state—otherwise there are no connections at all. So, we need some version according to which people follow or take account of rules but do not do so consciously. Neilsen sinks or swims on his ability to make this claim clear and plausible. Moreover, this sort of claim has to make sense vis-à-vis ordinary speech. Neilsen's scheme must be able to countenance claims on the order of: "in *this* empirical instance, X was rational because he took account of principles 1–15—or some combination—in the same way he used language in that situation, that is, automatically, unreflectively."

So the analogy must be sustained for the position to make sense. But there are two things wrong with it. Both reduce to the claim that Neilsen is trying to obtain the advantages of universals without defending them as such.

First, Neilsen cannot use *nativism* in the manner of (say) Chomsky (1965, 1968) without contradicting the spirit if not the letter of the ceteris paribus qualification. Nativism is more compatible with apriorism, exceptionless universals. The whole point of nativist accounts is that grammatical rules do not depend upon situations—precisely the "absurd" view Neilsen wishes to avoid. So, if we want to say that taking account of a rationality rule is something like using a grammatical rule, we mean something other than nativism. But what do we mean?

Second—and this is the formidable argument—the only way to make the analogy with language rules work for rationality rules is to take the ceteris paribus seriously and the only way to do this would be to allow rationality to be tied to *the most exhaustive sort of relativism*. I can prove this by spelling out, and granting for the sake of argument, the most extreme caveat.

Grant these things: (1) language development proceeds, alternatively utilizing native and acquired operations; (2) the proportions of these are unknown; we cannot conclusively settle "nature versus nurture"; and (3) language acquisition logically requires some "private language" of a complexity at least as great as the language learned (Fodor, 1979). We are granting quite a lot. These premises are all in dispute; but if we grant them, we put Neilsen's argument on its most favorable footing. If it cannot be sustained when these things are granted, it is in serious trouble indeed.

Granting these three points, there are still strong arguments about the effects of socialization. Language learning entails building schemata for dealing with *adaptations to situations* (Ryan, 1974; Ervin-Tripp, 1976; Habermas, 1970a, 1970b). Also, expressions are *indexical* and use the background assumptions necessary to all communication (Garfinkle, 1964, 1967; Gamson, 1974; Cicourel, 1974). Socialization into a language community is inter alia the learning of recurring patterns of situations for which forms of utterance are appropriate (Applegate and Delia, 1980; Bauman and Sherzer, 1974; Blum and Gumperz, 1972). So granting more to nativism than is necessary, the definition of situation remains central. A society is an organization of ceteris paribus qualifications.

Neilsen's principles thus could not operate as universals in any usual sense. What is important is their modifications through the ceteris paribus (see Lukes, 1970; Hollis, 1970a, 1970b; Bennett, 1964). If we accept the analogy with language rules, we have made rationality principles "instances" of the ongoing dialectic between conventions and intentions. To use the principles (for example, to understand or evaluate utterance) we should have to focus on the intended-toward utterance. If we plug any variant of this reasoning into a field theory, we find ourselves with an exhaustive relativism. For purposes of descriptive studies, there is nothing wrong with this result. We might, strictly speaking, refer to fields as recurring uses of ceteris paribus qualifications. Their rationality theories inhere in these uses, not in their rules. Neilsen's scheme works best tied to an empirical program and least well when serving universalistic aims.

I thus hope to have proved that justificational views of rationality are based upon untenable assumptions. No particular account can be defended over and against other rationality theories. It is proportionately implausible to assume that critics can employ particular accounts as standards by which to judge the arguments of field actors. We must therefore direct our attention to the field standards themselves as phenomena interesting in themselves.

Universals of Rationality

Owing mostly to the influence of the later Wittgenstein and to a disaffection with nominalism, it is no longer fashionable to equate words with names and to use physical objects as models for universals. Nonetheless, the generality of claims—the breadth of their foci and ranges of convenience—are abiding concerns. Many contemporary theorists (see Wilson, 1970; McKerrow, 1982) take it to be a modest expectation that any theory of rationality that says anything at all will turn out to be a universally obtaining one.

Against this expectation, I submit (4) that a universal of rationality will be trivial, so abstract as to say nothing of individual cases.[2] I start by considering Toulmin's views, on the assumption that the case against deduction does not need rehashing and that Toulmin has produced a cogent program which turns on a universal.

A fashionable claim nowadays is that universals relate to particulars by "warranting their warrants." Principles of application become warrant-establishing arguments (Toulmin, 1958). If we accept this as a design for universals (as I do), we face infinite regress unless the ultimate warrant for warrants is itself a complete argument. By "complete," I mean that the final warrant itself would have to be justified by *evidence.* If the final warrant is to be anything but a dogma, it cannot just sit there, sans evidence, as a self-evident principle. Toulmin's impartial standpoint of rationality will have to be exemplified by a full argument, including evidence.

This gets tricky. What sort of evidence justifies ultimate warrants? It cannot be field dependent unless we posit an ultimate field. If this is how Toulmin sees his impartial standpoint, he is doing roughly what the earlier theorists did when they made mathematics or physics invariant fields, or "master sciences." The evidence for an impartial standpoint would have to be such that no other field could legitimately claim that *its* evidence (and standards) disconfirmed the proposed invariant standards. If the impartial standpoint is tied to the substance of individual fields, it will have to be defended in terms of a "great chain of being" à la Lovejoy. The past failures of the ists and their isms to produce such a chain suggests that it is in principle doubtful that we should try to arrange argument fields hierarchically by virtue of some unifying principle underlying their subject matters.

This problem does not leave us stranded. We retain two options: the relation of universals to particulars might be explained by virtue of (1) principles of systematization independent of individual actors; and (2) processual principles of discourse. I opt for the second; Toulmin has opted for the first.

Toulmin clearly places much stock in his Darwinian metaphor. Argument fields are "conceptual ecologies." It is plausible that his impartial standpoint will somewhat resemble a generalization drawn from the recurring themes in ecologies. I have elsewhere criticized this thinking (Willard, 1980a, 1980d, 1981a, 1981c); and in lieu of rehashing those arguments, I shall proceed here as if the following conclusions have been proved.

Here is where Toulmin's program stands. He seeks a universal standard as a principle of conceptual change. It must be universal because only a universal will avoid the relativ*ism* inherent to field theory, and he seeks an impartial standpoint of rationality (ISR) with the widest possible focus of convenience and a universal range of convenience. The ISR must explain why conceptual change is *worthy*. There is the sociological sense of worthiness, that is, an idea is thought worthy of belief by conventional standards, and a universalistic sense of worthiness, that is, an idea *is* worthy of belief by invariant standards. This is the standard dispute in the philosophy of science; and Toulmin opts for the "rationalist" side: to explain worthiness in sociological terms collapses to relativism; Kuhn and Collingwood are criticized for this failing. Toulmin has not produced his ISR; it is arguably the case that he has not proved that it is in principle possible to do so (Willard, 1980d, 1981a). The juridical analogy is pivotal, the organizing basis of the ISR (to be discussed in the next chapter). But it works for him because he ignores *discretion;* if discretion is taken seriously, the analogy turns against Toulmin's in-principle argument for the ISR. The analogy can be made to say that the body of law comes out of situational definitions; judges make decisions and then find law that justifies them. No ISR will succeed on the basis of *that* analogy. Take discretion seriously, and the sociological account of conceptual change is unavoidable. As it is, Toulmin's field theory describes the most extreme sort of relativity; and it is not clear that he has the theoretic resources for securing his ISR as a warrant for all warrants (see Burleson, 1979b).

If an economist says that X leads to Y, what makes his claim true or false is the facts of the field of economics. What gives those facts meaning is their uses by economists. What makes the claim rational is the degree to which his argument corresponds to standard practices in economics. What will an ISR add to this? The most promising line, I think, is that an ISR might say whether the economist has *proceeded* rationally, that is, used a procedure of reasoning and arguing that is a precondition of rational discourse in any field whatever. The ISR will not tell us whether the economist's claim is true or false, good or evil—only that it was gotten correctly.

This is why an invariant principle of rationality will be substantively trivial; it will have no significant impact upon the *results* in particular fields. It will not be a principle of truth or of the good; it will never tell an actor, "choose X rather than Y in *this* situation." Nor does it do any of these things secondhand, around the corner. Many theorists believe that a processual principle is to be defended in lieu of defending a great chain of being but that it will do *the same* things the grand systems were supposed to do. They want to cling to the old isms without defending ontological arguments: follow procedure X and you are "more likely" to reach the truth or the good. This is a way of keeping the faith in "justifying" without defending specific justifications. Weimer (1979) might have called this "neo-justificationism." It is as if we still believed Aristotle's curious argument that, when both sides are properly presented, the truth has a natural tendency to triumph over its opposite; the act of justifying is itself what rationality is; we will not hash out the results but will take them for granted. So free and open debate is said to produce either truth or the next best thing.

Such arguments fail for the same reasons the grand systems did. If I ask how you know that debate produced the correct outcome, you court the same infinite regress (or collapse to faith) that the grand systematizers did; you will not have defeated the tu quoque; you will only have relegated it to the background. *If I press you* (and that is the key—paradigms become clear when their proponents are pressed), one of the three results will come out of the background. The claim that debate produces knowledge thus courts the skeptical critique.

So, here are the things that an ISR or any invariant principle of rationality will *not* authorize:

1. *X is true because it was rationally obtained.* "Rational" is a code word for

how it was reached; so such claims are always circular; what is crucial is the particular system being defended, not rationality. No system has avoided the tu quoque or infinite regress. In principle, we have no reason to think that a universal of rationality will tell us that this or that is true.

2. *X is good because it is rational (or has been rationally obtained).* "Rational" is again a code word for something else, usually a system of deriving a principle. The same reasoning used in (1) applies.

3. *Scientific "progress" is conceptual change that is rational.* Again, "rational" is a code word for something else, usually a particular justificationist scheme explaining conceptual change in scientific communities. These schemes are traditionally contrasted with "sociological accounts." Indeed, the dispute between the conventionalists and the "rationalists" reduces to a squabble about "correct" (that is, justified) change versus mere conventionalism (Laudan, 1977; Bartley, 1964; Weimer, 1979). But the grounds of this dispute are incorrectly understood if rationality is in a nontrivial way a sociological concept. The real dispute turns upon whether progress can be anything but conventionally defined. This is the old ontological dispute wearing a lab smock. The tu quoque, infinite regress argument, and circularity challenges work with equal effectiveness in this sphere (Weimer, 1979). The rationality construct badly serves this dispute because the "sociologists" have perfectly tenable views of rationality as conventionalism (for example, Kuhn, 1970a, 1970b; Weimer, 1979). If they are tenable, the dispute is not about rationality at all. To dispute this claim, the advocates of invariance would have to defend the view that there is a single universal of rationality. *Enter the tu quoque!*

4. *This or that particular warrant is warranted.* Toulmin's ISR in principle might give a warrant for the abstract idea of warranting claims, but it will not give warrants for particular warrants. This limitation applies to Habermas's felicity conditions of discourse and the idea that claims are redeemable through discourse. This thinking warrants the idea of a warrant, but no particular warrant. Habermas's thinking coheres with the reformed views of presumption and reflexiveness to be defended as universals of rationality But it is substantively trivial, that is, so abstract as to say nothing about particulars. Habermas's views do seem to complete Toulmin's broad aim for an ISR (Burleson, 1979b); and there is a way to stretch his views so as to make them fit into a conventionalist, nonjustificationist view of rationality such as Weimer's (1979) "comprehensively critical rationalism."

5. *This or that particular choice is best.* If I choose to believe X, not Y, or to do N rather than L, I do so referring to the facts of my field; it is the facts of the field that make my choice rational or not; this in fact is how my choice will be judged. If I choose to reject a new claim, I do so by virtue of conventional field standards. If you dislike my choice, a universal will not "justify" your condemnation without a demonstrable reason

why I should care about it. That reason would have to refute my field's standards or at least say why they are inappropriate to my choice. This is the minimum result of field theory. No one possesses unarguable qualifications for evaluating the standards particular to given communities of discourse.

If these arguments are sound, a universal of rationality will be modest indeed. It will be a processual principle that can successfully be said to obtain across fields.

All fields argue in one way or another. But it does not follow that principles of argumentation are invariant. Since there are cultures and traditions that do not recognize argument, negotiation, or debate in any Western sense, Western principles of good debating are not universals of decision making. The idea that truth might emerge from disputation entails the notion of compromise, that the truth lies somewhere between the extreme positions in debate. Cultures and fields that do not use or understand the idea of compromise, of "if-then" reasoning, or of hypothesis testing do not fit easily into Western thinking about argument practices. Argument practices might be said to be invariant Western traditions—they arguably are, since every field uses these principles in one form or another; all are committed to the idea of testing ideas in free and open disputation. But little beyond this point can be defended: other cultures reject this sort of thinking. Bear in mind that, for example, Japanese students of English are taught academic debate so that they might learn the ways of reasoning in a *completely alien culture.* To them the idea of disputation aiming at a result is utterly foreign. So principles of good argument are broadly employed processual principles in the West but do not survive even mild relativistic arguments.

We are close to understanding why the rationality notion is muddled: it has been asked to perform jobs that other terms perform better, and it has been bogged down in ontological disputes. As philosophers debate scientific progress, they drag rationality in as a name for invariant principles. As the arguments for invariance have not survived, so rationality has seemed to be in trouble. The preceding arguments suggest that rationality should be cut off from these familiar disputes, mostly because they are not going anywhere. If rationality is to be a useful notion, we need to identify the results and processes that fit its focus of convenience.

"Not Obviously Lunatic"

Since there are remarkably few uncontroversial claims to be made of rationality, it may prove helpful to start with particular field practices that square with our claims about the rhetorical character of the notion. Is there a recurring theme across fields respecting rationality? This question is not posed as a preliminary to a *consensus gentium* argument. The scholastics tried to prove the existence of God on the grounds that all people in all cultures believe in a God in one form or another. The temptation is very powerful to try something similar with recurring themes in fields, that is, to prove that rationality universally *is* this or that because this or that feature is a recurring theme in all fields. But stupidity, greed, envy, incompetence, and dishonesty are plausibly recurring themes in all fields in all cultures at all times. Thus, theorists who seek a common consent (consensus gentium) universal of rationality are likely to be disappointed. For present purposes, at least, the search for recurring themes in fields is a preliminary to generalizing about them. For instance, we learn something about the sociological roots of rationality by inquiring into similarities in their conceptions of rationality.

In ordinary parlance—and ordinary fields—there is a sense of rationality that may prove to be more sensible than more high-powered ones. Ordinary folk reserve the term "rational" to describe people who are not self-evidently lunatic. By this view, there are straightforward paradigm cases of irrationality: mass murderers, people so disoriented they cannot care for themselves or cannot socially function, people who talk to themselves or who violate in other ways the standard conventions underlying communication practices. This sense of irrationality is not so simple as disapproval of someone's reasoning processes. In fact, people with many serious thought disorders can work syllogistic problems, think logically and lucidly, and do most or all of the things we ordinarily associate with "rational reasoning." So for this ordinary sense of rationality and irrationality, the kind of reasoning or the certainty of the premises is irrelevant. It is the result that counts. Now, I think it is the result that counts in any case, and there are obvious parallels between this ordinary parlance rationality and more technical approaches. As a descriptive matter, it is the result actors name when they say someone has proceeded rationally. They express approval of the result or of the orthodoxy by which it was reached. The result and the process are not deviant.

A parallel of considerable power can be drawn between this ordinary sense of the rational and the rationalist position in the philosophy of science. While the squabble between the rationalists and the sociologists has turned upon alternative views of the nature of progress, both sides buttress their claims by pointing to clear-cut cases of new ideas that either clearly fall within a field's orthodox beliefs or clearly fall outside them. What neither side explains is (1) why, when two theories do the same work equally well, one is picked over the other, and (2) why some theories are ruled out even when they are not grossly deviant from conventional views. A plausible—though not complete—account is that every field (ordinary and disciplinary) has a vaguely defined line between acceptable and unacceptable thought and procedure; this is a fuzzy boundary, subject to continual adjustment and incremental change; it rarely receives reflective attention except in what Kuhn calls revolutionary times. The vast bulk of conceptual change occurs within such fuzzy boundaries—and one clear way of describing any field's line would be to say that things falling outside it are "obviously lunatic." If this is plausible, we should find fields entertaining ideas "in principle," that is, because they are not obviously lunatic; field actors would hear out ideas with which they disagree if they meet this standard but shout down the ones falling outside the fuzzy line.

It might be objected that this is "true but trivial" because it does not settle the *rationalist versus sociologist* dispute. But if this account explains at least some of the cases in which theories are accepted or rejected which the two camps cannot explain, it is nontrivial. Also, to term the ordinary parlance view trivial is to imply that one's own view of rationality is superior—which in turn presupposes that one can defeat the tu quoque and the usual skeptical questions.

It might also be objected that the ordinary parlance view makes rationality a "loose concept" (Black, 1970), but let us think this idea through. The rhetorical view of rationality implies that rationality *is* a loose concept as it is actually used, that it is a fuzzy and imprecise notion. Its foci and ranges of convenience will vary across fields. Its clear-cut cases will similarly vary, and the situations for which it is deemed appropriate will prove highly variable. "Not obviously lunatic" fits just the sorts of distinctions disciplinary and ordinary actors often apply, for example, the astronomer who believes that it is rational to discuss the moon's effects on the tides but that astrology is irrational.

Goffman's dramatistic views may prove helpful here. One way of thinking of rationality is as a mask, a facade, a role one plays. Entering a field is perspective taking—this inter alia involving learning the accepted ways of doing things in a field. Every field has standards, however loose, that say "this is how economists argue," "this is how psychologists evaluate data," or (recall Hare) "this is how analytic philosophers argue." Rationality becomes a matter of demeanor, appearance, poise and approach by which men display their "fit" into a going social order (see Goffman, 1959, 1963, 1967, 1969, 1971).

Rationality thus names ideas that merit entertaining—not ones that have to be agreed with, but ones that deserve attention. This function is analogous to that of Rokeach's (1960) description of "open and closed minds"; but my purpose in using this analogy is *not* to say that being closed-minded and dogmatic is "irrational." Nor am I trying to say that people equate disagreement about ideas with "being irrational." Some may do so, but my embryonic research into field practices shows that the term "irrational" is rarely tossed about willy-nilly at any idea with which someone disagrees. In ordinary and technical fields alike, people disagree widely but do not call their opponents "irrational."

Dogmatism applies to procedures and practices as well as to ideas. We do not seriously entertain the thinking of madmen just because we think them mad. Notice that this argument need not turn upon arguments about any particular standards of deviance and about particular ways of coming by these beliefs. Rokeach assumes that dogmatism is related to cognitive consistency tendencies and (thus) that people are closed-minded when new beliefs are highly "distant" from their own—"distant" meaning the degree of inconsistency. While this may be so, methods of advocacy may also deviate from orthodox practices in ways that cause ideas to be rejected; research methods may be so deviant from conventional wisdom that their results are rejected out of hand.

An atheist, arguing with a fundamentalist, may term his opponent's ideas "irrational" because of how he reached them, for example, if he claims to have had a divine revelation. The results of the revelation are not seriously entertainable because they were attained "irrationally." A behaviorist might reject findings based on free-response data because the methodology that produced them is so deviant from what he takes to be orthodox research practice. An analytic philosopher (think of Russell's criticisms of Bergson) might deem an intuitionist's arguments irrational, since they were not gotten by orthodox analytic procedures. In each case, the implicit definition of "rationality" *is* whatever the namer uses as a method. Perhaps the starkest example is the confrontation between religious fundamentalists and biologists culminating in the Scopes trial: both sides were dogmatic enough about the superiority of their methods that dialogue—disputation in any genuine sense—was impossible. That famous conflict turned more upon methods and sources than upon sheer disagreement about evolution: the fundamentalists thought that scientific methods diverged too sharply from literal interpretations of the King James Version; mirror opposite views of "the rational thing to do" thus clashed in that courtroom.

This statement, it seems to me, comes closest to describing the unvarying *results* of rationality judgments; rationality is shorthand for "not obviously lunatic" or, in the evolution-fundamentalism dispute, "not obviously evil." Rationality seems to be a name men use for "legitimate claims." Legitimate claims are those "justified" in orthodox ways. We could take the disputes among philosophers of science and say that there are parallels to all of the competing views in the working logics and orthodox practices of argument fields. While some fields might never use the term "rationality," they nonetheless do or do not grant legitimacy to points of view on the basis of their own faith in some standard.

Perhaps the best proof of this thinking is that "irrational" is a term reserved for powerful, emotional confrontations wherein crucial assumptions are thought to be at stake. Scientists who are puzzle solving in what Kuhn has called "normal science" disagree among themselves, but they do not toss "irrational" out indiscriminately. They reserve this big gun for genuine confrontations of paradigms, revolutionary matters in which their background assumptions are called into question. Fundamentalism questioned the very bedrock of biology; Russell questioned the very core of Bergson's thinking; some free response techniques call the behaviorist's laboratory techniques into doubt; and atheists and fundamentalists each call the very bases of the other's beliefs into question. "Rationality" thus seems to be a powerful name that men use when the social decorum itself is attacked; minor lapses are not usually cast out as being "irrational."

In sum, it is plausible to see "rationality" and "irrationality" as loose terms of art for describing deviants; they reflect different substantive issues in different fields, but they share the function of naming people who have not observed the amenities, acknowledged the standard rituals, or paid service to the usual pieties. The two terms are loose concepts because field's lines between the acceptable and the "self-evidently lunatic" are fuzzy and implicit. There are clear-cut cases (for example, the difference between arguing from probability that there might be extraterrestrial life and claiming that one has been taken for a ride in a flying saucer) as well as unclear ones (for example, entertaining sharp disputes within a community without charges of "irrationality"). Both sorts of case presuppose that the fuzzy line has or has not been crossed.

Presumption

The foregoing suggests that "rationality" is a way actors in fields express their views of change. The word typically crops up when actors are expressing their attitudes toward differences between conven-

tional and new ideas. We might well expect that the greater the difference, (1) the greater the likelihood that the new idea requires
change, and (2) the greater the likelihood that attention will be paid to
whether the advocate of a new idea has crossed the line. While the
content of these judgments is field dependent, the practice of expressing attitudes toward change is invariant. A reformed conception of
"presumption" may do justice to this thinking, that is, stand for the
invariant features of postures toward change. In keeping with our
preference for holistic explanations, the presumption notion should
square with the psychological and sociological senses of "field."

The Psychological Case

Kelly (1955) proposes that people construe things so as to enhance
their predictability, that they make interpretations so as to elaborate
their cognitive systems. This he calls a "principle of elaborative
choice" to denote the two directions cognitive elaboration can travel,
namely, a person can restrict and narrow his field of attention and take
comfort from the greater precision of his constructs, or he can broaden
his concepts by tolerating fuzziness in particular constructs in order to
expand the range of events for which his system is appropriate. In both
cases, the person is choosing to interpret something on the basis of the
fit of that interpretation into his cognitive system.

One aspect of judging new ideas is assessment of the jeopardy they
imply for elements of one's cognitive system. A plausible inference
from this is that actors will accept ideas that do not appear to jeopardize many elements and will reject those that jeopardize too many
elements. When change is seen as threatening, it is usually because
previously held interpretations will have to be jettisoned to accommodate the new idea. If a new idea threatens a pivotal element in one's
system, it may be seen to jeopardize the entire system. Procedural and
processual discriminations are often pivotal elements of such systems;
they are regnant definitions of appropriate procedures for evaluating
lower-order claims. Novelty is most likely to be seen as threatening
when it jeopardizes such broad in-principle elements of a system. Thus
Kelly (1955) insists that *"threat* is a characteristic of a construct's
relation to the superordinate constructs in a system. A construct is
threatening when it is itself an element in a next-higher-order construct which is in turn incompatible with other higher-order constructs upon which the person is dependent for his living" (p. 166).

For instance, to ask an astronomer to accept astrology might be
asking too much, namely, that too many broad procedural principles
be surrendered. The burden of proof for such a change would be so

great that no advocate of astrology could discharge it. Kelly (1955) states the matter this way:

> One maintains his construct system by clarifying it. Even one's own system is stabilized or controlled in the manner in which outside events are controlled. This means...that one controls his system by maintaining a clear identification of the elements which the system excludes as well as those which it includes. The moment one finds himself becoming involved in any way with the excluded elements...he becomes aware of the onset of incompatibility and sees these new clutching associations as threats. Like a wounded animal, he keeps facing his enemy. [P. 167]

A person's posture toward change—in this case, new ideas—is thus composed of a continual guardedness against elements that jeopardize important discriminations. We may infer that everyone uses an implicit theory of change in just the way they use implicit theories of personality and causality. Our name for these implicit theories of change can be "presumption."

Discourse communities (fields) also employ implicit and explicit theories of conceptual change. It remains to be seen how these differ from psychological ones. A sociological sense of "presumption" must square with the psychological sense because the psychological sense is the necessary condition of the sociological. But the sociological sense of presumption will cohere as well with the notion of social comparison processes—which makes it broader and more complex than the psychological sense. On the grounds that we may learn something important from considering this relationship, let $presumption_1$ be the psychological sense and $presumption_2$ be the sociological sense. When using "presumption" sans subscripts, we shall mean both. Respecting both, we seek a fleshed out (particularized) version of what many sociologists call the "Weber Thesis." We want to use Kelly's notion of jeopardizing constructs to explain why conceptual change is often glacial.

Presumption$_2$

The first crude formulation of the $presumption_2$ notion was premised upon the Whig view of history (Butterfield, 1965). This curious doctrine held that historical progressions were natural movements toward perfection (the British society of the time being the paradigm case of historical completion). Things "are as they are" because historical development has made them that way. It was not that we live in "the best of all possible worlds" but that any state of affairs at a given time is presumptively the best now attainable. By this reasoning, the British Idealists became apologists for the established order —Bradley's ethics being a case in point. The Idealists were "justifying the established social order; they were sanctifying tradition by making it reasonable; in a way they were justifying all traditions by making them right for their time and place, and then adding a fillip to their self-rightousness by making theirs the best because it was the latest" (Ross, 1951, p. xii). That is, "man is to be understood in terms of his institutions. These contain a kind of collective wisdom, for they embody the ways in which the race has solved its problems"(1951, p. xi). It followed from this notion that each individual occupied a station in life (hence Bradley's notion of "my station and its duties"). Persons who occupy lower stations and duties in life do so because it is their historical niche.

The thinking of Spencer and Bradley in England and of Sumner in America is little more than an embarrassing footnote, though Social Darwinism influenced an array of theorists who departed from the most extreme versions of the Whig view. Efforts to bring social theory into the service of nationalism and religion are properly held in some contempt today. But this thinking is important because it provided the roots of Social Darwinism (which must be considered in accounts of field theories of "progress"), and it generated the theory of presumption.

Whately is usually credited with inventing the idea of presumption. His is a thoroughly idealist conception, locating rationality in the systemic structure of society, just as Bradley located historical movements toward perfection in the British society of his time. The present system—what *is*—is as it is because of the continual perfective movements of history. So, what *is* is presumptively rational and good—our highest attainment so far.

Change, then, is always a slow, careful, rigorous, and tenuous matter. Things should remain as they are until good and sufficient reason is given for change. Good and sufficient reasons should represent a prima facie case for change. Thus, prosecutors have the burden of proof, not the defense; political change must be opposed in principle until the most rigorous burdens have been discharged.

This classically conservative view of change was thought to be a criterion of rational decision making. Presumption$_2$ operationalized rationality in the procedures and processes of a society. So viewed, it squared with the two reason-giving definitions of rationality ("have reasons" or "have good reasons"), and for our purposes it shares the weaknesses of those views. Whately believed that one could know good reasons when one saw them—which opens him to the familiar skeptical criticisms. Whately had no field notion or anything like one. He lacked the theoretical resources for making the merits of reasons field dependent. Presumption$_2$ was invariant, and so were the criteria for "good" reasons.

A more complex presumption$_2$ is needed here. It must fit the facts of presumption$_1$ and square with our field theory, a tall order. It implies that the content of a particular presumption is field dependent (that is, that the values given to orthodoxy, authoritative appeals, consistency, validity, and so forth are characteristics of the social traditions of particular fields rather than a priori universals) and that this is the most precise and usable sense of presumption.

Whately's conservative view of presumption$_2$ is oversimple. It imputes conservatism in principle to all fields (it does so just because Whately lacked the field notion). Goodnight (1980) has distinguished between the liberal and conservative presumptions$_2$ in a useful way. The conservative presumption$_2$ is Whately's; the liberal presumption$_2$ is its mirror opposite. The liberal view, Goodnight says, emphasizes the powers of entrenched interests, human frailties, and the inertial weight of uninspired leadership as the sources of the content and form of social institutions. A society's structure at any given time is as likely to be an accident (owed to incompetence, greed, and stupidity) as it is to be a product of intentional projects or perfecting historical forces. If there are intentional properties to institutions, they are likely to be evil and self-serving ones. Historical forces do not "aim" at anything, let alone perfection. A society's present state likely reflects the needs of the moment of preceding epochs. So the liberal presumption is to embrace change in principle unless there are good reasons for avoiding it.

Both senses of presumption$_2$ parallel accounts of "progress." As the "rationalists" and the "sociologists" dispute the nature of scientific progress, they equally assume the exhaustiveness of their explanations (that is, the truth of the matter is that change is due either to conceptual improvement *or* to convention and orthodoxy). It is more plausible to assume that different epistemic communities employ different senses of presumption$_2$ and (thus) different postures toward change. Some are more open-minded than others and are appropriate to different ranges of phenomena. It is pointless to call one "correct" and the other a delusion. They are merely different postures toward change, different senses of rationality, with different views of "progress." Sharply different examples can be produced by "rationalists" and "sociologists" because they draw from fields that proceed by virtue of incompatible orientations toward change. This means two things: (1) some fields differ from other fields because they use one or the other principle of presumption; some philosophers, because they see that "bad arguments" are ever-present threats, are attentive to new arguments *in principle*, that is, in the absence of good reasons not to, they take up new thinking readily; some scientists, conversely, equate tradition with sound research and new proposals with deviance; thus, they embrace new thinking only once a burden of proof against change has been discharged; and (2) some fields may function by a dialectical tension between both senses of presumption—which explains Kuhn's claim that there are defenders of the status quo continually at odds with the revolutionaries during periods when normal science is disrupted and also explains Toulmin's criticisms of Kuhn's distinction. If both senses of presumption are operating in a field, we can find examples supporting both views—making the revolutionary view appear to collapse with the normal science view.

While the presumption idea was originally intended to cast judgments on ideas per se, it is more appropriate to judgments about methodologies. This suggests that the liberal and conservative burdens of proof turn equally upon matters of methodological judgment. What overcomes a burden of proof is not necessarily or exhaustively the "coherence" or "consistency" of a new idea—many philosophers of science, in fact, equate a simple sense of cognitive dissonance with pressure for change. They say that what is inconsistent or inconsonant is the new idea in itself. This aspect may be less important than how the idea was gotten. Burden of proof, then, should mean *how* something is proved, not merely the standard of proof, quantitative or qualitative, that men want an idea to meet. That someone can discharge a burden of proof at all presupposes a shared standard of proof. If a church tribunal accuses a man of heresy on mystical grounds, physical evidence will hardly refute it, however strong the evidence may be judged by some objective standard. If a man is accused of sloppy science or weak arguments, his results will not count for much, however sharply they may challenge existing ideas. So it is plausible to claim that presumption is a posture toward change that embodies a person's or a field's attitude toward a procedure of proof.

With these considerations in mind, let us consider how the idea of presumption does as a universal. It *is* a universal if we cannot think up some fields that have no presumptive standards. The Western traditions, of course, seem universally to follow presumptions, liberal or conservative or both; the phrase "requirements of justification" is a philosophic term of art which seems to have counterparts everywhere. Every scientific field has its requirements of justification; every school of thought in philosophy does; every social science does; and so on. We are all familiar with the argument that there are other cultures that share none of the West's beliefs about argumentation; we have Ayatollahs who possess no views of negotiation, compromise, or debate familiar to the West. We have tribal standards of self-evidence and Eastern mysticisms—a veritable shopping list of counterexamples to the old claims of the absolutists (see Lukes, 1970; Jarvie and Agassi, 1970). But while few if any argument principles are universals, it is less clear that presumption is not. There are religious orders which share nothing of the scientific notion of proof but which have *a* burden of proof. If I say that I can be changed in my beliefs only by miracles, that is a burden of proof—a stringent one to be sure, but a burden nonetheless. It is a posture toward change.

I am trying to stretch a Western concept into a universal. How sound this is depends upon how hard we have to stretch: we have tribal men who use magic and the evidence of the senses (Werner, 1957). While the content of their judgments differs markedly from that of their Western counterparts, they share the possession of a standard of evidence, an implicit theory of evidence. They believe that something *is* when certain things happen, when their implicit theories of evidence are satisfied. So we have something very like presumption everywhere. To make this point conclusive we should have to examine every field in every culture empirically. I shall not attempt to do so here because the present argument seems prima facie sound. The empirical work is needed anyway if my arguments about the sociological character of rationality are valid (see Winch, 1958).

So presumption is plausibly a universal. Moreover it is a standpoint (here I am following Toulmin's phrase "impartial standpoint of rationality" to see how presumption might fill his bill as a successful impartial standpoint). It is at once obvious that presumption specifies in advance how strong evidence must be and how rigorous warrants must be to justify change (or to avoid change). Presumption is thus a posture men take to evaluate suggestions, a point of view toward what shall constitute sufficient evidence in a given case. The standards of evidence are field dependent; each field will have its own substantive standards of what a good reason is—but what is universal is the practice of taking this stance. Demanding evidence, then, is a standpoint; having specified standards—whatever they are—is a psychological and public perspective one takes. It is a posture toward justification and verification. This is why Weimer's arguments about the justificationist tradition do not bear upon the present view: he makes abstract arguments about justificationism as a metatheoretical posture. But whatever the merits of his claims—and they are considerable—men nonetheless use metatheories for evaluating proposals. Presumption is a good name for them, that is, for the practice of imposing a burden of proof.

Is presumption an "impartial" standpoint? Speaking loosely, the idea of a burden of proof comes as close to being a priori as any system of empty symbols. Its injunctions are invariant; it applies equally to all advocated change; its direction (liberal or conservative) is constant; and even if a field changes presumption theories, it changes the constancy of its thinking. As a stance fields take, presumption plays no favorites. It is nothing but an abstract claim that every advocate must have good reasons, leaving up to the fields what good reasons are.

Let us finally ask whether presumption is a self-sustaining notion, whether there are any overarching concepts that subsume it. This is the nub of the matter: presumption seems abstract enough to successfully subsume all of the other concepts. Argument theories, the specific views of good argument, are far more specific than presumption; in every case, presumption seems to give them meaning rather than the reverse (though *in practice*, argument practices may exemplify a view of presumption). While it seems forced to try to defend argument practices as universals, the abstract notion of presumption seems more easily defended. So it subsumes argumentation. Are there other candidates that might be regnant to presumption? The obvious traditional choice would be a particular system of reasoning (for example, geometry, mathematics, and so forth)—but these have not worked out as universals because, inter alia, they cannot illuminate particular cases of situated discourse. But in every argument interaction we may find something akin to presumption operating, that is, people proceeding by implicit theories of evidence and burdens of proof.

In the last section I shall tie the presumption notion into a reformed view of role taking. It needs saying here that argument fields are perspectives actors take; they are brought to life by the defining activities of actors who use their standards. So when presumption operates, an actor has taken a particular stance toward events, a field's point of view. "Speaking as an economist," or as any other ist, means that the speaker enters the institution of economics of psychology or analytic philosophy and uses that field's judgmental and veridical standards to test his thinking. One's burden of proof will take its form and content from the conventional practices of the relevant field. An actor would not know his burden of proof unless he successfully took the perspective of a field. Presumption is not a thing nor a monolithic universal: it is the conventional standard of proof in a field.

This is why I have made such a point of the importance of ordinary argument fields (Willard, 1980a, 1981a). Ordinary speakers, as opposed to their disciplinary counterparts, may develop argument standards ad hoc; they may need one field's, then another's, and then another's standards as an ordinary argument progresses. Arguments about abortion typify this pattern; we might argue drawing on biology, police science, medicine, morals, religion, political science, and so forth. If biology has an implicit theory of evidence differing in kind from, say, that of ethics, then arguers may encounter confusions if they use the one set of standards to judge generalizations from the other field.

The upshot is that a successful universal of rationality is bound to be substantively trivial, that is, saying nothing about this or that particular action. Presumption is a shorthand term for every field's burden of proof that comes close to describing the effect that people often use the word "rationality" to describe. It refers both to meeting a field's expectations about protocol, orthodoxy, and "being not obviously a lunatic" *and* to the distance between a proposal and conventional wisdom.

The Study of Field Conventions

I turn now to claim 5, that the grand ontological disputes are irrelevant to argumentation, that is, that in doing field studies we embark upon a social scientific project aimed at understanding field conventions on their own terms. This claim requires that we entertain the merits of abandoning justificationism—both as a general posture of criticism and in terms of particular critical practices.

The Critical Posture: "Comprehensively Critical Rationalism"

Having argued that criticism cannot be justificational because justificatory systems are tenuous, I now argue that getting out of the justification business frees critics to do the explication necessary to understanding conventional practices. Weimer (1979), relying heavily on Bartley (1964), goes very far by advocating "comprehensively critical rationalism," which makes science a comprehensively critical process: "*All* its conjectures, including the most fundamental standards and basic positions, are always and continually open to criticism. Nothing in science is immune to criticism or justified fideistically, by appeal to authority" (Weimer, 1979, p. 40). This, says Weimer, breaks the power of the tu quoque, because the question of how we know things is no longer appropriate: the scientist can answer that he does not—indeed cannot—know in any sense satisfactory to formalists. The tu quoque is defeated by exposing its illegitimacy, that is, its assumption of a standard of knowledge too rigorous to meet. Weimer is making just the argument that Rescher (1977a) makes about skeptical challenges based upon hyperbolic standards of knowledge. Like Rescher, Weimer lacks the notion that skeptical challenges are *parasitic* to the knowledge claims being made. Unlike Rescher, Weimer lacks the field notion—which means that for him, the tu quoque is a dangerous argument only to absolutists. It seems more useful to say that tu quoque arguments are challenges field actors make across field boundaries; they occur when claims are made about the superiority of particular field standards. It is plausible, for example, to say that many fields partly define themselves by their skeptical postures toward other fields (or, at least, that they define their organizing problems in terms of the failures of other fields). Because Weimer lacks the field notion, he fails to see that even though critics and scientists need not be in the justification business, the people they study *are*.

Most anything can pass as criticism for Weimer. He sensibly argues that there are times one had best be dogmatically committed to a position to argue its merits effectively. Criticism would thus look like Aristotle's arguments for the benefits of debating both sides of questions. This view of criticism is so broad that it includes all of the familiar claims made for argumentation. Weimer says that what is adequate criticism may vary from case to case. This being true, Weimer has an empty view of rationality; it says "be critical" but does not tell this or that actor in this or that context how to do so. In this respect, his view is inferior to the present equation of rationality with presumption: this equation tells every situated actor how to proceed, though it is silent about which reasons are good ones. Tied to our field theory, presumption displays the epistemic posture of particular groups.

What is important is that, though we are no longer in the justification business, the people we study *are*. "Comprehensively critical rationalism" is one picture among many we might draw of working logics and field practices. Presumption is consequently a better organizing universal in that it fits every order of activity, including the practices of people who would disagree with the very idea of comprehensively critical rationalism. For instance, Catholic theologians might say that there are essentially contested concepts, incapable of being solved, that must be taken on authority and faith—and *this is the rational thing to do*. That is, it is rational to accept certain things on authority or faith if there is no other way of resolving them and one's life would be disrupted if one tried continually to settle them. There is nothing illogical about such claims; they are even plausible when we disagree with them. Comprehensively critical rationalism might, then, be too open-minded for some arenas of thought and action.

In fairness, Weimer is talking about science and I am holding him to a broader standard, that is, whether his critical view can be a universal of rationality. He makes no such grandiose claims, and his arguments vis-à-vis science are plausible. The rub is this: we need to think through how we are to place scientific views into broader schemes. Many of my arguments about argument fields (Willard, 1980a, 1980d, 1981a, 1982) turn on the claim that science is a poor organizing paradigm for epistemics, not because of its weaknesses, but because it is unrepresentative of *most* working logics.

It seems plausible to see Weimer's view of criticism as something that can fit into our present view of presumption. Certainly one variation of the critical view would have it that critical decision makers take account of their burdens of proof—behaving as justificationists, as it were. Weimer's arguments have to do with how philosophers of science should define the norms of good science; and for this they succeed. The present argument is very different: a universal of rationality will succeed if it adequately describes the situated practices of field actors and if it can be made to give advice in all contexts falling within its focus of convenience. Presumption meets this standard; Weimer's view of criticism does not; its focus of convenience is science; its range of convenience might go into a few fields outside science, but surely not all. It *is* a statement of presumption, that is, it says just how seriously we are to take the status quo—we are to hold it always subject to attack, we are to take nothing on faith. We do no injustice to Weimer's thinking to see it as a species of the genus presumption.

"Comprehensively critical rationalism" is thus seeable as a plausible posture theorists and critics might take when they are using the field theory emerging here. They might adopt this posture not as a grand ontological faith but as a working assumption about the thinking that may best serve explication. "Justification" is something people do that is worthy of study, not to decide which principles of justification are best, but to understand the process on its own terms. Regardless of the fate of the tu quoque as a grand ontological challenge, it is a sociological practice of great importance to explanations of how things pass muster as knowledge. In this sense, *skepticism lives;* it arises whenever one social actor challenges another; its force is as strong as the epistemic claim being challenged; its implications are features of the assumptive frameworks involved.

The Critical Program

Now, what does a critic do when he is no longer busy with justification? If he abandons his aim of saying things are "correct," "right," or "good," what is it that he *does* do? Moreover, are these new things matters that were precluded in an innocuous way, because there was insufficient time or space to do them, or are the new things matters that were *logically incompatible* with the old preoccupation with justification and universalism?

To start with, taking the perspectives of situated actors *on their own terms* was logically incompatible with justificationism. One could not do both—especially when an actor's views contradicted (or in some way did not square with) the critic's assumptions. The essential job of criticism was to measure the degree to which the actor fell short of a standard; and it did not matter (by definition) whether the actor would agree with the standard. The slogan that typified this thinking was *tout comprendre, c'est tout pardonner*—a slogan that does not make sense unless one assumes that the critic's perspective is in some sense "superior" to the perspectives of the people studied. This assumption of superiority has taken several forms.

First, *critics make situated utterance fit into broad conventional categories.* Our isms here are, inter alia, naturalism, materialism, and positivism (and, of course, idealism, however it is made to mesh with the other isms). The idea is that critics focus upon overt, tangible acts; they are not to be bogged down in "idiosyncrasies" of specific actors. Thus formal logic could be used to evaluate situated utterance; broad moral claims could serve as standards to judge actions; and "idiosyncrasies" were desiderata, an "insoluble mire," which could only clutter criticism and research. This is a perfectly logical outcome of universal schemes: idiosyncratic meanings are irrelevant to an ordered universe. Second, *no particular point of view could be interesting.* When individuals differed from a grand scheme, they were at fault, not the scheme. They had "idiosyncrasies" that could be fiated out of critical analyses. There was *no point* to understanding a situation as an actor saw it. Third, *situations had characteristics independent of participants' definitions of them.* The whole shebang collapsed without this assumption; the actors in a context could see the situation either correctly or incorrectly; if they saw it incorrectly, this was of no consequence to the broad scheme because they were by definition in error. Tangible, concrete, obdurate situational characteristics were thus the focal point of critical judgment: the critic described the situation and showed how the actors misunderstood it. It can go without saying that they always did; omniscience is wonderfully successful. Fourth, *actions and words "are what they are" and "mean what they mean."* They are not problematic. Their intended-toward character is unimportant. If this is surrendered, an actor's intentions might not square with a grand system. If they do not square, and the actor's views are taken seriously, the grand system might be inapplicable to the studied event; and if so, the whole ism is threatened. So criticism consisted of making particulars fit into broad systems, however much they might have to be forced.

The consequence of these beliefs was a view of research and criticism that could not take situated viewpoints seriously. "Idiosyncratic meanings" were to be avoided at all costs; if they contradicted a general scheme, the critics possessed no principle for defending their perspectives as superior; the tu quoque lurked at every turn.

I do not mean to say that all critics were so simpleminded. Many in fact thought that critics had to demonstrate the "validity" of their judgmental standards. They had to labor long and hard to justify mere disagreements with the situated actors they studied. When critics assumed that burden of proof, they spent their efforts defending the burden rather than doing criticism. This practice was needlessly expensive. The whole matter turned upon the implicit assumption that the critical job was to render judgments upon thoughts and actions. Thus, the preceding assumptions are logical outcomes of the universalist point of view. There was no evading them: critics could not take an actor's point of view on *its* terms without courting a fatal confrontation.

Bruyn (1966) has produced an account of participant-observational research that can undergird a reformed view of criticism. One can, in fact, substitute "critic" and "criticism" for "researcher" and "research" and obtain as an interesting result a powerful case for regarding criticism as a process of perspective taking:

> Since the observer plays a natural, interdependent role in the culture he studies, sharing in the life and becoming involved in the activities of the people he observes, new methodological problems are necessarily set up to be solved which have not been previously encountered. Unlike the traditional empiricist, the participant observer must view a culture just as the people he is studying view it, including reflecting on the social process in which he is engaged. This means he sees goals and interests of people in the same way that the people see them, not as functions or experimental causes as would the traditional empiricist; it means that he sees people in the concrete reality in which they present themselves in daily experiences, not as abstractions as would the traditional empiricist; it means he senses that these people act freely within the scope of what they see as the possible, not as determined agents of social forces as the traditional empiricist would see them. [P. 22]

The aim is to understand people on *their* terms, to understand *their* sense of community as they achieve it in daily life, to take their intentions seriously. The researcher does more than merely describe the purposes of the people he studies; "he knowingly adopts these purposes as his own. The observer may intentionally allow the purposive values of the people he studies to invade and infuse his descriptions of their everyday life—he may allow their ethics to guide his own conduct. These purposive factors, he finds, become not only part of his data but also part of his methodology" (Bruyn, 1966, p. 41). This approach requires a bracketing of broad ontic disputes about (for example) "determinism" and "freedom":

> The participant observer can accept the voluntaristic model as a methodological guide...more readily than he can the deterministic model, for the former expresses more accurately what he observes in the daily lives of people who make decisions. The subtleties of decision-making are great, however, and often involve something different from a rational consideration of means and ends. Rationality is only a construct from which man often deviates and which by itself cannot serve to explain the actions of man. The observer...is in a position to document where rationality does not apply empirically to the subjective lives of his subjects and to develop other key constructs which may be incorporated into a theoretical viewpoint more compatible with what we now know is a very complex human reality. [P. 46]

The actors in fields, we may say, do bracket the grand disputes; they proceed *as if* things are manageable. Bruyn thinks of rationality as a universal, but we may make his argument say that a more complex (rhetorical) model of rationality is needed. What is important is his assumption that we cannot understand any particular action without understanding how the actor intended toward it—which requires that we take the perspective of the actor on its own terms.

Let us suppose that someone says, "abortion is a horrible crime." This claim has a conventional structure that can be analyzed for certain purposes; the results would be uninteresting for our purposes. For our purposes, someone is making an argument; and we want to know what he means by it, what he expects it to do, and what guidelines he is using to evaluate his own claim as well as counterarguments. If we start with the idea that utterance is context embedded, we cannot take that claim on its face, as it were; it is ambiguous; its meanings depend upon the speaker, the person spoken to, the reference, and the background assumptions in use.

It is not irrelevant whether the speaker is a priest or a left-wing politician: the one might mean "the practice of abortion per se is a horrible crime" and the other might mean "the way women have to get abortions is a horrible crime." Now we *might* say, if the leftist speaks the sentence this way, he *means* one thing but intends another; he is merely unskilled at expressing himself. But have we said anything interesting? I propose that it is trivial that we might take anyone's utterance and make it mean something that would surprise the speaker, that is, trivial *for us*—if we do it, we have not proved anything. If we want to know how people in fact argue, we need to look at *their* arguments; their arguments are often ambiguous and "ill-framed." Still, it is worthwhile knowing what *they* mean.

Let us reform the example to say, "the priest said, 'abortion is a horrible crime.'" Knowing the official title of the speaker may or may not help: the priest may be a dissident left-winger; plausibly, he may mean "the way women have to get abortions is a horrible crime." Notice that I can make the following logical but comprehensively banal judgment: "the priest is wrong, abortion is not a horrible crime; it is a minor crime, since it is a misdemeanor." There is nothing wrong with my logic; the conventional meaning I get out of the claim is "there, in the talk." So the claim is "incorrect." I shall not belabor the silliness of this result other than to say that it is a *reductio* of conventionalist views when they are taken to be exhaustive accounts of meaning. One wretched result might be that we may start disputing the meaning of "horrible," especially whether I have legitimately cast it into legal parlance. It will hardly matter which of us gets the better of it; several dictionaries countenance using "horrible" to mean "great," "significantly bad," or "very evil."

Let us further flesh out the example: "the priest said to his fellow graduate student (not a priest), 'abortion is a horrible crime; life is too precious to be wasted like that.'" We are fleshing out the linguistic context, but have we gotten any further in figuring out what the priest means? I submit we have not: he *still* might be a leftist priest bemoaning the loss of life in back room abortions and *not* making a "right to life" argument. As is often the case, arguers call forth more information about assumptions than do other interactants; so let us say that the priest is challenged: "You can't mean that literally; more babies than mothers die." And let us say the priest replies, "That's not true."

What is not true? Does the priest mean that babies are not human, and therefore cannot be weighed against the loss of life for the mothers? Or does he mean that there are more mothers who die from back room abortions than babies who die in legal abortions? Or is he drawing a distinction between "babies" and fetuses? He is actually doing none of these things. I hand-recorded such an exchange between two graduate students discussing "categorical statements." They had left a classroom where the subject was established and had entered another room continuing the discussion. None of their statements had the "logical force" it appeared to have. Once we see the statements as they did, they make sense; one can make sense of the exchange completely apart from their intentions, but one will have obtained an entirely irrelevant result. This is not unlike an example I pursued vis-à-vis field-based talk (Willard, 1981a): Russell and Strawson argue about "the King of France is wise" and how that claim might be paradoxical. Both miss its intended-toward sense, that is, how they in fact use the claim as an *example;* the logical force and significance of "the King of France is wise" have nothing to do with kings, France, or wisdom. They have to do with the force of an example of a paradox.

These examples prove two things: (1) intentionality matters; and (2) intended-toward meanings are the starting place of research and criticism *for us.* Conventional meanings are complex enough; but they are ambiguous when choices are possible; since choices are usually possible, we cannot know what a speaker means unless we assess his perspective. Perspective taking is thus the starting place for understanding situated utterance. Since a definition of situation gives meaning to utterance, it is essential to know what it is. This very approach is ruled out of the universalist schemes, since a given definition of situation is "idiosyncratic."

In sum, argument theorists and researchers cannot justify saying that they study the nature of objectivity, validity, and justification as if these terms were monolithic, real entities. Whatever else they are, these terms describe social practices worthy of study. Argument fields are resources people use when they "go and get" objectivity; they are stances, points of view, frameworks of assumptions that permit judgments. These frameworks need to be understood on their own terms; we need to see how they work by participating in them, working out their consequences. We cannot do so if we remain in the justification business.

Perspective Taking

I turn now to claim 6: perspective taking, construed broadly to encompass the reformed view of presumption, is the most precise and usable view of what rationality is. Mead's view of perspective taking has been extensively discussed (Meltzer, 1972; Kolb, 1972; Blumer, 1969), and I shall not rehash these familiar themes. It is enough to say that Mead proposed, as a comprehensive theory of mind, that "I-Me" interactions make up an inner deliberative forum; the "I" being the person's own ongoing lines of action, the "Me" being the imported reaction of relevant others. Hence the fundamental character of rationality is the "temporary inhibition of action" to assess the reactions of others and to accommodate one's own actions to those assessments. In this way, perspective taking has been said to be the fundamental communicational process by which children are socialized into language communities (Delia and O'Keefe, 1979) and the basis of "strategic adaptations" of communications to others (Delia and Clark, 1975, 1977).

Mead's thought is not being used intact here. He believed that mind was emergent from social processes; almost none of his followers and students do. One can see this most clearly in Blumer (1969), who selectively interprets Mead's thinking so as to ignore the behaviorism that was at the core of Mead's scheme. There is nothing wrong with doing so as long as we are aware that we are doing violence to Mead's intentions: perspective taking can be a strictly conditioned process *if* we follow Mead in thinking that mind is emergent from social processes. It becomes a process of *successive developmental choices* when we drop the emergence notion (see, for example, Werner, 1957).

Though this idea is sometimes couched in formidable jargon, it is a rather simple and straightforward view: men display their rationality by accommodating to (taking account of) the perspectives of others. They do so by taking the perspectives of single others and of the "generalized other"—which Mead held to be "society" as a global and diffuse notion. Field theory would have us think of the generalized other in the plural, that is, that there are many social perspectives that the actor can and does take. Anyone can think "as an economist, a psychologist, and an atomic physicist" from time to time.

Argument fields are perspectives waiting to be taken. They are organizations of assumptions that a person might pick up and use when he deems them appropriate to the matters at hand. *Appropriateness* is an interpretation men make as they decide which standards best fit the needs of the moment, which standards have foci of convenience that do justice to the events in question. The matter of first importance in studying argument fields is these judgments of appropriateness—when we know how these work, we shall know why this or that field attracts followers.

We come closest to expressing the ambitions traditional thinkers have had for the rationality notion when we speak of people *adapting to situations*. We have said that all action is context embedded and that intentional meanings stem out of definitions of situation. These arguments imply that we accommodate their activities to social expectations and to events at hand. Loosely speaking, every situational adaptation comes out of a dialectic between social expectations and the idiosyncratic requirements of this or that context; and we shall learn much about this balancing act as we study actors making such decisions. It is not the picking up and using of a field's standards that is rational but the *choosing* of them. It is not an actor's place in a context that makes him rational, but his attempt to decide what is appropriate. When a man chooses to understand events as, say, an economist and not as, say, a psychologist, he is doing something that ought to be of consuming interest to us. He is engaging in the most precise sense of "if-then" reasoning, namely, the choice of this or that field's judgmental and veridical standards implies that an actor implicitly or explicitly thinks through the possibilities of "given the ground rules of language X, my reasoning will go this way; given the rules of language Y, my reasoning will go this way."

Presumption is a good shorthand term for this process. It expresses the need not to behave willy-nilly, to accommodate to situations and to other people (assuming that these are separable). It is a way of saying that communication activities are social comparison processes in which people try to attain objectivity. I have elsewhere (Willard, 1979a) argued that objectivity is always a subjective accomplishment, and the present argument fleshes out this thinking: people choose to subject their subjective interpretations to objectified social standards; their choice act manifests their rationality; "presumption" is a word that can stand for their interpretations of a need to objectify.

This "universal" is substantively trivial. It says nothing about this or that choice, what reasons should be accepted, and which actions should be done. Field standards do this work—and that is a full-blown relativity with which epistemics as a field needs to grapple. Nothing in this argument entails that wrestling with relativity in the old justificationist sense cannot be done. As far as I can see, the felicity conditions of discourse and the idea that choices can be redeemed through discourse (Habermas, 1970a, 1970b, 1971, 1973, 1975, 1976, 1979) is a justificationist view that can fit into the present account. The idea of a background assumption such as "redeemable through discourse" is itself a perspective to be taken; it uses a sense of presumption in a normative way that does not contradict our descriptive sense here. I am merely proposing a different program from that of Habermas, a descriptive one which studies the situated choices that animate argument fields. Such descriptive work will ultimately augment or undermine the grander aims. For instance "freedom" is a fundamental value in Habermas's thinking, but how does it work out in practice? If descriptive work finds situations in which freedom is counterproductive (in any number of senses), important modifications in the counterfactual view of discourse would have to be made. More likely, we might find that freedom is not monolithic, not always at every level of decision making, a useful thing; there might be stages in decision making where closure and ruled options are preferable. So the descriptive program is worthwhile despite our desires to do something grander.

Conclusion

Rationality is a word people use to name decision-making processes and results of which they approve. Its roots are in the communication processes that make communal life possible. The most basic of these are the definition of situation and perspective taking. All activities are context embedded; all ordinary expressions (at least) are indexical, and the paradigm case of rational activity is a person's temporary inhibition of a developing line of action in order to assess the expectations of others. In so doing, a person enters a field.

Presumption$_1$ names a person's need to objectify his thinking. Presumption$_2$ names the communal tradition's standards of objectivity and justification. Fields consist of the defining activities of their actors—these social comparisons often occurring in arguments. "Rationality" and "irrationality" are words fields sometimes used to name practices and results falling inside and outside fuzzy boundaries between acceptable and obviously lunatic actions. Actors display their rationality inter alia by proceeding competently with the orthodox projects of their fields. By the present view, they display their rationality most fundamentally by the perspective taking that makes movements in and out of fields possible. The working hypothesis is that such an "ordinary parlance and practice" view of rationality will illuminate the psychological and sociological senses of "field" and the relations between them. Since arguments are often explicit instances of such accommodations, they are useful foci of the empirical program with this aim.

Most people seem to think that there is a great difference between social practices and the verities of the world. Practices are social accidents, the chimera of daily life that (like Plato's shadows) need to be penetrated if we are to reach the Great Truths. But there is nothing wrong with proceeding on the opposite view. If our field theory rings true, it is possible that social practices are the verities. Even if they are not, we must study them on their own terms so that we would know a verity if we saw one.

We will not know the plainest verity if we lack a conceptual vocabulary for describing it. A precondition of such a vocabulary is a language for describing social practices that is not muddled by the value judgments common to traditional accounts. Argumentation should make some progress toward building this vocabulary (and the conceptual apparatus behind it) by studying the ways field actors in practice justify and verify. So proceeding, the search for universals will cease to be a dramatic train of events (not unlike UFO sightings) and will become a more prosaic—but arguably more useful—descriptive study.

Rationality is but one example of this broad agenda. It might turn out, as Aristotle thought, that rationality is a moving principle in humans which links them to the cosmos. It might also turn out that rationality is nothing but a word expressing social approval. This approval—which is a procedural value differing across fields—might turn out to be what shall have to serve as our universal (poor ragged little thing!).

The grand schemes by their nature ruled out successful descriptive work. Argument criticism could be nothing but a tradition of breast beating, since everything in ordinary life fell short of the formal standards. The perspective of the situated actor could not be taken seriously in itself. By "taken seriously," I do not mean merely "studied." They were studied but thought to have no philosophical importance.

So let us play the hunch that rationality is a human invention bearing social and cognitive consequences. If it speaks to man's place in the cosmos, it does so by illuminating his ongoing practices and the assumptions on which they are based.

3 The Nature of Argument Fields

The problem of defining the relationships between knowledge and social practices is a doubly difficult one. It presupposes that one has ready and dependable senses of knowledge and of social practices on which to base comparisons. If either or both are in doubt, the relations between them become increasingly obscure. If proponents of particular theories of knowledge and of social practices have divided into warring camps, the problem of drawing relationships is compounded twice over—sometimes to such a degree as to make us doubt that the project is worth the trouble. We might expect to find that schools of thought within epistemology and within the sociology of knowledge have gone their respective ways, each (with but a few exceptions) more or less ignoring the other.

At first glance, the notion of argument fields bears the ambiguous stamp of this schism. It is sufficiently ambiguous, and its attendant concepts are sufficiently elastic that it may be called into the service of very different projects. Viewed one way, the field notion exemplifies the implications of relativity. It says that the truth of any claim and the rationality of its exposition depend upon the working assumptions of different communities of discourse rather than upon the systemic imperatives of a universal logic. Seen this way, the field notion makes relativity an indubitable fact and becomes the basis of a relativism and a consensual theory of truth and rationality. Viewed another way, the field notion is a way of generalizing about relativity across and within cultures, the ways knowledge is balkanized. This becomes the explanatory base for finding universal, impartial, and invariant principles of knowledge and rationality. Relativity is given its due but is thought not to issue in a relativism or consensual theory. Thus the field notion has been fitted into broader positions respecting the relations between knowledge and social practices—merely another weapon in the arsenals of the relativists and the universalists.

A second look at the field notion reveals that it is capable of being enormously more complex. It can be defined so that the two views of relativity and relativism are not incompatible and are, rather, two sides of the same coin. It can be defined in such a way that the problem of the relationships between knowledge and social practices is subsumed and redefined. By this account, dependable views of knowledge and of social practices are obtained from considerations of their relationships. It is their relationships that give them their character.

Consistent with the holism of the psychological and sociological senses of "field," I propose that fields are built upon trusted relationships between practices and knowledge (between procedures and their outcomes) and that fields are in part definable by what they take these relationships to be. Consistent with the view that objectivity is a subjective accomplishment, I want to make the field notion overarch the traditional points of dispute and to glean from this a sense of what universals of knowledge and rationality look like, defined in field terms.

A Tale of Two Theories

I shall pursue two parallel projects, namely, an elaboration and critique of Toulmin's views and the development of a holistic alternative appropriate to our epistemic agenda. My aim is to acknowledge a profound debt to Toulmin while diverging in important respects from his thinking. Excepting perhaps Foucalt (1970, 1972), Toulmin has devised the most elaborate field theory based upon epistemic aims. Pointed appraisal of his program may thus yield alternative views of considerable breadth and power.

In considering Toulmin's views and in raising objections to some of them, my intention is to weave a tapestry of issues against which an alternative field theory can be set. The skeletal outline of our figure will emerge from the ground of exegetical and reforming arguments about Toulmin's thought. That is to say, we can develop in broad outline the alternative field theory as a corollary to particular criticisms of Toulmin's scheme. This will prove to be a productive entertainment because Toulmin has organized his field theory around two seminal insights, namely, (1) the assumption that an adequate theory of collective concept use cannot explain the stability of concepts with one set of terms and their variability with another (1972, p. 412), and (2) the view that historical and cultural relativity creates intractable problems as long as "rationality" is thought to be a feature of conceptual or propositional systems rather than of procedures (1972, p. 478). These, it seems to me, are the felicity conditions of a good field theory. My objections to Toulmin's views concern the choices he makes in fleshing them out.

For clarity, let me specify at the outset the nature of these objections and point to the rough outlines of the alternative theory that emerges from them. I shall argue that Toulmin's formulations of the field notion and its conceptual relatives are not well suited to the analysis of ordinary utterance—because his organizing exemplar of knowledge is science. In *Uses* (Toulmin, 1958) the field notion is obscure, and in *Understanding* (Toulmin, 1972) the rational enterprise notion (the clarified successor to the field concept)[1] is poorly suited to the analysis of ordinary practices and utterance because (a) conceptions of argument utterance do not fit easily into Toulmin's field divisions, and (b) the exemplar of a rational enterprise—a compact discipline such as atomic physics—directs our attention away from the context embeddedness of arguments and thus does not permit a holistic account of the psychological and sociological senses of "field."[2]

Assembled against Toulmin's account will be a field theory that uses the notions of communication and perspectivity to explain conceptual stability and change in the same terms. Its main assumption is that a precondition of something counting as knowledge is its fit into a theoretical framework that so regards it. The alternative field theory is an attempt to describe this fit, interfield differences in frameworks and fits, and the social processes which these comprise. A guiding principle is that conceptual frameworks are not *things* or in any sense reducible to the usual terms of the history of ideas. They are not impersonal conceptual ecologies; they are generalizations we make about practices. Thus the sharpest comparison of Toulmin's views with my own appears when we consider the jurisprudential analogy as a paradigm case of an argument field.

In the broadest possible terms, the alternative theory goes this way. The field notion turns upon the idea of drawing distinctions; it consists of many different distinctions which serve a variety of aims. The particular distinctions which best serve our epistemic agenda are:

1. *Fields are real sociological entities.* The field concept thus overarches traditional terms such as "group," "organization," "social framework," and "social relationship." I shall draw four distinctions among these terms.
   (A) *Encounter fields.* Relations among strangers, conversations, particular interactions.
   (B) *Relation fields.* Sustained clusters of encounters; spouses, close friends and acquaintances, professional associates; relationships are built upon background assumptions that allow their discourse to make sense.
   (C) *Issue fields or schools of thought.* Larger groupings based on the stances men take toward ideas. These fit the broad labels often used

in movement studies, for example, "proabortion," "scientology," "behaviorism," "Freudianism," and so forth.

(D) *Normative fields.* A reformed variant of the "reference group." This overlaps and interplays with the other senses of "field." It is a particular way of looking at the other three kinds of fields; it exemplifies the ways actors take influence from social groups.

Overlayed on these senses of "field" is a distinction between ordinary and disciplinary fields. This captures the difference between (say) a group organized around political action goals and one whose activities center upon the epistemic project of "getting better."

2. *Field theory studies "objectifying," not "objectivity."* This idea ties the sociological to the psychological sense of field. Activities within fields are social comparison processes (as I have already argued).

3. *Fields are psychological perspectives,* alternative ways of construing phenomena. Field theory thus fleshes out Mead's "generalized other." A field is a body of logic and entailments an individual can choose to abide by. The two previous chapters have fleshed out this notion.

4. *Fields are domains of objectivity.* They are organized around historical successes with problems; people have faith in them because they are trustworthy checks against subjective interpretations. Thus:

(A) To enter a field is to be "constrained," that is, to surrender a measure of one's freedom to the entailments of a field's concepts and traditions.

(B) Fields are schools of thought; they are isms of which the actor becomes in appreciable respects an ist.

(C) The "as if" maxim: people treat fields as if they are accomplished bodies of knowledge; if their internal disputes are too severe, they permit no "objectifying"; they are unworthy of trust.

5. *Fields are essentially rhetorical;* the source of "authority" if a field's standard is the faith actors have in its standards and experts. The explanation of actors' orientations to their fields is best explained as a slight twist of the old *fides proecedit intellectum:* one believes in a field as a precondition of understanding the field's phenomena. One implication is that fields may be partly defined (that is, cut off from each other) as *audiences.* Most of this reasoning appeared in the previous chapter; I shall thus restrict the discussion here to the audience.

6. *Fields are frameworks of assumptions,* that is, background assumptions and norms which facilitate particular activities. Thus to know a field is to know its cardinal virtues, its ideals, its paradigm cases of excellence.

7. *Fields cannot be equated with their documents;* documents display parts of issue fields but reveal little about real social entities.

At issue here are the sources, uses, and effects of public standards which countenance knowledge. By "knowledge" is meant in every case that which in one way or another passes muster. Passing muster occurs in the psychological field but has corollaries in the social arrangements we want to call fields. Since the world is a complex place, phenomena which are thought to differ in kind, communal traditions—which are based upon different assumptions, foci, and purposes—are proportionately various. Since humans cannot construe events in precisely the same ways, the social arrangements we call "fields" are phenomena which reflect the evident necessity of social comparison. Fields have the shapes they do as historical residua: people devise social structures to check their private interpretations against communal standards; their historical successes are embodied in social entities, fields.

My aim in the arguments to follow is not to use one doctrine to bludgeon another. Instead, I want to prove that it is legitimate to build an epistemic agenda upon a broader base than Toulmin apparently does and to conceive of knowledge more broadly than is standard in the literature. One can readily discuss the epistemic effects of argument narrowly and do nothing actionable as long as one does not claim to have exhausted the subject. If, however, one has readily at hand a set of concepts that permit a broader view, one might as well see what work they will do.

One can premise one's conception of knowledge on the simplest case reasoning we have already discussed. One would say that since the sciences are the most straightforwardly successful epistemic enterprises, scientific knowledge may serve as the paradigm case of knowledge. On the other hand, one can just as easily insist that far harder cases plausibly fit into knowledge and (thus) that broader concepts are needed. I propose, for example, that a person's attributions of internal states to others (person perception) fit plausibly into our ordinary sense of what knowledge is. It is far harder to study; but its outcomes are often more important to a person's immediate prospects than other senses of "knowledge." To include person perception in epistemic concerns is to speak more directly to the human bases of knowledge and to pose more sharply the question of what it is to know.

Toulmin's Theory

Field theory is the anthropological aspect of the "three faces of philosophy," the other two being formalism and criticism (Toulmin, 1976). Many recurring disputes result when theorists defend one face to the exclusion of the others, and Toulmin opts for accepting all three as legitimate postures toward particular matters. His assumption is that the three may complement one another if they are wedded by virtue of careful considerations of their respective foci and ranges of convenience. Thus while one may legitimately consider arguments as propositional serials for certain purposes, one must also consider them as human activities and procedures. Working as philosophical anthropologists, we aim to relate someone's claims to the "characteristic contexts within which those claims are naturally at home" (1976, p. 169). To understand a claim, we have to understand both the words in the claim and their "relevance to the corresponding aspects of life" (1976, p. 169). Our focus is on the common ground that facilitates intelligible discussion. The field concept is intended to convey the diversity of the activities and associated points of view upon which propositions depend for their intelligibility.

But the facts of diversity taken alone lead to skepticism and relativism. Thus the critical face of philosophy is to consider not merely that things are done in thus and so ways in this or that field but—more fundamentally—"on what conditions such activities are *possible and justifiable at all.* What concerns the philosopher, in short, is not just the *actual historical and cultural conditions* of rational argument in different fields of experience; rather, it is the *general preconditions*, without which there could be no such argument" (1976, p. 206). The anthropological or "commonsense" project opens the door to critical considerations of worthiness. We need to transcend "mere anthropological reporting, about how scientists, art critics, and the rest *in fact* act and talk" and "recognize how and in what respects the work of such people enables them to *achieve* something substantial" (1976, p. 228). The study of relativity, then, must not yield a relativism.

It very much matters what the relationship between the anthropological and critical faces of philosophy is said to be. If the anthropological project is exhaustively the precondition of the critical, one's universals of worthiness might turn out to be a mere counting *not* of individual noses—that happens within fields—but of communal noses in a contemporary version of the consensus gentium argument. In fact I think Toulmin's search for an impartial standpoint of rationality may turn out to have this outcome. But this claim is complex and must await a purely exegetical exposition of his views. Another possibility is that the anthropological project might yield a relativity of sufficient power as to force modifications of the critical purposes. Again, I think this is a plausible interpretation, but it must emerge as a corollary to particular criticisms of Toulmin's views—to which I now turn.

Rational Enterprises

Imagine a pyramid of rational enterprises—these fields being arranged on the pyramid according to the "compactness" of their knowledge. The pyramid's top comprises the most exact, rigorous, and unified enterprises, the "compact disciplines"; their conceptual repertories are exposed at every stage to "critical reappraisal and modification." They are compact because disputes can be adjudicated by veridical and judgmental standards (by judges whose expertise is verified by their facility with the standards) which are generally agreed upon. Atomic physics is the extended example. Though Toulmin does not survey all candidates, he leaves the impression that not many disciplines are compact. This is one justification for the pyramid metaphor—which is mine, not his: it narrows at the top, implying that the compactness region contains fewer enterprises.

Immediately below the compact are the "diffuse" disciplines—their knowledge procedures conform only "loosely" to the rigors of compact disciplines. Diffuse disciplines are exemplified by sciences "containing" different schools of thought, contending veridical and judgmental standards as well as different problem foci. Despite differences, the competing schools within the diffuse disciplines retain commonalities that permit dispute among the alternative views. Thus they are high on the pyramid, having elements of compactness, but at a broader point in the pyramid (because there are more of them). Remember, we are moving *down* the pyramid.

Next come the "would-be disciplines," displaying few if any shared standards because they contain competing schools of thought so hostile to one another or making such different assumptions that they cannot be said to share a problem focus, let alone veridical and judgmental standards. Examples include many of the social sciences, such as psychology and sociology. These enterprises are potentially disciplinable if they can unite under a shared point of view. Toulmin sometimes uses "would-be" and "diffuse" as interchangeable terms, implying that they are the same categories. I stipulate here that there is a distinction because it allows for progressions upward toward compactness. There are, I should think, differences between a discipline containing ten schools of thought and one containing only two— the former (possibly) being characterized by more total resistance to compactness than the latter. Thus as one moves downward on the pyramid, problems are less sharply defined (and problem foci less likely to be shared); veridical and judgmental standards are more likely to be contested—themselves matters of disputes rather than being the agreed-upon arbiters of disputes; and there are fewer (or weaker) professional associations among actors in the disciplines. One is confronted more and more with personal rather than communal goals vis-à-vis knowledge: compact disciplines have only one set of standards; diffuse disciplines have many incompatible systems of thought.

At the pyramid's base are the nondisciplinable fields—lacking shared problems, often overlapping with one another, and taking their character directly from the personal perspectives of their actors. These fields are not and cannot be disciplines because their argument standards are features of personal points of view. Because these fields are at the pyramid's base, we conclude that they are more numerous than the compact disciplines. These fields of argument are not easily classifiable, partake of many subject matters, admit of myriad alternative interpretations, and take their character from the circumstanced interpretations of arguers. For locutionary ease let us call them "ordinary fields."

As we pass down the pyramid (from compactness toward diffusion) we reach a point at which the word "disciplines" no longer applies. The would-be disciplines retain the word "disciplines" because they aim at some goal which unites their views of knowledge with the broad assumptions made by the compact disciplines. What, then, is the principle of division? It can be described by saying that disciplines aim toward improvement—toward expanding and making more precise their knowledge. Their veridical and judgmental standards have evolved with this aim in mind. Despite substantive disagreements, actors within disciplines (accomplished or would-be) aim at greater compactness. For example, Freudians and behaviorists might disagree about most issues but share the broad goal of making the field of psychology "better." No such aims are manifest in ordinary fields because they are defined by the situated psychological activities of arguers rather than by clearly hewed-to veridical and judgmental standards. Ordinary arguers aim at greater predictiveness in their *personal* construct systems but do not share with, say, atomic physicists the goal of making a public veridical or judgmental system more compact.

The pyramid metaphor is appropriate to Toulmin's system (though it bears repeating that the metaphor is mine, not his). Toulmin sensibly assumes that knowledge takes different guises, that it is both public and private, and that it manifests itself publicly at markedly different levels of exactness, precision, and consensus. He believes that consensus is fundamental to public interaction but is disinclined to reduce knowledge to mere voting. Thus the shape of the pyramid represents the progressive narrowing toward the top, the comparative rarity of compactness. As we move downward on the pyramid, we encounter a great range of fields for which passing muster on knowledge *is* a matter of counting noses.

Toulmin stipulates that this hierarchy is not a value scale, that compactness does not make atomic physics a *superior* (in any number of senses) field. Compactness is a nonevaluative description of the state of agreement vis-à-vis a field's judgmental and veridical standards and its problem foci. To state that one field is less compact than another thus might mean only that the less compact discipline deals with less tractable problems.

This reasoning is not as clear as one would wish. If compactness is that toward which disciplines aim (in "getting better"), the notion of compactness is certainly not value free; it becomes a measure of epistemic success consistent with a consensual theory of truth. Compactness is *not* the contrasting pole *to* but a high achievement *of* consensus. It can be achieved by arbitrary and narrow-minded procedures, for example, when religious orders achieve compactness by ruling out opposing viewpoints, as John Paul II has done with his renegade theologians. Catholic theology *is* a compact discipline. It raises (I shall argue) special problems for Toulmin's overly scientific model of knowledge.

We need not settle this question now. Compactness is one sort of distinction among fields that we may draw. It may not prove to be the most central, however, and we can proceed with a discussion of fields, keeping an open mind about its value-free nature. Whether it is value free may depend upon the sort of work that we think the compactness distinction does. Thus we might expect that the compactness notion is most value laden as a sociological distinction and least evaluative as a metatheoretical distinction. If, for example, social scientists model their work after the positivists, the fact that their disciplines are not compact is a trenchant criticism. Conversely, if by the verstehen view the social sciences are held accountable to less rigorous models of knowledge, the compactness distinction might be nonevaluative.

The pyramid is also valuable for displaying differences between the direction of Toulmin's thinking versus my own. Toulmin may be said to start at the top, working downward to explain knowledge, while I advocate starting at the base with the ordinary fields, working upward toward the compact disciplines.

Theorists working downward on the pyramid use the principles of compactness to explain diffusion, whereas those working upward use the notion of argument per se to explain how greater compactness is achieved out of the diffusion of ordinary talk. If one looks downward one is bound to use the notion of compactness (and the exemplars of compact disciplines) as conceptual lenses for understanding the diffuse disciplines and ordinary fields; one will see diffusion in terms of its differences from compactness and will thus overlook differences in kind across fields. Working upward, one is bound to see compactness as a special accomplishment, a refinement of ordinary processes (in the sense that it was earlier argued that syllogistic and propositional logics are rarefied and exotic attainments are built upon ordinary inference and utterance). If one peers downward, one takes the compact sciences as exemplars of knowledge and sees the lower-order fields as deviations from the exemplar.[3]

The Program in Uses

The field notion started with the intuition that people in different social traditions *use* terms and claims in different ways. These differences were first understood by Toulmin in terms of a rough sense of logical types, that is, that there are nontrivial differences among arguments because they refer to different orders of objects and because they are put to different uses. It is unlikely that Toulmin has retained this commitment to logical types (see Willard, 1981a). But this early commitment bears mention because it contributes to the central problem in reading *Uses*.

Uses gives only the sparsest exposition of the field notion—the bulk being devoted to examples which Toulmin apparently takes to be self-explanatory in light of a not-too-precise sense of logical types. These examples are, however, ambiguous and equivocal in ways I shall shortly explain. *Sans* examples, the field notion is immediately fraught with difficulties. Toulmin aims to *depsychologize* argument to the extent that a field can be described in terms of its history of ideas—impersonally and abstracted from individual circumstances. To do so is a serious error. It forces us to bracket the psychological sense of field and to focus upon written records; it assumes that the truth conditions of claims cannot reside in the psychological field, and it ignores situated discourse.

I shall later defend the claim that texts often cannot stand alone, that the meanings of statements depend upon the intentions of the speakers. There is no doubt that the meanings of statements can be analyzed apart from the intentions of speakers, if for no other reason than that the language system possesses its own systemic mandates. I stipulate only that such analyses may be useless for understanding *situated* utterance. If one only grants that textual analyses can arrive at meanings which would surprise the speakers, one has granted that the role of textual work is limited *for argumentation's purposes.*[4] As a descriptive matter, we cannot know the meaning of a proposition (and of a total argument) without knowing how the speaker intended toward his utterance. We can assign meaning to his statements (as situated statements) only by confidently describing *his* definitions of situation. For argumentation's purposes, then, the goal of de-psychologizing argument is a profound error.

Why does Toulmin insist upon this aim? I see at least two reasons, although the matter may be more complex. These two reasons serve at least to identify differences between his program and my own. First, his aims are normative rather than descriptive, and I think he might not grant that secure descriptive work is a precondition of normative speculations. Second, Toulmin aims at salvaging some features of a universal logic (in the form of whatever content the impartial stand-point of rationality may have). Hence he is not centrally interested in understanding situated utterance or specific situations. These two reasons bear closer examination.

The program in *Uses* is normative. The rules of logic are *"standards of achievement* which a man in arguing can come up to or fall short of, and by which his arguments can be judged." Logic is not concerned with a person's manner or techniques of inference: "Its primary busi-ness is a retrospective or justificatory one—with the arguments we can put forth afterwards to make good our claim that the conclusions arrived at are acceptable..." (Toulmin, 1958, pp. 8 and 6). These claims are not to be understood in terms of appeals to a priori logics but in terms of field theory: retrospective justificatory arguments take their form and content from the relevant facts of the fields in which they occur.

What is at issue here is whether such a normative program is prema-ture and/or arbitrary. It seems to presume that the fields with which an evaluator of arguments must work are more or less perfectly under-stood: the facts of a field must be relatively well understood, straight-forward, capable of being looked at, and amenable to systematic exposition. Here we have the first indication that Toulmin's conceptual lens focuses on the most compact disciplines and that this distorts his thinking about ordinary fields. As one moves down the pyramid, the degree to which the facts of the field are understood and consensually confirmed decreases. At the base of the pyramid are the ordinary fields for which no secure consensual agreements obtain; there will be more dissension than continuity. Thus descriptive work must be the precon-dition of normative evaluation: I do not see how one person can evaluate another justifiably without convincingly demonstrating that he knows what the other person thought he was doing. Normative programs court arbitrariness at every turn unless they are securely based upon empirical statements about the phenomena being evaluated.

I am not parroting the Vienna Circle view that theoretic statements must be traceable to descriptive propositions. The weltanschauungen assumptions embraced already suggest the more plausible view that description is embedded in broader assumptive frameworks—it always reflects expectations and prior assumptions. Thus value-free and theory-free research is not possible. The description-evaluation dichotomy by this view is a false opposition. Evaluation presupposes that the evaluator can defend an interpretation of a situation. It is in this spirit that I have urged argumentation theorists to start with descriptive matters, recognizing all the while that careful theoretic work leads to the best descriptive work. This does not entail a "violation" of Hume's law so much as a recognition that its interpreters (as opposed to Hume, who I think did not see it in quite the same way that subsequent analysts have seen it) have assumed a false dichotomy. Every "is" that ever was has been derived from an "ought," and every "ought" that ever was has been derived from assumptions about what "is." The degree to which a field's norms inform its discourse is thus a descriptive question; the degree to which a theorist is unable to describe the effects of a field's norms upon specific actions is the degree to which his defense of a normative system is arbitrary.

The second reason for depsychologizing argument is to salvage some sense of a universal logic. This merits a close look, since it bears directly upon the relevance of Toulmin's program for argumentation. It is at least worth considering whether his preoccupation with the stable normative features of fields may have closed off from him the obvious importance of situated action. One can hardly doubt that such closure has occurred, given statements such as this one: "If one thinks of logic as an extension of psychology or sociology, the notion of logical form remains impenetrably obscure—indeed it can be explained only in terms of more mysterious notions, being accounted for as a structure of relations between psychic entities or social behavior patterns" (Toulmin, 1958, p. 43). Let us pose now (leaving the answer for later) the question, if logic is not an extension of psychology or sociology, of what is it an extension? If we ultimately say that it is an extension of nothing but itself, we are back to Frege. If it is not an extension of psychology or sociology or an absolutist scheme, we are running out of candidates. Ultimately I shall claim that for Toulmin logic *is* an extension of sociology. So far, at least, he possesses no other theoretic resource for explaining its sources.

The distrust of psychology has long explained the attractiveness of absolutist schemes, especially mathematical logic. It appeared to offer the only clear, easily understandable description of logical form. Since Toulmin wishes to eschew a sharp distinction between logic and epistemology, epistemology is perforce expected to divorce itself from psychology: "The problems of epistemology, if psychological at all, are pretty clearly not psychological questions of any ordinary sort" (1958, p. 211).

This is a rather inchoate statement, taken as is. Presumably the field notion is to undergird the special sort of psychology Toulmin has in mind; and there can be little doubt here that the field notion is being asked by Toulmin to bear substantial theoretic weight. We are after a comparative logic for which "validity is an intra-field, not an inter-field notion. Arguments within any field can be judged by standards appropriate within that field..., but it must be expected that the standards will be field dependent, and that the merits to be demanded of an argument in one field will be found to be absent...in another" (1958, p. 255). This is sensible, but does it square with the following? "Yet to turn logic into a branch of psychology...makes it too subjective and ties it too closely to questions about peoples' actual *habits* of inference. (There is, after all, no reason why mental words should figure at all prominently in books on logic, and one can discuss arguments and inferences in terms of propositions asserted and facts adduced in their support, without having to refer in any way to the particular men doing the asserting and the adducing)" (1958, p. 5). Such things can doubtless be done. But what are the implications of this point of view? First, it must mean that fields can be understood *uniquely* and exhaustively in terms of written documents. Second, we do not need to look at instances of a field's operations in order to understand it. Third, we can analyze the meanings of statements without references to a speaker's intentions. These conclusions are all well and good for logic, since logic has no relation whatever to empirical activities—it neither takes from empirical generalizations nor contributes meaningful statements to empirical work. But that is the whole point of Toulmin's trenchant critique of the absolutists.

I earlier argued that argument theorists who pursue the "middle course" are able to utilize the full argumentative resources of relativism to attack the absolutists and the full arsenal of absolutist arguments in attacking the relativists. The present problem exemplifies this flexibility. Fields are being treated (in and of themselves) in the same way that the absolutists treated all phenomena. Toulmin accords the working logics of fields a status (within their respective fields) analogous to the status of the a priori logico-mathematical principles of absolutist schemes. Thus, many of my objections below resemble Toulmin's criticisms of absolutism.

So the question is this: of what are fields composed? As far as I can see, Toulmin's formulations do not permit a coherent answer. If the norms of fields are not psychological, sociological, or absolutistic and a priori, it is uncertain what they can be. What Toulmin does (I shall argue) is depend upon a special sense of "sociological" which is essentially absolutistic ("structuralistic," if you will), achieving within fields the stability and coherence provided by the old logics while sustaining only at the level of lip service the relativity which ought to be at the core of field theory.

My own answer to the question is drawn from Chicago School interactionism: fields take their character from the ongoing activities of actors within them. Daily life of nearly every sort is constituted of individuals pursuing their own developing lines of action and simultaneously accommodating to the expectations of others. Thus, *a field is best understood by reference to a paradigm instance*. We ought to be able to look at some circumstance (in which actors engage in some activity) and say that they belong to thus and so field. The appeal to thus and so field should help us in some way to understand what they think they are doing; it should illuminate their activities. Otherwise, I do not see what value the field notion has for argumentation. *If* fields are made up of the ongoing activities of actors "in" them, then it will be those activities which serve to carve one field off from another—which means that a field-centered logic will be incoherent without reference to situations and circumstanced statements.

It is now appropriate to turn to a more specific exposition of Toulmin's thinking and contrasts with our proposed alternative. The issue is whether the foreclosure of psychology is premature or arbitrary, whether it vitiates the field notion for our purposes, and whether it leads to the absolutism which Toulmin has attacked. I shall proceed with the comparative exposition, keeping in mind the distinction between Toulmin's purposes and our own and the genuine ambiguity about whether this distinction can be maintained. I shall also keep in mind that the implicit issue is about the makeup of fields—we are after the most precise and rigorous account of the relations of psychology, sociology, and absolutist principles and the bearing of the field notion upon situations.

The field notion was introduced in *Uses*, although its importance has only gradually become apparent. Toulmin proceeds from the sensible view that arguments take many forms and that it is questionable whether a common procedure can be sufficiently general to assess all kinds of arguments in all fields. The old notion of comparative stringency (whether one can compare the standards of argument across fields) is vulnerable, since any such judgments would themselves require warrants which are invariant, that is, which apply equally well to all arenas of discourse. This is the indubitable fact of relativity with which we must grapple, the hard fact to respect: whether or not a statement is true depends upon how we look at it; how we look at a statement depends upon what we think we are doing; and what we think we are doing depends on the field to which we belong. These claims are mine, not Toulmin's, although the field notion—as an empirical phenomenon—is used by him to attack traditional logic. Two arguments are said to belong to the same field when their data and conclusions are of the same logical type; and they are said to belong to different fields when their data and conclusions are of different logical types.

I have elsewhere argued that the logical type notion is inappropriate to argument studies (Willard, 1981a). My basic argument was that one cannot derive useful sociological distinctions from logical distinctions except by making fields redundant to language categories, epiphenomena of the structure of a language. I concluded that if types are taken seriously, fields cannot be and that linkages between the field notion and logical types stretch the logical distinctions far beyond their foci and ranges of convenience.

Instead of belaboring these criticisms, I shall argue here that the type notion is premised upon discredited assumptions, namely, Russell's view that philosophy's main job was "correction," translating grammatically incorrect (or otherwise misleading) statements into "correct logical form." Such correction was held to be the hallmark of analytic philosophy, the theory of descriptions. The analysts, including the Wittgenstein of the *Tractatus*, Ryle, Wisdom, Stebbing, and Moore, assumed that the structure of language reflected the real structure of the phenomena represented. If one could delve through incorrect descriptions, one would arrive at correct statements. Behind this was a theory of meaning which held that the meaning of a statement was reducible to its method of verification. Hence the verificationist doctrines were born: a statement had no meaning if it could not in some sense (there were disagreements about which sense of verification was prior or most appropriate to different classes of statements) be verified. The theory of logical types suggests that the objects and concepts named by language have their direct counterparts in the world and that they take their "correct" logical shape from their relations to these objects, that is, relations being exemplified or operationalized by the methods of verification needed for a given linguistic unit.

It was the Wittgenstein of the *Investigations* who put the torch to this account by stipulating that investigations into the grammar of language bore no clear relation to real phenomena. This broadside against traditional ontology has reverberated to the present day. It rejects the picture theory presented in the *Tractatus* and has been the basis for broad-based attacks upon the whole range of analytic views of language. The so-called "linguistic turn" (Rorty, 1967) proved to be an S-curve in which many theorists first embraced, then veered away from reductionism (for example, Wittgenstein, 1953; Wisdom, 1931–1933; Strawson, 1950; Urmson, 1956; Ryle, 1966).

To use a theory of logical types as the basis for defining argument fields seems to require the following untenable assumptions: (1) that meanings are stable across situations, that is, that there are no important differences between intentional meanings and conventional ones or at least that the range of choice is narrow enough to permit confident guesses about situated meanings; (2) that language in itself has an essential structure apart from situated employments; and (3) that it is isomorphic of reality. These are bankrupt notions. Weitz (1966) describes their status cogently:

> After the *Tractatus*, Wittgenstein and others began to question all the fundamental doctrines of this theory of language. That language has or that we must presuppose that it has an essence—i.e., a set of necessary and sufficient properties—and that language is a picture or a structurally isomorphic mirror of the world are denied. In the *Investigations*, the refutation is total and complete. Indeed, the whole theory is now seen as an illusion. Imposed upon language by language itself. If we turn the whole examination around, i.e., if we "look and see" how language functions, we find that language does not function as a picture or mirror, but—if a metaphor is needed—as an enormous toolbox, replete with the most diversified assortment of tools, practically none of which resembles those things in the world to which they may be applied. We also discover that words and sentences as such, i.e., independently of their specific uses, do not refer to or name anything; rather it is in the context of their employment that some words are used to name, others to classify, and still others to prescribe; and sentences are used variously to refer, describe, emote, persuade, etc. Meaning, too, it is seen, is not a relation between words and things, but must be construed as the rules, regulations, conventions, and habits that govern the actual use of expressions. [Pp. 10–11]

Two things need saying here. First, rules, regulations, conventions, and habits do not fit readily into the notion of logical *types*. Second, although Weitz might eschew this reading, rules, regulations, conventions, and habits are field dependent in some cases and more broadly conventional in others. Genuine ambiguities prevent clear and consistent distinctions between field and invariant conventions. It could go without saying that rules, regulations, conventions, and habits cannot stand alone: they gloss over situational uses of themselves. Thus grounding the field notion in a theory of logical types seems unpromising at best.

In *Uses* the bulk of the exposition of the field notion is devoted to examples. The proofs in Euclid's *Elements*, the calculations in the *Nautical Almanac*, and taxonomic arguments such as "this is a whale, so it is a mammal" are all presumably representative of different fields because their subjects and objects are of different logical types. Other examples are: (1) "Harry's hair is not black, since I know for a fact that it is not red," (2) "Peterson is a Swede, so he is presumably not a Roman Catholic," (3) "This phenomenon cannot be wholly explained on my theory, since the deviations between your observations and my predictions are statistically significant," and (4) "Defendant was driving at 45 m.p.h. in a built-up area, so he has committed an offense against the Road Traffic Acts." Other field examples include ethics and aesthetics.

Since fields employ different procedures and techniques of argument, it is important to identify those features which are unique to individual fields and those which are invariant, which cross all fields. No special term is given for elements which cross some but not all fields; perhaps one is needed. Toulmin introduces the distinction between the force and criteria of modal terms to address the dependent-invariant distinction. A term's force consists of the practical implications of its use: for example, a term like "cannot" includes a generalized injunction—something is ruled out. This is contrasted to the reasons or standards by which actors decide that a term is or is not *appropriate* for use in given circumstances, that is, the term's *criteria*. The force of modal terms is invariant, while their criteria are not.

Thus the idea of meaning is discarded. The assumption is that the force-criteria distinction cuts across and draws finer distinctions than a global term such as "meaning." No reference to situated intentional meanings is needed (since, presumably, language follows its systemic mandates irrespective of situational and intentional problems). The distinction, then, is essential to the depsychologization program, and I shall later take sharp issue with it. It will suffice for now to stress that the field examples in *Uses* should be distinguished by virtue of the criteria for their modal terms.

The ordinary field notion makes little sense unless one can draw clear distinctions between fields. However, it is often difficult to separate logical types from sociological conventions; and once sociological conventions are admitted into the calculus, the field examples blur into one another. As *types*, the examples nonetheless blend together in unclear ways, thanks to their traditions of use.

Euclid's proofs can be (and were) employed in special ways by an array of disciplines. Ethical theorists, biologists, metaphysicians, economists, and a host of other specialists used the proofs as invariant principles. The *criteria* were the same (or at least similar enough to call the distinction into question). The appeal to invariant principles is the same, regardless of the intentions behind it and regardless of the field in which the appeal occurs. What is interesting here is that the *force* of some modal terms appears to have been field dependent, while the criteria, the standards of appropriateness, appear to have been invariant.

The calculations of the *Nautical Almanac* could be employed with equal diversity. Statistically significant relationships (and propositions about them) also display this characteristic. They exemplify the ambiguity of the force-criteria distinction: (1) "statistically significant" relationships have the same criteria across most fields which use statistics, that is, they are appealed to for the same reasons; and (2) the practical implications of a statistically significant relationship can vary across fields, that is, while a term like "cannot" is a general injunction, an idea like "$p<.01$" takes its implications from the uses made of it. The terms blur because of genuine ambiguities inherent to the distinction—ambiguities which parallel the ambiguous relationship of logical types and sociological practices. Viewed one way, criteria are sometimes invariant and other times dependent, and force is sometimes invariant and at other times dependent. I am confounding certain elements of meaning with force and criteria—making the matter less neat than Toulmin would like; but the point is that the distinction does not explain the uses made of statistical statements by situated speakers in varied fields.

It is probably justified to distinguish between the discipline of statistics and the ways statistical ideas are picked up and used by other disciplines. Since argumentation is mostly interested in the *uses* of statistical arguments made by arguers in varied fields, this distinction is worth underscoring. The discipline of statistics is arguably a compact discipline, an amalgam of professional associations and traditions sharing common problem foci (for example, reducing mass data to meaningful and manageable generalizations, understanding frequency distributions, normal probability curves, measures of central tendency, variability measures, and correlation coefficients). It is a self-contained rational enterprise—its veridical standards are widely agreed to and rigorously specified. It comes as close as most fields to being an a priori science; and the self-descriptions of statisticians sound suspiciously similar to the old self-descriptions of logicians. For the most part, statistical arguments are *warrant-using arguments*. Thus there is an important difference between statistics per se as a rational enterprise and the uses of statistics by other fields and in the ordinary fields.

The varied disciplines that pick up and use statistical principles do so in such varied ways that the force-criteria distinction is genuinely ambiguous. First, some fields treat statistics in the same way that argumentation is used to treat logic, as a body of invariant a priori principles. This is an interesting phenomenon, viewed from argumentation's perspective, because it reveals the nature of the warrants in these fields. It also illuminates the collapse of force into criteria into one another, that is, insofar as a behavioral psychologist uses statistics as an a priori body of principles, no meaningful distinctions between force and criteria can be derived. Second, criteria are often defined in such a way that they are indistinguishable from force. For example, significance tests are understood similarly by all who use them, that is, their practical implications (force) are the same. If we appeal to them because their practical implications are the same, that is, on the same grounds (criteria), then for all practical purposes there are no differences between force and criteria. "$p < .01$" means what it means; it has the same force and criteria wherever it is used. One appeals to a statistical relationship on the basis of its force.

No one would disagree with the claim that "$p < .01$" is a "significance correlation"; but let us imagine a disagreement about whether "$p < .01$" *is significant*. If two fields disagree about whether "$p < .01$" is "significant" (as opposed to being, say, a "vague association"), then they may be said to agree on criteria but to differ about force—the opposite of Toulmin's intentions for the distinction. If a physicist and a psychologist are arguing about the theoretic implications of a correlation "$p < .01$," it is not unlikely that they would agree that it is a statement of significance (that is, they agree on criteria, that it is a statement to be appealed to in thus and so circumstances) but that they would disagree about whether the correlation is a "significant" one. The physicist might say "$p < .01$ falls far short of true significance (namely, $p < .0001$)." That is a dispute about the principle of appeal to correlations (that is, based on the practical implications of a level of significance) involving no disagreement about criteria, the psychologist and physicist agree that one appeals to correlational evidence in thus and so cases. Thus *force is field dependent, while criteria is not.*

Notice that this argument can be alternatively constructed so that one person might say that "$p < .01$ versus $p < .0001$" is a dispute about criteria because it depends upon one's standards of "significance," that is, one's criteria consist of the minimum standards of significance one places upon correlations before one uses them. This makes the practical implications of the argument (force) nothing more than the claim that "$p < .01$ and $p < .0001$" are both significance statements, that is, their practical implications are the same, but fields will differ in their willingness to use .01 versus .0001 correlations.

If the two arguments are equally plausible, the force-criteria distinction is genuinely ambiguous. If the first argument is marginally more convincing (which I think it is), the distinction is vitiated, since "force" is field dependent, while "criteria" in some cases is not. If the second argument is the more convincing, the distinction seems again to be confounded with "meaning," since one must assign motives to the arguers in order to understand the distinctions being drawn.

Toulmin's most sustained examples for the force-criteria distinction are modal terms such as "probably" and "cannot." If my arguments about statistical statements are convincing, "probably" is mired in ambiguity. I add here only the idea that in ordinary fields, which sometimes use statistical arguments, the force-criteria distinction is even more questionable. For ordinary arguers, a proverb like "figures don't lie, liars figure" brings credibility issues to bear upon the justification of a statistical warrant or datum; it illustrates the sense that for situated actors, while figures mean what they mean, the uses to which they may be put, the sense that can be made of them, can vary in important ways, depending upon the motives of the arguer.

The term "cannot" is based on suspiciously congenial examples. Toulmin uses a *situated* illustration while taking the situation to exemplify all uses of the term. "You cannot be sick" means different things when uttered by a train steward and by a physician. The steward is on a train, not in a physician's waiting room, when speaking; the physician is in her office, not on a train.

The first statement is a claim for social niceties rather than a use of a generalized injunction, and the second is not an injunction at all. A statement such as "you cannot be serious" is similarly an evaluation, not an injunction. If we take this at face value, "cannot" is a logical type and means what it means regardless of the situation in which it is uttered. We shall want to contrast this statement with the plausibility of our developing brief for the importance of the definition of situation.

The field exemplars in *Uses* draw their criteria and force from the psychological processes of the speakers. The *meaning*, force, and criteria of "statistically significant," "I know for a fact," and "Peterson is a Swede" stem from the intentions of the speaker who is in *this* situation, trying to do *that*. Each can display the same force and criteria across many contexts. Thus, the force-criteria distinction blurs definitions of situation and is proportionately valueless for the analysis of ordinary talk.

This ambiguity (and the differences between Toulmin's intentions and my own) can be illustrated by a look at "Harry's hair is not black, since I know for a fact that it is red." For argumentation's purposes, the phrase "I know for a fact" is as important and in some respects more crucial than "Harry's hair" and "black" and "red." "I know for a fact" is simultaneously datum and warrant for certain claims. It exemplifies an arguer characterizing his own knowledge. It crosses fields, since we would not be surprised to hear atomic physicists or truck drivers saying the same thing. The phrase is an invitation to other arguers to ask for more information about a person's cognitive processes and definitions of situation. "Harry's hair is not black" can be said to differ (as a field exemplar) from "Peterson is a Swede" by virtue of "I know for a fact." Thus every statement of virtually every sort can be something "I know for a fact." This means that force-criteria distinctions are valueless—the more global term "meaning" is needed to understand what it is, in a certain circumstance, for the speaker to "know for fact."

Thus the distinction is irrelevant to ordinary discourse and arguably so even for disputes in the compact disciplines. It does cut more finely across some distinctions than does "meaning," but it is rather a blunt instrument for argumentation's purposes. It rules meaning out by fiat and of necessity ignores the context embeddedness of statements. The distinction doubtless works in the compact disciplines, and perhaps my claim reduces to the familiar argument that the natural and social sciences have subject matters which differ in kind. MacIver (1942) and Weber (1947) among others have made eloquent cases for this distinction on the grounds that events and objects have *meanings* for people—these meanings being the core research problem of the social sciences. Schutz (1954) has stated the case succinctly:

> ...[T]here is an essential difference in the structure of the thought objects or mental constructs formed by the social sciences and those formed by the natural sciences. It is up to the natural scientist and to him alone to define, in accordance with the procedural rules of his science, his observational field, and to determine the facts, data, and events within it which are relevant for his problems or scientific purpose at hand. Neither are those facts and events pre-selected, nor is the observational field pre-interpreted. The world of nature, as explored by the natural scientist, does not "mean" anything to the molecules, atoms, and electrons therein. The observational field of the social scientist, however, namely the social reality, has a specific meaning and relevance structure for the human beings living, acting, and thinking therein. By a series of commonsense constructs they have pre-selected and pre-interpreted this world which they experience as the reality of their daily lives. It is these thought objects of theirs which determine their behavior by motivating it. The

thought objects constructed by social scientists, in order to grasp this social reality, have to be founded on the thought objects constructed by the commonsense thinking of men, living their daily life within their social world. [Pp. 266–67]

Cicourel draws from this reasoning the conclusion that "the precise measurement of social process requires first the study of the problem of meaning in everyday life. Social inquiry begins with reference to the commonsense world of everyday life. The meanings communicated by use of ordinary day-to-day language categories and the nonlinguistic shared cultural experiences inform every social act" (Cicourel, 1964, p. 14). I take this to be the precondition of successful social research in general and of field studies in particular.

The force-criteria distinction is intended to circumvent the problems and ambiguities of the term "meaning." Meaning is too psychologistic; it introduces obscure variables into logic. But what is at issue is whether Toulmin avoids "meaning" merely by fiat. "Linguistic context" (like its conceptual offspring "substantive context") is irremediably ambiguous *unless* one assumes that language is imported into every situation intact, in more or less precisely the same ways, and that it "means what it means" irrespective of individuated definitions of situations. I do not see how we are to defend a theory of logical types or the force-criteria distinction without embracing these assumptions. Moreover, once we accept these assumptions, I see no recourse to saying that individual cases are deductive instances of generic rules of language.

This rings false for several reasons. First, if we grant that there can be and often are differences between what a situated speaker means and what the things he says mean, we need the notion of "definitions of situation" to serve as a principle for explaining these differences. A term such as "probably" could display countless gradations toward certainty in ordinary parlance; there are no special reasons to believe that "linguistic context"—understood in the abstract—would reveal these intended gradations. Second, only the most extreme versions of linguistic determinism permit us to deny that situated speakers face *choices* in their selection and management of language. Once talk of choices is allowed, "linguistic context" must account for them. I do not see how it can do so without the idea that speakers intend toward the things they say. For our purposes the most fundamental sense of linguistic context must be the intentional meanings of situated actors. Thus, third, we can avoid linguistic determinism only by allowing that definitions of situation affect meanings—which forces us to regard definitions of situation as the core presupposition of "linguistic context." The logical type theory and the force-criteria distinction permit no situational analyses; they assume more or less complete commonality across contexts.

It is thus to the psychological perspective of the situated speaker that we must turn to derive a useful conception of argument fields. The field notion ought to illuminate phenomena which without it would be obscure. The phenomena so exposed are the elements of situated argument. Toulmin's terms are conceptually neat but perfectly arbitrary escapes from the problems of grappling with situated meanings.

Implications for the Alternative View

Let us take stock of where our thinking seems to be leading. We have carved the field notion into two broad domains, "disciplinary" and "ordinary." For the disciplinary fields we have retained most of Toulmin's vocabulary and the idea that these fields are pyramided according to their compactness. We have distinguished the disciplines from ordinary fields by virtue of the disciplines' collective commitment to "getting better," and we have argued that this aim toward compactness unites professionals even when they share little else. Actors in ordinary domains do not share this epistemic aim (which is not to say that they have no epistemic aims at all) because they are centrally concerned with action. Most popular movements unreflectively presuppose knowledge; they take their concepts more or less at face value; they do not want to improve their knowledge so much as to enhance the effectiveness with which they seek to attain social and political goals; their actors do not centrally see themselves as contributing to a body of knowledge so much as they see themselves *using* facts which can be taken for granted. We need not insist upon the *disciplinary versus ordinary* distinction as a hard and fast rule permitting no exceptions. Fringe cases which overlap both domains will doubtless emerge (for instance, it is hard to tell whether pronuclear and antinuclear power arguments uniformly fit into one or the other category). Nonetheless, we have a rough idea that there are important differences between experts arguing with experts about their shared knowledge and its probative status and laymen arguing with laymen about lines of appropriate action. This distinction seems plausible enough that we can probably proceed without disaster to use it to illuminate some more specific distinctions.

Let us say that the disciplines and ordinary fields (alike) can be broken down into fields which differ according to the kinds of communication processes we emphasize and according to our analytic interests. Our aim is to point to several different senses of "field" which serve different analytic interests and which stand for different aspects of social life. Again, we are after not hard and fast distinctions (for reasons that will shortly be clear) but rather rough and ready guidelines which may clarify our thinking about the relationships of argument to epistemics. Let us say, then, that the two broad rubrics (disciplinary and ordinary) consist of at least four different senses of "field," namely, encounter fields, relational fields, issue fields, and normative fields. In considering the utility of these distinctions, we should keep mindful of the possibility that we are merely proliferating jargon. At bare minimum we want our distinctions to prove faithful to the empirical facts of social life and to make genuine contributions to our capacities for formulating and answering epistemic questions.

It might be objected—even before we have defended the different senses of "field"—that the fourfold conception of "field" makes the concept too broad—that it embraces virtually all aspects of social and professional life and (thus) loses its defining power. If we are to answer this objection, the case for theoretical holism needs to be re-emphasized. We are concerned with an array of concepts that bear upon questions of knowledge, and a case has been made for explaining these ideas by virtue of unified set of constructs, the main ones being communication and perspectivity. The sociology of knowledge ruled by these constructs is thus inevitably broad. Our preliminary assumption is that the problem of knowledge consists not of a single agenda of logically related items but of a broad-based offensive consisting of several parallel lines of inquiry. Our four senses of "field" are designed to call attention to these parallel inquiries, to suggest the importance of each, and to illuminate the relationships among them. By all odds, they should expand the defining power of the field concept—not merely by applying the term to a range of hitherto unconsidered domains, but by tying these different empirical domains (and the analytic procedures appropriate to them) together into a coherent epistemological package. Let us see if this can be done.

An *encounter field*—using "encounter" in its usual sociological sense (Willard, 1978a)—consists of the definitions of situation, coorientations, and issue assumptions brought to bear by arguers in a single encounter. Two strangers at an airport may negotiate a temporary relationship by appeal to conventional etiquette; the substantive presuppositions behind their arguments will reflect these definitions and coorientations. They will "call on the facts" when necessary; and we should not be surprised to find such arguers explicitly negotiating judgmental standards for purposes of "getting on with the argument." Thus the encounter field notion calls our attention to *particular arguments*.

Why study encounters? We are proceeding on the assumption that arguments have epistemic effects—that the very idea of argument is essentially an epistemological notion. The proof of this assumption (presumably) resides in particular arguments. If argument is epistemic, we can surely discern these epistemological effects in particular empirical cases. Moreover, it is insufficient merely to know that arguments are social comparison processes which lead to new beliefs for the arguers; we want to know how and why arguments create knowledge. Having labored to produce unified conceptions of argument interaction and utterance (and having labored to prove that one must know what an arguer *means* by an utterance), we surely have to try this thinking out in particular cases. This trial, it seems to me, is the necessary condition of being able to say that argument is epistemic. It is also (as we shall see) a pivotal component of explanations of the effects of ordinary issue fields upon situated thought and action.

Relational fields involve actors united in longer term relationships. Spouses, for example, evolve special conceptual ecologies and background assumptions that support highly elided and implicit exchanges (see Jackson and Jacobs, 1980) as well as recurring (long-term) arguments that "flare up" and "simmer down" (Willard, 1980e). Trials, for reasons to be seen, are relational fields because they take their character from the personal and professional relationships among legal actors. Issue fields, ordinary and disciplinary, are animated by ongoing interactions of their actors. Relational fields, then, embrace many encounters; they are social relations which give meaning to and are given meaning by particular interactions (Argyle, 1964, 1970, 1973; McCall et al., 1970; Goffman, 1959, 1967, 1971, 1974; Blumer, 1969; Bruyn, 1966; Douglas, 1970a). The relations among legal actors in any particular trial may thus reflect a dialectic between their interaction histories and their definitions of situation in the particular case. We may take this dialectic to be paradigmatic of the relational bonds undergirding all fields—disciplinary and ordinary alike.

Why study relationships? The argument will gradually develop here that issue fields are not things but generalizations we make about certain organized congeries of activity; issue fields, in sum, are animated by the activities of their actors. These activities are informed by relational fields—making relationships a central concern to the sociology of knowledge. In the last chapter, a case will be made for seeing criticism as the study of the effects of presuppositions; and nowhere except in encounters and relationships are presuppositions so clearly brought into relief. Thus, the study of relational fields is the study of how an issue field's substantive concerns actually affect situated action.

Issue fields, let us say, are substantive domains—both disciplinary and ordinary. Disciplinary issue fields correspond (roughly) to Toulmin's diffuse or would-be disciplines—falling in the middle of the pyramid—although his vocabulary is (arguably) less precise than the terms I shall substitute. Disciplinary issue fields (I shall say) are schools of thought, paradigms, or theoretical orientations. A "Freudian," "behaviorist," or "constructivist" is a person distinguishable from other people by virtue of the beliefs he holds and the ways he conceptualizes the phenomena he studies. While the methods for distinguishing among issue fields must be considered at length below, it may suffice here to say (crudely) that issue fields differ from one another because they concern themselves with different subjects (though no appeal to the theory of logical types is intended by this claim). Ordinary issue fields are not utterly different from their disciplinary counterparts, but genuine distinctions can be drawn. By "ordinary" issue field I most basically mean the sides a person takes on social and political issues and the interpersonal bonds one builds by virtue of his positions on issues. What rhetorical theorists have traditionally called "movements" would fall into this category. Typifying examples might be the pronuclear and antinuclear power movements, "creationism," proabortion and antiabortion movements, the ecology movement, the John Birch Society, the women's movement, the PTL Club, and so on. The intuitive idea is that ordinary folk (for a variety of reasons) enter substantive domains and that the ideas of these domains are taken to vouch for the claims they make in situated discourse.

How do issue fields—ordinary and disciplinary—relate to encounters and relationships? We do not (strictly speaking) want to say that issue fields are the genus and encounters and relationships the species because (a) we have imputed great importance to the definition of the situation and perspectivity, and (b) the genus-species relation will not square with the empirical claims (made below) that issue fields are animated by the situated activities of their actors. An issue field, then, is not the same thing as a "history of ideas." A history of ideas can be surveyed independent of particular thoughts and actions; but the description of an issue field requires (we shall see) reference to the practices and recurring situations which animate it. While a history of a field's ideas might be an important step in what we want to call "field study" (while, in fact, it might prove indispensable to the critical program we shall advocate), it cannot for our purposes be taken alone. Thus we shall not assume that particular encounters and relationships are merely microcosmic copies of the broader issue fields the arguers refer to (even though we would not be surprised to see some arguers treat their interactions as if "Freudianism" and "behaviorism" were doing battle). Rather, we shall proceed on the assumption that issue fields are generalizations we make about particular practices—inductive results. We are as interested in the practices as in the ideas which inform them; and our studies of issue fields are pursued in the service of the broader aim of understanding the social organization of knowledge. A history of ideas can only be a part (though an important one, to be sure) of this enterprise.

Normative fields may prove to be the most troublesome concept; and it might turn out that they often collapse into issue fields (that is, they will turn out to be indistinguishable from issue fields). Nonetheless, while I want to say that the substance of someone's arguments is drawn from the school of thought deemed relevant to the subject at hand, many speakers have broad allegiances which cross issue field boundaries. While it is best to focus upon "behaviorism" or "constructivism" rather than on "psychology" to understand the substance of an argument, there are nonetheless valuable insights to be gained from knowing the importance a speaker attaches to being a professional "psychologist" or "an academic" or a "secular humanist." The intuitive idea is that, while the issue field—one's school of thought—is a source of *meaning*, a normative field is often a source of general values. Thus by "normative field" I mean something akin to the old notion of the reference group. Thus normative fields are general social and professional orientations which affect people's estimations of appropriate behavior. The intuitive idea is that they often differ in kind from one's issue field (in the sense, for example, that a lawyer's sense of his professional obligations and status differ from his intentions in a particular trial).

Let us turn first to the idea of *issue fields*. I shall start with the disciplines—my core claim being that Toulmin's vocabulary is less precise than "schools of thought," "paradigms," "theoretical orientation," or "point of view." A second goal will be to specify the senses in which the disciplinary issue field notion does not by itself illuminate situated utterance. It bears reiteration that this is not a plea for discarding the history of ideas so much as for assigning it a clear position in argumentation's theoretic and analytic hierarchy.

Let us start by asking whether it is more important that a man is a professional psychologist or a "Freudian," a sociologist or a "structuralist," a member of the Speech Communication Association or a "constructivist." It will pay to proceed cautiously because, for one thing, the question itself may be illegitimate, that is, it may pose a false dichotomy; for another, there may be some higher unity that we have unintentionally ignored. More likely, I think, is the possibility that the cogency of the question may depend upon the purposes behind it, that is, one may be more important than the other with respect to one matter but not to another. If our question asks why a person attends one professional convention versus another, professional definition might be more important than issue orientation; and this is almost certainly a phenomenon of interest. If our question, conversely, asks why a person reads one journal rather than others, follows one tradition of thinking rather than others, and footnotes certain people rather than others, one's issue orientation is arguably more important.

Thus we can proceed as if our question—as posed—is legitimate. Since we want to know where the premises of arguments come from as well as the presuppositions behind a person's definitions of situation, it is plausible that knowing whether a person subscribes to one school of thought rather than another would be valuable. Just as we can legitimately pose the question, we may also cautiously proceed to answer it. That is, we can legitimately pursue the claim that, for argumentation's purposes, understanding what arguments *mean*, a person's issue orientation is more important than professional alignments (although we need not assume that the two are ever mutually exclusive).

From Toulmin's vantage, one wants to know if a person is a "psychologist," "sociologist," "rhetorical theorist," "philosopher," and so forth—more or less on the assumption that human knowledge is divided into rational enterprises which correspond to the bureaucratic divisions expressed in a university course catalog. My position is rather different. One will grasp the sources of arguments when one knows if a person thinks he is a "Freudian," "behaviorist," "constructivist," or "existentialist." Further, "existentialists" appear in a variety of professional domains, that is, they are psychologists, sociologists, philosophers, and communication theorists. Thus, people who share a school of thought have more in common with others in the school than they do with fellow professionals who follow other visions.

Many of my arguments will be similar to Toulmin's statements about the diffuse and nondisciplinable fields, but I draw different conclusions. He recognizes the importance of differing schools of thought within these fields—that is the defining characteristic of "diffusion" versus "compactness." But Toulmin overstates the case for professional stability within the respective professional domains and proportionately underplays the need for understanding the relations between psychological processes and schools of thought. My claim is that if a man says he is a "Freudian," he is saying something important about his sociological orientations, his definitions of situation, and his own judgmental and veridical standards. Thus the examples below illustrate that "psychology" or "sociology" are less useful field parameters than "Freudianism" and "behaviorism." I shall start with aesthetics, since that example appears first in Toulmin's works.

Toulmin uses aesthetics in *Uses* to illustrate a difficult case, a professional discipline which contains competing paradigms. His position is this: "In these fields, more often than in most, the answers to questions remain matters of opinion or taste. Aesthetics is an obvious field in which this is liable to happen, though even there it is easy to exaggerate the room for reasonable disagreement and to overlook the cases in which only one informed opinion can seriously be maintained, e.g., the superiority as a landscape painter of Claude Lorraine over Hieronymus Bosch" (1958, p. 20).

Several comments need to be made. First, it is difficult to take this example seriously, namely, the comparative merits of Bosch and Lorraine as *landscape* painters. A more uninteresting disagreement is difficult to imagine (though a comparison of Poe and Pound as short story writers comes to mind). The example is "true but trivial." Second, differences between aesthetic schools are for the most part as complex as they are unbridgeable. Theorists like James, Santayana, Prall, and Dewey (despite differences among them) can easily be contrasted with the likes of Langer, Ducasse, and Weitz, who (despite differences among them) can be contrasted with the "psychologists" such as Pepper, Croce, Spingarn, and Nahm. The differences between these schools are not matters of taste; they are differences in the presuppositions behind their arguments.

Notice that most of these theorists have produced work which spans professional lines (as Toulmin conceives them), for example, Langer's thinking (like Santayana's, Dewey's, and Pepper's) has been incorporated into paradigms in psychology, sociology, and communication (as well as many others). This seems to support the "school of thought" interpretation of field rather than the professional association view.

Notice also that the differences between these divergent theorists and the *practitioners* of art are usually if not always insoluble. It has often been explicitly recognized that the differences between theorists and practitioners are so profound that little agreement has been attained even about the rough outlines of the "field" of aesthetics.

Notice further that it is sometimes insufficient to name the different paradigms, for example, the "separatists," "psychologists," "semanticists," or "metaphysicians." Differences even within these schools are sometimes profound. Within aesthetics, for example, Sartre and Merleau-Ponty are both "phenomenologists," but some (not all) of the differences between them are chasmatic. This fact raises difficulties for the school of thought interpretation of fields; and we will do well to keep mindful of them. One line of thinking would have it that the broad rubric of "phenomenology" embraces many divergent orientations (as it indeed does) but contains enough common threads to permit clear discussions of the differences. Another line would have it that Sartre and Merleau-Ponty have produced works which themselves constitute fields. Both interpretations seem plausible for certain purposes, and it may be sufficient for now to say that theorists and researchers say they are working from "a Sartrian framework" or some such and that so saying they are defining their personal fields of argument. If critics say "the Sartrian framework is not the best phenomenological perspective," they are trying to broaden the field, to bring in additional and presumably better judgmental and veridical standards.

The aesthetics example thus seems to tell us several things: (1) it is not especially revealing about the nature of argument fields to name aesthetics a "would-be" or even "undisciplinable" field, that is, doing so tells nothing about aesthetic arguments; (2) the "professional discipline" of aesthetics is nearly unrecognizable: aesthetic work overlaps many other disciplines, aesthetic theorists are often in different academic departments, and substantive disagreements between the competing theories are so profound as to make "aesthetic discipline" a contradiction in terms; and (3) aesthetics seems to exemplify the comparative value of looking at schools of thought rather than professional associations to understand fields of argument.

Our next example is psychology, and my claims are the same as for aesthetics. Toulmin recognizes the often profound differences between the competing schools of thought within psychology, but he draws from these differences only the generalization that psychology is not compact, and he says nothing about psychology as an argument field. My arguments below bear a strong resemblance to his comments about psychology, but I draw the conclusion that "psychology" is too broad and vague a term to be useful as a field exemplar and that its individual schools of thought are superior models.

The differences between Freudian, neo-Freudian, S-R and S-O-R behaviorist, cognitive, third-force, constructivist, psychobiological, and sociobiological psychologists (as Toulmin recognizes) reflect often profound paradigmatic differences in (1) problem foci, (2) definitions, (3) assumptions about theory, (4) research methodologies and techniques, and (5) even modes of inference. For example, *repression* is a core problem for a Freudian but nonsense to a behaviorist; theory-free observation is assumed by a behaviorist but held impossible by a constructivist; and free response data is dependable research for a constructivist but chimera to a behaviorist.

The arguments of these divergent schools may employ data and conclusions of different logical types. Proponents of laboratory research sometimes scoff at arguments based on participant observation, introspection, or other "qualitative" approaches. Some theorists see statistical work as a limited, relatively minor part of the field of psychology, while others see it as the core. Differences between physicalism and humanism stem in part from differences in standards of appropriateness for the data, warrants, and conclusions of arguments: George Kelly's problems are not Carnap's: one does not shift from Carnap's views to Kelly's because (to use Toulmin's criterion) Kelly's model better solves Carnap's problems; Kelly rejects most of Carnap's concerns as unworthy of good psychological theory, for example, reducing psychology to the language of physics is not for Kelly a problem better solved by constructivism; it is a program held to be valueless once one accepts the assumptions of constructivism.

At a high level of abstraction, Kelly and Carnap (and the other divergent theorists) might be said to share a common commitment to truthful research and to understanding human nature. But how useful is such an abstraction? If it disguises fundamental theoretic and practical differences, it is counterproductive. It will not do to unite these different schools under the banner of "science" because (1) they differ fundamentally in their conceptions of science; (2) such a procedure would elevate the scientific metaphor to invariant, a priori status in a manner akin to traditional logic—a program that field theory per se calls into question; and (3) the procedure would lead to trivial comparisons, that is, if asked to compare B. F. Skinner and D. Bannister as *scientists*, I might justifiably reply that this is analogous to comparing Bosch and Lorraine as landscape painters *or* that their conceptions of science are so different that to force-fit them under this generic banner does violence both to them and to the rubric of science per se.

Hence psychology seems to prove the same claims we advanced for aesthetics. The schools of thought within it are better exemplars of argument fields, they illuminate more precisely the presuppositions behind arguments than does the gross label "psychology." This does not require that we ignore the fact that a "Freudian" is a "professional psychologist" rather than, say, a communication theorist: rather we use the "Freudian" orientation to define, for that person, what it means to be a psychologist rather than using "psychology" to define what it means, for that person, to be a Freudian.

Our next example is sociology, which seems to work in the same ways that aesthetics and psychology function. Again, Toulmin explicitly acknowledges the diversity within the professional discipline; again, the divergent schools are better field exemplars than the professional discipline. I can perhaps illustrate this point by looking at two branches of a single perspective (among many possibilities) within sociology, namely, the differences between Iowa School and Chicago School symbolic interactionism. These traditions display markedly different assumptions about research, causality, statistical work, variable analysis, and other matters. They sometimes define their problems with the same terms but define the terms so differently that it cannot be said that they focus on the same problems. Both deal with the "self," but the followers of Manford Kuhn and of Herbert Blumer define "self theory" quite differently. These differences, Meltzer and Petras (1972) say, are organic and systematic:

> While Blumer's image of man dictates his methodology, Kuhn's methodology dictates his image of man. Thus, Blumer begins with a depiction of man's behavior as entailing a dialogue between impulses and social definitions in the course of which acts are constructed. He proceeds to recognize a level of interaction devoid of social definitions and reflecting sheerly spontaneous behavior. Holding these two preceding ideas, he questions the extent to which human behavior is predictable. And finally,...he must urge a methodology that combines scientific and humanistic elements.
>
> Oppositely, Kuhn starts from a scientistic concern. This, though joined with his symbolic interactionist orientation, brings him to...a basically deterministic image of behavior. In the service of both scientism and determinism, he denies to the I any role in conduct, thereby dismissing the possibilities of both emergence and nonsymbolic interaction. [P. 54]

Discussing the dim possibilities for rejoining the two perspectives, Meltzer and Petras stress that the Iowa and Chicago Schools address essentially different problems. Iowans focus on *operationism* (reflecting their determinism and positivism), while Chicagoans insist upon conceptual clarity as a prerequisite to operational definitions. There are no professional unities between the schools: "As in the past and present, the two schools may continue the pattern of taking little cognizance of one another and of going their separate ways. This pattern is evidenced by the fact that representatives of each school rarely cite the works of the other school. This type of parochialism is fostered by the fundamental and perhaps irreconcilable divergence of the schools on the methodological level" (Meltzer and Petras, 1972, pp. 56–57).

Sociology thus displays the diffusion we have imputed to aesthetics and psychology. Its professional boundaries are less useful than its schools of thought to describe the presuppositions behind arguments. Its isms are standpoints, conceptual lenses—perspectives from which one may organize and give meaning to phenomena. To know that a person is a psychologist or sociologist is to know little about his presuppositions and values. To know that someone is a behaviorist or constructivist is to know far more about his organizing point of view, the superordinating system by which he makes events meaningful. Schools of thought, then, are the best exemplars of argument fields. When *A says X*, we go far toward understanding what *A* means by saying *X* by knowing *A*'s issue field.

Notice I do not say that knowing *A* to be a "Freudian" exhausts the study of what *A* means when *A says X*. The issue field notion cannot by itself explain circumstanced action, that is, it reveals a person's broad orientations but not particular definitions of situation. It is not as if one can read the central tracts on (say) Freudianism and thus know how a Freudian will define a particular situation. Historians of ideas can use the issue field as an organizing principle which stands alone because they are not especially concerned with particular contexts; they are uninterested in explaining fields *as going concerns*. The rhetorical theorists who study "movements" can also use the issue field as a history of ideas (though they are more obligated to look at situated uses of ideas—documents often make little sense until one understands how their ideas are vivified through practices). But argument theorists can make no such claims. They are neither historians of ideas nor movement theorists.

If a Freudian and a behaviorist argue about *X*, it is oversimple to equate the particular argument with *Freudianism versus behaviorism*. We need to know what they think they are doing. Their issue fields may help us with this task; but they cannot exhaust a situation. To assume that they could is to assume that (1) the ism is a united front, that is, consists of a few core ideas that can be represented in short statements, and (2) the arguers are more or less perfect replicas of the ism. I should think that (2) is decisive. Incompetence, stupidity, and ignorance are surely common enough traits; a plausible inference from this is that it is imprudent to assume that any particular actor is a replica of an issue field. Mannheim discovered that no person was the bearer of a complete (or accurate) ideological system—a historical experience worth remembering when we seek ways of using the issue field notion. The prudent course is to see issue fields as rough general guidelines, as preliminary guesses about a person's presuppositions, as hypotheses to be tested against other observations.

The Jurisprudential Analogy

The jurisprudential analogy is central to Toulmin's exposition, his most extended exemplar of a field. Properly revised, it may be central to our own view as well. The reformed analogy can explain relational fields. The need for reforms in Toulmin's analogy merits discussion because it may illuminate the differences between his field theory and the present view. This comparison will buttress the claims that sociological views of fields must cohere with the psychological sense of field; the notion of meaning cannot be ruled out of the working logics of fields; fields do not exist in their documents; and Toulmin's exposition works best for the compact disciplines. Comparing the two analogies will also clarify the things we want field theory to do. It will point to the need for a descriptive construct that illuminates the meanings of claims and the reasons given for them by arguers—not arguers in some abstract sense but as critics usually find them: situated, dealing with events. The reformed analogy should thus augment the holistic view. We can see it as a way of generalizing about recurring themes in definitions of situation.

Put crudely, Toulmin sees the legal analogy as describing the field of law as exemplified by the traditions embodied in the language of the law. I want the analogy to focus upon the ongoing practices of legal actors as constitutive of the field. Toulmin emphasizes the constraints upon legal action imposed by the body of law and tradition; the reformed analogy stresses the context embeddedness of particular decisions. Toulmin sees the body of law as a conceptual ecology which informs particular decisions; the reformed analogy makes discretion the definitive element of legal activities (appeals to the law being done post facto to justify decisions arrived at for reasons peculiar to particular situations). The reformed analogy makes individual trials its field exemplars rather than the "legal profession" or the "body of law."

There can be little doubt that the analogy is central to Toulmin's exposition. One may ask, he says, whether it is an analogy at all: "When we have seen how far the parallels between the two studies can be pressed, we may feel the term 'analogy' is too weak, and the term 'metaphor' positively misleading: even, that law-suits are just a special kind of rational dispute, for which the procedures and rules of argument have hardened into institutions" (Toulmin, 1958, pp. 7–8). We are to take this analogy rather literally. Thus, "logic (we may say) is generalised jurisprudence. Arguments can be compared with law-suits, and the claims we make and argue for in extra-legal contexts with claims made in courts, while the cases we present in making good each kind of claim can be compared with each other" (1958, p. 7). Jurisprudence's task is to describe the essential features of the legal process. Logic is to pursue a parallel path to describe the procedures by which claims are put forward, tested, and judged. It is from this parallel that a general impartial standpoint of rationality is expected to emerge.

Organizing Model: Trials "versus" Bargaining. For Toulmin the trial is central to explanations of legal processes. Yet trials are relatively rare occurrences. Their rarity confronts us with a special problem of deciding whether plea bargaining rather than trials best exemplifies the field. The vast majority of criminal cases are bargained, and most civil cases are negotiated out of court. Toulmin (1972) tells us to understand a rational enterprise by examining its professional associations, problem foci, and organizing activities—advice which directs our attention in jurisprudence not to the trial but to bargaining. Bargaining is how the daily business of the law gets done. Thus I shall proceed with two claims: (1) bargaining—the core legal process—supports a psychologistic view of legal procedure and dovetails with the interactional view of argument; and (2) trials cannot be abstracted out of the broader spectrum of legal activities which eventuate in trials.

Claim (1) entails little more than the assumption that bargaining is a form of interpersonal communication, taking its character from the perspectives of interactants. These coorientations (we have said) are emergent interpersonal attributions. Negotiation of all sorts entails such defining activity. Thus to know a bargain is to know the motives of the bargainers: prosecutors will be guided as much by social and political constraints as by legal precedent, and the defendant will interestedly pursue the lowest possible level of punishment.

Claim (2) implies that trials reflect the psychological perspectives of legal actors and that they follow extralegal paths. So viewed, trials cannot be contrasted with bargaining in the way Toulmin leads us to do, that is, they function by virtue of the same principles. Toulmin recognizes the difficulties of generalizing about trials. There are differences between civil and criminal proceedings, common law versus statute, and between the sorts of evidence relevant to different cases. We can underscore this with Toulmin's words: "To establish negligence in a civil case, wilful intent in a case of murder, the presumption of legitimate birth: each of these will require appeal to evidence of different kinds" (1958, p. 16). This is a crucial test, since the defining characteristic of fields is to be the content of their data and conclusions. If different trials devise their own standards of evidence, they may be fields in and of themselves.

The Importance of Discretion. Trials are rooted more in discretion than in precedent. While we should be mindful of the possibility that this is a false dichotomy, there is probably nothing wrong in proceeding under the assumption that they are not, that is, that the difference between discretion and precedent is fundamental and that it strikes at the heart of the jurisprudential analogy.

Davis (1971) has stressed that discretionary actions are far more important in jurisprudential conduct than rules: "Even in something generally supposed to be so much controlled by law as the administration of criminal justice, administrative discretion is far more important than rules. All the rules that call for punishment can be nullified by any one of five sets of discretionary power....We have not yet found a way to eliminate discretion with respect to arresting, sentencing, prosecuting, paroling, and pardoning without destroying the crucial values we want to preserve" (1971, p. 18). Discretion causes most injustice, but the jurisprudential system could not possibly function without it except at the expense of essential values. Rules alone never suffice. In fact, they are sometimes the least important aspects of a trial. The discretionary interpretations made by lawyers, judges, juries, and other legal actors are the actions which actually constitute a trial. Discretion is a tool that is "indispensable for the individualization of justice.... Rules alone untempered by discretion cannot cope with the complexities of modern government and modern justice. Discretion is our principle source of creativeness in government and law.... In a government of men and of laws, the portion that is a government of men...often tends to stifle the portion that is a government of laws. Perhaps nine-tenths of injustice in our legal system flows from discretion and perhaps one-tenth from rules" (1971, p. 25). Most American law, Davis argues, springs from adjudication—from creativeness in the process of deciding particular cases: "The crucial point in the process is discretionary power to be creative in particular cases" (1971, p. 21). The very idea of individualized justice thus turns upon discretion (1971, p. 19): "When discretion shrinks too much, affirmative action is needed to recreate it. For many circumstances the mechanical application of a rule means injustice; what is needed is individualized justice; that is, justice which to the appropriate extent is tailored to the needs of the individual case. Only through discretion can the goal of individualized justice be attained" (1971, p. 19). The most fundamental characteristic of a trial, then, is the discretion available to the legal actors and their uses of it.

Discretion is a psychological matter. The judge exercises powers across the breadth of the trial process, only a few of which are specified by law; and few legal scholars would be comfortable with the claim that judicial discretion is unrelated to the judge's psychological processes. Trials have political aspects, for example, depending upon the party affiliations of the judge and prosecutor and their perceived publicity stakes in securing guilty verdicts. They display these aspects *not as pathological disintegrations but as routine features of daily conduct.* A judge's ruling on the admissibility of evidence may depend more upon his fears of being overturned (as a purely political matter) or upon his perceptions of the probity of the evidence than upon judgments about its legality. A prosecutor's decision to bring a case to trial may stem more from the case's difficulties vis-à-vis plea bargaining or from its publicity value than from any special judgments about the merits of the case per se. Thus with respect to Toulmin's desire to depsychologize argument, the discretionary aspects of the trial metaphor encourage a very different—quite psychological—approach to argument. The discretionary analogy implies that processes of argument directly reflect the processes of reasoning which produce them.

Psychologizing the Metaphor. As with the aesthetics example, Toulmin makes his case with respect to extremely broad and proportionately uninteresting features of the analogy. In approaching trials he paints, as we say, very broad strokes. Certain features are held to be common to all trials, be they civil or criminal: "There must be an initial stage at which the charge or claim is clearly stated, a subsequent phase in which evidence is set out or testimony given in support of the charge or claim, leading on to the final stage at which a verdict is pronounced" (Toulmin, 1958, p. 16). With this statement the robust analogy has paled considerably. Toulmin's words say little more than Aristotle's claim "you must state your case and you must prove it." At best Toulmin's statement describes a relatively trivial aspect of trials, their chronology, and says nothing about their content.

The legal analogy, saying nothing about trial content, does not contribute to the field notion. The statement that trials consist in chronological stages amounts to little more than saying "someone gets charged, arguments are made, testimony is given, decisions are reached." This notion is not interesting; nor is it descriptive of trials as they occur. This statement says nothing about the criteria for modal terms in trials, although a psychological approach to discretionary justice does hint at the criteria for applicability in terms like "probably," "possibly," and even "cannot."

Toulmin's legal analogy also does not seem to illuminate the nature of argument well. My formulation of the analogy suggests that the relationships between claims and the evidence for them is *always* psychological. "Leaps" from data to claims are movements made by thinkers—which means that they obey the matters of the thinkers' cognitive systems. These are discretionary leaps, if you will, which take their character from the definitions of situation and other interpretations made by the thinker. So the legal analogy must be "psychologized" to the extent that personal definitions are seen as fundamental to the decisional process. Every trial becomes a negotiated relational enterprise—a self-contained field in the sense that interpersonal relations create relationships and encounters which can be carved out of the broader social system. Trials borrow from the penumbra of meanings around case law; but stare decisis almost never consists of simple deductive reasoning from statutory law to the case at hand; in this respect trials are not analogous to individual experimentation in science, that is, they are *not*—nor were they intended to be—special cases of a general rule. Stone (1964), after arguing that stare decisis consists of *choice making* at the discretion of legal actors, stresses that the range of choice in the law is constantly expanding:

> For the universe of problems raised in judicial choices at the growing points of law is an expanding universe. The area brought under control by the accumulation of past judicial choices is, of course, large; but that does not prevent the area newly presented for still further choices by the changing social, economic, and technological conditions from being also considerable. And it has always to be remembered that many occasions for choice arise by the mere fact that no generation looks out on the world from quite the same vantage point as its predecessor, nor for that matter with the same eyes. A different vantage point, and different eyes, often reveal the need for choice-making where formerly no alternative, and perhaps not even any problem, were perceived at all. [P. 281]

The practices of legal actors are not deterministically shaped by the background assumptions of the profession or the weight of case law. Legal actors doubtless share values, traditional commitments, bodies of knowledge, and professional standards; but every trial is in certain fundamental senses unique—reflecting the exigencies of events, the purely personal definitions of situation made by the various legal actors.

Force and Criteria versus Meaning (Discretion). Our discretionary reformulation of the legal analogy assumes that the force of modal terms—again to use Toulmin's vocabulary—is not constant across trials; our arguments about discretion's prominence support this interpretation. My claim is that the notions of force and criteria blur into one another when the legal analogy is taken seriously. A term like "cannot," for example, is understood by Toulmin to imply a generalized injunction: "what is common to all the statements [that is, the implied sanctions] remains. Each of them can be written in the following pattern...: 'P being what it is, you must rule out anything involving Q; to do otherwise would be R, would invite S.' The form is common to all the examples: what vary from case to case are the things we have to substitute for P, Q, R, and S." Jurisprudential examples include statements such as "you can't force a defendant's wife to testify" (Toulmin, 1958, p. 29).

Thus Toulmin's focus is upon the rule structure, while the discretionary reformulation focuses upon individual interpretations. Now let us see what happens to this modal "cannot" vis-à-vis both interpretations. First, there are obvious exceptions to the statement, that is, "you cannot force a defendant's wife to testify unless in a divorce or other civil proceeding." In a divorce any spouse literally can refuse but in another—equally literal—sense cannot. Some judges refuse to find for litigants who refuse to testify; their preferences become well known; thus an informal rule outweighs formal legal protection. Discretion in every legal context sometimes means that defendants must routinely disregard many of their "rights" to meet the practical requirements of success. The state putatively "cannot" deprive defendants of trials, although it routinely does so through bargaining. Moreover, defendants routinely bargain away other "rights" in order to secure the best possible treatment from the state. The "cannots" in the structure of the law are thus vague outer limits or flexible guidelines rather than specific instructions guiding the conduct of legal activities. Pragmatically the force and criteria of "cannot" collapse to *meaning*.

There *are* "cannots" in the language of case law; but they are vivified by the "understandings" among legal actors and defendants which grease the operations of the system. We turn not to the language of the law so much as to the understandings among legal actors to grasp the essential form and content of the judicial process. Interpersonal understandings compose the framework of informal argumentative agendas and the implicit judgmental structure of the bargaining and trial proceedings. "Cannot," in sum, has *meaning*—which cannot be ignored.

The "Healthy" Legal System. The foregoing arguments all presuppose that discretion, not rule following, is the core characteristic of the legal system as it routinely operates and that our legal analogy ought to be based upon routine rather than ideal operations. The theoretic importance of this first assumption—which I think is decisive—is clear when we try to evaluate the examples, that is, try to decide whether they are in fact exemplars of the legal process or are "unhealthy" examples. Toulmin believes that "unhealthy" examples can be discarded; he stresses that his study is of the legal process in "a healthy state"—not in terms of its "pathological disintegrations." I shall defend two claims with respect to this statement: (1) the discretionary and extralegal aspects of trials are not pathological disintegrations; they are the core bases of trials, the routine procedures which make up the field;

moreover, this is as it ought to be, that is, a judicial system premised solely on precedent and containing no discretion would itself be pathological, and (2) while there is nothing wrong with pinning the metaphor to *ideal* processes, claims about descriptive accuracy cannot be made by virtue of the metaphor; and, as (1) implies, rigorous precedent following is *not* the most defensible ideal.

Perhaps the most interesting feature of the Scopes trial was its routine departure from traditional legal practices and principles. Both Bryan and Darrow used data and conclusions that were extralegal; indeed, some of their most important arguments were sociopolitical and theological. Bryan worked from a point of view that largely identified the interests of law and revealed religion, while Darrow worked from a freethinker's position, decidedly more political than legal, which viewed legal matters through the conceptual lens of civil libertarian political principles. Case law was not especially relevant; and few references to it proved decisive (or interesting). If we recall that the court had no *Sheppard* v. *Maxwell* guidelines to follow, the conduct of the trial—which took place in a volatile social context—was not unarguably an instance of "pathological disintegration." Indeed, the interplay of social, political, and legal issues—in ways that become clear below—was rather typical of the trial process although exaggerated by the publicity the trial received. The judge made no profound errors (though he might have been overturned on *Sheppard* grounds, had they been available); the defendant was found guilty of breaking a law he admitted to breaking; a minimal fine was imposed, reflecting the fact that the trial was an intentional test-case on the parts of both sides. It was, in sum, an attempt to affect precedent, but hardly an instance of precedent following.

The Leopold-Loeb murder trial similarly illustrates extralegal arguments occurring in a relatively well-conducted trial (which took place in the context of the most inflammatory sort of pretrial publicity and hostile community sentiment). We would stretch things perhaps too far to call the trial a disintegration. The verdict did not reflect the hostile climate of public opinion. Darrow's pleas for clemency were premised upon a popular rather than legal conception of justice. Case law is irrelevant to that classic summation and (as well) to the final decision. Yet it is not uncommon to see this trial used as a paradigm case of "getting justice." This example (and the Scopes trial) vivifies the preeminence of discretion; neither trial is unarguably a pathological disintegration.

My claim is not that precedent is irrelevant or unimportant but that discretion is far more important. It is the ordinary, routine, commonplace way precedents are selected and used to justify decisions made on entirely different grounds. Precedent is a way of rationalizing decisions already arrived at by processes peculiar to a trial. It affects individual trial agendas insofar as legal actors avoid "straying too far." "How will this work out on appeal?" is thus a recurring question. Precedent is a backdrop against which the trial plays itself out. But it is nothing more than a backdrop. Like all scenery, it supports the action, contributes to the mood, but supplies little of the dialogue. Every trial thus creates a particularized argument field. It builds its interactions out of such materials as the sociopolitical climate, the degree of publicity, the bargaining events which led to the trial, the prosecutor's motives, the judge's assumptions and procedures, the jurors' definitions of what it is to be a "juror," and the implicit background assumptions, the taken-for-granted scenery which facilitates communication.

Comparative Claims about the Two Legal Analogies. I can perhaps clarify the results of these arguments by setting forth a series of claims comparing Toulmin's rule-centered analogy with the discretionary analogy being defended here. This will permit further elaboration of the discretionary view as well as a clearer understanding of the implications one chooses to abide by in adopting one or the other analogy.

I. *Toulmin's analogy is prima facie trivial.* It says only that charges are made, evidence is produced, and decisions are reached. This obscures the means of argument as well as the meanings of arguments. The import of this analogy is that every claim carries an implicit or explicit burden of proof. But this says nothing substantive about why people in particular cases see one reason as better than another. The analogy is thus less explicit than our view of *presumption.*

Ia. *The discretionary analogy is nontrivial.* It says that all trials proceed when legal actors weigh competing claims on their attention and allegiance. Decisions are negotiated settlements springing from defined contexts. Trials are (thus) situations created by actors to accommodate to events. The discretionary judgments which permit a trial to proceed are thus exemplars of arguments in general. People rarely blindly follow rules—discretionary interpretations being the more common case. So the discretionary analogy directs our attention to these interpretive procedures.

II. *Toulmin's analogy does not describe the relation between general argumentation and particular arguments.* It makes arbitrary assumptions about the relation of jurisprudence to particular trials. But it is empirically implausible to say that trials are deductive instances of general principles of law, just as it is erroneous to claim that decisions are deductively derived from stare decisis.

IIa. *The discretionary analogy explains this relationship.* It more plausibly describes the relation of general jurisprudence to particular trials. The scenery metaphor is the key: precedent affects trials if legal actors think ahead to the accounts they will have to render to justify their acts; precedent is thus a rationalizing resource.

III. *Toulmin's analogy makes discretion a form of deviance.* If law is rule following, discretion is deviance. Rule following becomes the essence of jurisprudence and (thus) the model of legal argument.

IIIa. *The discretionary analogy makes rule following a special case of discretion.* This is more faithful to the empirical legal processes on which we want to model our views of argument. Davis's arguments are plausible; discretion is the core legal fact to respect—which makes rule following "deviant," to put the matter loosely.

IV. *Toulmin's analogy is an unattractive ideal.* A legal system of rule following would be a moral monstrosity. Rules can only generalize; trials particularize—which is inevitably a discretionary process.

IVa. *Discretion is a better ideal.* As Davis says, were there no discretion in the system, affirmative action would be needed to create it. Justice, equity, and fairness issue from situated choices people make; they cannot issue from rule following.

V. *Toulmin's analogy obscures argument as interaction.* The body of law is a conceptual ecology—which makes communication processes tangential to conceptual change. Since precedent is taken to be the central criterion, legal actors and their special interpretations are more or less interchangeable.

Va. *The discretionary analogy illuminates interaction.* Coorientations among actors are assumed to endow each trial with its character, to create its argument agenda. Each trial is unique owing to the definitions of situation which animate it.

VI. *Toulmin's analogy is tautologous vis-à-vis utterance.* It says that every claim must have a reason. The analogy is redundant.

VIa. *The discretionary view pins utterance to situated definitions.* The things people say mean many things, but they also mean what the speakers want them to mean and what the hearers take them to mean. If a text may contain meanings which would surprise the speaker, critics cannot exhaustively depend upon texts.

VIII. *Toulmin's analogy does not explain argument fields.* It treats "law" as a unified monolithic enterprise and thus obscures particular trials. We could understand "the law" but misunderstand a trial, just as we may understand behaviorism but not the arguments of a given behaviorist in a particular context. Only loosely could "the law" be said to be an argument field, that is, in the first sense of "issue field," defined earlier as the history of ideas.

VIIIa. *The discretionary analogy exemplifies argument fields.* The ongoing practices of legal actors are what make up trials. Trials *are* circumstances especially created to satisfy certain human purposes. Trials exemplify relational fields: they are negotiated circumstances created by the actors who work within them. I shall later argue that there are analogues to the trial at nearly all levels of human enterprise (compact through ordinary). If we take the pyramid at face value, the compact enterprises are those for which instances replicate or approximate quite closely the shared ideal. There is a narrow gap between the communal veridical/judgmental standards and the actual practices of actors within the enterprise. Compactness means that any individual trial exemplifies the "language of the law" construed broadly. The diffuse disciplines—to pursue our metaphor—hold different conceptions of trials; there are contending schools of thought, and we are apt to find several different varieties of trials. Moving down the pyramid, we encounter more diffusion; we would expect that trials would be unique in and of themselves. The ordinary fields would create their own argument fields across the normal processes of creating social relationships. Notice that we are using the jurisprudential analogy to illuminate the nature of argument fields rather than the reverse. This adds a conception of diffusion that we might otherwise have missed: law is a loose framework (akin in this respect to many other sociological traditions) within which myriad permutations occur, that is, discretionary latitudes are so broad that grasping the framework is not to grasp the individual situations. Toulmin, I think, believes the law to be more or less compact—at least as social enterprises go—whereas our arguments imply the reverse: it is of necessity diffuse because it is brought to life through the ongoing practices of legal actors.

IX. *Toulmin's analogy does not explain differences between "justified" practices and mere conventions.* As I said, the impartial standpoint of rationality has been left for the third volume of *Understanding;* and, if my arguments are sound, we are likely to get little more than some rehashed version of presumption, that is, the impartial standpoint is likely to be a substantively trivial proposition. Empirically, the legal analogy puts the torch to the impartial standpoint because legal knowledge *is* a matter of convention. Stare decisis, which ought to exemplify the stable and enduring core of the history of legal ideas, displays great variability vis-à-vis specific decisions. Moreover it is arguably the case that rule following per se is a poor exemplar of justification, that discretion is a superior model of situated arguments out of which justificatory statements spring.

IXa. *The discretionary analogy equates justification with convention.* Moreover, there are layers of convention envisioned by our analogy. One has broad professional conventions, the standards of professional conduct learned in law school, the contents of law books, and the social beliefs held about legal actors. There are the conventions of individual courtrooms, the practices of individual judges which compose the expectational frameworks of trials occurring within their courts. There are the sociological conventions of the communities within which trials occur; and we assume as a fundamental tenet of our analogy that trials are never held in vacuo apart from the social and political traditions of the communities. Again, our analogy does not assume corruption or criminal behavior on the parts of the legal actors: rather, the actors are, among other things, members of their communities; they proportionately reflect the prevailing standards and myths that bind communities together.

XI. *Toulmin's analogy does not work except by assuming an idealized legal logic.* If the analogy is to have descriptive power, we are forced to assume that individual trials are instances of generic legal language and logic. *Within* the field we have precisely the idealized logic that Toulmin has been at pains to attack across fields. Now, if there are no invariant logics, how are we to suppose that within fields logics are nonetheless invariant? Why should this be so? First, Toulmin would not assume it to be so in anything but the compact disciplines—which leads us back to the earlier claim that the analogy as he formulates it does not work unless law is presumed to be compact. Second, if the law is not a compact discipline—I assume that my arguments about the importance of ongoing activities are plausible—we are left with the uncomfortable belief that idealized logic is being arbitrarily assigned to the legal analogy.

XIa. *The discretionary analogy assumes that working logics are hashed out through the process of organizing trials.* There are doubtless commonalities across trials; but each trial negotiates its own argumentation standards, its permissible lines of argument, and its own judgmental/veridical standards. Such individuated justice is the whole point of trials. Were discretion not the core of the system, individual cases could be handled by clerks who check the facts of cases against checklists of criteria.

XII. *Toulmin's fear of relativism limits the usefulness of his analogy.* My claim is that he falls victim to his own criticisms of traditional logic. The plausibility of my arguments above determines the force of my claim here that his own words (aimed at traditional logic) stand as a criticism of his (1958) formulation of the legal analogy:

> [F]ormal logic has indeed lost touch with its application, and…a systematic divergence has in fact grown up between the categories of logical practice and the analyses given of them on logicians' textbooks and treatises.

...once, however, we recognize the sources of the deviation between working logic and logical theory, it becomes questionable whether these problems should have been raised in the first place. We are tempted to see deficiencies in these claims only because we compare them with a philosopher's ideal which is in the nature of the case unrealisable. The proper task of epistemology would be not to overcome these imagined deficiencies, but to discover what actual merits the arguments of scientists, moralists, art critics, or theologians can realistically hope to achieve.

The existence of this "double standard," this divergence between the philosopher's question about the world and the ordinary man's is of course a commonplace: no one has expressed it better than David Hume, who recognized both habits of mind in...himself. Usually the divergence has been treated as a matter of pride, or at any rate tolerance; as a mark (at best) of superior penetration and profundity in the thought of philosophers, or (at worst) as the result of a pardonable psychological quirk. It is almost mean of one to suggest that it may be, in fact, a consequence of nothing more than a straightforward fallacy—of a failure to draw in one's logical theorising all the distinctions which the demands of logical practice require. [Pp. 9–10]

Within jurisprudence this applies in spades to Toulmin's analogy. While there are commonalities across trials, an idealized logic cannot account for them. If these are important continuities, we shall surely come to recognize their status by virtue of how they are construed by actors in individual trials. *Working* logics are trial logics.

XIIa. *The logic and language of generalized jurisprudence are broad repositories of ongoing practices.* Here, my arguments parallel Toulmin's views of working logics. Generalized jurisprudence is merely a special accomplishment—possibly bearing little relation to any specific trial. For argumentation's purposes, it is thus the trial that is of interest, not the history of ideas of the field of law.

XIII. *Toulmin's analogy links the rendered verdict too closely to rule following.* His aim for the analogy is largely to expose the nature of rational decision making; but precedent following per se is an unattractive foreclosure of situated judgment. If rule following is the core attribute of rationality, the analogy is unneeded: a military metaphor is more appropriate. With respect to moral matters, Toulmin has stressed that situated judgment consists of dealing with the events at hand either by reference to a rule (if one is available) or by innovation. The same can be said of trials, although Davis's arguments would imply that reference to rules is a second-order line of reasoning. We need not insist upon dichotomizing the two, however.

XIIIa. *The discretionary analogy assumes that rules are selectively used.* Every trial hashes out its own balance between general rules and special adaptations to the events at hand. Trials decide, among other things, whether the strict application of a rule would be just. This is as it should be, since strict and invariant rule following would be unjust. Balancing a rule against the needs of the events at hand is a discretionary decision-making process that is not itself circumscribed by rules.

McKerrow (1980b) has objected that the juridical analogy and the conceptual ecology (Darwinian) analogy are not intended by Toulmin to describe the same phenomena. The juridical analogy is to focus upon the critical function of reason, while the ecological metaphor emphasizes population shifts in a conceptual ecology. If I understand this argument correctly, it sees the ecological metaphor as part of the history of ideas and the juridical metaphor as a communicational notion. While such a distinction might be successful, it is not quite Toulmin's intention. The legal analogy depends upon the common core of rules and assumptions that endow trials with stability and predictability: the "law" is itself a conceptual ecology which lends specific uses of it (trials) procedural and substantive stability. The analogy is thus incoherent unless a conceptual ecology is assumed. Trials are analogous to individual experiments in science by this reasoning; each individual act (in both cases) exemplifies the general field.

Moreover, McKerrow's argument misses a common thread in the two analogies, that is, ignores their shared enterprise in exposing the grounds of rationality. *Understanding* clearly ascribes rationality to the conceptual stability and innovation in rational enterprises. *Uses* ascribes the same properties to the judicial system. The *critical* function of the reason is surely no more exposed in trials than in scientific experiments (at least in Toulmin's view). On the whole, I am inclined to accept the analogical relation between experiments and trials.

Now, the exemplar of rationality is supposed to be the *considered* ways in which men change their minds: the standards of innovation they employ as well as their resistances to ill-considered ideas. The Darwinian analogy is full-blown here. The legal analogy does not work for Toulmin unless the same view is taken of trials: we are interested in the balancing act each trial creates, weighing rules against circumstances. *This implies that discretion resides at the core of legal rationality.* A discretion-free legal system would be the apotheosis of rationality.

XIV. *Toulmin's analogy blurs the width of discretionary parameters.* In spirit, trials exemplify rationality because of their common features—not their innovational qualities. If discretion is the core of the process—the argument might go—anarchy, chaos, and capriciousness are the hallmarks of the system. McKerrow has made this argument in terms with which I think Toulmin would agree: "Although judges may and do exercise discretionary power, they do so only within the context of an established set of precedents or guidelines for behavior. To say otherwise would be to convict judges of practicing whimsy or capricious judgment, and would reduce the judicial system to anarchy" (McKerrow, 1980b, p. 406). Hence, the "judge who roams too far" will be reprimanded, McKerrow argues, and "in ordinary argument, the person who roams too far is equally subject to the sanctions applied in the particular community he chooses to argue in" (1980b, p. 406).

Does McKerrow's thinking draw blood from the case for discretion? How are we to square this reasoning with Davis's arguments that discretion is the core process of law? One promising line is to weigh some ambiguities in the above argument carefully, for example, the notions of "roaming too far" and what constitutes "whimsy" and "capriciousness." Carefully considered, these terms suggest that McKerrow's argument is deficient: one can roam quite far without roaming "too far."

It is commonplace to say that precedents are broad parameters of action. We find such statements in many orders of legal texts and essays; and conventional wisdom has it that most sorts of precedents are actually quite broad. It is not altogether too fanciful to say that judges who avoid public drunkenness, sex scandals, and writing their opinions in iambic pentameter (as one judge recently did) are free to do most everything else in their courtrooms. A vast body of literature, for example, attests to the range of discretion in *sentencing*. The breathtaking array of sentences for the same crimes led many state lawmakers to pass minimum sentence laws: what had gotten one year's probation in one district was getting twenty-five to life in the next. Thus, "roaming too far" actually says little about discretion, since one can roam a great distance without going "too far." Further, what constitutes "too far?" Presumably writing a verdict on a prostitution case in poetry "goes too far," although this was a purely discretionary ruling, that is, there are no explicit rules prohibiting poetic verdicts. "Too far" often reflects nothing more than community (rather than legal) standards to such a degree that only the most bizarre and abhorrent actions are apt to be sanctioned by the legal system. The *Sheppard* trial went "too far"—but surely McKerrow would be uncomfortable in defending *Sheppard* as a typical instance.

There are, for all practical purposes, *no* restraints on prosecutorial discretion; the power to bring or not to bring charges (and to determine the nature of the charges) is a core determinant of the quality of justice. Prosecutors, if they can in any sense be said to be constrained, are held in check by the political forces in their communities rather than by legal rules. Only the most outrageous criminal behavior is apt to be sanctioned. None of the above arguments about discretion need to involve outrageous, criminal, or bizarre actions: this is why the phrase "abuse of discretion" is often used by appellate courts.

McKerrow's argument thus poses a false issue: discretionary parameters are exceptionally broad without entailing the extraordinary sorts of abuse he lists. No illegalities or moral outrages are entailed by discretionary decisions about (1) whether to charge; (2) what bargains to make about the nature of the charge; (3) what lines of testimony and orders of evidence to admit; (4) which arguments jurors should or should not hear; (5) how to instruct the jury; (6) what sentence to reach as well as which verdict is most appropriate. These are but broad labels for decision points which contain countless opportunities for discretionary judgments.

XIVa. *The discretionary analogy does not reduce to anarchy—it is not a caricature.* It rests on the argument that discretionary parameters are very broad—not on the assumptions that capriciousness and whimsy can rule trials. It is empirically difficult to distinguish legitimate discretion from whimsy, which tells us how broad discretion actually is. Moreover, the discretionary analogy does not imply that precedent is unimportant or that the history of legal ideas embodied in case law has no effect upon the conduct of trials. It says that precedents are picked up and used—selected according to how they serve the needs of the moment. Stare decisis is proportionately a rationalizing process. Legal actors may work with an eye to how well their actions can be rationalized, an influence not to be underestimated. In this respect our reasoning dovetails with Toulmin's belief that moral reason involves situated judgment about rules and unique features of a context. Our analogy assumes that there is a constant dialectic between case law and specific trials (explaining the stability across trials, their differences, and the indubitable fact that case law itself changes over time). Each trial is part of an ongoing interplay between rules and the needs for innovation; the rationality of the system—if such there be—resides precisely in the fact that this vital interplay is a feature of the discretionary scope available to legal actors. The evolutionary analogy works very well here, once we assume that a trial is an instance of pressure toward innovation and that the fact of discretion is what will ultimately be said to display or not to display rationality. Later, turning to moral implications of field theory, I shall make precisely this argument vis-à-vis ethical evaluation.

XV. *Toulmin's analogy reduces legal practices to instances of the language and logic of written law.* The definitions of situation made by legal actors are more or less irrelevant to the rendering of verdicts (if the analogy is to hold together). Intentional meanings must be more or less equated with conventional meanings. Thus, law reduces to the written documents of the field.

XVa. *The discretionary analogy assumes that conventions are selectively used.* Definitions of situation lead to the selection of certain intentional meanings rather than others; every trial negotiates its special meanings; no trial is "just a carbon" of the general language of the law. Adaptations to convention can be convenient facades employed by legal actors to justify decisions they have reached by very different means. Exhaustive focus upon conventional legal language will proportionately ignore context-embedded speech: individual trials will be commensurately misunderstood.

Rules, Roles, Relations, and Situations. These comparative arguments presumptively prove the wisdom and attractions of a discretionary legal analogy. These claims dovetail into the emerging theory of utterance and argument fields. They cohere as well with the methodological views appropriate to the field theory, namely, with *triangulating* (Denzin, 1970) toward fields of discourse with a variety of interpretive as well as causal research methods. The indubiety of discretion weighs, I think, against claims for the primacy of convention. It does not make conventions unimportant, just as our field theory does not. It merely insists that conventions are animated in situations.

The discretionary analogy is a superior conceptual lens through which to view an array of social practices. It more satisfactorily accounts for the key elements (and their interplay) of situated decision making. Let us say that the following terms best express these key elements: *rules, roles, relations,* and *situations.* Our faith in symbolic interaction and personal construct theory combined with our doubts about deterministic accounts lead to the following theoretic statements about these terms.

Rules (in law and everything else) are explicit and implicit. Explicit rules are typified by written documents; and they share the characteristic of being generic rather than specific, that is, we do not possess a law against murdering John Doe because he is sleeping with our spouse, but we possess a generic sanction against murder. Now, if I kill John Doe, the court does not blindly apply some rule schedule to the act to arrive at an appropriate point on a checklist to determine the appropriate verdict. *Justice* is not, as it were, contained in the rule; it is created through judicial discretion. My claim that killing Doe was justified and that I thus merit mercy is not per se a legal claim: it is an invitation to examine the circumstances; and we are usually rather willing to say that a trial which ignores the purported circumstances cannot produce justice.

Roles are both sociological labels and personal constructions of public expectations. There are public standards for the behavior of "prosecutor," "defendant," "lawyer," "juror," and "judge," although these are not explicitly codified in a written code. Judicial rules of conduct are especially broad prohibitions (and sanctions) for the most extreme versions of "misfeasance, malfeasance, and nonfeasance." Personal definitions thus exert decisive influence upon the actual practices of legal actors: the prosecutor construes, for example, community expectations; and he might well decide that they outweigh abstract legal definitions. Defendants also weigh competing role definitions and arrive at some satisfactory balance between legal expectations and the needs of the moment. Lawyers must often tread careful lines between protecting their clients and breaking laws; and they occupy ambiguous roles as counselors and officers of the court. Their personal balancing acts, then, are what lead to their actions. There is a vast body of literature attesting to the complexity of the jurors' self-definitions, the influence they take from other legal actors, and their final balancing of social expectations versus their personal definitions of the issues at hand. For them, the term "role" exemplifies their personally constructed definitions of the perspectives of others. Finally, the judge weighs understandings of "what it is to be a judge" against personal political ambitions, social pressures, and abstract notions of the requirements of "justice." It is thus empirically unfaithful to reduce legal actors to passive occupiers of structurated social roles—more or less interchangeable units of a larger social structure.

Relations are only broadly specified in written law, that is, judges cannot have financial interests in the cases at hand, and so forth. The career relationships between attorneys and judges, their interactions over hundreds of trials, directly affect their relationships in any given trial. We shall not go too far wrong in assuming that legal actors display the same order of relations with other people that we customarily ascribe to social actors in general. To assume that these interlaced relations are somehow bracketed or tossed aside as legal actors enter the courtroom is surely naive. Perhaps the most clear-cut example presently available would be pornography cases in which explicit law now holds "contemporary community standards" to be the touchstones of judgment for deciding whether certain materials are offensive. Here we have the language of the law specifically asking judges to remain "citizens of their communities." Presumably, opinion polls or the judges' intuitive sense of community will are to stand as the criteria for judgment. In general, it seems reasonable to assume (as we do with respect to each of the other key terms) an ongoing dialectic between a person's definitions of social expectations, legal expectations, that is, the standards of the professional guild, and personal goals.

Situations are only broadly circumscribed by written law, in the sense that *Sheppard* v. *Maxwell* or *Nebraska Press Association* broadly describe the grounds of permissible press coverage. Every *rule* and *role,* however, is open to alternative construction, depending upon a given definition of situation. Justice is a product of the system that does not spring from rules, roles, or relations so much as from the definitions of situation made by the relevant legal actors. It does not seem too farfetched to say that trials are in fact negotiative processes for arriving at definitions of the situations that led to trial. *Relations,* of course, often comprise background assumptions of definitions of situation; and as such, they are part of the assumptive framework upon which individual trials are built and sustained.

To recapitulate, a satisfactory legal analogy must accord discretion its due. Toulmin's analogy makes structuralistic assumptions about the rules, roles, relationships, and definitions of situation that make up trials. It assumes that individual trials are special cases of general rules and that situated legal reasoning is a special case of the conventional legal code. It emphasizes the enduring core of statute and tradition at the expense of innovative adaptations to situations. The reformed analogy emphasizes that the field of law is an issue field (à la history of ideas) animated by particular relational and encounter fields (trials and bargains). Discretion is the most satisfactory paradigm case of rational action: it emphasizes the adaptive character of judgments, the ways conventions are brought to bear upon circumstances and fitted to the needs at hand. So reformed, the analogy augments our developing view of argument fields.

Ordinary Issue Fields

The jurisprudential analogy proves that issue fields should not be confounded with relational and encounter fields and that the relational field—embodied in the reformed trial metaphor—is the central concern of argumentation. In its disciplinary guise an issue field is a discipline's history of ideas, the backdrop for its practices.

It is now appropriate to elaborate the ordinary sense of issue fields and to consider whether the claims made of disciplines apply equally to them. In general I want to argue that they do and that individual arguments cannot be equated with impersonal conceptual ecologies.

With respect to ordinary fields, we shall have to tolerate considerably more diffusion and looseness because ordinary fields take ideas from many different disciplines and put these ideas to work in the service of aims peculiar to the sphere of action. By *ordinary issue field* I mean the public issues around which people unite and the social movements which they enter. Obvious names come to mind: the Moral Majority, the pronuclear lobby, the proabortion and antiabortion movements, creationism, ecology, the military-industrial complex, astrology, the dope culture, and the like. These are complex fields because they draw data and claims from a myriad of disciplines. They choose the facts they draw upon according to their particular purposes. Those who favor or oppose abortion thus might draw from sociology, psychology, ethics, theology, police science, and medicine (to name a few), depending on the sorts of claims they want to make. The proabortion and antiabortion movements possess no disciplinary counterpart (while other ordinary fields, for example, antinuclear power movements, do). If ordinary advocates use the generalizations of one discipline to contradict the claims of another (for example, "these biological facts contradict that claim of Catholic theology"), there exist no accepted veridical or judgmental standards for adjudicating the dispute. The theological perspectives may be the only ones that assume for themselves overarching status, the "right" to settle disputes between conflicting disciplinary claims. This self-assigned status is itself a matter of controversy—meaning that the abortion issue is largely a dispute about the nature and scope of an argument field.

Notice that instead of calling "abortion" a field we are (roughly) dividing up its warring camps. The data and claims of the proabortion and antiabortion sides are too incommensurable for us to lump them together. It is more plausible to say that one's orientation to an issue constitutes one's entry ticket into an issue field. There are (possibly) five or six identifiable positions on abortion. Insofar as these positions take different things to be facts (and assess what can count as a fact in different ways), they are distinguishable ordinary issue fields.

Let us call one of the positions the "Catholic View." Our assumption is that for those defining themselves as Catholics, the antiabortion message is spoken (as it were) with a single voice. This statement uses a special view of the facts which is at odds with most of the other abortion-related fields. The facts in this field have their guarantor in authority: the fact that a fetus is a complete human being depends not on biology but on dogma. If one believes in papal infallibility (or an orthodox variant thereof) one has one's facts ready made as doctrinal matters. For our purposes, the most relevant facts are not the biological nature of the fetus but the nature of Church authority (that is, the sociological patterns of allegiance to authority, the communication strategies that hold the Church together). These are the topoi on which "right to life" arguments are premised; they affect every interaction insofar as one's self-definition is shaped by defining oneself as a Catholic.

Let us call another of the abortion positions the "women's movement." Here the relevant beliefs are about neither the fetus nor authority. The core assumptions are about the autonomy of women and the implied limitations of the powers of government to dictate personal choices. Thus *rejection of authority* is a central line of argument. With respect to virtually every "Catholic" belief, the women's movement takes positions that cannot be reconciled. Neither side abides by a judgmental standard by which the opposing positions could be adjudicated. We have (in a catch phrase) incommensurable paradigms. Arguers in either field, when they confront the foe, act as caricatures of Kuhn's scientists working under the aegis of different paradigms. They do not share enough common assumptions to argue productively. Neither side is likely to win converts from the other. Both sides therefore aim their appeals at "the public."

Goodnight (1981) has argued that the pervasiveness of argument fields (and the specialized assumptions and truth conditions they embody) threatens to destroy "the public." He is likely correct in this estimate. When advocates of these two abortion fields address the public, they do not submit to judgmental and veridical standards common to the public; they refuse to be judged except by their own field standards. Thus, for example, advocates of technological programs (antiballistic missile systems, defense spending, cost-benefit accounting for health and education) hold themselves accountable not to the public but to their fields. Of course, the public is not a thing but an abstraction, and it is difficult to guess what the public's judgmental standards might be. Likely, field actors bring their own special standards to bear upon issues when they see themselves as part of the public. Goodnight has nonetheless posed a problem of considerable importance—one which field studies may be able to solve. If there are recurring argument practices that work out for the best across fields, these are standards worthy of the public. A general theory of argumentation may thus be inferred from field practices (corresponding to the special sense of presumption defended here).

I shall elaborate the case for this toward the end. It seems to me that the truth conditions of claims cannot, for the public, reside in particular disciplines. If it does, we shall have nuclear power engineers claiming special privilege and recombinant DNA researchers believing they are accountable only to their colleagues. The public is a useful abstraction, therefore, for displaying the sorts of generalizations we want to draw from field studies. To prove this, I shall emphasize the notion of deciding *which fields merit attention*—not which ones are "right," but which ones ought to be listened to.

To return to the main thread of argument: our approach to ordinary issue fields makes no assumptions about the orientations of individual arguers to them. We do not expect to find the professional collegiality common to the professions; nor do we expect to find the epistemic goal of "getting better." A Catholic arguer is not interested in making dogma epistemically better; he is interested in picking it up and using it for particular purposes. What is key here is that he defines himself as a Catholic. There are certainly normative elements to Catholic theology (to which I shall shortly turn). What is of interest here is that the ordinary issue field notion can stand without assuming professional or collegial relations among actors.

The true believer is of interest politically, rhetorically, and ethically, but is not central to definitions of ordinary fields. It is plausible to assume that it is a characteristic not of a field but of a person which leads to fanaticism. While true believers are of intrinsic interest and while our field theory might yield insights into their orientations to issues, our definition of issue fields does not need to be tied to them.

The critical aim is thus to understand arguments (partly) by fitting arguers and their claims into their sociological niches. If one analyzes abortion arguments, it is surely necessary to know that one speaker is a Catholic, another a liberationist, and to know how seriously they take these labels. We need *not* assume that a Catholic perfectly replicates Catholic theology (likewise with any speaker and field). As we argued with respect to the disciplines, we need only assume that ordinary issue fields are preliminary guesses about what A means when A *says* X. Ultimately, we must know how a speaker *uses* a field's ideas (which is why we have termed criticism a form of role taking).

Normative Fields

We require a concept that explains the tissues of orthodoxy and rhetorical alignment that bind argument fields together. The idea of normative fields may serve this aim if we clearly specify at the outset that we are not adding another real social entity to our list. We need instead a particular analytic focus upon these fields, a way of looking at them that illuminates the ways they hang together. Thus, by normative field I mean something akin to the traditional sociological notion of "reference groups." It should apply in equal measure to ordinary and disciplinary fields of every sort.

The normative field notion entails two distinct but interdependent levels of explanation for the existence of fields. First, it emphasizes the bare fact that communal traditions of practices are organized around shared ideals and norms. In this sense, to know a field is to know its cardinal virtues, its paradigm cases of excellence, its exemplars. Second, the normative field notion directs our attention to the rhetorical bases of norms and ideals, the ways they tie the actions of different people together, the ways they countenance and justify particular activities.

On the basis of the interactionist view of group life, I assume that when we choose to look at the reference group functions of argument fields, we shall not regard them as static structures with rigid and easily identifiable characteristics (of which the individual is a facsimile). The first crude formulations of reference group theory failed because they stipulated that structure determined activities; they considered broad structural schemes at the expense of ongoing activities. They posed such a deterministic view that they could not explain: (1) how and why individuals deviate from groups, (2) how and why individuals maintain memberships in many groups and how they weigh off or prioritize group allegiances, and (3) how and why groups change over time. They assumed as well that social boundaries were straightforward, rigidly defined, and easily described. Because they saw individual activities as determined by the structures, they did not focus upon the ways individuals move in and out of groups, organize their activities within groups, and balance their obligations to and trust in different groups. They lacked, in sum, the organizing benefits of the "psychological field."

It seems more sound to think of "reference" groups as communal traditions people refer to, for one reason or another. This leads us to ask about their reasons and the sources of their faith. We shall want to say that people refer to communities of discourse because they define particular situations in appropriate ways. It follows ex hypothesi that *it is the nature of relational and encounter fields that illuminates the character of normative fields rather than the reverse.* The nature of norms is bound to be academic unless one can account for their influence; and one cannot explain normative influences without looking at situated actors making use of them.

Within the disciplinary fields, compact through diffuse, we should not be surprised to find intricate, interwoven patterns of normative influences. Any professional will take norms from professional associations (as Toulmin stipulates), collegial circles (which may differ greatly from the professional associations, that is, the person may be a member of a splinter or special interest group), institutional colleagues, political and social associations, and perhaps many other lines of influence. The physician may ask what it is to be "a physician—in a philosophic sense," a member of the American Medical Association, a Catholic physician, a member of the right-to-life interest group, and so forth. The list could be as broad as an individual's range of interests. The same list could be drawn up for any professional.

It is the individual cognitive system that makes sense of these interwoven influences, that is, defines them, decides their applicability to situations, and resolves incompatibilities between them. The "liberal—Democrat—Baptist—Chief of Gynecology—at a Catholic hospital—serving essentially Catholic clients" may have some interesting thinking to do with respect to a public position on the abortion issue. The "atomic physicist—liberal—Democrat—employee of the N.R.C. (National Research Council)" may have an equally cumbersome weighing task if he has doubts about nuclear power. Now, it is definitions of situation that force these individuals to weigh their values against one another; the physician and the physicist can ignore their ambiguous positions as long as no events occur to challenge some part of their normative structures. It is thus by accommodating to situations that the physician and the physicist will be forced to weigh values; it is through arguments that this weighing process is sometimes made public.

The same reasoning applies in spades to the ordinary fields. While some people doubtless select some reference group as an unyielding standard against which to assess other arguments, others demonstrably do not. For some, being a Catholic resolves all ambiguities about abortion, while for others, because they have already doubted that structure for other reasons, being a Catholic is not sufficient. They innovate, as it were—ad hoc their way toward some accommodation to the abortion issue. If this indeed happens, it more or less follows that we will best understand norms by understanding how individuals use them—applying them intact or modifying them or even disavowing them—to deal with situations.

This may suffice to introduce the normative field notion. We shall return to the claim that fields are essentially rhetorical in fleshing out the alternative theory. I leave for the last chapter a discussion of the far-reaching consequences of this thinking, for example, the powerful relativity described by this view and its implications for interfield disputes. The organizing question there will be whether one field can—in any justified sense—evaluate the claims of another. Since criticism is itself a field, can critics "justify"—by their own standards—evaluating the activities in other field?

*Depsychologizing Argument: To Refute Emotivism Is Not to
Refute Subjectivism*

Our developing account of the various senses of "field" assumes that
meanings are situationally defined and intended toward. So viewed,
arguments are psychological processes; and to study them, we must
inevitably grapple with subjective meanings. Hence, at the level of
loose labels, our program differs from Toulmin's by virtue of rejecting
his aim of "depsychologizing" argument. Yet, the distinctions to be
drawn here are not quite so straightforward, and it is perhaps now
appropriate to draw our distinctions as carefully and explicitly as we
can.

Toulmin distinguishes—and I agree—between logic as a public form
of utterance and inference as private thought or ratiocination. This
distinction works well enough as long as we avoid untenable assumptions about the characteristics of logic. If we assume, as I think
Toulmin does, that logic takes its character from language, then we are
bound to confuse conventional and intentional meanings. If, that is,
argumentation is restricted to the study of conventional meanings
displayed in the structure of language and speech acts, it will miss the
very character of *situated utterance*. If one only grants that any conventional utterance "contains" alternative choices for interpretation and
that situated actors attach intentional meanings by virtue of their
definitions of situation, then one is more or less forced to admit that
purely conventional accounts are relatively worthless as sources of
information about situated speech acts. I therefore choose to construe
the logic-inference distinction as a "public-private" dichotomy and
nothing else, that is, the distinction reveals nothing per se about either.
We have no secure bases for believing that thought is nothing but silent
speech, just as we cannot prove that speech is equivalent to thought. I
shall not bother to try to prove either, since given the present view, the
public-private distinction obscures the essential differences between
ratiocination and speech.

It is apparent from this difference that Toulmin and I do not agree
about what is at issue when there is discussion of depsychologizing
argument. Subjectivism is, for him, thorough surrender, the counsel of
despair; for me it constitutes the starting point of argumentation
theory. "Psychology" is thus equated with subjective "doctrine" and
rejected. "Subjectivism" for Toulmin is a philosophic doctrine which
despairs of impartiality—a categorical surrender to solipsism. My
view is that solipsism is the natural state of affairs which many activities aim at "solving"—overcoming, ameliorating, bridging.

Toulmin attacks the subjective doctrine for an obvious defect: it it is
true, there is nothing to be said when two people disagree about the

value of an object or action. Indeed, "no subjective theory can give any account of what is a good reason for an ethical judgment, or provide any standard for criticising ethical reasoning" (1964, p. 29). Two things need to be said about these pronouncements: (1) they ignore the capacity of field theory to define and explain the grounds and warrants of arguments within fields—thus without further work, field theory is sufficient to explain given orders of situations while assuming that no ethical universals—except perhaps the fact of ethical judgment—are possible; and (2) Toulmin is attacking an especially vulnerable version of subjectivism, that is, behaviorism. This last point merits elaboration, since it serves to identify more clearly the points of dispute.

Toulmin's exemplars of the subjective doctrine are Ayer and Stevenson—the emotivists—which means that subjectivism is construed uniquely in terms of moral *responses*. Stated pejoratively, when a person says "*X* is good," he does nothing more than describe the state of his glands. Thus, "if X is a word for a subjective relation, and two people are asked, 'is this X?' they will answer in logically *independent* ways: each will say whether X describes the effect of the object on *him*. They may without contradiction give opposing answers..." (1964, p. 32). Comparisons are thus impossible if subjective statements are logically independent.

This is an unfairly narrow vision of the possibilities of psychological accounts or "subjectivism." Stevenson and Ayer produced accounts which assumed the value of psychological behaviorism—moral statements, so viewed, are *responses*. Our own view, based upon constructivism and interactionism, says that all of the main assumptions of behaviorism were false or poorly stated. Higher mental processes—at a minimum—are not *responses* but *predictions*, that is, in the sense that all behavior is experimental. The man-as-scientist metaphor is at the forefront of our thinking here. Moral statements are like all other statements in at least this respect: they are implicit predictions rather than passive responses.

One can thus be a thoroughgoing relativist and not commit oneself to any version of emotivism. The man-as-scientist metaphor, in fact, leads to a conception of moral reasoning that permits agreement with Toulmin's (1964) description of situated judgment:

> Given two conflicting claims...one has to weigh up, as well as one can, the risks involved in ignoring either, and choose "the lesser of the two evils." Appeal to a single current principle, though the primary test of the rightness of an action, cannot therefore be relied on as a universal test: where this fails, we are driven back upon our estimate of the probable consequences. And this is the case, not only where there is a conflict of duties, but also, for instance, in circumstances in which, although no

> matter of principle is involved, some action of ours can nevertheless meet another's need....
>
> So it comes about that we can, in many cases, justify an individual action by referring to its estimated consequences. Such a reference is no substitute for a principle, where any principle is at issue: but moral reasoning is so complex, and one has to cover such a variety of types of situation, that no one logical test (such as appeal to an accepted principle) can be expected to meet every case. [P. 147]

Such situated balancings, to be sure, are characteristic of life; we assume an ongoing dialectic between general rules and situational/ innovational necessities. The man-as-scientist metaphor thus permits each key link in this reasoning. Our only caveat, although it may be unnecessary, is that general rules will be field dependent—rooted in the facts of individual fields. This reasoning implies, incidentally, that one will best understand the ranges of convenience of general rules once one grasps their interplays with given definitions of situation.

Hence we can share with Toulmin the distinction between two sorts of moral reasoning. Faced with conflicting claims, a person can appeal either to an accepted principle (staying with the man-as-scientist metaphor, say, a "law") or seek to assess the probable consequences of the claims, that is, reason that X will lead to Y (that is, he can frame hypotheses and test them). We thus have reasons for individual acts distinguished from reasons for social practices—both realms being assumed to feed into one another in the sense that reasons for social practices represent the long-term experience of a society (or field) exemplified by a lawlike statement, for example, on the whole, and with some exceptions, honesty is the best policy.

Toulmin's attack upon subjectivism is thus not a strong case against psychological approaches to argument. He attacks only a narrow and especially vulnerable brand of psychology—emotivism, rooted as it is in behaviorism—and seems to hold all versions of relativism hostage to the admittedly unattractive implications of emotivism. I incline to Emmet's (1966) distinction between "hard" and "soft" relativism; and her distinction is worth elaborating here because it points the way toward defending relativism while rejecting the chief assumptions of behaviorism:

> Relativism in the "hard" form would be the view that moral principles are causally dependent on something else.... In a "soft" form it would be the view that, although there are distinctive moral factors, these are interrelated within a culture with other factors...so that they vary according to these. The difference between the "hard" and "soft" forms of relativism would be that for the former, morality is a resultant of other things; for the latter, there are genuine moral elements in a culture, but the form these take will be affected by other elements and vice versa,

while the whole complex will make up a particular culture with its social structure. [P. 91]

Like Emmet, I incline to the soft version; and her development of the notions of "rules," "roles," and "relations" fits nicely into our own thinking about how situated actors, through their ongoing defining activities, give form and meaning to these phenomena. Behavior within these concepts need not be construed as "responsive" in any behavioristic sense.

This is why I have stipulated that role taking is the fundamental resource of critics and researchers. One understands the facts of a field by participating in it. Bruyn (1966) thus argues that an observer studies meanings which exist in the minds of people other than himself by empathetically taking their roles as though they were his own; he participates in "the natural processes of communication extant in the culture he studies." One "goes native"—as it were—to understand the unique communication system of a field. One tries, that is, so far as is possible, to become socialized into the field under study. Every field should display its unique "rules, roles, and relations" and special understandings about situations. These are unique to fields because they are themselves shaped by the ongoing communicational practices unique to the fields. If one can become socialized into the communicational practices of a field, one will come to understand the background assumptions which make up the rules, roles, relations, and situations which are unique to given fields.

The goal of "psychologizing" argument, then, is a matter of putting first things first. Arguments—as they happen empirically—*are* psychologically grounded, that is, they are psychological coorientations when we construe them as interactions and they are intended-toward utterances when we treat them as statements or "argument products." Constructive alternativism suggests that any statement is capable of being alternatively construed; and, if this is so, then critics and researchers are engaged in role taking par excellence. They must therefore be able to defend their attributions to the perspectives of the situated actors they study. *This* is the hard "fact" of relativism which we must respect: statements occur in situations and are intended toward by speakers according to their definitions of situation. It is this hard fact which confronts argumentation and which field theory should equip our domain for solving.

To recapitulate, relativism is a problem, not a solution—although we often see it used as a solution to the problems of absolutism. Our view is that relativism is the indubitable fact of human interaction with which argumentation must deal, that is, by explaining the ways situated actors in fact do overcome subjective limitations, the ways they create objectivity out of the materials of social intercourse. Toulmin has attacked only a special—and especially weak—version of relativism (emotivism) which is based upon behaviorism. Since no assumption is made here that human behavior is primarily responsive, it is untenable to claim that moral (or other) normative statements are responsive. Situated humans are creative and innovative. Rules, roles, relations, and situations are *interpreted*, and argumentation is most centrally the study of such interpretations. An argument field (in the senses elaborated here) is nothing more than a group's publicly articulated interpretations. Only by fiat will philosophers arrive at a conception of fields "untainted" by psychology: fields exist in the ongoing activities of the people who work within them. These activities are psychologically grounded. The goal of "depsychologizing" argument amounts to saying that we want to account for human social life without reference to psychological statements. This is a bizarre closure of our thinking and a point of view that will serve argumentation poorly. It is tantamount to saying that we want a theory of communication untainted by the facts of social life.

The man-as-scientist metaphor is our particular conception of relativism. It describes the socially grounded human dealing with uncertainties in a future that needs predicting. The study of the ways men ameliorate or learn to live with the problems of relativism is the study of alternative approaches to knowledge, since knowledge is nothing more than human creations. These approaches are artifices different fields have contrived to deal with the phenomena that interest them. Since such contrivances cannot be understood apart from their uses in situations, the case for holism remains convincing. The psychological and sociological senses of "field" are interdependent; each explains the other.

The Alternative View

The tapestry is perhaps sufficiently complete and the skeletal outline of the figure upon it sufficiently clear for us to put flesh on the bones. This will be a complex proceeding because the figure is a multidimensional one. No neat singular definitions can describe it, and no single side of it can adequately depict it. We shall have to surround it, rather in the manner of cinema Indians circling a wagon train, and check our thinking from time to time by occupying particular wagons in the circle to regard the circling Indians.

We want to distinguish among real social entities in ways that bear usefully upon epistemic matters. This will prove tricky because no single encompassing principle is at hand to give us an objective stance that also respects the differences and interrelationships among fields. In various ways and to different degrees, every field uses induction, deduction, arguments from analogy and sign, qualitative and quantitative data, scientific and humanistic arguments; their languages have grammar, syntax, and semantic orders that often do not differ; their procedures and practices are sometimes similar enough to make us wonder whether the field idea can be sustained at all.

Quite apart from the problem of distinguishing among fields in ways that respect their differences is the problem of selecting distinctions appropriate to the empirical and analytic work we want the field construct to guide. Our capacity to distinguish among human groups and practices is virtually limitless. As the sheer variety of competing rubrics attests, the purposes for which we draw distinctions often differ. The minimum condition of a successful field theory, then, is that we be able lucidly to specify the sorts of distinctions it uses, how these relate to other distinctions in the literature, and the sort of work we expect our particular distinctions to perform.

Distinctions and Distinctions

Doing field theory is a way of insisting upon particular distinctions for particular purposes. In itemizing the characteristics of argument fields, one moves from distinction to distinction—some being empirical distinctions among the situated practices and traditions of actors in real social organizations, others being normative distinctions among the postures critics and analysts can take. While these are different distinctions, some being theoretical, while others are metatheoretical, they should be of a piece, part of a unified epistemological package. Let us consider how they may be made so.

The numerous rubrics for distinguishing among groups and practices (see the introduction) by no means form a unified body of theory or knowledge. They use distinctions that sometimes overlay and overlap one another, that sometimes differ in kind and cut differently, that are sometimes redundant, and that are sometimes incompatible. Some distinctions, in fact, bear no envisionable relation to some of the others (for example, while an epidemiologist might distinguish between smokers and nonsmokers who live in New Jersey, it is hard to see how this would fit with, say, people who believe in behaviorism versus people who believe in Freudianism). The purposes of the distinctions differ so greatly that a field theory will have to pick and choose from a Chinese menu of distinctions.

Perhaps the worst way of selecting distinctions is to think in terms of hierarchies. Consider, for example, the relationships among three sorts of distinctions. Ethnographers distinguish "speech communities" which are said to be built from norms for language use. When we see a group of people sharing "rules for the conduct and interpretation of speech, and rules for the interpretation of at least one linguistic variety," we have a speech community (Hymes, 1972, p. 54; Gumperz, 1962). Comparative ethnography thus utilizes particular distinctions which facilitate ethnographic and linguistic studies across communities. These distinctions, however, differ greatly from (and thus blur if we blend them together) certain sociological distinctions, for example, among groups and institutions, among disciplines and rational enterprises, and among social movements. These distinctions, which cross the linguistic boundaries of the ethnographer, do different work and serve different interests. The relation between ethnographic and "institutional" distinctions is so unclear that we cannot confidently say whether they are compatible or not. Now add to this confusion a third sort of distinction: the various schemes for distinguishing among practices and groups by virtue of rhetorical principles. Viewed one way these schemes fit either the ethnographic or the sociological distinctions; viewed another way they fit neither. We might define a rhetorical community by virtue of its leaders and spokesmen, the frequency of interaction of its actors, its totems and pieties, and its recurring definitions of situation. Except for frequency of interaction (which is discredited on other grounds), we can construe the rhetorical elements ethnographically, sociologically, or in markedly different ways, for example, by saying that rhetorical elements cross ethnographic and sociological boundaries.

These three ways of distinguishing among groups and practices ought to mesh but do not. Each is an intuitively plausible account which guides promising empirical work. But as empirical descriptions, each account's distinctions so overlay or overlap the others' distinctions that it is hard to make sense of their fit. One obvious solution would be to cast them into an Aristotelian hierarchy. Many field theorists, I think, have some such arrangement of fields in mind. But a hierarchy poses insuperable difficulties. The regnant set of distinctions—whichever of the three we choose—will blur the valuable distinctions of the others, for example, the speech community notion obscures the boundaries of rhetorical and sociological communities, the sociological boundaries would blur the rhetorical and ethnographic, and so on. To arrange empirical descriptions in hierarchies presupposes that clear genus-species relations can be drawn; but the three present examples can be alternatively construed (depending on our assumptions) to be genus to and species of each of the others.

Think of a field theory as a particular selection of distinctions. While there are countless distinctions among groups and practices that might be made, a field theory picks and chooses certain distinctions that combine to accomplish particular purposes. Thus the ethnographic, sociological, and rhetorical accounts do not have to mesh, given certain aims. By the present view the sociological and rhetorical accounts take precedence over the ethnographic, not in the spirit of ruling ethnography out, but because we want to focus upon substantive domains. If (say) the rules of conversational implicature (Grice, 1975; Jacobs and Jackson, 1982) seem invariant in our field scheme, to cross field boundaries, this does not make them less interesting; it merely rules them out of the ways we have chosen to define field boundaries.

Our purposes are epistemic; one of our aims is to understand interfield differences in methods of passing muster on knowledge claims; another aim is to understand interfield disputes. We must select distinctions appropriate to these tasks. The case for holism (that is, for aligning the psychological and sociological senses of "field") leads us to think of fields as real sociological entities. This in turn yields a principle for selecting distinctions appropriate to an epistemic field theory: the distinctions drawn by social actors will be of central interest. We are not limited to these, but empirical work can start with them. If someone says, "I am a Freudian psychologist," we focus upon both labels. "Psychologist" may define someone's normative field; "Freudian" may define the issue field. Toulmin's disciplinary approach captures only the former, while we have attached considerable epistemic importance to the latter.

Every distinction has the virtue of calling our attention to something and the defect of obscuring other things. In critiquing Toulmin's reliance upon academic divisions, I proposed that issue fields cross academic boundaries in important ways and are obscured when we think of the world as having the shape of a university catalog. I also argued that Toulmin's distinctions obscured interfield borrowing, importations of the Indeterminacy Principle being a paradigm case. These criticisms amount to saying that Toulmin's distinctions obscure more than they illuminate for epistemic purposes.

Thus while field theories might be based upon a variety of assumptions, the focus here is upon this intuition: people who move in different social organizations focus upon different substantive "bodies of knowledge" and take things to be knowledge in different ways because they engage in practices that in some respects evaluate knowledge differently. They are substantive domains possessing enough unique characteristics that we can define them; but they are rarely "sovereign" entities (cf. K. Farrell, 1981). To the contrary, our expectation is that the most interesting things about fields are their overlaps, interminglings, borrowing practices, and disputes.

Relations among Field Theories

The problem arises of deciding what sorts of claims our framework can yield. If particular distinctions of other field theories successfully fit into our own framework, do we want to make combative claims about the primacy of our view over the other rubrics? Are we entering the bustle and clamor of competing theories with the aim of creating a voice that will silence the others? Since all of the rubrics use distinctions that are to some degree interchangeable and for certain purposes capable of being surrogates of the others, it is tempting to cast our theory into an imperialistic stance with regard to the other rubrics.

My inclination is to resist this temptation. For one thing, the imperialist stance presupposes that differences among the rubrics stem from errors and imprecision in their makeups or that the different theories are merely alternative ways of describing the "same phenomena." The emerging field theory here demolishes such claims. Moreover, it is prima facie plausible to start from the assumption that every theory is merely a working out of the implications of a starting point. This assumption makes it pointless to slug it out toe to toe with all of the other rubrics. We need to do so only vis-à-vis the views that share our aims—which is partly why so much attention has been paid Toulmin here.

A hermeneutic posture seems appropriate. If the reality of a literary work may consist of all the interpretations we can wring out of it, it seems plausible to assume the same of social distinctions. The variety of theoretical approaches may thus be construed to reflect the limitless range of possibilities for drawing distinctions and working out their implications. An epistemic field theory may be seen as a working out of the implications of particular distinctions rather than as a doctrine which rules the other rubrics out. Thus in adapting reformed versions of certain elements of the other rubrics to the present view, I shall not argue that mutatis mutandis they become the exclusive property of the view. In arguing that field theory can overarch many of the other rubrics, I shall not be claiming that it is the only correct doctrine or, for that matter, the only viable field theory. My concern is with producing a plausible view of the social foundations of knowledge and of the ways people organize their activities around judgmental and veridical standards.

In Defense of Fuzzy Distinctions

In defining fields as real social entities, we are led to think of them as constellations of practices organized around one or a few dominant assumptions. While a field's various theories, traditions, and practices might seem diffuse, stratified, and compartmentalized, we ought to be able to tie them together coherently under a unifying paradigm or world view. It should be possible to discern recurring themes in the practices of particular social communities. These will include understandings about the range of activities to which certain ideas are appropriate, exemplars of excellence and success, particular theories accounting for relationships among the phenomena the field finds interesting, and exemplars of adequate and ethical procedures.

"Field" thus overarches terms such as "group," "organization," "frameworks," and "social relationships." Understanding fields to be real social entities means that we make sociological claims as a first analytic step. We impute unity to a group of people, that is, we say that they unify around particular beliefs, interests, purposes, judgment and veridical standards, rhetorical appeals, authorities, social relationships, and political aims. We shall want to say that this social unity stems from the trust field actors have in the things which unify them. Exemplars of this trust should be apparent from observations of a field's practices.

It may prove wise to run a loose ship respecting the boundaries we draw between these real entities. The early group theorists floundered upon attempts to make very rigid distinctions among social arrangements and to prove a deterministic relation between groups and individuals. They found themselves unable to explain how and why individuals moved among groups (variously) taking influence from them. It seems clear that people move freely among groups, accommodating to their different requirements in different ways for different reasons. They make choices about the *appropriateness* of fields to situations—a social comparison process of central interest here. Since the boundaries between groups are as sharp or blurred as people make them, we should not view field theory as the building of rigid and static structures bearing clear demarcations among social activities. Field theory will not be a massive isomorph of social structure "plodding through time intact."

A considerable tolerance of fuzziness is thus needed—not because inadequate empirical work has failed to solve the "fuzziness problem" but because fuzziness is simply a fact of social life (O'Keefe and Benoit, 1982). Toulmin's use of academic divisions avoids fuzziness at the price of obscuring intuitively obvious features of social life. Any scheme which makes social boundaries clearer than they in fact are will do the same. Rowland (1981a) uses Ven diagrams to suggest certain relationships among fields. While this approach is lucid, the present view proposes a rather different view: as if a Ven diagram consisted of circles overlaid upon circles in four or five dimensions, the outlines of the circles being continually in motion, some lines fading and disappearing into other circles while new ones emerge.

It is virtually impossible to conjure up this sort of Ven diagram, especially with multiple dimensions and changing textures. This fact indicates the incongeniality of sharp distinctions to the holistic account we seek. It seems better to assume that fields are continually in process, their configurations and boundaries with other fields continually evolving and fluctuating. Constellations of practices are configured differently, thanks to the special adaptations they require of actors' defining activities. They use distinctions that cut differently, assumptions that yield special working logics, and traditions of practice organized around different purposes (Rowland, 1981b). Sociological thresholds of cohesion are neither necessary or sufficient conditions of their existence (or of defining them). We should expect fields to display every gradation of tight- and loose-knittedness, different patterns of association, and different authority structures. Apart from the difficulties of finding a principle of cohesion that does justice to these differences, it is infeasible to look for a rigid doctrine that (in defining interfield differences) will not do violence to the activities and assumptions that make fields possible. Relational fields, for example, have a legal cohesion (in the sense that the relations among spouses are defined by the state and encumbered by legal obligations). But this sort of distinction is too gross to do useful work: we commonsensically do not equate particular marriages with the legal arrangements that legitimize them; we look instead to the social relations among spouses, their special understandings and practical traditions. Legally, every "marriage" is equally cohesive—which proves that the legal boundaries are relatively unimportant to the epistemic distinctions we want to draw.

Thus traditional sociological distinctions such as membership, organization, and cohesion (taken alone and construed as exhaustive criteria) are too rigid for defining argument fields. If we add to this view the consideration that *informal* social structures are interdependent with formal structures, we are left with the conclusion that our thinking must respect the looseness and fuzziness of social arrangements.

Social Interaction

A critical, analytic, and empirical focus upon social interaction can encompass the differences and interrelationships among fields, respect their fuzziness, and point to recurring themes within them. It is appropriate to the commonsense realities actors confront in daily life and to the ways they organize their experience and define situations. It expresses the context embeddedness of all activities, the continual dialectic between conventions and intentions, and the importance of the definition of situation as the foundational frame of meaning. It is the starting place for explaining how and why actors appeal to particular frameworks to objectify their thinking—it is a way of seeking the recurring themes in these practices.

Think of fields as living, breathing organisms. People breathe life into them through their activities. To describe fields is to describe these animating activities—the assumption being that fields exist of and in ongoing practices; they *are* their activities. Communal life is comprised of the accommodations people make to one another, their temporary inhibitions of their own developing lines of action (Mead's "I") to assess the expectations of others (Mead's "Me"). Such "temporary inhibitions" of action are viewable as the paradigm case of "minded behavior" (see Meltzer, 1972, p. 13). Following Mead, we may say that minded behavior is a social communicative process, that is, arising as individuals enter particular social settings and groups. Perspective taking is thus a process of referring or appealing to a particular framework of assumptions, namely, a field's background awarenesses and explicit assumptions. Fields, then, are viewable as perspectives one can take, stances toward events, interpretive schemes appropriate to particular classes of occasions. They exist because people use them (inter alia) to objectify their thinking. This does not mean they are adopted in the same ways and for the same reasons. We shall want to distinguish between people "in" an activity tradition (for example, the scientist "in" a research tradition) and people who pick up and use a body of knowledge, bringing it to bear as a matter of convenience upon an event. There is also a useful distinction to be drawn between someone who *serves* a body of knowledge and one who picks up and uses a corpus. Both are *using* the field to give meaning to practices, but the former defines his activities in terms of contributions to the field, while the latter regards the field's facts as ready-made proofs to be picked up and used.

If fields exist in action, they are not objects, and object language is inappropriate to them. Again, a parallel with group theory is helpful. The first crude group theories equated groups with things. Such thinking proved too rigid, and the sociological notion of groups gradually loosened to accommodate to the obvious fact that people do not stand about in canisters. It became apparent that groups were not inflexible, unyielding, or clearly bounded phenomena; they proved to be of varying kinds and to display great differences in their methods and degrees of cohesion. The early theories lacked the interactionist notion of groups existing in the action of their members. This created an over-determined picture of group life in which the norms, values, and rules of groups were presumed to determine the behavior of the people "in" them. They consequently did not see *action* as the source of stability and change. Hence the interactionist's critique: "A gratuitous accep-tance of the concepts of norms, values, social rules and the like should not blind the social scientist to the fact that any one of them is sub-tended by a process of social interaction—a process that is necessary not only for their change but equally well for their retention in a fixed form. It is the social process in group life that creates and upholds the rules, not the rules that create and uphold group life" (Blumer, 1969, pp. 18–19). Thus a group "does not function automatically because of some inner dynamics or system requirements; it functions because people at different points do something, and what they do is a result of how they define the situation in which they are called on to act" (Blumer, 1969, p. 19). It is better, then, to view groups (and fields) as traditions of joint action, as arising out of the background of ongoing activities of people. Blumer thus stresses that "one is on treacherous and empirically invalid grounds if he thinks that any given form of joint action can be sliced off from its historical linkage, as if its makeup and character arose out of the air through spontaneous generation instead of growing out of what went before" (1969, p. 20). The focus must be on the continuities, the underlying historical threads that make joint action possible. Our shorthand term for these continuities among activities is "fields."

It is obvious that this equation of fields with activities does not square with defining them (essentially) as histories of ideas (cf. Foucalt, 1972). A history of ideas can ignore situated discourse and can proceed without regard to particular thinkers (in the sense that "Kant-ian" philosophy is studied apart from Kant's personal history). A history of ideas is contained in documents. It is physically bounded, having obdurate characteristics. Objectively correct readings of it are in principle possible (either in the hermeneutic or deconstructionist senses). Such a history of ideas is very like Toulmin's conceptual ecolo-gies. It leads us to think of a corpus, a body, a unit of thought. We thus explain renewal, criticism, new discoveries, dissonant findings, and resistance to change in terms of the logical characteristics of concepts (and their interrelationships in a conceptual ecology).

This thinking is for our purposes defective. First, it rules practices (and the facts of communication) out of fields. It makes fields lifeless, obdurate structures which do not depend upon the actions of people for their meanings. There are two serious weaknesses to this approach: (1) whether objective readings of documents are possible or not, documents pragmatically mean what they are taken to mean—which explains why disputes about their meanings constitute important parts of a field's ongoing activities; and (2) it requires a disjointedness of theory and practice, that is, if we equate a field with its documents, we have no useful way of defining its practices (aside from the obviously unacceptable line which makes practices deductive instances of written concepts or the equally unsatisfactory stance which sees them as the same things as documents).

Second, the history of ideas inevitably collapses field boundaries (the obvious sociological distinctions we want to draw) because ideas (in the abstract and in terms of pragmatic uses of them) overlap in confusing ways. Interfield borrowing is commonplace. But if we ask who "owns" the Indeterminacy Principle, we might be led to ask who uses it most—which is silly. It seems better to see how concepts appear in practices, how they are *used* for particular tasks and purposes.

Third, objectifying a body of knowledge in terms of its written documents obscures just the epistemic phenomena we take to be central to understanding how knowledge is passed upon, namely, "progress," "innovation," and every field's pressures toward stability or change. These are at best only symptomized in documents, never exemplified. It is in the domain of action that ideas are hashed out and used; new meanings are progressively devised to meet specific requirements—which means that we dare not ignore how field actors adapt their concepts to situations. One *can* explain progress through a field's documents, but one could not know whether the documents revealed the reasons for conceptual change. In principle, one could not know whether the progress discernible in documents was the same thing as the progress in practices which produced the literature.

The histories of ideas of fields are useful resources for understanding aspects of particular ecologies. But such histories cannot be the central theoretical and empirical base for an epistemic field theory. They are the spoor, not the animal. Obviously we shall want to know how a field's documents affect its practices, but we must as well discover how a document's ideas are transformed into practices and how new documents emerge as summaries of these transformations. Thus a history of ideas constitutes an important but not a central part of field studies. It must square with the broader view that fields are living, breathing aggregations of flesh-and-blood people whose activities are conjoined by shared assumptions and aims.

Maxims of Epistemic Postures

It is tempting to equate fields with accomplished states of knowledge. This temptation bears scrutiny. It may illuminate a dispute—an implicit one, to be sure—about what sorts of jobs field studies might do. Theorists who have despaired of structuralism but who want to salvage its most promising features are tempted to view fields as manifestations of a single, invariant, unifying thread. Foucalt has called this a search for a "fundamental teleology" or "profound continuity" undergirding all approaches to knowledge. Field relativity is, by this account, merely apparent. We can bore downward through the layers of social practice, peeling away Russell's "layers of misconception," or "emancipating" ourselves from "false consciousness," to arrive at the fundamental, invariant link uniting apparently discontinuous practices.

This thinking is defective, though it might turn out to be true. Its main weakness resides in the practices it permits. Boring through layers of social practices implies that the layers themselves are relatively unimportant. Chasing fundamental teleologies implies that one is crashing through a thicket of irritating but basically irrelevant underbrush. One cannot make sense of such assumptions unless it is also assumed that the people who take conventions to be correct are wrong, while the analyst is in a privileged position. But the analyst who takes this posture vis-à-vis any field has to break the power of the tu quoque and to avoid in some minimally acceptable way the usual skeptical challenges we might expect the field actors to raise. Since analysts cannot do this, their merry chase amounts to hunting foxes for food.

It is prima facie plausible to consider the conditions of epistemic success in social groups—and to do this as a distinctively social scientific entertainment. We can seek the social, psychological, and communicational prerequisites of knowledge claims in order to better understand their places in human associations. Our organizing question might be, to borrow from Grice (1975), *what fundamental, necessary assumptions make knowledge possible?* Just as Grice points to the maxims underlying the very possibility of talk, so we need to consider the maxims which are necessary conditions of *justified true beliefs* as we have defined them.

The *As If* Maxim. Having argued that fields are social groups with boundaries and conceptual ecologies more negotiable than static, I want to argue that there is a sense (consistent with the sociological sense) in which fields *are* accomplished bodies of knowledge or "domains of objectivity." I refer to the ways actors *use* fields *as if* they are accomplished, as "facts" taken as true, as not-to-be-questioned assumptions and background awarenesses. They use fields to objectify their thinking, as points of reference for social comparison, to check their private interpretations against communally validated standards. Plausibly, they do this with different degrees of confidence. They might proceed axiomatically, plausibly, or tentatively (and by every gradation we might conjure up between these terms). But whether one's assumptions are self-evident axioms or rough working hypotheses—however modest one assumptions may be—they are taken *as if* they are guaranteed by an *accomplished*, dependable standard.

The *as if* maxim is thus a necessary but not sufficient condition of a field's success—necessary, since even modest assumptions about a standard's dependability require a bracketing of doubts, and not a sufficient condition because it does not explain how or why an individual chooses a particular guarantor. The *as if* maxim thus says that a field cannot exist unless people enter it *as if* it is in some sense capable of authorizing claims and vouching for assumptions. This captures the rhetorical bases we have already attributed to fields. It implies that a first step in describing a field is to describe the *as if* assumptions people construe it to authorize.

The *Accomplishment* Maxim. The *as if* maxim directs our attention to the things an individual thinks a field authorizes. The *accomplishment* maxim points to the public epistemic posture a field takes, its conditions for success and its claims to have met them. So viewed it is a continuistic notion: some fields claim that their knowledge is axiomatic; others claim only to possess rough working hypotheses; others make claims falling between these extremes. These public claims say much about a field's *sense of accomplishment*. To consider these often flattering self-portraits, we need not become bogged down in considerations of a field's "objective accomplishments." What *we* might say about a field's epistemic successes might be irrelevant to defining the field.

This distinction is worth insisting upon. To ask why someone chooses a guarantor for his inferences or claims is always to ask (by the *as if* maxim) why he *trusts* the standard. One source of faith in a standard is one's assessment of how it works out pragmatically: one trusts a research standard because of its results or an assumption because of its predictions. Thus scientists sometimes say that the test of a good theory is the number of empirical problems it poses and (presumably) solves. The viability of a research tradition inheres in its effectiveness, the problems it succeeds with. So we have fields continually debating the effectiveness of competing views, and we have people trusting field standards to different degrees. A sense of accomplishment is thus the social counterpart to the *as if* maxim—and as

such the essential public posture a field must take. It is embodied in
the claims a group makes about the things authorized or vouched for
by their beliefs.

We might use Toulmin's term "compactness" as a shorthand expression to describe a field's epistemic success. "Compactness" would
thus refer to the degree to which a field's standards are uncontroversial, taken as true, not-to-be-questioned final arbiters of disputes.
Atomic physics, Catholic theology, creationism, and (in fact) any field
accorded powerful allegiances and trust by its actors would be "compact." We thus use "compactness" as a sociological/rhetorical term
denoting the degree to which field actors have closed ranks around a
standard—this phenomenon being characteristic of both disciplinary
and ordinary fields.

The *Progress* **Maxim.** Having explained the epistemic motive for
entering fields and the public postures fields take toward their epistemic success, I turn now to a purely internal presupposition that
bears importantly upon the first two maxims. The *progress* maxim
suggests that fields adopt particular theories and procedures by virtue
of their fit into historically trusted frameworks and that this *fit* depends largely upon the progress a new idea or procedure seems to
accomplish. Does it pose interesting new puzzles or circumvent vex-
atious problems for disciplinary fields? Does it make things run
smoothly? Does it secure power for political fields? Since not all fields
wash their dirty linen publicly, we need an explanation of the *internal*
view of a field's successes.

I have drawn this thinking from Laudan's (1977) view of research
traditions, by which he means a set of ontological and methodological
do's and don'ts. Formally, *a research tradition is a set of general assumptions about the entities and processes in a domain of study, and
about the appropriate methods to be used for investigating the problems
and constructing the theories in that domain"* (1977, p. 81; italics in the
original). A "field" in our sense might contain many research traditions or (conversely) might be the same thing. The focus is upon people
engaged in projects, embarked upon particular lines of inquiry. Given
their starting assumptions, they can be said to "progress." A successful
tradition, Laudan says, leads by its component theories (which may be
inferentially incompatible) to the adequate solution of an increasing
range of problems (1977, p. 82). As the range of success expands, the
actor's faith in the guiding assumptions of the tradition increases: I
trust X because X solves my problems. A good standard is thus one with
a broad but precise focus of convenience.

Laudan's views are intended to explain scientific knowledge, although we need not stretch them much to see their applicability to ordinary domains as well. The notion of "success" might not mean "range or focus of convenience" if a field is concerned with action rather than with epistemic growth. But the idea of progress does not need to be construed exclusively as a disciplinary prerogative or taste. It is more prudent to assume that ordinary actors enter fields for at least some of the same reasons that disciplinary actors do (that is, to objectify), although their proximate aims may be political action rather than epistemic betterment per se. Thus we can use the progress notion without making science our paradigm case of knowledge. We can focus instead upon congeries of practices, each having different aims and methods as well as a standard for defining progress respecting these.

One might claim that as fields mature they coalesce into broader, more universal fields—thus defining "progress" as the process by which fields perfect themselves out of unique existence. This claim is defective on (inter alia) historical grounds. Fields have improved and multiplied rather than the reverse. We possess no credentials for saying that this diffusion is a "progress" whose underlying unity has yet to be discovered. This thinking requires a retreat to absolutism without providing new weapons for defending the position. A teleology of fields is just as regressive, circular, and vulnerable to skeptical challenge as the absolutisms it might be thought to replace.

Like rabbits, fields have merged and spun off progeny. In Aristotle's time, *theoretical and practical reason* were the main divisions of activity. This Eden was successively invaded by more particular distinctions; for example, after Bacon we had "scientific" versus a number of other kinds of reasons as well as distinctions within science. As particular domains broke into discreet balkanized fiefdoms, we had as many "sciences" as there were research traditions. More and more schools of thought arose to demand allegiance from actors in many domains. We could plausibly infer from this that "progress" can be equated with particularization. The movement toward atomization proceeds until a particular research line (or tradition of practice) breaks off—in roughly the way Kuhn speaks of revolutions. It is at tiny interstices of particular research and activity traditions that cross-pollination is most apparent. And it is from the smaller balkanized segments that thinkers leave one weltanschauung for another. There is an ebb and flow of ideas which progresses both toward coalescence and reduction (though for particular people the two cannot happen simultaneously).

This reasoning does not need Kuhn's (1970a, 1970b) distinction between revolutionary and normal science; nor does it require Toulmin's (1967a, 1967b, 1970, 1972) evolutionary account. Revolutions may be

quiet, retrospective observations or flashy and dramatic confrontations, depending upon the epistemic environment in which they occur.
Evolution may or may not be the case: particularization is in one
important sense the opposite of evolutionary "growth." Traditions
develop as much as matters of taste and convention as of conceptual
adaptation. Moreover, the movement toward reduction can be as regressive as it is progressive.

Remember, we are saying that disciplinary life is an exotic embel-
lishment of ordinary life. We thus do not speak of a field's *objectivity* as
if this concept yielded some invariant insight into the epistemic attainments of fields. We have a sociological/rhetorical sense of "compactness" to explain the objectivity of fields. Thus, for example, in
describing the objectivity of the sciences we are making a claim about
the trust and faith scientists place in their judgmental and veridical
standards. This is a plausible claim, no matter what else scientists
may say about their objectivity, that is, our sociological argument is
prima facie nontrivial. Thus it will not do to refute this (as Suppe
[1977] critiques Kuhn) as being a collapse to subjectivism or relativism. If the sociological argument is nontrivial, this criticism is beside
the point. Just as ordinary fields blur and sharpen their boundaries,
slide together and break apart, happily coexist and snipe at one another, so the disciplines fluctuate in and out of one another, redefine
their subject matters, and alter their routine practices.

"Progress" may thus be seen as the change we see in the broad
outlines of fields. So viewed it includes accumulation and disintegration, not as a Yin-Yang dialectic—that would be the meekest sort of
retreat to Hegel—but as organizing patterns by which actors order
their activities. Within traditions there may be progress of just the sort
the Vienna Circle positivists emphasized. Or there may be something
like an enduring commitment to criticism (comprehensively critical
rationalism) and a faith in revolution for its own sake. We shall find (I
think) that the social and professional worlds contain pragmatic counterparts of virtually every philosophic doctrine ever propounded. This
is not just a cute locution. While grand theorists have looked for *the*
theory to explain growth, there have been examples supporting every
contending view; the disputes have been spirited, to say the least. Our
field theory suggests that there are utilitarian, rationalist, nativist,
nominalist, authoritarian, dialectical, and existential fields—fields
reflecting every ist and ism we can conjure up. Field actors pick up
grand theories and use them—making life imitate art and philosophy.
The order we study is thus man-made, not in the trivial sense that
people think their theories up, but in a deeper sense that fields are
attempts to work out the implications of starting points.

The *What If?* **Maxim.** A field is a constellation of practices built up from a *what if?* preface. It exists because actors treat particular ideas as plausible or valid starting points. They flesh out the scenario suggested by the starting point's logic. They do just what Kelly's man-as-scientist metaphor says individuals do, that is, regard events in an experimental manner. If individual behavior is experimental, group behavior is likely the same. A person, we may say, enters a field because he likes its hypotheses or because he has one of his own the field seems to explain. He thus enters a communal tradition which bases its activities on working out the implications of particular starting points. The man-as-scientist metaphor suggests that actors retain hypotheses because they seem to be borne out by events. The scientific parallel is the notion of problem solving: scientists retain ideas because they suggest interesting puzzles and solve important ones. They retain larger paradigms because they like the puzzles. When these cease to be interesting, they move on to other things, for example, moving from behaviorism to constructivism not because behaviorism has been conclusively refuted but because constructivist puzzles are more interesting.

The *what if?* maxim depicts actors as following particular lines suggested by particular starting points. They might be in Laudan's research traditions or in political action groups. These lines often (though not always) take on a life of their own, leaving the broader social structure in which they arose panting in their footsteps—not quite the vision Parsons had in mind. Albeit brief and dogmatic, this sense of "progress" is at least worth trying out: it coheres with our view of social practices and traditions and is compatible with our thinking about the blurred boundaries between fields.

The *Attention* **Maxim.** Having argued that fields are essentially rhetorical, that is, that they draw cohesion from epistemic authorities and the attractiveness of their practices, and having argued as well that a field's sense of accomplishment is a pivotal part of the rhetorical glue binding it together, I want to argue here that fields are seeable as *audiences.* The intuitive idea is that a group becomes an audience by virtue of its intentional choices to *attend to* particular communications. I have elsewhere (Willard, 1982) criticized Foucalt's (1972) emphasis upon the *speaker*—saying that it blurs ordinary fields, ignores overlaps in subject matters, uses cases which are too clear-cut (for example, physicians "speak for" medicine), and blurs issue fields. Taking the audience notion as an organizing principle, we can more easily say that fields in part define themselves by their choices concerning sources—the organizing question being "to whom shall we pay attention?" While some fields define themselves by choices about *who* shall speak, for example, Catholic theology is largely organized around assumptions about the appropriateness of claims to speakers, others do not. All fields, however, attend to communications. To point to the speakers, journals, popular sources, and tracts to which a group attends is thus to go far toward defining the group.

This reasoning squares with our holistic account. The psychological field is most basically a field of attention. Attending to people and events is a constructive choice—which means that the decision to listen to someone inter alia is an epistemic posture. The decision to listen is (arguably) the basis of social comparison and thus foundational to the special use of the man-as-scientist metaphor we have chosen to employ. This dovetails into the sociological sense of "field" by virtue of the assumption that people band together in part because they listen to the same communications; they accord respect to the same people and ideas; they share a view of who and what merits serious attention.

In defining fields as audiences and in emphasizing their rhetorical dimensions, I am using "field" to subsume the sociological notion of "community." The intuitive idea is that group cohesion, the sense of "we-ness" usually thought to be the necessary condition of a community, is a constructive accomplishment of social actors accommodating their lines of action to one another. Shared assumptions about the people and ideas meriting serious attention is surely foundational to such accomplishments. The audience notion thus means that fields are rhetorically achievements and that this is the most fundamental thing to be said about them.

Toward the end I shall tie the *attention* maxim to the field of criticism—replacing the usual justificationist questions with the principle of deciding which fields criticism ought to attend to. While naive actors may well make such decisions using the language of "right and wrong," "correct and incorrect," there are no reasons critics should follow suit. The organizing question (better stated) is, "To which fields should we listen?"

The *Constraint* **Maxim.** Having argued that a person's entering a field is a constructive accomplishment, an interpretive choice, I want to augment this thinking by considering the social contracts actors implicitly and explicitly sign when they enter fields. My claim is that the decision to enter a field is a decision to accept constraints, to surrender a measure of one's freedom, to accept a starting point and to abide by the consequences. A perhaps oversimple example may serve to introduce this view: if you and I sit down to a game of chess, we fully expect one another to abide by the rules; we expect as well that both of us must adopt strategies and "see things through." There are no "takebacks." We decide upon our strategies and sink or swim with them. The game would be impossible without this contract.

Consider a person making a decision. We might expect that among the lines the decider thinks through will be alternative strategies for deciding. Such hypothetical calculations will be as crude or sophisticated as the person's attainments permit. The person might ask, "Shall I make a cost-benefit calculation?" So asking, one is led to think through the implications, the outcomes of such a starting point. The decider is picking and choosing among relevant fields—the organizing question being "which rules are best to abide by in solving *this* problem?"

Remember that we have distinguished between actors *in* fields and those who pick up a field's ideas selectively. In the present case we have a person considering which strategies are best to pick up for a particular problem. The constructive alternatives are to "go and get" some objectivity in this or that field. My claim is that we may learn much about popular uses of field notions (and about the nature of the public) by considering the reasons why actors go and get objectivity from particular fields. Our decider is considering alternative epistemic postures (although the sort of weighing being described here is itself an epistemic posture). His final choice, then, is a decision to live with the consequences (though *not* a promise not to squeal about them). It is a decision to abide by a particular set of constraints based upon one's assessment of the outcomes.

A person's decision to enter a field, that is, to become a field actor, is analogous (though presumably one makes life choices on a broader base of considerations than a field's utility to a single situation). Whatever the reasons, people become professional economists, psychologists, engineers, and philosophers at least in part because of the attractiveness of these fields; and they adopt particular schools of thought because (inter alia) they like the puzzles, the people, and the consequences. The decision to become (say) a Freudian is thus a constructive choice to abide by the consequences of a line of thinking, to put one's ideas at risk vis-à-vis a particular group of people and their standards. The standard expectation in the disciplines is that one agrees implicitly *not* to squeal about the consequences. The contract is to submit one's thinking to the judgments and evaluations of others and to abide by the judgmental and veridical apparatus trusted by the group. The *accomplishment* and *as if* maxims explain the attractiveness of this contract.

This thinking leads to an especially useful view of freedom and determinism. It is based upon Kelly's (1955) view, which says that regnant constructs determine subordinate ones by giving them meaning. Since cognitive elements are hierarchically arranged, it is thus plausible to say that we are as free as we think we are. Unexamined assumptions are what enslave us. "Each little prior conviction that is not open to review is a hostage...[we give] to fortune" (1955, pp. 21–22). People who reflect upon their points of view and who cast their thinking into broad principles rather than rigid rules are more able and apt to choose alternatives that emancipate them. Thus Kelly stresses that theories are the thinking of people seeking freedom from events. Freedom from events is the ability to *predict* them successfully—which is the same thing as saying that one is free of events when one can successfully interpret them. Theories are interpretations (and broad interpretations of interpretations). An idea which controls another idea is free of that idea; determinism is thus the control a higher-order construct exerts on a subordinate one.

To enter a field is to adopt its theories. In one sense, this is a constructive choice to surrender one's autonomy to the adopted theories, namely, the agreement to abide by the consequences. In another sense, entering a field might be seeable as an effort after freedom: because a field's assumptions and procedures give order and coherence to events, they endow the field actor with freedom from the events.

It very much matters how reflective a person is in deciding to enter and to act in a field. If I take a field's beliefs as immutable axioms, as not-to-be-questioned truths, I surrender a large measure of my freedom; if I unreflectively take a field's beliefs and procedures *for granted*, I surrender virtually all of my freedom respecting the events relevant to the field. In both cases it is I (and no one else) who has handed freedom away. If I am a true believer, I have decided that the advantages of fanaticism outweigh those of freedom.

We might well expect great variability among fields in the degree of reflective thinking they encourage. A few disciplines are founded on continual questioning of their presuppositions—something like Weimer's "comprehensively critical rationalism." Most disciplines (plausibly) take things for granted (in the sense, that is, that particular schools of thought orient themselves around at least a few not-to-be-questioned assumptions). The ordinary fields doubtless display the same variations. We might expect to find popular theologies based upon rigid doctrine (popular Catholicism) as well as upon freethinker values (popular Unitarianism). In every case, however, people enter fields because they are in some sense "accomplished," because they in some sense appear to *authorize inferences*. Our assumption should be that anything which can authorize an inference *determines* (with the same power by which it authorizes) the inference. This happens, not as a sociological determinism like structuralism, but as a process of constructive choices. One might gain or lose freedom by adopting a theory, depending upon the decisions one makes about the theory's power. Since even the most modest assumption about a theory's power requires some allegiance to the theory's entailments (why else adopt it?), every decision to abide by the consequences of a field's standards is a surrender of private alternatives.

Freedom and determinism are thus alternative outcomes of every person's and every field's epistemic posture—two sides of the same coin, really. Both have advantages and disadvantages, depending upon a person's aims. Social arrangements are obviously created and sustained when people surrender at least some of their freedom. Social contracts thus embody the foundational arrangements of a field: the willingness of a field's actors to abide by the consequences of the field's starting points is the sine qua non of the field.

Justified True Beliefs

The truth condition of a claim, the positivists said, inhered in its fit with the facts. The maxims undergirding alternative epistemic postures essentially say the same thing. When *A says X*, we ask why *A* feels authorized to say *X* and whether *A*'s feeling authorized is licensed by the epistemic framework *A* abides by. This is tantamount to saying that whether *X* is true depends upon its fit with the field's facts. This is more a substantive matter than an offshoot of logical *form*, since the form of an argument guarantees neither its truth, goodness, or propriety (excepting, of course, the grossest fallacies). If we ask whether *X* is *defective*, while we might be asking a formal question, we are more likely posing a substantive one, namely, how *X* fits with the facts.

We can appropriate the language of the positivists as long as we keep our rhetorical, psychological, and sociological aims squarely at the forefront. Since our question (among many) is why *A* feels justified in saying *X*, we should not be surprised to find that *A says X* because *X is a fact; X* is a fact because *N* guarantees it (that is, some field assumption or procedure guarantees *X*). The truth conditions of every such claim thus inhere in a field's *facts*. No grand formal principles work quite as well as the notion of "facts." Nor do formal principles explain why fields abide by different facts (since, that is, each field we have looked at seems to use similar formal principles and procedures). Thus whether a sociological claim can contradict a psychological one (to take a standard example) depends upon which field we use as a conceptual lens for weighing the two.

A field's facts have their ancestry in the field's historical facts, its history of ideas. Pragmatically, this works out to be a history of *practices*. We are assuming that people take things to be facts because of their fit to particular lines of action in particular circumstances. The cumulative experience of a group (of using certain facts certain ways) thus comprises the field's facts.

This yields a rhetorical-sociological variant of the familiar analytic view of justified true belief. *A says X;* is *A* justified in believing *X* and does he believe *X* for the correct reasons? *A* has a justified true belief if (1) *A* believes *X;* (2) *X* is a fact; and (3) *A* believes *X* for the correct reasons. *X* is a fact by virtue of its fit into an epistemic framework that so regards it; *A* is correct in believing *X* if he believes *X legitimately,* that is, in the field's authorized manner. *A* believes *X* as the result of the rhetorical elements we have been discussing. All three stages of the justified true belief are the *figure* we have set against the *ground* of the field's facts.

The language of positivism is thus a good way of speaking (literally) about claims and inferences—as long as we remember that we are not doing ontology. Thus we can say that *A believes X* (correctly) because *X* is true, that is, legitimized consensually. *How* consensual legitimation occurs is thus an organizing question for criticism; and how disputes among different consensual traditions are to be looked at becomes the organizing problematic of critical epistemology.

The Critical Turn

Our figure has emerged from its ground. Claims and inferences about knowledge have been set against the backdrop of the sociological entities in which they occur. Justification has been fleshed out as a rhetorical process which presupposes certain rhetorical accomplishments, namely, the senses in which fields are taken to authorize, legitimize, or warrant particular claims. Fields have been conceptualized in terms of the people and actions animating them. This emphasis on social life yielded the conclusion that to say *fields* authorize claims is roughly to say that *A* feels authorized to say *X* because his companions or colleagues buttress *A*'s views. A field *is* a conceptual ecology; but it is also (and more basically) a practical ecology, a tradition of practices. A field's pragmatic history thus informs its conceptual history; it says what the facts are.

Let us imagine an interlocutor who, having followed our argument this far, raises an objection of the following sort:

> You are shamming. All you have done is dress consensualism in a new costume and reassert the old skeptical objections to universalism. You

have a principle of sociological association (namely, rhetorical alignments) but no principle of knowledge. The net result is a banality: different fields have different facts because they have different pieties.

This objection is not implausible, but we have a weapon or two.

Field theory proposes an empirical project of understanding how
field actors pass muster on knowledge and why particular substantive
domains take different things as facts. "Consensualism" by itself
merely proposes the tautology that there are social differences, that
things taken as true are so taken because they are consensually validated. Field theory goes several steps further by its insistence upon
empirically grounding our understandings of consensus. It poses the
problem of relativity (we shall see) in an especially productive way.

But we have not merely reasserted the familiar skeptical litany
against universalism. The facts of interfield differences are far more
powerful skeptical weapons against universal claims than the broad
skeptical doctrine ever was. The broad doctrine of skepticism cannot
survive the shift to practice; but field differences not only survive the
shift, they emerge as flat, powerful objections to universalist claims.
They require that the broad doctrinal disputes be set aside in favor of
an empirical project aimed at elaborating our understanding of these
differences.

The claim that we have no principle of knowledge is thus defective.
In the shift to practices, we have concluded that the principle of
sociological association (the rhetorical glue binding fields together) *is*
the principle of knowledge. So proceeding, we have set out the preconditions of any successful (and nontrivial) universal, namely, that it
account for incommensurable epistemic frameworks and that it do so
without resort to justificationist principles (these having been undermined by the bare fact of interfield differences). We have thus gone far
toward describing a critical project based upon considerations of
interfield disputes.

Given these replies, let us say that our interlocutor amends his
objection to say something of this sort:

> I grant that you have a powerful relativism here, but I am not prepared to
> admit that you avoid banality. You do just what you used the arguments
> of Rescher and Toulmin to prove that skeptics do: pose a standard of
> *universal* knowledge "so hyperbolic" (Rescher, 1977a) that your field
> theory is bound to undermine it. There are enough straw men here to
> constitute a fire hazard.

This is implausible. We want to know how arguments work, what their
claims mean, and why people use them as they do. An important part

of this problematic is understanding how people take things as knowledge. So no straw men have died here: the traditional tools of analysis have been said to be inappropriate to the rhetorical/sociological inquiries necessary to field studies. Aspersions have been cast upon any field which claims that its special analytical tools are universally valid—which is not a banality if the claims themselves are nontrivial.

Now, our interlocutor might opt out of the dispute at this point because we have taken an empirical tack. But let us say that he instead argues:

> I grant you your pretensions, but not your accomplishments. You have climbed off one skewer onto another. In proving that your project is not banal, you have posed a problem you cannot possibly solve. You are reduced to the counting of noses—and you have done it in such a way that you cannot avoid concluding that this is all there is to say. Your epistemic postures are merely "love it or leave it" claims; what is true is what is voted to be true—the sole epistemic objection one can raise being to flee a field.

This objection displays, perhaps, one virtue: it emphasizes that our interlocutor is still thinking like a justificationist. He assumes that our posture toward interfield disputes must be to "solve" them, to referee them. Since we have argued that no critic has the credentials for such refereeing, it would seem that we have silenced criticism.

I hope to prove in the next chapter that the principle of attention (buttressed by certain other principles of interfield discourse) can equip the critic with useful analytic tools and embark him upon a project of asking, not which fields are best, but *to which fields epistemics ought to listen.* For now, there is no need to defeat each contending epistemic field on its own ground; we need only decide which fields merit our attention—which fields so conduct their internal affairs and their disputes with outside fields that it is worth our while to deal with them. If this project succeeds, the present objection is itself banal.

But let us say that our interlocutor is not satisfied with this promise:

> Provisionally granting that you will succeed with nonjustificational principles of critical epistemics, you have answered only part of my objection. You have utterly closed off the possibility that truth is *not* merely the counting of noses. You are pretending to say what knowledge *is.* In rejecting universalism, you have said that knowledge *is* what the *authorities* and *consensual* agreements of any field say that it is. If (tomorrow) a field decides that the earth is square by a 51 to 49 percent majority, you shall have to say that this decision must stand.

There are several confusions in this objection. First, our field theory does *not* "reject universalism" but brackets it. The argument on which I have depended has been that universal projects have not succeeded and do not appear likely to; the argument has *not* been that universalism in principle cannot succeed. While field studies *might* prove that this is so (and while we have argued that this is not an intolerable consequence), it is equally plausible that field studies might yield their own universals. Thus, the present field account does *not* "utterly close off" the possibility that truth is not merely the counting of noses. Nor does our field theory place any special value in majority votes. To borrow Lippmann's claim, the only difference between 51 and 49 percent of a field's votes is that 51 is bigger than 49.

To claim that things are thought to be true (or good or trustworthy) because a field's authorities and consensual conventions vouch for them is to make an empirical claim about our epistemic situation. It is not to say that consensualism inevitably rules out universals. A sociological field theory does imply that judgments of epistemic worth are tightly interwoven with authority and consensus and that disentangling them from "genuine" judgments has so far proved impossible except by recourse to arbitrary principles. But this is neither to exalt nor to condemn authority and consensus. Strictly speaking, the argument goes this way: (a) knowledge, as we now conceive of it, is largely a matter of authority and consensus; (b) this is neither generally good nor generally bad—majority and minority views are equally capable of being right; therefore, (c) every field attentive to its epistemic best interests must continually consider the grounds of well-founded consensus—the kinds of consensus that get the field's business done. It is pointless to debate whether a field should seek impersonal and universal guarantors of knowledge; many of them do for reasons that are beyond critique from us. My claim is that knowledge is in fact balkanized and that critical epistemics ought to consider carefully the problems this divisiveness raises. Put crudely, it is our present epistemic situation that we seek to know the truth in contexts ruled by authority and consensus. The study of authority, consensus, and legitimation (their uses and misuses, good and evil, utility and disutility, and their effects—good and bad—upon attempts to secure trustworthy invariant standards) is thus the twentieth century's principle epistemic project. It is our present epistemic situation that we do not know (for sure) whether there is a difference between genuine and conventional claims; we have no agreed-upon principles for drawing such contrasts.

So the study of epistemic conventions is an urgent and justified project. It neither applauds nor condemns authority and consensus. Its aim is to consider their empirical nature, thereby better assessing the prospects for improving or even supplanting them. To argue—as I have—that a sociological field theory can replace the older justificationist accounts is not to reject the ultimate aims of those accounts. It is merely a call for an empirically accurate epistemic self-portrait. It is not that Frege or Russell was wrong but that their projects did not succeed with empirical examples. Field theory thus urges a different project, pinned to the idea of understanding interfield differences by studying the cases in which these differences are displayed most clearly, namely, in interfield disputes.

But our interlocutor might well reply along these lines:

> Now you are trying to have it both ways. On the one hand, you say that it is in principle possible that authority and consensus will turn out to be the whole story—we might have to vote on your theory! On the other hand you say that sociological field theory does not rule universals out. But in making your case for the balkanization of knowledge you have so framed the matter that *to defend the idea of fields is to legitimate them.* Take the example of the confrontation between creationists and evolutionists: both sides retreat into the special assumptions of their fields, the creationists taking comfort from their divine revelation, the scientists taking comfort from their scientific method. You have so designed your project as to legitimize this practice; you underwrite it; you end up saying that the *scientific* claims made by the creationists are just as good as the scientific claims made by the scientists.

I want to make several replies to this objection. First, to argue that knowledge is balkanized is neither to approve nor to disapprove of this state of affairs. Nor does it amount to a universal claim that knowledge is *inevitably* heterogeneous. Many of the sciences, after all, use each other's data and proceed along interchangeable lines—this owing mostly to their shared trust in the scientific method. It is conceivable (though not certain) that the sciences might gradually relegate our sociological field theory to the realm of long-past stages in the evolution of knowledge. But they have not done so yet; and within the social sciences it is just as conceivable that the balkanization of knowledge will never be transcended. Thus, to claim that there are communities of discourse which hold incommensurable views is merely to point to an empirical fact with which we must work; it is not to say that incommensurability is inevitable in all fields.

Second, the present objection is based upon a misunderstanding of the creationist and evolutionist arguments. Strictly speaking, the two sides advocate things which do not (by either field's standards) contradict one another except as political postures. The facts of evolution are (for now at least) pretty indisputable; but these facts refer to developmental matters; movements from simplicity toward complexity, processes of adaptation and assimilation. Whether these facts bear upon a theory of *creation* involves arguments far removed from the facts—arguments which are vastly more "underdetermined by the data." Thus I hope to draw from principles of interfield disputation certain judgments of the creationist dispute which will disprove the claim that a sociological field theory underwrites the practice of retreating into one's field. Put loosely, the present theory permits a judgment that, in this case, both sides of the *creationist versus evolutionist* dispute misargue their cases. And it does this while fully respecting the creationist's claim that scientific method cannot refute revelation and the scientist's claim that revelation cannot refute data.

Third, the present scheme does not in any case underwrite an advocate's "retreat into his field." The principle of attention, to be elaborated in the next chapter, suggests that we decide which field merits our attention by considering the utility of the argumentation practices. Retreating into one's field, I shall argue, is among the least useful argument practices; and the fields which beat such strategic retreats (arguably) do not merit serious attention by students of knowledge. We may study them for purposes of understanding how fields of discourse hang together; but this does not require that we take their pretensions seriously when we consider the grounds of well-founded consensus. The value of our field theory is that it provides a clearer way of looking at interfield disputes—clearer by virtue of the fact that it does not require taking sides.

Finally, the present objection assumes too much about the usefulness of scientific knowledge as a paradigm case of knowledge per se. The *creationist versus evolutionist* dispute is largely a political debate—borrowing as many premises from political science and morals as from biology. Our concern with *ordinary fields* and the disputes among them is thus unaffected by the present objection even if we granted it. A sociological field theory directs our attention to the ways social actors in fact employ judgmental and veridical standards to test their thinking. Even if the case of scientific knowledge were clear-cut (which it is not), knowledge of other matters is just as important and often far more urgent. Problems of the quality of life, of government policies and neighborhood harmony, of world peace or nuclear war turn largely upon assumptions and communication practices in the ordinary fields. What the sociology of fields does is insist that such matters be seen as foundational aspects of the larger epistemic agenda.

Perhaps the final sort of objection might be raised: "But even respecting ordinary fields, you sound like 'Son of Feyerabend.' You propose an irretrievable radical subjectivity (you have, after all, defended psychologism) and an irremediable anarchy between fields." This objection confuses the case against absolutism with the empirical claims about our present epistemic situation. For reasons that the next chapter will clarify, no *general* skepticism is justified by our sociological field theory. While radical subjectivism is in one sense true (as a literal description of one's perspective), we have also proposed that subjectivism is a problem with which actors grapple and with which they often succeed by processes of social comparison. As a *practical* matter, actors make radical subjectivism untrue (except as an abstract, academic question). The skeptical doctrine (I shall argue) rings hollow when we focus upon field practices. Case-specific skeptical arguments (see Rescher, 1977a, 1977b) are always possible in and across fields. They often crop up in interfield disputes—which is why we should study them. After all, while there are many lurid examples of incommensurable interfield postures, there are as many examples of fields arriving at solutions to their disputes.

Now let us assume that another interlocutor has weighed the objections we have considered and our answers to them and that he raises an objection of this sort: "Your answers to these objections confirm what I have suspected from page one: you talk like a relativist, but you do not really believe it. You have just handed back to the absolutist all that he hoped to gain. You seem to be defending the view that relativism is merely false consciousness. Despite your claim to get out of the justification business, you are still in it; relativity is merely a waypoint on the road to universals." My reply is that the present position is somewhat deeper than the objection. Since when must epistemic decisions amount to taking sides among doctrines? What if both absolutism and relativism are true—each depending upon the other to make sense? We are proceeding, after all, on the assumption that relativity is our hard fact; we have expressed a willingness to live with the consequences if relativisms turn out to be the whole epistemic story; we have merely not closed the door on the possibility that certain epistemic successes might let us deal adequately with relativity. Our continuing claim has been that radical subjectivity is a correct description of individuals but that it is a problem social actors successfully deal with when they enter social arrangements. Why could not the same be true of interfield disputes?

There is another reply which philosophers have often used against objections of this sort: this is no objection at all unless the interlocutor is himself a relativist who believes that there can be (in principle) no exceptions to relativism—a paradoxical position in that it proposes an absolutistic relativism. Now our interlocutor might well say that he does not care whether his position is paradoxical (since, for example, he believes that the world is paradoxical). But if he takes this line, as many relativists do, it seems to me that he has opted out of the dispute: he is saying (in effect) that any solutions to relativity must be false consciousnesses. While we certainly cannot refute him, he certainly can raise no objection if we ignore him. There is arguably nothing wrong with studying the ways fields get their business done and inquiring into ways of improving these methods; and whether the relativist is correct or not about our insincerity as relativists, there is nothing writ in stone which says that a relativist cannot try to solve relativity. Since interfield disputes often pose urgent problems, we have decided to bracket ontology and to proceed with the business of considering the nature of (and solutions to) these disputes. This project places us on the relativist's side, although it does not force us to be doctrinaire about it.

Sociological field theory is relativistic mostly because it is non-justificational. We do not want to muddle our attempts to understand interfield disputes with the broader aim of securing universals; we do not want to hold description hostage to our prescriptive preferences. Thus it is pointless to referee interfield disputes. It is our present epistemic situation that ordinary and disciplinary fields are often if not always beyond critique (excepting, perhaps, the sciences which use each other's data). Field theory—as defined here—thus raises serious objections to universalist's schemes. But it raises as well the possibility that the hoary dispute between universalists and relativists might not look years from now quite the way it has looked in the past. Perhaps the best test of the utility of the present sociology of knowledge is whether it puts the whole dispute on a new footing.

4 Criticism: The Epistemics of Argument and the Argument of Epistemics

The leitmotif throughout this project has been that if one takes relativity to be an indubitable fact, one becomes—however much one resists it—a relativist. But relativism (traditionally conceived) is merely a doctrinaire form of despair. It gives rise to a general skepticism, a questioning of all knowledge claims in principle, that virtually precludes useful analysis and research. It mires the sociology of knowledge in endless disputes about the relations of genuine to social knowledge. And it permits the inference that critics must resist relativity at all costs because the relativism thought to be the inevitable outcome of relativity is so thoroughly skeptical as to demolish the familiar assumptions of justificationist criticism.

The guiding aim of these inquiries has been to produce a relativism which does not fall victim to the worst of these sins. The theoretical move which sent us along this path appeared in our decision to set ontology and universalism aside. This decision, we argued, avoids the intractable problems posed by justificationism. Since we are not preoccupied with saying whether a field's beliefs are correct or incorrect, the way is cleared for more precise and rigorous observations of how fields pass muster on knowledge. This approach opens the door to a distinctively rhetorical explanation of knowing.

The early sociologists of knowledge preferred to believe that their work explained the *genesis of error*—a belief that goes back as far as Bacon's Idols (Stark, 1967). Truth, they thought, was a unity owing nothing to social practices. The happenstances of social life were of epistemic importance, to be sure, but only as impediments to knowledge. The heirs of Mannheim and Durkheim assumed the burden of justifying the alternative reading, namely, that individuals are the most usual sources of error, while society is a living correction. Argument scholars have divided along similar lines, and the results of their disputes have been as unsatisfactory as those of the more venerable dispute. A century of deliberation has brought neither field closer to plausibly relating knowledge or error (either) to the individual or to society. The problem was (and still is) that universalism and consensualism are two utterly distinct fields, taking different things as facts and different empirical postures as valid.

So our aim has been to set the facts of relativity out in such a way that we do justice to interfield differences but still have something of interest to say about how people pass muster on knowledge. Taking the facts of communication and perspectivity to be central to this project, we have proceeded to develop a picture of social differences along lines suggested by the field notion. This task was made easier by the decision to omit the value judgments entailed by seeing one or another field as a source of error. It was facilitated as well by a more modest conception (than is usual) of the problem of knowledge. The problem is not (as Toulmin puts it) that man knows and knows that he knows. Rather, man often doubts that he knows but must *act* (as if he knows). Our aim is to understand how people express and ameliorate their doubts; the empirical focus which serves this aim is upon argument interactions and the things said in them.

This posture toward the social grounds of knowledge is a rather immodest promissory note—which has come due. In this essay I want to take stock of the promises made, the debts paid, and the theoretical collateral that remains mortgaged. The reader who has stayed with me this far has doubtless granted many premises (provisionally and reluctantly) in the hope that I would make good on them. It is time to repay such indulgence in its own coin.

I shall start by considering the critical apparatus suggested by our field theory. On the assumption that methodological decisions should cohere with theoretical claims about the phenomena to be studied, I shall sketch the epistemic implications of the field theory and try to match them to particular features of a reflective view of critical inquiry (D. L. Swanson, 1977a, 1977b). Since field theory *has* skeptical implications, I shall organize my arguments around a consideration of which features of traditional rhetorical criticism our theory calls into question. My claim is that we may avoid a morass of intractable problems by abandoning the notion of critical *evaluation*.

Consistent with this thinking, I shall introduce critical principles which (I shall say) satisfactorily solve the problems we have posed. I hope to get beyond the obvious (and banal) claim that "rhetoric is epistemic" (or that "epistemics is inevitably rhetorical") by considering the social conditions in which epistemic differences are most often brought to light, namely, disputes, arguments, interfield confrontations. I hope to prove that critical principles can be found which say something of interest about such confrontations—something that illuminates aspects of knowledge and knowing that we have not already seen. These principles (I shall say) are consistent with our assumptions about the epistemic conditions of argument. If they prove plausible, that is, if they offer the promise of a criticism better outfitted to glean insights into the facts of consensus and dissensus, we shall want to call them the "argument of epistemics."

Criticism as Interfield Argument

We know by experience that moral and utilitarian judgments are ubiquitous in daily life. People evaluate their fellows humanely or harshly along value and pragmatic dimensions. It is the hallmark if not the necessary condition of disciplines that they be able to pass confident and decisive judgments upon the abilities and activities of individuals. Cardinal virtues, exemplars of excellence, and the minimum competencies which legitimize an actor's place in a field presuppose that the normative component of social arrangements is of fundamental importance. With respect to the disciplines, the normative and judgmental assumptions and practices are virtually definitive elements. Judgmental and evaluative standards and practices thus figure prominently in field studies of every sort but acquire decisive importance vis-à-vis disciplinary issue fields.

The centrality of evaluation can be explained largely in terms of the functions some fields serve as domains of objectivity. Some fields, especially the disciplinary ones, are able to authorize claims and legitimize practices because they are able as well to judge competencies and appraise performances. To describe such fields is in part to describe what it is like to proceed competently within them. This in turn presupposes that such fields employ critical standards capable of being understood, strived for, and abided by and that these standards bear directly upon field practices. Every field has its own "city of truth" (Toulmin, 1976) which authorizes critical evaluations of arguments and practices and which countenances particular methodological criticisms.

In disciplinary fields, the interrogatory character of the rites of passage by which novices are accorded full membership presupposes the necessity of evaluation, that is, of fixed, agreed-upon minimal competencies. The inquisitorial air in doctoral examinations or the reliance upon formal standardized examinations exemplifies this perceived necessity. Both methods presuppose that a person applies for admission into a field—the price being meeting the standards. The ticket for entrance into many ordinary fields may differ in some respects from that of the disciplinary fields (one might, for example, merely have to declare one's affiliations or willingness to abide by certain rules; or one might have to "witness" in the fundamentalist way) but it shares the presupposition of the disciplines that evaluation is a straightforward and basic way of arranging communal activities.

We might expect that differences in what fields take to be knowledge stem mainly from differences in their methods of evaluation. But this is imprecise because it ignores the fact that fields are substantive domains. Put crudely, the inquisitorial practices of fields do not display consistent differences in method so much as divergent purposes, substantive foci, and authority preferences. Our reformed version of presumption makes it a broad field-invariant evaluative posture which leaves it to particular fields to define the substance and scope of particular burdens of proof. That a person demonstrates competency in verstehen theory and methods cuts no ice with a behaviorist who identifies competency with particular achievements in quantitative work. We are prone to praise competence qua competence, but with exceptions, for example, we might prefer incompetent to competent criminals and enemies. I might respect your competence at mathematics but say that it is irrelevant to doing my work. Evaluation, then, is less a purely formal matter than a substantive and purposive practice employed by interested parties in particular substantive spheres.

This poses two different but related problems. The first can be seen as a particular way of describing interfield relativity. Let us call it *the problem of interfield communication* and stipulate that it takes two forms, namely, difficulties posed by imported concepts and problems of substantive disagreements between fields. So viewed, the problem of interfield communication constitutes the core concern of epistemics because it forces consideration of how different substantive domains borrow one another's concepts yet retain differences in the things taken as knowledge. The second problem is a particularization of both forms of the first, namely, *the problem of critical evaluation*. Criticism is a field, a substantive domain which simultaneously borrows concepts from other fields and presumes to evaluate practices and claims in other fields.[1]

Both problems must be faced squarely. If they are genuine, they require a radical rethinking of the grounds of critical evaluation. If they are insoluble, they require that critics abandon the practice of evaluation. In either case, they pose a tricky agenda. They require consideration of the implications for criticism of the theoretical moves we have made already.

The Problem of Interfield Communication

People reveal things about their inferences and assumptions *when* pressed—and so do argument fields. Inquisitorial and disputative demands occur in arguments, within and across fields. We shall be most interested in arguments across fields, since these may reveal just how incommensurable different fields' standards and facts are.

Skepticism: The Doctrine versus Case-Specific Objections. It belabors the obvious to say that field theory yields a relativity that vitiates most traditional justificational schemes. It may prove more enlightening to consider what kind of relativity this is and what sorts of skeptical questions it poses. Relativism and skepticism are not equivalent doctrines, though the former is sometimes ammunition for the latter and the latter sometimes a ritual piety of the former. Neither in fact needs to be seen as a doctrine at all. Relativism—at least the sort that issues from field theory—is an empirical catalog of sociological differences; skepticism is a posture one takes toward particular knowledge claims. Relativism is a self-sustaining empirical account, while skepticism is always parasitic to the assumptions of the *people* it questions.

Relativism, as defined here, is an acceptance of sociological differences, this acceptance taking several forms. Differences are accepted as being important in themselves, as bearing sometimes decisive importance for philosophical claims about knowledge, and as being insoluble in traditional justificational terms. To gloss, it is not inconsequential that different pragmatic traditions use principles (substantive and formal) that yield different knowledge claims. This is true in two senses. Often, though not always, field actors confront conceptual problems of bewildering complexity which are owed to interfield differences. Their solutions to such problems, even when they become predatory raids upon particular fields, are thus of continuing interest to students of fields. Second, this relativism poses horrendous difficulties for criticism. It forces reconsideration of the very grounds of criticism and raises the specter of a skeptical critique so powerful as to render anything but the most banal criticism inarticulate. It questions, that is, the very possibility of criticism.

If skepticism is nothing but a philosophical doctrine, field theory allows us to ignore it. In the form given it by Hume, it threatens only philosophers and among them only the ones seeking invariant justificatory principles. It cuts no ice in the ongoing pragmatic activities of fields.[2] Qua doctrine, skepticism is a paradigm case of an academic question; the leap from the armchair to a field of activity, of *practices*, is a freeing move: it turns one's attention to the ways field actors in fact bracket their doubts, deal with events, and secure perfectly legitimate "progress" whether or not the skeptical doctrine succeeds on its own terms. If skepticism is a doctrine, it is a field based on grounds and assumptions congenial to it. At issue is not whether skepticism can critique other fields but whether other fields should bother to listen. It will soon be clear why field theory inevitably assigns to the skeptical doctrine the same burdens of proof impinging on any field that presumes to critique another.

Silencing the skeptical doctrine by focusing on practical methods and their pragmatic outcomes is now standard fare. Toulmin (1976) premises his "critical face" of philosophy in answer to the relativism and skepticism of the anthropological face by such a move. Rescher (1970, 1973, 1976, 1977a, 1977b) uses a full-blown argumentation theory as a methodological route bypassing the skeptical doctrine. Both propose justificationist schemes based upon attendance to the practical outcomes of procedures, and both take scientific method as a pradigm case of pragmatic success.

Rescher (1977a, p. 85) rightly argues that a Pyrrhonian victory will be "altogether Pyrrhic" because, inter alia, it is purely hypothetical. Though he ignores the parasitic nature of skepticism (that its strength depends upon the breadth and absolutism of the claims being critiqued), Rescher (1977a) nonetheless makes a powerful case for the shift to practices:

> On his home ground of purely theoretical argumentation regarding abstract possibilities, the sceptic's position is no doubt secure and irrefutable. By refusing to accept the standard probative grounds *as grounds*—as capable of constituting a rational basis of warrant for acceptance—the sceptic assures the security of his system. He thus wins an easy—but empty—victory because he sets up a standard for "knowledge" so hyperbolic that he *systematically denies evidential weight to those considerations which alone could be brought to bear in making out a case to the contrary.* [Pp. 86–87]

This criticism is similar to "closure" (Willard, 1982)—a field practice to be discussed below, although Rescher arrives at it by a route special to his own theory. Of interest here is its central consequence, namely, its requirement that doctrinal skeptics address the particularities of other fields, that they argue their points on a *case-specific basis.* This is dictated by the most efficacious methods of argument—which the skeptic cannot deny without surrendering his own grounding in argument. The need for rational argumentation is the skeptic's core assumption (that is, the justification for particular critiques of, say, absolutist systems). In the practical sphere, the familiar litany of skeptical doubts are ignored on the assumption that results speak for themselves, and the skeptic cannot deny this without grappling with particular cases.

Rescher thus concedes that the skeptical doctrine cannot be defeated on its own grounds—something we may take to be true of any field—but emphasizes that the shift to practice (which many skeptics have taken to be the main reply to the doctrine) is a shift to a particular kind of practice, not practice as such. We have universals of presumption and burden of proof—Rescher's exposition of these being remarkably congenial to our own. "In affecting to disdain *this* the sceptic must now turn his back not simply on the practice of ordinary life, but rationality itself" (1977a, p. 94). The skeptical doctrine, by its own lights, makes no sense apart from the "standard machinery for assessing probative propriety." The debate process, which is central to Rescher's disputational model of inquiry, is thus seen as the facilitating condition of the skeptical critique—just the sort of practice which the skeptic's standard abstract litany cannot ignore. So, "the sceptic thus runs afoul of the demands of that very rationality in whose name he so high-mindedly claims to speak" (1977a, p. 95).

The skeptical doctrine can be set aside because (1) it has been redefined on justificational grounds by Toulmin and Rescher, and (2) nonjustificationist views of criticism are even less vulnerable. Particular skeptical questions—stemming from the skeptical posture as opposed to the doctrine—have to be hashed out on a case-specific basis. This fact does not diminish their power. It remains to be seen whether particular critical enterprises can survive case-specific skeptical critique. But the dispute becomes more manageable by making the burden of proof on the critic more reasonable. Critics who make absolutistic claims, of course, must deal with the doctrine as well as the posture of skepticism. The skeptical doctrine has not been defeated; what Rescher and Toulmin have done is narrow its focus and range of convenience. Critics who make far-reaching exhaustive claims about their work may find themselves beset by the doctrine operating at full power. Every critic, let us say, faces skeptical questions parallel and proportional to the claims he makes. The successful critical theory will be one which survives the skeptical critique appropriate to it.

The Relativity of Fields. In emphasizing the differences among fields, we must not overlook their similarities. Many fields, for example, share general conceptual and procedural assumptions to a sufficient degree that arguments between them may be cut-and-dried substantive disputes which look just like intrafield debates. If two fields share a rough and ready sense of scientific method, this may facilitate clear and straightforward interfield disputes. Thus, for example, psychologists and biologists might debate the merits of particular materialistic claims *if* they belong to issue fields which vouch for the presuppositions behind the claims (the biologist thus finds more commonality with a behaviorist than with a constructivist). Because scientific method crosses many field boundaries, it is tempting to regard it as a regnant overarching principle (as Rescher and Toulmin do in their respective ways). But sharp field differences suggest a more prudent course, namely, assuming that successful universals are content free (for example, presumption). While scientific method may unite some fields, it divides or is irrelevant to others. Presumption fits all fields because it is left to the fields to endow it with content.

Field theory yields the bare fact that anything can be legitimated, given the sociological/rhetorical conditions necessary to its success. This claim is innocuous enough until its implications for criticism are considered. It forces reevaluation of the bases and purposes of criticism and opens the door (as we have seen) to skeptical objections of an especially serious sort.

We have already set out some useful examples. The first contrasted neo-Kantian ethics with cost-benefit analysis, the interesting feature being their mirror-opposite views of whether values can be reduced to quantities (or the language of quantity). Disputes between the two fields are not academic possibilities: they happen often as decision makers weigh the competing claims of value-oriented proposals and the cost-benefit analysts. Since these competing claims are premised upon incommensurable assumptions, they cannot properly speaking be "weighed." Decision makers can only opt for one or the other.

Our second example contrasted the Catholic antiabortion movement with the women's proabortion movement. In this case, the two fields do not embrace incompatible facts so much as facts which are so different as to defy comparison at all! No productive grounds exist for weighing their competing claims; the organizing claims of both possess no *truth conditions* in the standard sense. Neither side is completely willing to submit to the sciences, since both retain the option to interpret scientific findings selectively. Thus, each field places itself beyond critique from the other.

The third example stems from military discourse as we might weigh it against particular ethical principles. Imagine that one might use Sartre's view of evil (the abstraction of that which is concrete) to condemn the general who says, "We had to destroy the town in order to save it." Both fields proceed as if they are beyond critique from the other—the general arguing that "war is hell (and thus) anything goes," the moralist claiming that ethics is prior to (that is, is authorized by) some principle to critique the conduct of war (or the making of military claims).

We might draw another example from the colorful confrontation between "creationists" and "evolutionists." Both sides impute religious fervor to the other; both accuse the other of closed-mindedness and censorship; both accuse the other of justifying claims fideistically; neither side can translate the other's claims into a common language authorizing comparative arguments (and settlement). Both sides thus address (rather than each other) the public—the former trying to gain political power, the latter trying to keep it—an interesting reversal of the Scopes trial. The creationist side can be defended against the evolutionist's attack in a perfectly consistent and forthright way (see Jacobs and Laufersweiler, 1981). If one equates one's intuitions with revelation, the evolutionist has no resources for defeating one's claims. While the creationist is—indeed—wrapping himself in the mantle of "God speaks to me," the evolutionist is just as vulnerable on his own grounds if the creationist argues that the faith in scientific method is merely another religion—a secular one to be sure—but a religion nonetheless. Both sides have guarantors of their knowledge; neither guarantor can (in any obvious way) be compared to the other by virtue of a common language that would authorize a solution.

Critics will get nowhere trying to *settle* these disputes. With what field will they take sides? In each case, the critic cannot take sides with one field versus the other: the guarantors of the critic's claims would *be* the favored field's standards. The critic would become just another advocate in an insoluble conflict. By the universalist account, the critic might propose a field regnant to the contending fields. It would be regnant because its judgmental and veridical standards can arbitrate the dispute at hand. But the pervasive skepticism we set aside in the shift to practices would arise again (at full power), just as it has done with respect to every absolutistic system. Critics would fare no better. No critic could prove his bona fides for settling an interfield dispute of the sort we have described sans a full-dress philosophical development and defense of a successful universal.

So much for justificationism. Fields use different facts. If one set of facts does not square with another, it is up to the fields involved to see if they can set things aright. If *public claims* based on these incompatible facts are made, it is best for the critic to try to make sense of the confrontation rather than trying to settle it. The problem of interfield communication, then, poses the problem of critical evaluation in a blunt way. Critical evaluation is suspect in the senses we have specified; taking sides in interfield disputes places the critic on argumentative ground he cannot justify; thus it is appropriate to ask whether critical evaluation can in any sense be justified.

The Problem of Critical Evaluation

The merest glance at the argumentation literature reveals that evaluation is the pivotal component of its self-definition as a field. Its historical preoccupations are captured in the question, "What is the force of the better argument?" The thrust of this question has been generally conceived to be evaluative, which has uniformly been taken to mean that argumentation is a "normative" discipline (Wenzel, 1980; Balthrop, 1980; McKerrow, 1977, 1980a, 1982). The early formulations did not use "normative" to mean the study of argument norms in communities of discourse; argumentation was an applied logic aiming purely at drawing judgments of ordinary discourse. Lately, a preoccupation with Toulmin's thought has legitimized the sociological reading of "normative," although this is widely thought to mean that field theory is an obstacle to be overcome: the relativity of fields is a smokescreen which obscures the invariant principles which vouch for decisions about "better arguments." Because fields are not taken seriously, criticism is widely thought to turn upon evaluations, the critic's justifications for saying that particular arguments are right or wrong, good or evil, rational or irrational, mundane or great.

This organizing view is owed to a belief in universals and to the view of argumentative *risk* associated with universalism. The universalists base their thinking on an animus for relativisms and feel proportionately obliged to keep the field idea at arm's length. Taking fields (and their differences) seriously immediately calls evaluative standards into doubt, not by appeal to skeptical doctrine but by case-specific skeptical arguments. Veatch (1962) and Toulmin (1972, 1976) thus organize their objections to relativisms on the ground that they vitiate evaluation. Veatch reiterates a classic objection to relativism which says (to gloss) that to accept it is to admit that the fascists cannot be answered when they mockingly claim that logic and rational appeals can justify even genocide. But this objection hardly refutes the claim: it only says that relativisms are not true because it would be horrible if they were; the need to evaluate is equated with a need to reply to the fascists, a fallacy if there ever was one. Toulmin similarly justifies his middle course between absolutism and relativism by (1) the well-argued view that absolutism obscures working logics and situational adaptations, and (2) the *taken-for-granted* ground that relativism vitiates evaluation. In both cases, the central objection to relativism is its consequences for evaluation.

Universalism thus stems from a sturdy hope that the facts of fields will not turn out to be the whole story. Relativism is eschewed as a "counsel of despair," a "surrender to chaos," a "loss of coherence." These apocalyptic phrases make sense only in reference to the consequences for evaluation. Thus, even those who grant that field theory describes a relativity retain an abiding "animal faith" in universalism, not because they have good grounds for believing it but because the consequences of surrendering it are not to be borne.

This continuing search for invariant judgmental principles is reinforced by a confusion of a field practice with the organizing concerns of criticism. Because to argue—in most fields at least—is to risk one's self, that is, to place one's views at risk against some societal check, it is mistakenly thought that every arguer is at risk vis-à-vis the critic's standards. Arguers in fields *do* put themselves at risk, as an implicit or considered decision; but they do so vis-à-vis their *field's* standards. Critics conclude from this that the risk of arguing must be a universal, thereby assuming that every arguer is at risk of *the critic's* standards.

Field theory guts this assumption. If the critic's standards differ from a field's, the critic has no grounds for proving their superiority. Nor can the critic confidently presume a taken-for-granted right to evaluate a field actor on the grounds that the speaker is—in a general sense— "at risk." The speaker does not put himself—in a general sense—at risk.[3] The critic can define the critical perspective *entirely* in the field's terms (which many contemporary critics in fact do) to authorize evaluations by virtue of the "risk" notion. Leaving aside the objection already raised (that this makes criticism indistinguishable from reflective theorizing in fields), the additional objection arises that the critic must completely abandon universalist aims to take this posture. One could examine cost-benefit arguments only in terms of that field's presuppositions (and be similarly limited with respect to each of our examples).[4]

We avoid these problems by (1) giving fields their due, seeing them as self-contained bodies of implications which may not fit our own preferences, (2) the muddled notion of "risk," that is, by realizing that because a speaker risks his field's standards, this does not mean he incurs risk from the critic's, and (3) realizing that criticism is itself an argument field.

To regard criticism as a field has far-reaching consequences. It puts the universalism issue into a more useful perspective. If critics claim to traffic in principles which overarch the procedures and practices of other fields (and thereby authorize evaluations of these procedures and practices), they are describing the critical field in the same terms the absolutist philosophers used to define philosophy (in essence, they are equally pretentious claims). They thereby incur the same burdens. Arrayed against them are the skeptical doctrine (in full bloom), case-specific skeptical demands, and the tu quoque. The outcome is a forgone conclusion.

Quite apart from these standard objections to making any field regnant to others is the pragmatic probability that the critic instead of being rebutted would be ignored. The critic who chides the general for "abstracting that which is concrete" will likely not be answered with a full-dress defense of the autonomy of military discourse from philosophy. More likely the general will shrug and go his way, crediting the moralist with ignorance of the "war is hell" assumption which justifies particular military claims.

Thus, taking evaluation to be the cornerstone of criticism requires a universalism that cannot be defended—at least on justificationist grounds. The risk argument works best when the particularities of fields are ignored and least well when it is assumed that arguers put themselves at risk vis-à-vis their field standards. If criticism is itself a field, it incurs the burdens impinging on any field claiming regnancy over other fields—these burdens being undischargeable, given present theoretical resources. The result is that field theory will prove unpalatable to people who believe relativity to be merely a temporary setback in critical development. Thus the present state of Toulmin's theory (namely, without a fleshed-out impartial standpoint of rationality but with the promise of one) is thought to be a transitional one. Since critics are unlikely to succeed with the burdens that defeated the absolutists, they are apparently happy to cool their heels while waiting for Toulmin to hand them a legitimizing concept.

Preconditions of Evaluation

The disciplines are not invariably dependable conceptual models for understanding epistemic and evaluative practices. They lead to the assumption that because fields (especially the disciplines) are founded on evaluation, this automatically authorizes the critic's assumption that every arguer is at risk of *his* standards. Oftentimes the contrivances of mundane social life are surer guides to our thinking, and this may prove to be the case with respect to evaluation as well. Plausible sociological generalizations may illuminate the narrower concerns of the disciplines (if it is granted that the disciplines are sociological entities).

In the mundane sphere, it is a serious business for one person to evaluate another. If I call you "evil," "stupid," or "narrow-minded," I attack the bases of your moral worth or your autonomy as a choice-making animal. Notice, for instance, how prone we are to tell children that name-calling is as evil as assault, on the grounds (presumably) that strong criticism is a sort of violence. Notice as well that traditional sociological explanations of the evils of labeling apply here: to name someone a "pervert," "deviant," or "unintelligent" has profound consequences for the namer and the named.

It might be objected that a false analogy is being formed here; critics evaluate arguments, not people. The literary critic's focus upon the work rather than the author seems to be a clear-cut case. But this objection has at least four weaknesses. First, it is unsound because rationality is said (in virtually all of its guises) to be a human characteristic. That my argument is rational is thus said to symptomize my rationality. Common locutions in ordinary and philosophic parlance thus include "being rational" and "to be rational is to behave thusly." The importance of rationality is what it says to and about the speaker. The proof of this is that to deny it one must turn it around, that is, say that a person can make a rational argument without being rational. But this is implausible: "the irrational man said rational things" makes rationality a trivial characteristic of his speech. To defend this one would have to prove that rationality inheres not in people but in language and logic—as if these systems were not human productions. Even the strictest absolutists ended up with the very different view that rationality consisted in a person's use of a system.

Second, the objection clashes with the plausible pedagogical claim that students learn logic in order to *be* rational. The Greco-Roman tradition has held rationality to be a virtue—in one sense or another—and irrationality to be a vice. While there are disputes about the nature of virtues and vices, it is passably safe to say that they are thought to be human characteristics. It seems needlessly complex to insist that vices and virtues be characteristics of languages as opposed to people.

Third, the objection blurs the intentional character of situated utterance. To stipulate that rationality inheres in arguments, not people, requires that one ignore intended-toward meanings and their adaptations to definitions of situation. One perfectly trivial observation defeats this notion: people often use arcane and specialized meanings; thus any statement is capable of being rational or irrational, depending upon the intentions toward it. If the meanings of utterance are simultaneously conventional and intentional (and if one grants that these sometimes differ), explanations of rationality will most easily succeed when they make it a characteristic of intentional meanings. To say otherwise is to say that rationality does not speak to situated choices.

Fourth, the objection cannot take sustenance from distinctions between public and private reasoning (for example, Toulmin's). As an exegetical matter, Toulmin couches his discussions of rationality in personalistic terms, not as an expositional accident, but as a considered claim that being rational is something a person does. The focus is thus upon what a *person* does in considering conceptual change.

So the objection that critics evaluate arguments, not people, is no objection at all. The literary analogy is implausible because evaluations of situated utterance differ *in kind* from literary criticism. While a novel might be seen as a self-contained object, situated utterance cannot (because its meanings are intentional and context embedded). It seems pointless to grapple with the consequences of "the irrational man said rational things" or "the rational man said irrational things" solely to defend a critical practice. Both statements might be true in certain exotic cases (for example, the rational man said irrational things in order to appear irrational for strategic purposes); but even these cases require that rationality be seen as an attribute of humans, not impersonal systems.

So we are on arguably sure ground in calling evaluation a serious matter. The analogy between critical evaluation and social labeling seems plausible. It is further buttressed by considering that the clinician who labels a patient "deviant," "dangerous," or "perverted" usually does so by reference to considered *judgmental standards.* He compares the present case with relevant social norms in much the same way critics compare instances with broad standards. Both labeling and evaluation have the same *political* effects (Szasz, 1961, 1970). Labeling homosexuals "perverts" is a political move affecting their legal rights and the obligations of "normals" toward them. Labeling minorities "unintelligent" functions similarly. Analogously, the surest thing to be said of the term "irrational" is that we use it to name people with whom we sharply disagree, this being as true of academics as of ordinary folk. Analytic philosophers, for example, termed certain intuitionists "irrationalists" or "antirational." Doing so served the political function of naming deviates, of carving one side away from mainstream (orthodox) thinking.

This view squares with field theory. Convention and orthodoxy are (even in Toulmin's view) foundational to the ongoing operations of fields. Veridical and judgmental standards thus serve political as well as epistemic functions. Nor are these functions consistently distinguishable. If they were, the problem of distinguishing worthy (justified) claims from merely orthodox ones would not constitute the core dispute in contemporary epistemics.

There are parallels as well between the usual objections raised against labeling and critical evaluations. For instance, the claim that labeling becomes a self-fulfilling prophecy applies equally to calling someone irrational. It is a way of cutting off dialogue between dissidents and the defenders of a paradigm. It affects how the named people see themselves and how the namer sees them. The burden of rejoinder is usually upon the person named, since fields are presumptively correct.

The Price of Evaluation

Having proved that evaluation is a serious business, I want to prove that it is needlessly expensive. It is, for example, paradoxical, muddled, and untenable if criticism is seeable as a field. In considering these claims I hope to illuminate the ways critics confound the distinction between universal and field-based norms.

The Necessary Evils Paradox. Necessary evils are not necessarily paradoxical, but this one probably is. The paradox emerges when we rehash Veatch's arguments about answering the fascists. Recall that we judged his reasoning to be tangential to the probity of relativistic claims (and to the claims of particular relativisms). Veatch's claim reduces to saying that relativity must not be true because relativisms have intolerable consequences. One could grant the evils we have imputed to labeling and name-calling but could plausibly argue that it is necessary to answer the fascists. Doing so yields the necessary evil. Evaluation may be a bad business, but it is essential for certain purposes (which we might gloss to read, "it is necessary to do evil to evildoers"). The arguments by which this is justified thus authorize evaluation in general. We are to take the good with the bad.

What is happening here is that an obviously evil domain is assumed to require universal standards of good and evil to answer it. The reasoning works like this: (1) field theory is an extreme relativism; (2) given Nazi assumptions, Auschwitz *was* a good thing; (3) if humans generally believed that genocide is a good thing, only a deviate could doubt it; and (4) if field theory is taken seriously, there are no answers to the fascists. The weakness resides in (4). Let us see how.

We escape this paradox not by accepting one or the other side of it but by adjusting our thinking. The paradox exists only if one equates answering the fascists with the purely theoretical aspects of critical evaluation. We have said that field theory studies how actors in fact judge and verify and that such empirical matters should not be muddled with universalism. We have set aside the pardonable but untenable expectation that when people do evil things, the cosmos rather than mere field actors should answer them. The truth or falsity of particular relativistic claims does not turn on the fact that people in fact *did* answer the fascists and that they did so because they argued a variety of matters out in particular ways. Whether genocide is (grandly, ontologically) evil is beside the point that people decided that it was for reasons drawn from particular fields of discourse. The judgmental and veridical standards (and the argument processes that animated them) which guided the answers to the fascists are thus of paramount interest to students of knowledge. The villain, then, is evaluation. Abandon the aim of saying which fields are right and wrong, of *arbitrating* interfield disputes, and you avoid the necessary evils paradox.

We reach this result only by assuming that social practices are just as "real" as any of the entities that have been supposed to be universals (and that abstractions about social processes are just as interesting as the postulated essences thought to be universals). The communicational activities which animate fields (and the psychological processes which feed and are fed by them) have real consequences, that is, in the standard interactionist sense (drawn from W. I. Thomas) that "situations defined as real are real in their consequences." Consider, for example, that if we ask whether there is such a thing as rationality, we can easily affirm it if we construe the question as a sociological one. There is abundant evidence that field actors in fact believe that rationality is a real attribute of their thoughts and actions. If we take the question to be a broad ontological query, we are drawn back into the endless disputes about essences. By reentering these disputes, we shall obscure the social phenomena (and research) that might illuminate the recurring themes in field activities which embody rationality. We might be led to think that how people in fact did answer the fascists is in itself uninteresting.

So far I claim to have proved that evaluation introduces a necessary evils paradox into argumentation and epistemics (and thus into criticism). This diverts our attention from what field theory does best, namely, descriptive work dealing with how people in fact evaluate the claims and actions of their fellows.

The Muddle: Obscuring the Definition of Situation. I turn now to the related claim that evaluation—taken to be the core critical project—obscures the importance and nature of the definition of the situation. Fields (we have said) are conventionally organized ways of defining situations. So the importance of the present claim is that it points to a misdirection of sociological thinking and (proportionately) to a poor use of field theory. I can perhaps clarify this claim by considering Asch's (1957) arguments against relativism. My claim is that when one is preoccupied with refuting relativisms in order to salvage the "right" to evaluate claims one wishes to reject, one argues one's case on the least productive grounds.

Asch offers well-conceived arguments which prove that relativists often carelessly argue their own positions and that they assume (rather than carefully argue) too many things. They often, Asch says, blithely *assume* that diverse evaluations of the "same act" are unquestionable proof that different evaluative principles are being used. Asch then turns to what I take to be a seminal claim, namely, that many differences among men are attributable to the differences in their circumstances; but the fact that men adapt to circumstances is itself a universal. This is a seminal idea because it can be made to say that the definition of situation, role taking, the temporary inhibitions of action as the perspectives of others are assessed, all compose universals of context-embedded activity. But Asch draws from this sound reasoning a view that contemporary field theorists cannot successfully work with, namely, that "the essential proposition of ethical relativism states that one can connect to the *identical situation* different and even opposed evaluations." (Asch, 1957; emphasis added). I underscore "identical situation" to flag Asch's commitment to the belief that situations themselves have objective knowable characteristics. He does *not* mean by definition of situation what the symbolic interactionists mean; the phrase "situations defined as real are real in their consequences" would have no meaning for him.

Asch is dependent upon just the sorts of assumptions all evaluationists must use. He assumes that relativism is a monolith. Field theory in any other than an innocuous rendering says precisely the opposite—there should be as many variants of relativism as there are fields trafficking in it. He assumes also that we need the concept of a "human nature" (an invariant nature) to *evaluate* moral claims; and he assumes that this is so because relativists—by their nature, one would suppose—despair of evaluation. He reaches this claim by arguing that relativists miss the importance of situations. Since he lacks the idea of fields, he reduces relativity to different situations.

Field theory is a deadlier enemy than the one Asch confronts, since it cuts across and through "cultures." So "cultural relativity" is too gross and combinatorial a phrase; it blurs interfield differences within cultures. Field theory does not need the "culture" concept to describe relativity (though field theory could use it to describe broad differences between societies). The field theory vocabulary is more precise, since it shows that cultures are not monolithic, that they are balkanized into communities of discourse; and *this* relativism is far more resistant to Asch's objections than the gross relativity he attacks.

What leads Asch astray is that he formulates "the problem of relativism" on the implicit assumption that it is a "problem" of evaluation. In briefest compass, (1) cultural diversity is a fact; (2) it undermines absolutist claims; (3) the "profound conditioning" effects of social conditions have been overlooked by relativists, leading them to ignore the *psychological content of situations;* thus (4) the fact of cultural diversity does not countenance the claim that values differ—it only proves that people respond to different situations. The importance of these arguments is that they bear upon the invariance of human nature—this being understood in turn to bear upon the viability of evaluational claims; the disputes between absolutists and relativists, then, take their importance from an implicit need to evaluate, to compare cultures and their practices and to make value judgments about their differences. The fact that infanticide is rejected by one society but embraced by another is important only because it endangers universalistic proclamations about infanticide; otherwise it would be only a curiosity.

Field theory assigns greater urgency to descriptive work aimed at understanding argument fields and allows us to bracket universal evaluations. Notice what happens to Asch's arguments when a defense of evaluative schemes is no longer defined as the core problem. First, unencumbered with the need to make evaluative comparisons, we can look at different fields on their own terms. By discarding evaluation, we discard a pernicious traditional idea (namely, *tout comprendre, c'est tout pardonner*). This rather standard view is *coherent only* as a justification of ethnocentrism. Take the claim as is, and the only justification for looking at alternative cultures is to describe their weaknesses vis-à-vis one's own culture. Second, we can look at deterministic ideas more open-mindedly because we no longer need them to salvage something; Asch *needs* the deterministic conditioning view to link situational characteristics to the human actions they produce— and notice how this rules the definition of situation idea out of his thinking, that is, it will not give him the sort of invariant human nature his arguments require to refute the relativists' claims about value diversity. The need to defend evaluation, then, leads to uncritical acceptance of a certain view of "psychological content" of situations. Asch has so framed his arguments that he must defend conditioning and situational determination of behavior at all costs; he is in this fix because he assumes that the main point of a universal must be evaluation.

If it is the way of the world that universals exist and can be understood, it is nonetheless possible (field theory makes that "probable") that these universals might not be what traditional theorists have expected. That humans define situations and act according to their definitions may be universal, but the contents of definitions may differ in nontrivial ways. The contents manifestly differ across fields in far stronger ways than early relativists may have thought—which is a generous way of saying that absolutist schemes were brought down by the weakest versions of relativism. So however the ontological issues turn out, man's efforts after order will persist, and this, too, is the way of the world.

Proceeding this way, I am assuming the merits of some familiar arguments. These bear mention here to clarify the present claims:

1. *The "multiple realities" arguments are strong.* Schutz and others have hashed these out; to paraphrase Goodman, it makes no sense to speak of *the* way of the world; there are as many ways of the world as there are persuasive visions of it (Goodman, 1960). It is the nature of art works to be as varied as the interpretations made of them (Gadamer, 1976); and likewise, epistemic claims are always constructed alternatives (Schutz, 1967).

2. *Field theory is an especially strong variant of the multiple realities argument.* Brown's argument will do: "Reality becomes richer and more varied in the multiplication of forms of its symbolic expression. This is not progress, gradually encompassing more and more reality un-til...Being has been encircled and conquered. It is rather progress in the respect of progressive revelation, in which each theory, each world view reveals another immanence in our own world, in which each vision of reality provides an additional perspective into our capacity for objectification" (Brown, 1977, p. 39–40).

3. *To understand multiple realities, one must understand how ideas pass muster.* Judgmental and veridical standards are the glue binding argument fields together; they are continually reconfirmed through use (Farrell, 1976, 1977; Goodwin and Wenzel, 1979; McKerrow, 1980a). We thus say the same things of fields that we do of psychological perspectives; there is a sameness to how actors take the perspective of a field and how researchers do (Cicourel, 1970).

4. *Multiple realities are incomplete, that is, continually changing.* We often say this about a person's perspective, and since fields are accomplishments of the defining activities of their actors, we must say the same of fields. This notion squares with the *accomplishment* maxim because the fact that a framework is not fully accomplished does not mean that one cannot treat it *as if* it were accomplished.

These claims are familiar turf and need no belaboring here. They combine to suggest the importance of context embeddedness and (thus) the importance of the *adaptive* character of human activities.

"Tout comprendre, c'est tout pardonner" made sense only because of the implicit commitment to evaluation undergirding it. There were some points of view thought to be so deviant from acceptable standards of morality and conduct that they should not be understood on their own terms. There was something intuitively distasteful about taking Heidreich's worldview on *its* terms and finding that it logically held together; this seemed to be an utter degradation of values. It was (rather) a discrediting of logic as a sociological and psychological model. If logic was the language of the cosmos and Heidreich's point of view was logical, the result was not to be borne. To try to see things as Heidreich did was tantamount to legitimizing his thinking. This meant, inter alia, that the critical aim had to be to condemn Heidreich—a goal that rather ruled out understanding that point of view.

Consider a less clear-cut case. We often study "cults" as if our naming them "cults" legitimated certain criticisms. But one man's cult is another man's religion; the use of "cult" merely exposes a critic's pieties and sociopolitical preferences. The assumption (presumably) is that cults of which I disapprove should not prove to be well founded; they should be illogical or based at least upon beliefs bizarre enough that I can condescend to the field. If my own critical assumptions turn out to be as dependent on faith as the cult's assumptions are, I am doing nothing more legitimate than what children do when they point at people they do not like and call them names.

To make sense, then, the evaluationist line requires untenable assumptions about the objects of criticism and about the privileges of the critical stance. The standard skeptical objections arise respecting these; and the usual result ensues. Respecting particular critical acts, these are case-specific skeptical objections (which are thus not vulnerable to the replies which limit the power of the skeptical doctrine).

The Fruitless Effort Argument. To continue with case-specific skeptical objections, I turn to the claim that attempts to justify critical evaluations are fruitless efforts. The cumbersome arguments critics must make (to justify their assumptions) inevitably obscure explicative work. The results of these arguments are largely inconclusive, although it usually works out that even conclusive judgments are trivialities.

This argument has been extensively considered by literary and art critics. Eliot (1960), reacting to the futility (and misdirectedness) of evaluative criticism, argued that judgments and appreciations had replaced explication and comparison for the "dogmatic and lazy mind." Evaluations, he argued, could not be part of the critic's "serious business" (see Wimsatt, 1963). Seeing criticism as elucidative and explicative is now standard fare among the critics who three decades ago concerned themselves with judgments about "greatness," "correctness," "morality," and the like.

The problems which literary and art critics recognized long ago are far more urgent for critics who deal with situated speech. A critic's standard must be adapted to the situation being studied, and to evaluate action the critic must argue that the critical standard is more appropriate to the situation under study (or in some other sense better) than the points of view of the involved actors. This often issues in banalities of the "if only he had known" variety. A standard critical argument for historians might say, "General Smith's error was in not occupying Hill-14; the enemy was not there, but Smith erroneously thought the enemy was there; now let us hash out whether this was a culpable error or not." What goes wrong here is that the critic is so preoccupied with making proclamations that General Smith's way of seeing the situation will be obscured. Likewise, rhetorical critics often argue that speaker A should have made argument X rather than Y. Such claims are always inconclusive; but if we consider the conditions under which they might prove conclusive, we shall see that the essential precondition is that the critical claims be innocuous.[5]

Our multiple realities argument combined with Kelly's (1955) view of *constructive alternativism* (saying that every event is open to alternative construction) are case-specific challenges to any critic's claim to produce a conclusive (and correct) evaluation. Since critics who *judge* actors and events have to meet the skeptical challenges and tu quoque argument writ small, they devote more of their time to hedging their bets than to doing criticism. Strictly speaking, such judgments are most easily justified when they appear in critical essays— essays in the old sense: the critic makes no pretense of objectivity but is an advocate defending a particular position. But of course, the critics who want to make evaluation the center of the critical enterprise rarely see it this way. They seek universal standards of judgment— absolutism writ small. Any judgment, then, is bound to be one scenario among many—and not demonstrably better than the others.

But let us suppose that a conclusive judgment is possible, that a critic could conclusively say that General Smith erred. What would this teach us? A plausible inference is that we would learn nothing of interest: military science does not extend its knowledge by knowing that Smith erred in thinking that *that* hill was unoccupied; there is nothing about this case which will tell General Jones that *this* hill is unoccupied. Knowing that persuader A *should have* argued X does not tell speaker B whether X is the best argument in B's situation.

It is often said that we learn from experience, but let us think this through. The lesson for the general is to have good intelligence operations—a maxim we could arrive at without looking at any particular situations. The lesson for the persuader is that argument X did not work in *that* situation—which does not speak to its usefulness or propriety in *this* situation. To draw lessons from experience—which is what explicative criticism seeks to do—is to perceive their recurring themes. Were every situation utterly distinct, completely unique, we could have no *experience*. Our experience consists of the recurring themes we see in events (Kelly, 1955). To construct these recurring themes requires that we place interpretations upon the events—as Kelly says, compare and contrast them to other events. This requires that we see General Smith's situation as the general saw it. Our license to critique the general surely presupposes that we know what the general thought he was doing.

Critical epistemology—as the field of epistemics is conceived here—thus aims at a hermeneutic posture studying the alternative constructions people place on events. It aims to produce a body of knowledge about such interpretations, a fleshed-out sense of the constructive alternatives available (and usable) in different situations. So viewed, criticism is capable of "progress" or epistemic growth. But if its aim is to elaborate our understanding of how people construe events, it will be best served by avoiding the fruitless search for evaluative principles. Evaluation presupposes the critics can *justify* their judgments, that is, can defeat specific skeptical objections. Yet even if conclusive evaluations proved possible, the precondition of making them is extreme situationalism—which trivializes the evaluation, that is, makes it impossible to perceive recurring themes uniting the situation under study to other similar situations. To perceive unifying threads among situations is to see them as their actors saw them. Abandoning the preoccupation with evaluation will facilitate this aim.

An Example of Practical Criticism. Let me try on a metaphor—which can be taken rather literally. In aviation it is often said that only general rules for weather flying can be propounded, because no two situations are the same. That is, within any pilot's realm of experience, no two weather conditions ever have been or ever will be the same. There can be no rules such as "one can safely fly through a hole of five miles width between cumulonimbus clouds." Sometimes yes, sometimes no; the winds are never the same. So the "lessons of experience" are problematic. An organizing article of faith among pilots is that whether X makes it safely through a five-mile breach in a squall line bears little if at all on Y's chances for doing the same, even a few minutes after X's passage. So the rule is "go and see; play it safe," without specifying what "play it safe" means. The tenor of this reasoning is that one adapts to situations rather than follow general rules. The only valid general rules are *so* general that they make little sense until plugged into specific contexts. "Play it safe; go and see" tells a pilot he may go and look for a breach in a squall line; but it is up to him whether to try it. Nothing in the general rule tells him whether he should. Since weather changes rapidly, the fact that *X* made it through minutes ago is no guarantee that it is still safe.

Pilots fly their planes with appalling frequency into weather they cannot handle. After crashes, investigative teams perform what can only be called "criticism." They assess what happened and try to judge how the pilot *erred*. Sometimes they decide that a pilot broke one of the general rules (in principle), that is, he did not play it safe; he took undue chances. Most times this is a banality; the scattered debris proves that the pilot took chances and that the odds were bad. One could reach this conclusion without seeing the crash site. Other times specific causes are mentioned: "The pilot error occurred as positive control was lost after entering a downburst or wind sheer condition." The lesson is that we should avoid downbursts. But this conclusion is trivial. All trained pilots know to avoid downbursts; they merely do not know how (other than to avoid flying at all when thunderstorms are scudding about).

The general rules tell a pilot to be safe, but not how to be safe on particular occasions. Since particular occasions are only roughly similar, and never the same, it is nearly always banal to conduct lengthy investigations to conclude that a pilot erred in thinking he could get through *that* gap in a squall line. We could get this conclusion from newspapers. It has no cautionary value, since *that* gap will never exist again. Thus the evaluations most easily made of pilots who crash are authorized by rules so general and abstract that the breaking of them means little if people get away with it and the pointing finger at pilots who do not get away with it has no pedagogical value. Since *that* gap in a squall line will never exist again, the best general rule is "try not to crash."

I belabor this metaphor because it is appropriate to the hermeneutic critical epistemology I have in mind. The things we say of weather are plausibly analogous to the things we must say of social reality. Just as weathermen deliberate not about particular situations but about the sufficiency of interpretations, so social critics will learn little from rules so general as to apply across all situations. A "wrong" argument in situation *X* may prove to be the best argument in future contexts; so the general rule which proves that an argument is wrong will be so abstract as to make no useful predictions about future situations.

There is a more productive line which our metaphor can illustrate. Accident investigators often try to reconstruct the processes of *judgment* (the pilot's thoughts) which lead to an accident. This is a corollary development to the pedagogical aim of teaching good judgment rather than general rules. The organizing question is something on the order of, "Why did *A* think he was playing safe when he was not?" This is a process of perspective taking in which investigators try to see the whole flight from the pilot's point of view—to accept his logic and see how it works out. In a spirit analogous to weltanschauungen thinking, the investigators take the pilot's starting point as a theoretical starting point to work out the operations of the flight presumably as the pilot did. Their concern is not centrally with assigning praise or blame or with belaboring the obvious, for example, "positive control was lost due to ice buildup on the control surfaces; this proves that one should avoid ice." The aim is to say why someone proceeding in a certain way permitted a given situation to develop. The search is for working principles of judgment—ways of thinking that would help a pilot avoid thinking he was playing it safe when he was not.

The investigators of air crashes have a self-evident error scattered on the ground before them, whereas social researchers often have the reverse (if, for example, they want to discuss the strengths and weaknesses even of successful enterprises). But just as accident investigators sometimes find nothing wrong with a pilot's judgment (and thus find themselves faced with an inexplicable crash), so the very idea of error is problematic in social criticism. The fact that arguments succeed once but fail afterward can mean nothing unless the situations in which the successes and failures occur are *understood*—the precondition being seeing the situations as the participants saw them. While general rules are sometimes helpful (for example, persuasion is enhanced by emphasizing the speaker's commonality with the audience), there are nontrivial exceptions (for example, credibility sometimes requires that the speaker be *different* from the auditor [Delia, 1976a], depending upon the auditor's *orientation* to the situation).

The lessons to be drawn from instances concern interpretations. We may plausibly assume that a person's actions stem from his constructions of his alternatives (Kelly 1955, 1961, 1965, 1969, 1977) and that a crucial aspect of these alternatives is their perceived appropriateness to a situation (Fransella, 1972, 1977; Goffman, 1959, 1961a, 1961b, 1963, 1967, 1969, 1971, 1974). Since every situation can be alternatively construed, the different interpretations people in fact place upon events are of central interest (see Adams-Weber, 1969, 1979; Argyle,

1964, 1970; Bannister, 1966, 1970; Bannister and Fransella, 1971; Fransella and Bannister, 1977; Bernstein, 1958, 1964a, 1964b; Delia and Grossberg, 1977; Delia, O'Keefe, and O'Keefe, 1982).

By this view criticism is the mode of epistemology which aims at illuminating the effects of assumptions. It seeks to understand the reality of events by explaining the alternative constructions that may be placed upon them. Its subject matter is the range of interpretive possibilities presented in situations, the cognitive effects of different interpretations, and the stances actors in fact adopt (Zimmerman and Pollner, 1970; Wax, 1967; Weber, 1949, 1962; Turner, 1974; cf. Abel, 1948). Our holistic view directs our attention to the ways individuals make their social activities and cognitive arrangements square with one another (Schank and Abelson, 1977; C. Taylor, 1964; Wyer and Carlston, 1979). "Every form of existence has its source in some peculiar way of seeing, some intellectual formulation and intuition of meaning" (Cassirer, 1946, pp. 8–9). Since all events are open to alternative construction (Kelly, 1955, 1969, 1977; Cohen, 1962; Friedrichs, 1970), it is never a matter of indifference which interpretations people choose to organize events. Having said that adaptations to situations are virtually definitive of human activity, we are led to say that criticism's most basic job is the explication of the effects of assumptions upon situational adaptations (Gross, 1960; Gurvitch, 1971; Gurwitsch, 1964, 1966). Since the reality of a point of view consists of the alternative interpretations that can be made of it, criticism is (properly speaking) the working out of the implications of alternative interpretations (DuFrenne, 1946, 1953; Outhwaite, 1975; Polanyi, 1958, 1966; Polanyi and Prosch, 1975; Rabinow and Sullivan, 1979; Psathas, 1979; Pollner, 1970; Remmling, 1973; Schutz and Luckmann, 1973).

One can draw parallels between this hermeneutic critical project and certain views of literary criticism (Booth, 1979; Davis 1978; Iser, 1978). But the study of the effects of assumptions requires a focus upon particular circumstanced activities—the more precise model being qualitative sociology rather than literary criticism. This thinking has been extensively discussed (see Brown, 1977; Douglas, 1970a, 1970b, 1971, 1972, 1977a, 1977b; Denzin, 1970; Filmer et al., 1973; Garfinkle and Sacks, 1970; Gendlin, 1962; Gidlow, 1972; Glaser and Strauss, 1964, 1967; Goldthorpe, 1973; Murphy, 1971; Park, 1969; Znaniecki, 1934, 1940, 1952, 1955). We need not present anew a case for qualitative sociology and criticism; the world does not need another one (Schwartz and Jacobs, 1979; Becker, 1970; Gouldner, 1970; Filstead, 1970). Our parallel with aviation accident investigations hints at the particular critical project appropriate to our aims, namely, the reconstruction of situated judgments. The idea is to understand situations by understanding how people define and adapt to them.

Criticism as Perspective Taking

They said, "You have a blue guitar,
You do not play things as they are."

The man replied, "Things as they are
Are changed upon the blue guitar."[6]

Some claims ring true even when subjected to vastly different interpretations. A case in point is Aristotle's justly famous claim that all
men by nature desire to know. If we ignore Aristotle's teleology and
monism, we can gloss this claim to say that people seek to predict and
control events. As Kelly's man-as-scientist metaphor says, humans are
forward-looking calculative beings who base their interpretations
upon the recurring themes they discern in events. They construe
events so as to enhance their understandings of them; they make
cognitive decisions about the appropriateness of particular constructs
to particular events. They objectify their subjective interpretations by
putting them to social tests, by trying them out on other people, by
weighing them against communal standards. A plausible inference
from this is that there is an ongoing dialectic between a person's
assumptions and his particular adaptations to situations—this dialectic expressing most exactly how argument fields are brought to life.
Argument criticism is thus a way of studying the ways objectivity is
intersubjectively created and sustained.

Arguments—understood as social comparison processes—are sub-
ject-designed experiments in which arguers try out hypotheses and
evaluate results. They are interactions in which actors more explicitly
than usual bring alternative perspectives into conflict; their inquisitorial nature legitimates demands for warrants and evidence—
which often means that more total information about a person's cognitive processes is publicly available than is usually the case. Arguments
are thus congenial research foci. They display more vividly than any
other form of social action the processes by which people pass muster
on knowledge.

Criticism—generically—seeks to unpack the possibilities of its objects. Literary criticism probes the possibilities of alternative interpretations of literary works. Argument criticism looks to the
interpretations actually operating in the situations under study—thus
expanding the traditional hermeneutic focus upon the text. It necessarily attributes motives and intentions to speakers because it aims at
understanding the practice of objectifying by illuminating the effects
of definitions of situation upon particular argument utterances. While
the literary critic can unpack the possibilities of a text more or less
apart from the peculiarities of its author, the argument critic is

centrally concerned with the speaker. The focus is upon what Gadamer (1976) has called "the vast realm of the occasionality of all speaking," the context embeddedness of utterance. The assumption is that speakers use definitions of situation to give sense to their utterances—thus making utterance irretrievably indexical.

Nobody questions that a person's lived world is a subjective place filled with idiosyncratic interpretations, special assumptions, and unique constructions of events. What has always been at issue is whether sense can be made of these. For evaluationists, the worst to be said of a theory is that it "exalts idiosyncrasies." But this is perhaps too facile: if everyone has idiosyncrasies, idiosyncrasies are the rule, not the exception. Some theorists will grant this point but infer that it vitiates useful criticism and research. It is better (by this account) to see particular utterances as special cases of conventional meanings.

There is arguably a parallel between the evaluationists' dissatisfaction with idiosyncrasies and the everyday efforts of actors to objectify their thinking. Thus we have said that people enter discourse domains to secure objectification of this sort, to weigh their own ways of seeing against communal standards. Arguments are the public means by which such accommodations of the private to the social are accomplished. People adopt starting points and see how things work out.

A parallel case can be made for seeing criticism as the study of the effects of assumptions. Brown (1977) has said as much in interpreting Stevens's "Blue Guitar." "Playing the blue guitar is a figure for what pioneering artists, scientists, and other makers of paradigms do when they create new ways of expressing 'things as they are.' " Knowledge, Brown says, is largely possible because of the perspective-taking processes by which knowers are able to adopt new points of view. For instance, the researcher is presumed able to take another person's illusions as real money: "and then to ask how such 'illusions' are possible. The 'bias,' rather than being suppressed, is used as a source of understanding. The various voices do not cancel each other out, nor is the truth limited to those points on which they agree; instead, much as characters in a play, each voice enriches the others, each contributes to the dialectical construction of more and more comprehensive metaperspectives" (Brown, 1977, p. 69). These metaperspectives, Brown argues, organize the points of view of various actors into a "structured mimesis" of the field to be explained.

Explicating Points of View

I have elsewhere pursued a three-way analogy between cognitive development, socialization into argument fields, and participant observation research (Willard, 1982). My aim was to secure the same sort of holism by which the notions of argument interaction and utterance have been tied together here. The working assumption was that there are enough functional similarities among the three processes for them to illuminate one another. Of central importance (I argued) is the fact that all three processes turn equally upon perspective taking. Having argued that criticism is a process of perspective taking, I now want to point to its fit into this analogical arrangement. A plausible working assumption is that the three-way analogy buttresses and clarifies the claim that field studies involve the working out of the implications of starting points.

The Three-Way Analogy. The centrality of perspective taking to cognitive development, socialization into social domains, and participant observation can be proved easily enough. Our reasoning will square with that by which argument utterances have been said to be context embedded and intended toward. The result should be a broader unity in our thinking which ties together our conceptions of argument utterance and interaction with our developing view of criticism.

Perspective taking is a precondition and product of the symbolic exchanges by which children build interpretive schemes for predicting events (Ryan, 1974; Shotter, 1974). Development proceeds "orthogenetically," from relative simplicity and lack of differentiation toward cognitive complexity: hierarchic integration of constructs, greater articulation of them, and expanded differentiation among them (Werner, 1957; Crockett, 1965; Delia, 1976b; Delia and O'Keefe, 1979; O'Keefe and Sypher, 1981). "Decentering" is a precondition of socialization, since a child cannot enter the social world without increasing ability to adapt to the perspectives of others (Flavell et al., 1968; Clark and Delia, 1976; Delia and Clark, 1977) and an expanded repertoire of constructs for interpreting other people (Livesley and Bromley, 1973; Chandler, 1977). One symptom of this developmental progress is a child's increasing ability to strategically adapt persuasive messages to the perspectives of others (Clark and Delia, 1977).

While the particulars of cognitive development do not apply in every respect to socialization into particular domains, it is plausible to infer that socialization into an argument field works broadly like a process of development. Consider that the family (a relational field) is the group into which children are first socialized. I am not building a gemeinschaft-gesellschaft argument here or in any way saying that the family is a primary group which endows other groups with informing ideals. The family may be regarded as an argument field because it is organized around background assumptions, routines, and taken-for-granted beliefs to such an extent that it can be seen as a community of discourse. Cooley argued that the family was held together by an intense feeling of "we-ness." This classic view is appropriate to the field view emerging here. We can say that the precondition of entering an argument field is that a person construe things in roughly the ways other field actors construe them, that the person accept the field's starting points. Cognitive development and socialization into fields thus equally proceed as social comparison processes. In both cases, objectivity becomes a subjective accomplishment (Willard, 1979a) rather than the antagonistic opposite of subjectivity; it is a stance a person takes, a point of view toward a particular domain of phenomena. Entering a field is a process in which "the other"—in this case a group—is constructed by the individual to facilitate taking the perspectives of particular people in the group.

We can press this parallel farther by considering that socialization and cognitive development depend equally upon social interaction: just as social interactions with others provide children with the social comparisons necessary to elaborating their interpretive schemes, so interactions with field actors are the bases on which the uninitiated enter fields. Epistemic betterment is an *effect* of entering a field, though it may not be the person's reason for doing so. We have a battery of concepts for explaining the motives for entering fields ("identification," authority, security), and in many respects this parallels the choices children make in development. I have elsewhere spelled out the reasons for adopting a "smidgeon of functionalism" (Willard, 1980b), namely, that people enter fields with certain purposes in mind or because membership serves some satisfying aim. If the tasks and satisfactions people attribute to fields can be described, we shall have gone far toward describing fields.

To complete the three-way analogy, let us consider that participant-observation research (strictly speaking) entails a process of socialization into the groups studied. The researcher aims to be socialized in the routine manner of the field—thus being able to participate in the field's social processes *as* a member (Bruyn, 1966). Perspective taking is central to this research (Denzin, 1970). The researcher aims to make a series of controlled decisions for entering into ongoing social events and dealing with a field's actors *as if* he were one of them. This is a variant of our *as if* maxim: the researcher does not become so enmeshed in the field's activities that he loses sight of his research aims; nonetheless a central research aim is to understand what it is like to proceed *as if* the field's assumptions are true. One aims not to become a naive field actor but to assess reflectively the cognitive and social conditions of being a naive actor in a particular field. Broadly construed, such verstehen work has a long history (Znaniecki, 1940, 1952, 1955; Thomas and Znaniecki, 1958; Kluckhohn, 1940; Schwartz and Schwartz, 1955; Whyte, 1955; Junker, 1960; Reimer, 1937; Berger and Kellner, 1970; Waller and Hill, 1951; Emerson, 1970a, 1970b). Although such work has received severe criticism (for example, it is sometimes said that participant observation is discredited because its results are not generalizable), there is nothing in principle wrong with it. It seems to be the only sure way of discovering the rhetorical glue binding fields together (B. Anderson, 1974; Attwell, 1974; Denzin, 1970; Mehan and Wood, 1975; Psathas, 1973; Cicourel, 1974). It is a plausible means of gaining insight into the ways fields pursue their routine activities, organize their activities around conventionally approved procedures, and sustain the sense that "nothing unusual is happening" (Emerson, 1970b).

Thus the three-way analogy is plausible. The unifying thread is perspective taking as it is embodied in social comparison processes. Explanations of the three processes ought to be of a piece, and observations of all three ought to illuminate one another.

The Critical Stance. We can start with Gadamer's (1976) claim that understanding is rooted in an "unsuspendable historicity and finitude"—a claim which can be taken as a gloss of Kelly's (1955) experience corollary, which says that people construe events by perceiving recurring themes in them and by comparing and contrasting different aspects of them. This, Kelly says, is experience. It forms what Gadamer (1976) calls the knower's boundedness to his horizon as the ground of all understanding. It comprises what we have called the psychological sense of "field." The assumption is that a person's presuppositions are the conceptual lenses through which events are made meaningful, the grounds of the cognitive constitutive processes by which one fuses past, present, and future.

Since observation is never theory free, the critical stance is most basically rooted in reflective awarenesses of one's presuppositions. The critical act starts with the critic's considerations of his own values, aims, and assumptions (see Swanson, 1977a, 1977b; Rosenfield, 1968; Wander and Jenkins, 1972). This reflective awareness of the critic's values does not legitimate *evaluation* as the organizing aim of the critical act; it brings the critic's inevitable valuing of his own point of view to the forefront of attention. The more urgent interest is in the ways fields and their actors evaluate arguments. Criticism, we may say, is the study of valuing (and the alternative forms of valuing) but is not itself devoted to evaluation.

Since all events are open to alternative construction, criticism is a hermeneutic project of spelling out the available alternative interpretations of events. This conception squares with Gadamer's doctrine that criticism is possible because understanding is necessarily interpretive. This makes criticism a self-conscious form of understanding. It is *episodic* because every interpretive act is historically rooted and becomes (as well) a part of the historical ecology of the phenomenon studied, thus adding to its possibilities. It is *intersubjective* because every critical act requires reciprocating attributions, that is, making sense of utterances requires that one impute intentions to the speaker.

There are two senses of "constructive alternatives" active here. The first relates to the psychological field (and to differences among persons). It suggests that understanding events entails considering the alternative ways they may be seen and that field descriptions require "triangulation" (Denzin, 1970), that is, to describe fields we need to come at them from more than one perspective in order to offset the biases inherent to particular methods and points of view. The second sense of "constructive alternative" refers to interfield differences—but a distinction is needed here. In the natural attitude we might say that different fields construe the same things differently. Reflectively, however, we want to say that different fields see themselves dealing with different things because their organizing explanations lead them to think this way. But mutatis mutandis we shall want to retain the natural attitude sense of interfield differences. Fields *do* dispute among themselves about what they take to be the "same things." These disputes (I shall argue) form a fecund resource for understanding how people take things as knowledge.

We have looked at several maxims of epistemic postures and have described them as preconditions of knowledge. Individually and combined these maxims suggest that people enter fields to benefit from the advantages of communal accomplishments. Fields and their accomplishments keep problems narrow; they relegate things to the background of awareness; they authorize the taking of certain things for granted. This is why people enter them and use their principles; it is the "smidgeon of functionalism" to which we have repeatedly referred. It suggests that an important part of a field's ability to authorize or vouch for claims is its power to keep certain things implicit. When problems arise, things get explicit; when things are running smoothly, more things can remain implicit. A plausible inference from this is that criticism—*field study*, as we have defined it—is a progressive explication of that which is implicit.

This view squares with Gadamer's (1976) focus upon the implicit bases of speech. It points to the perspectivity intrinsic to utterance and to the necessity of our holistic view of utterance. Gadamer's view of linguistic context is sufficiently broad and pliable to include the non-discursiveness thesis. He says, for example, that language always leads behind itself and behind the facade of overt verbal expression; it is not coincident with that which it expresses; and there is a proportional limit to objectifying anything that is thought and communicated: "Linguistic expressions, when they are what they can be, are not simply inexact and in need of refinement, but rather, of necessity, they always fall short of what they evoke and communicate. For in speaking there is always implied a meaning that is imposed on the vehicle of expression, that only functions as a meaning behind the meaning and that in fact could be said to lose its meaning when raised to the level of what is actually expressed" (1976, p. 88).

Thus we have things unsaid but nevertheless made present by speech and things which are concealed by speech. The first means that "Relativity to situation and opportunity constitutes the very essence of speaking. For no statement simply has an unambiguous meaning based on its linguistic and logical construction as such, but, on the contrary, each is motivated" (1976, p. 90). The notion of things concealed by speech penetrates more deeply, Gadamer believes, into the hermeneutical conditions of language behavior. Lies, for example, conceal things: "The complicated interweaving of interpersonal relationships encountered in lies ranging from Oriental forms of courtesy to a clear breach of trust between people has in itself no primarily semantic character.... In the case of texts, for instance, a modern linguist would speak of lie signals by virtue of which what is said in the text can be identified by the intent to conceal. Here lying is not just the assertion of something false; it is a matter of speaking that conceals and knows it." Thus seeing through a lie is a matter of linking a concealment to "the true intention of the speaker." Lies are not the only concealments: speakers also seek to disguise errors (1976, pp. 90–94).

This reasoning leads Gadamer (1976) to a conception of context that more or less dovetails with the nondiscursiveness thesis and coheres as well with our views of intuition:

One of the fundamental structures of all speaking is that we are guided by preconceptions and anticipations in our talking in such a way that these continually remain hidden and that it takes a disruption in oneself of the intended meaning of what one is saying to become conscious of these prejudices as such. In general the disruption comes about through some new experience, in which a previous opinion reveals itself to be untenable. But the basic prejudices are not easily dislodged and protect themselves by claiming self-evident certainty for themselves, or even by

posing as supposed freedom from all prejudice and thereby securing their
acceptance. [P. 92]

Hence dogmatism is explained along the same lines Kelly uses to
explain the unwillingness of persons to jeopardize constructs because
of the perceived damage this would cause for the broader construct
system.

So conceived, hermeneutics aims at the understanding of understanding. Here, Gadamer's thinking dovetails with Heidegger's—and
perhaps this is the best evidence that our broadening of his conception
of language does minimal violence to his views: Heidegger's stress
upon the direct personal experiencing of being (as opposed to sensing
beings) completely depends upon an intermingled discursive and nondiscursive system; how else could angst be the regnant construct of an
ontological system? Gadamer invests considerable capital in Heidegger's thought, thus fueling our own interpretation.

What Gadamer unambiguously gives us is (1) a focus upon circumstanced speech as illustrative of the linguistic circle out of which
meanings arise—a view which coheres with our conception of the
epistemic functions of argument; (2) a cogent statement of the reasons
why criticism has to be a form of perspective taking; and, perhaps
most important for our purposes, (3) a plausible account of essence,
namely, the view that the ontic status of a text is never a single
interpretation but the myriad and arguably limitless possibilities, the
alternative constructions which can be placed upon a text. This last is
the essential contribution: the critic is to allow what is foreign and
what is his own to merge in the process of hermeneutical reflection
which draws the critic into a new linguistic explication of the world.
"In this process of finite thought ever moving forward while allowing
the other to have its way in opposition to oneself, the power of reason is
demonstrated. Reason is aware that human knowledge is limited and
will remain limited, even if it is conscious of its own limit. Hermeneutical reflection thus exercises a self-criticism of thinking consciousness, a criticism that translates all its own abstractions and also
the knowledge of the sciences back into the whole of human experience
of the world" (Gadamer, 1976, p. 94). It is most essentially a critique of
alternative ways of thinking, then, to do philosophy.

Notice that this reasoning fits easily into our view of rationality in
that perspective taking is the core critical process. If there is a unifying
nucleus to Gadamer's project, it is that alternativism (or indeterminacy) is the obdurate fact to work with and that human finitude is
an (apparently) insuperable barrier to understanding. Finitude means
that points of view are not transparent. While illuminating their
designata, they also shape and define them—which is why

weltanschauungen thinking stresses the importance of reflective awareness of one's own presuppositions. The organizing epistemic problem is that we find ourselves "under way within an entirety of speaking and thinking which always exceeds the horizons of our perspective" (Smith, 1980, p. xiii). There is an essential incompleteness in all descriptions. Reflective thinking does not expose all of the interpretive possibilities of events so much as it lays bare the potential range of alternatives. If the idea of rationality is to make sense, there must be some need for it. Gadamer plausibly locates this exigence in the obdurate facts of relativism and the related but conceptually distinct fact of human finitude (Gadamer, 1975). Thus our sense of the dialectical interdependencies between the psychological and sociological senses of "field" seems to have a parallel in Gadamer's views.

Our field theory thus yields a critical theory which places perspective taking at the core of the enterprise. The alternativity of fields requires a critical program aimed at understanding different presuppositional frameworks and the effects of these upon particular practices. The epistemic accomplishments of fields require a critical program aimed at describing the assumptions which make such accomplishments possible. The critical enterprise thus depends upon explication. The foundational move in any critical act is the taking of a starting point and the working out of its logic of implications (whatever that logic may be). In this, the critic's activities parallel the ordinary person's as he is socialized into a field. This means that an elaborated observational research project is needed as a companion enterprise to the sort of criticism advocated here.[7]

Explicating Interfield Disputes

People are apt to reveal the most about their thinking when they are pressed to give reasons, to account for themselves, to justify their claims. Since they are most often pressed to do these things in arguments, we have concluded that argument studies are especially promising resources for understanding the psychological field. Given the holism with which the psychological and sociological senses of "field" have been tied together, we shall obviously want to say that field actors display—in the most explicit way—their field's assumptions when they are pressed to do so. Thus we may learn much about fields and their epistemologies in considering how fields deal with one another. Put crudely, fields borrow concepts from one another, critique one another's practices, and make supremacy claims respecting one another's rights to evaluate certain phenomena (for example, claims of the ownership of concepts). What sense might critics make of these practices?

The Principle of Attention. The most helpful preliminary assumption critics might make is that they are themselves field actors. Criticism (we argued) is a *field* organized around particular aims and assumptions and devoted to particular practices. Its most basic practice is the study of interpretation and of the communal objectifying practices by which interpretations are legitimated. Every field (we argued) partly defines itself by deciding about appropriate *sources*— the question being "to whom shall we listen?" While naive actors often couch this matter in terms of "deciding who is correct," we need not see it that way. For our hermeneutic purposes, the most interesting aspect of attentional decisions is that psychological and sociological fields *focus* on one source while excluding others.

"To whom shall I listen?" is thus arguably the most important epistemic decision a person makes. Since questions frame the horizons of their answers (Ladriere, 1970) a person's decision to attend to the arguments of another is not a decision about what to think so much as it is a decision about *what to think about*. It is a decision about how the person will focus his attention—which is tantamount to saying that every decision about listening is a constructive definition of the boundaries of a person's horizon. Attentional decisions are thus far more basic to interpretation than decisions to accept influence—the latter presupposes the former (as a necessary precondition).

Analogously, fields define themselves by the people and ideas they attend to and focus upon. Thus, for example, we understand behaviorism best by looking to the positive philosophers of science and physicists to whom the behaviorists paid attention; we understand constructivism best by looking to the interpretive philosophers of science to whom constructivists attend; and so on. The spokesmen of fields are one manifestation of this, although we have rejected using the concept of the speaker to define fields. Some fields place great importance in deciding *who* shall speak—such decisions often turning upon the need for human arbiters of disputes.

An attentional decision is a commitment to enter into intersubjective processes—a decision to participate in communication processes. Field studies thus focus upon such decisions on the assumption that they reveal much about how a person or field *deliberates*. Deliberations, after all, often entail attentional decisions.

Interfield Borrowing. While attentional decisions are necessary preconditions of influence taking, it is nonetheless the case that people and fields exemplify their attentional decisions by the influence they in fact take. When one field borrows concepts from another, it speaks volumes about its own internal agenda and practices. Something like Gödel's incompleteness theorem thus obtains with procedural and conceptual ecologies. Inside and across fields, change occurs when someone decides (often by a crude utilitarian calculus) that a new idea does more good than harm. Such decisions may stem from methodological preferences, intolerance for incompatible findings, simple followership, or intuition. The parallel we have drawn between Kelly's views of personal constructive procedures and field processes suggests that the range of conditions under which a field's actors might decide to jeopardize their assumptive frameworks by importing new ideas is as large as the actors' constructions of their alternatives permit.

A plausible assumption is that just as actors enter fields for social comparison purposes, so fields borrow concepts from other conceptual ecologies to check their thinking or to avoid impasses. One way, for example, for a field to resolve its *determinism versus free will* dispute might be to import Heisenberg's Uncertainty Principle, or the Second Law of Thermodynamics, or some weltanschauungen principle. Such importation amounts to risking one's ideas against the checks of another field to reap the benefits of "progress." The epistemic motive is "to get better."

Borrowing Incurs Obligations. Let us say that there are differences between borrowing and theft. When one borrows something, one incurs obligations to the one borrowed from—these obligations being roughly analogous to the sorts of obligations one incurs in entering the institution of promising (Searle, 1969). Such obligations are rooted in the communications by which borrowing (or promising) is accomplished. That is, one takes certain postures toward other people when one borrows from them.

Fields incur obligations as well. When fields import concepts they *transform* them in ways dictated by their assumptions. But there are limits to such transformations. Imported concepts have no value unless they accomplish something new in the field, for example, settle disputes, surmount impasses. Imported concepts must thus be seen as having—to some extent at least—their own meanings. If fields borrow concepts to transcend local obstacles, the borrowed concept has to have some feature new to the field. This permits the inference that fields which import concepts assume the logical burdens of the concepts. If, for example, one uses the Uncertainty Principle, one buys into the assumptions that produced it and the conditions by which it is to be evaluated. Kelly's view of freedom and determinism—which we have used to elaborate a person's fit into communal traditions—thus explains concept importation. The decision to import a concept is a decision to take it in some respects on its own terms (why else import it?). The imported concept limits one's freedom by performing particular epistemic tasks. Thus if the Uncertainty Principle is devised by fallibilists, its use in other fields entails at least some commitment to abide by the consequences of fallibilism. I am not resurrecting a priorism here but making a claim about how borrowing usually works out. Fields which import concepts do so because they need new principles—ways of surmounting impasses in their internal logics. They secure these progressive benefits by hauling in concepts intact.

Consider, for example, that thinkers have historically selected aspects of the physical theories of their times. Kant appropriated Newtonian space and time to create the a prioris of cognition (see Feinberg, 1972), just as contemporary theorists wrestle with the Copenhagen Interpretation. The interesting outcome has been that thinkers who hitched their wagons to particular physical models did so by virtue of arguments that forced them to share the physical models' fates. Positivists, for example, used realism rather than quantum theories to argue that psychology should be based on the language of physics—which made them accountable to the arguments of physics and vulnerable to the doom of their philosophy of science at the hands of Bohr and others. "If the inherent realism of classical physics showed the sheer irrelevance of idealistic epistemologies, then the idealism espoused by Neils Bohr and others of the Copenhagen School showed the folly of trying to base philosophical positions on current science" (Fine, 1972, p. 3). I am less interested in pointing to particular follies than in illuminating the obligation Fine's argument exposes. It is rather as if the borrowing of concepts entails a social contract to abide by the consequences; it is a decision to listen to another field and to submit to a certain extent to that field's judgmental and veridical standards and practices.

The Principle of Nonclosure. The task at hand is to decide how broad the critical field of attention should be and which fields merit our attention, that is, which fields have concepts worth borrowing (and abiding by). Since we want critical activities to contribute to a unified and coherent body of knowledge, we cannot gad about, borrowing concepts willy-nilly. Nor dare we borrow concepts we are not willing to live with. Since our aim is to create a general account of the acquisition and uses of knowledge and of the place of communication processes therein, we shall want to look for concepts which fit the importance we have imputed to these processes. Remember that we have abandoned the aim of securing a single account of knowledge or of (consensus gentium) counting field noses to find points of agreement and letting those points stand as our epistemology. We want to accommodate to the differences among the ways fields pass muster on knowledge because we think it plausible that different modes of knowing are used by people because they are appropriate to different facts.

So in considering the framework and practices which shall constitute critical epistemology, we shall not be refereeing interfield disputes, that is, pointing to particular fields as being "correct" or "incorrect." The general skeptical doctrine will do us in (on our own grounds). The better organizing question is an attentional one, namely, to which fields should we listen?

This question should direct our attention to a principle that lets us make sense of the examples of interfield disputes we have surveyed (cost-benefit analysis versus neo-Kantian ethics, the antiabortion and proabortion positions, military versus ethical discourse, and creationism versus evolutionism). While we cannot settle them, we can decide how to look at them and how to advise other fields (or the public) to look at them. Since we have emphasized the rhetorical roots of such disputations, we require a concept that squares with the rhetorical facts as well as with our particular explanatory aims. Having said that fields are beyond critique, except on their own grounds, we require a principle which applies to the home turf of the fields we are interested in. It cannot be one that settles disputes; but it might be one that lets us look at the rhetorical postures of these disputes in a useful way. Since we have said that borrowing concepts incurs obligations (on the home grounds of the fields who borrow), this may yield the principle we need.

Let me use the term "closure" to stand for the practice of refusing an argument strategy to an opponent on the grounds that one's own argument strategy rules it out. This is the opposite of what Johnstone (1982) calls "bilaterality" (the principle that one cannot deny one's own argument strategy to another person). "Closure" occurs when one insists that one can be refuted only on one's own grounds. "You may argue only as I do." Closure does not mean that an advocate has had an idea fallaciously. Strictly speaking, it is not a fallacy but a refusal to abide by a procedural nicety.

Notice that our examples each involve fields which have effected closure. The formalist, for example, says that formal arguments cannot be refuted by empirical claims; cost-benefit analysts stipulate that objections to their arguments must be couched in the language of quantity; evolutionists stipulate that only the tests of scientific method can evaluate their claims; both sides of the abortion issue impose strict conditions upon what can count as a permissible argument; the creationists insist that revelation cannot be refuted; and so on. In each case we have bizarre confrontations between fields because the fields have effected closure; they are willing to abide only by their own rules; they put themselves at risk only vis-à-vis their own frameworks; they rule out argument forms which are alien to their own.

We are thus equipped with a principle of argumentation that speaks to the responsibilities of advocates. It depends upon saying not which fields are right but which fields epistemics ought to listen to, that is, which fields take epistemic postures worthy of our attention. We thus say that fields ignore the nonclosure principle at the risk of being arbitrary; they are not "wrong" but they make counterproductive assumptions about their argument obligations. We can say to the various sides of the disputes we have considered:

> You have reached a *stasis* that makes further dispute useless. This is bad because dispute is presumptively good. You achieved this stasis because both theories are too rigid and arbitrary, too self-contained, and too innocent of the facts of other fields. Both theories will be improved if you rethink not their facts (their substance) but your assumptions about the obligations you have to outsiders when you argue your positions. I cannot prove you wrong; but in saying what knowledge is I have no special obligations to take counsel from you, that is, because you acknowledge no special obligations to listen to outsiders.

The nonclosure principle is thus a rhetorical principle of cooperation which requires that fields take other fields seriously. Fields which borrow concepts have incurred this obligation *on their own terms* and are especially vulnerable to the nonclosure principle as an *objection*. Fields which do not borrow concepts are invulnerable to objections based on the nonclosure principle; but they cannot justifiably feel offended if we ignore them.

Our working assumption can thus read something like the following: *fields observing the nonclosure principle command our attention; fields which depend upon closure do not.* This is not a correctness principle but a decision about which fields have interesting things to say about knowledge. The importance we have imputed to argument processes as the grounds of knowledge, as the grounds on which people pass muster on knowledge, requires that we seek principles of rhetoric and communication which facilitate our understanding of these processes. Fields whose arguments survive because of closure presumptively can be ruled out of our epistemic framework.

While the question of closure is the question we want to ask to decide which fields critical epistemology might take concepts from, it is a question which any actor in any field whatever might pose. To gloss, any actor might ask: "To which fields and ideas do I wish to incur obligations? What are the obligations and are they worth the trouble?" Here the concern is with the focus and range of convenience of ideas and practices rather than (per se) with their correctness or goodness.

The question of closure may also undergird a public philosophy (although the outlines of that philosophy will have to await our attention in another work). The balkanization of knowledge described by field theory poses complex and urgent problems for students of the public sphere (see Cox, 1981; Goodnight, 1981). In particular, the "public" cannot be conceptualized as a monolithic entity, and the public sphere cannot be seen as clear-cut arena for which universal judgmental and veridical standards can be laid down. Put crudely, one might well ask whether the balkanization of knowledge has destroyed the public sphere. To gloss Goodnight's (1981) argument, we can imagine an objection of the following sort:

> The balkanization of knowledge means that speakers are no longer accountable to the public but only to their respective argument fields. If a policy maker advocates a policy which harms a particular group, he need not justify the policy to the affected group so much as he must speak to the specialized realm of discourse (the field) which vouches for his assumptions. Thus, cost-benefit analysis might justify abolition of the food stamp program; or purely technological arguments might favor increased use of nuclear power; or particular religious beliefs must justify censorship. The justifications of such arguments "retreat to their fields" rather than fitting into some broader public standards. Thus the uses of knowledge in the public sphere amount merely to power grabs; "justification" amounts to nothing more than speaking *ex cathedra*—in this case, from one's field.

This argument raises problems of considerable importance. It does not deny the empirical correctness of a sociological field theory; it points instead to the most dangerous implications of the balkanization of knowledge.

There has always been a correspondence between particular critical theories and certain public philosophies. So the criticisms we have leveled at traditional argument criticism bear importantly upon the concerns of a public philosophy. In denying the critic's bona fides for making evaluations of the traditional sort, we have by implication placed special limits upon the capacities of the public sphere to generate ways of solving interfield disputes. Recall that most of our examples have been of different fields vying for the attention of a third party—usually the public. The creationists do not (at least centrally) want to convince the evolutionists of their errors; they seek political power. The "prolife" forces are not so much concerned with changing the views of the proabortion forces as they are with outlawing abortions, with securing the political power necessary to this end.

So in considering the general posture of critical epistemics, we are by implication creating an embryonic public philosophy. Since the full exposition of that philosophy is beyond our aims here, we shall have to be satisfied with proceeding by virtue of a tentative assumption, namely, that the uses of knowledge in the public sphere are (pragmatically) indistinguishable from the manufacture of knowledge in particular fields. In considering the ground rules for making sense of and deciding upon a posture toward interfield disputes, we shall be hashing out methods which will prove appropriate to the public sphere as well. The tentativeness of this assumption should make us cautious—continually mindful that we might be dead wrong (that is, that the sociological field theory we are defending does—as Goodnight's argument has it—undermine the public sphere). But this is not an argument for avoiding field theory; our central pretence, after all, is that field theory is an empirical account. It is an argument that means (rather) that the development of a field theory is a first step in the development of a public philosophy and that epistemics is a field bearing important implications for political science and policy making.

So we may return to the central question of the nonclosure principle mindful that we are arguably doing three things at once, namely, defining the subject matter and central judgmental posture of the field epistemics, describing the critical posture any individual may take to confront particular problems, and making inroads into a public philosophy.

Given the ubiquity of interfield borrowing, the importation of concepts, "attending to" other fields may plausibly be said to be a fundamental component of every field's epistemic posture. Bear in mind that we have used the notion of the audience as one way of defining fields and that we have justified this project by arguing that people often define themselves as groups in terms of the sources of influence they choose to attend to. One way, then, of defining epistemics is to point to the fields that can and do speak to us and whose procedures and beliefs are capable of being argued about.

Perhaps an analogy will clarify this argument. Some fields (let us say) function like autistic children, being self-contained and unwilling or unable to communicate with others. While we might (being very liberal in granting some premises) grant that autism is an unpainful way of dealing with the world, we would never grant that an autistic person (assuming we might enter that world) demanded our attention and followership. Just as a naive social actor would never go to an autistic child for social comparison, so no sensible field will turn to another field whose internal definitions make it incapable of speaking or of being understood. Our field-defining question, then, is whether we shall take counsel from autistic fields.

If cost-benefit analysis and formalism (to take but two of our examples) so define things that they owe no accounts, no social comparison obligations, to outsiders, they have no obvious claim upon our attention or belief. Their disputes are of no special interest *to us* except as instances of stases that cannot be transcended except by changing modes of argument. In our examples, eschewing closure is what is needed. We have three ways of looking at such stases:

1. Can a field's epistemic views be defeated by its own logic?
2. Does a field succeed only by closure?
3. Does the act of borrowing incur obligations, namely, to attend to all arguments pertaining to the imported concept?

With respect to (1) we have familiar arguments. We might say to decision makers something like the following:

If you deem decision making a free enterprise, giving full and fair play to all competing claims, cost-benefit analysis is a data source incompatible with your belief. Cost-benefit analysis cannot be refuted on its own grounds; but it makes no valid claims on your attention (which is a disastrous situation for a field which defines itself as a field which *advises* policy makers).

With respect to (2) we would buttress our criticism with a claim of the following sort:

Cost-benefit analysis succeeds *only* by closure; it gets its results in no other way. It expects the public to abide by its decisions, but it entertains the public's values *only* on its own terms—in terms, that is, which make it impossible to refute cost-benefit calculations.

With respect to (3) we would conclude in something of the following way:

Cost-benefit analysis is a field premised on an assumed right to give advice to other fields (and in particular the public sphere). This, *by the field's logic*, entails the obligation of attending to counterarguments that do not fit its own quantitative language. Otherwise, cost-benefit analysis is taking the posture of parent to child—this paternalism being justified *only* by virtue of the field's closure.

In raising these arguments, we are developing a theory of accountability especially appropriate to the public sphere (although it applies to disciplinary fields as well). This accountability concept depends not so much upon evaluating fields on their own substantive grounds as upon evaluations we make of their interfield argument practices. These *are* evaluations, although they are nonjustificatory. They square, as far as I can see, with the general brief against traditional evaluation in criticism we have considered here. They are offshoots, that is, of our principle of attention.

To some formalist theories, the arguments would work in much the same way. With respect to (1) we would use the tu quoque and case-specific skeptical challenges appropriate to the claims we are considering. The power of our skepticism would be fueled by the breadth and power of the formal claims to knowledge which have been made. With respect to (2) we would point to the obvious: "If you in principle rule empirical claims out of discourse, no empirical field in principle owes you its attention; since epistemics is an irretrievably empirical field, it owes no debts to purely formal arguments." With respect to (3) we would conclude that fields which live by physical concepts can die by them as well.

Now let us consider the example of military versus moral claims. With respect to (1) we observe the general has imported other political concepts (for instance, "better dead than Red") and thus possesses by his own logic no principled reasons for rejecting counter claims out of hand. Once the door is opened to value judgments from outside, the "war-is-hell—anything goes" paradigm is beset with difficulties. With respect to (3) we say that claims such as "we had to destroy the town in order to save it" *are* imported value concepts; thus military science has no rationale other than argumentative expedience for picking and choosing among the value concepts it wants to let in. It does not matter that we cannot settle for once and for all the correctness of the general's claim. What matters is that policy makers in a free society can decide by virtue of the general's argument practices when his military claims merit attention.

In the case of creationists versus the evolutionists, our arguments work in the same ways. With respect to (1) we note that creationism's refuge in revelation cannot be evaluated by *any* logic. With respect to (2) we note that the creationist position succeeds *only* because it takes refuge in personal revelation; when arguing on scientific grounds (which creationists often do), the creationists solidly *lose* the argument that creationism and evolutionism are two equally acceptable theories; they are able to fight the evolutionists to a standstill *only* when they argue that scientific data cannot refute revelation, that is, when they adopt a privileged position through closure. With respect to (3) we would note that when creationists enter the domain of science, using scientific examples to buttress their claims, their public posture entails the obligation to abide by the consequences—something creationists have largely been loath to do. The logic of their position, that is, suggests that if they can prove creationism to be a theory coequal to evolutionism by virtue of scientific examples, they can lose the argument by virtue of scientific examples. With each step, we are evaluating the argument postures of the two fields—not saying that one is right and the other is wrong. What is interesting here is that deciding the relative correctness of the two positions is not—for epistemic or public policy purposes—necessary.

The principle of nonclosure combined with the principle of attention yields a relativism that respects interfield differences while explaining interfield influence taking. The three questions we have used to resolve our examples thus dovetail into the critical posture suggested by our field theory. The unifying thread is that critical epistemics is the study of the effects of presuppositions; and in every case, as we have dealt with examples which turn upon incommensurable presuppositions, we have employed principles which are equally appropriate to successful interfield disputes—disputes in which at least some disagreements are settled by appeal to commonly acceptable judgmental standards. Proceeding with our examples in this way, we have arrived at a clear and plausible sense of what the empirical focus of epistemics must be, namely interfield disputes.

Our general epistemic posture toward the fields of discourse whose practices interest us is captured in Weimer's (1979) notion of comprehensively critical rationalism. By this account, science is a comprehensively critical endeavor because *"all* its conjectures, including the most fundamental standards and basic positions are always...open to criticism. Nothing in science is immune to criticism or justified fideistically, by appeal to authority" (1979, p. 40). This may be an empirical overstatement, but as a normative principle it has much to recommend it. It equips epistemics with a way of proceeding with the study of disputes in and among fields that does not require taking sides. It yields, that is, a nonjustificational posture toward the objects of study.

Since argument is foundational to knowing, argument criticism of necessity becomes the pivotal preoccupation of epistemics. Field studies, we have said, are not ends in themselves but (rather) the preconditions of successful critical enterprises. These studies aim not at critique but at an understanding of the presuppositions which affect the premises and procedures of arguments. Epistemics' aim with respect to these premises and practices is to consider the arguments

which work out for the best. Argument principles get their justification not from *within* argumentation but from their successes in the
fields using them. Thus, while epistemics aims to accumulate knowledge concerning practical argumentation, to study the justificational
practices of fields, it is not itself a justificational field. To say otherwise
would make epistemics' posture toward other fields imperialistic.

It is plausible to see argumentation as the study of the accumulated
wisdom of fields respecting their argument practices. In this preoccupation, it is synonymous with critical epistemics as we have defined
that field. The organizing assumption is that, as fields change their
practices change; the test of argument principles is how well they
serve changing interests. Argument principles are not spun out of
empty logic or conjured up from thin air; they come from practices and
are judged in something like an act utilitarian way: fields, that is,
judge the usefulness of epistemic principles by assessing whether their
foci and ranges of convenience are adequate to the fields' problems.

The aim of epistemics is to study these judgments which fields make
and to consider the recurring themes in argument practices which
cross field boundaries. The ultimate aim is to consider (in general) the
utility of such practices and to derive therefrom a more precise and
detailed (and therefore more useful) epistemic self-portrait (Toulmin,
1972). This portrait will presumably never be complete: it can only
freeze its subjects in particular moments of their epistemic development; and in capturing them, it may prefigure future developments as
much as it itemizes the past.

Conclusion

I have aimed to strike a balance between the obvious facts of relativity and an appreciaton of the ways field actors ameliorate their
doubts. The search has been for a set of critical aims (and for an
empirical project and analytical apparatus appropriate to it) which
allows epistemics to bypass the fixed stance—a criticism, that is,
which does not confuse the epistemic stances of its objects with its
own, a criticism which is neither absolutistic nor generally skeptical.
Such criticism may operate in the service of a useful sort of relativism,
that is, a relativism which makes sense of the catalog of interfield
differences, which yields a way of looking at such differences that
illuminates which things are important about them and which
things are not.

The balkanization of knowledge described by our field theory poses
problems of greater urgency and complexity than the ones our predecessors grappled with; and—worse—it reveals that we are no better

equipped than our predecessors for dealing even with their more straightforward problems. After Krutch (1954) we may own to the fear that man's ingenuity has outrun his intelligence. Our field theory suggests that we can be satisfied with neither usual solution—that is (to gloss Krutch, 1954), we can neither say with Wells, "Let us get wise as soon as possible," or say with Thoreau, "Simplify." As Krutch says, "neither of these prospects—compulsory simplification or the long wait while Creative Evolution produces something better than man— seems very cheerful to us poor creatures of the hour. We may be pardoned if we cast about for some *tertium quid...*" (1954, p. 27).

The place of criticism in this general epistemic situation is to assess the general conditions of certainty and doubt and to study the disputational processes by which these are achieved. That interfield disputes will persist and that actors will continue to doubt that they know can go without saying. The search for confidence which these processes reveal thus becomes the unifying thread between the psychological and sociological inquiries necessary to understanding our epistemic condition.

So we have decided to live with the consequences of relativism—as a worst case scenario which we have acknowledged may turn out to be too pessimistic. This decision has opened the door to a variety of arguably useful projects. Moreover, our decision has not closed the door on some of the traditional questions of epistemics—indeed, it has lent them greater urgency by imposing them upon the background of the balkanization of knowledge. We still want to know how arguments yield knowledge. We want to know a good argument when we see one; and we want to know why it is true. Since the form of an argument cannot (except for the most obvious fallacies) help us answer these questions, we have turned to an empirically plausible sense of the truth conditions of any argument—its substantive fit into a going social order. Our tentative starting point is the assumption that the field-dependent character of argument is at once the source of truth and error. Thus it is to the social practices in which arguments arise rather than to propositional logic that we turn for answers to our questions.

Our critical agenda can be pinned to the notion that a well-founded consensus is a well-argued one. While the substantive probity of claims is continually subject to the ebb and flow of consensus and authority, argument practices are less so. The ubiquity of argument, not its objects, is the hard fact we must respect. In assessing our present epistemic situation, we can say (after Santayana) that we cannot pass, except under the illusion of a moment, to anything firmer or deeper.

Notes

Introduction

1. The term "tu quoque" is variously used. Strictly put, it replies to various knowledge claims by saying, "*you too* are vulnerable." Sometimes called the "two wrongs argument," the tu quoque argues that one's critic is open to his own argument. Skeptics thus impute irrational bases to rationality theories. Thus, Weimer (1979) uses the tu quoque as a label for the claims that rationality always entails irrational commitment, that people may make whatever epistemic commitments they choose, and that these commitments are beyond critique. A looser variant of the tu quoque involves using it as a label for infinite regress arguments as skeptics and absolutists debate one another. A still looser variation is as a term for "turning one's argument against one." There are two recurring themes in these three versions: it is a *process* of arguing about one's *presuppositions*. Thus, as an expositional convenience, I shall use "tu quoque" as a broad label encompassing the familiar features of skeptical arguments combined with the special features of field theory *as if* they are a monolithic objection. So viewed, the tu quoque is a tactic, a posture, a line of argument often present when knowledge claims of any sort are made—and an especially combative posture when absolutistic claims are made. It is a specter continually present in the interfield disputes when one field claims epistemic privileges or superiority over another field. If, for example, a moral theorist criticizes the businessman for ignoring rules of distributive justice, the businessman may skeptically challenge the importation of one field's (in this case ethics) standards into another field (in this case business affairs). I want to label such challenges tu quoque.

2. Criticisms and discussions of Toulmin's field concept appear in Willard (1980a, 1981a, 1981c), McKerrow (1980a, 1980b), and Rowland (1981a, 1981b).

3. A variety of "sociological" field theories have lately emerged (Gronbeck, 1981; Klumpp, 1981; Cox, 1981). Criticisms of the sociological approaches appear in Goodnight (1981) and Wenzel (1981).

4. My original definition used "propositions" rather than "positions." My intention was to illuminate the struggle in which people engage to render private cognitive processes into public languages. But "propositions" implies that argumentative positions are contained in statements alone—an implication which I have come to believe is entirely inadequate. For reasons to be

explicated in the first chapter, it is conceivable that a person's "position" might be nondiscursive even when he tries to express that position in discursive propositions. Because I do not want to limit the concept of argument to "propositions," I have substituted "positions" in the definition.

Chapter 1

1. It will not do to say that turn taking is an ordinary version of debate. Turn taking is clearly an organizational principle undergirding ordinary conversation (Jackson and Jacobs, 1978; Jacobs and Jackson, 1979, 1980, 1982; Bach and Harnish, 1979; Coulthard, 1977). Debates are artificially designed institutional procedures, not unlike legal proceedings, whereas turn taking is a pervasive organizational principle implicitly (as a background awareness) facilitating talk. Debate structurally prefers dissensus, while the routine grounds of everyday talk prefer consensus (see Jacobs and Jackson, 1982).

2. This task will prove especially difficult to carry out if the defender of simplest case reasoning also defends viewing argument fields as broad doctrines or as histories of ideas. If the visitor from space asked (let us say) what "behaviorism" is, we would seek the simplest instance rather than the broad doctrine. I advocate (but do not justify on simplest case grounds) that fields be exemplified through examination of particular circumstances in which they are manifested. I do not see how anyone can maintain the simplest case reasoning for defining arguments while simultaneously insisting that argument fields be described apart from their particulars.

3. I shall mostly ignore the familiar—often heated—disputes between methodological *holists* such as Mandelbaum and Gellner and *individualists* such as Hayek and Popper. Weltanschauungen assumptions wedded to field theory suggest that the dispute is unproductive and that the two positions seem most opposed when they are caricatures. Individualists often proceed from a distaste for metaphysical considerations, while holists merely want to retain the ability to employ macroexplanations. Holistic arguments do not preclude unified theoretical accounts of and research programs for the psychological and sociological senses of "field." The differences between methodological holism and individualism seem more apparent than real because both sides lack the notion of the focus and range of convenience of theoretical constructs. "Field studies" as defined here clearly presuppose a methodological individualism— the starting place being the construing person entering an argument field. The expectation is that such empirical work will coalesce in a broader theoretical framework in such a way as to prove both broad and particularized explanations of shared meanings and of the things communally taken to be knowledge.

4. Balthrop (1980) attributes to me a stronger and more exhaustive commitment to Langer's views than I have made. Langer says—and I agree—that presentational forms are "untranslatable." She concludes that presentational forms cannot be justificatory, cannot transmit ideational content, and thus fall outside the realm of shared representations. I disagree. While it may well be an outcome of Langer's views that presentational argument is impossible (or in a vague way a contradiction in terms), my own inclination is to stress the

interdependence of discursive and nondiscursive symbolism (see Tyler, 1978; Goffman, 1961a, 1963; Gurwitsch, 1964; Hall, 1966; Kelley, 1971; Kelvin, 1970; Landfield, 1971; Leiter, 1980; Lofland, 1976). We represent nondiscursive symbolism in daily life, indirectly and by action (Nisbett and Wilson, 1977; Nisbett and Ross, 1980; Philipsen, 1975; Psathas, 1979). People attach meaning to such representations (J. P. Anderson, 1977; Burleson, 1979c, 1981). Given the presuppositions, not of Langer's philosophy, but of the constructivist/interactionist view, nondiscursive symbolism is an integral part of argument. I have thus approvingly cited Langer's distinction (and her discussion of its implications for accounts of mind)—and nothing else.

5. "The Red Wheelbarrow" from *Collected Earlier Poems of William Carlos Williams* Copyright 1938 by New Directions Publishing Corporation. Reprinted by permission of New Directions.

Chapter 2

1. For instance, the various sciences share a broad but particularized sense of scientific method. This allows them in some cases to use each others' data. It is thus possible that such commonalities might eventually make field distinctions among the sciences unnecessary. The social sciences, however, are still balkanized into schools of thought to such a degree that their sharing of broad principles of scientific method seems less important than their substantive differences. Many nonscientific fields, of course, maintain that their enduring puzzles will never be solved by scientific research; and still others believe that their most basic concerns are matters of faith, not science, and that faith is (in its own way) just as rational as science. For these reasons (among others), I do not think that differences in views of rationality can serve as dependable markers of field boundaries.

2. This is a familiar argument in ethics. See, for instance, Shoeman (1974), who argues that a fundamental moral principle is "of far less moral significance than one would have thought or hoped it to be."

Chapter 3

1. I am using the terms "field" and "rational enterprise" as synonymous labels for the "disciplines" on the pyramid. I assume that the rational enterprise notion is a clarified successor to "field" but that Toulmin has not abandoned the field notion. He states flatly in *Understanding* that he is elaborating themes taken up in *Uses*. Had he wished to discard the field notion, he presumably would have done so there. The best evidence that "field" and "rational enterprises" are synonymous notions is that Toulmin and his colleagues use the two terms interchangeably (Toulmin, Rieke, and Janik, 1979, pp. 27–29, 34, 49), that is, in ways that suggest that the authors thought either word would do. McKerrow (1980b) argues that Toulmin has abandoned the technical sense of "field" in *Understanding*, since that work deals with the collective uses of concepts, not with individual arguments. This contention ignores the interchangeable uses of the terms (Toulmin, Rieke, and Janik, 1979) and the holism

of the "three faces of philosophy" (Toulmin, 1976), which uses both terms. It is possible that Toulmin has abandoned his early commitment to logical types but less plausible that he has jettisoned the intuitive idea of fields.

2. It might be objected that I am holding Toulmin hostage to a standard he did not intend to meet, that is, that he did not intend to produce a research exemplar for the analysis and criticism of ordinary discourse. My aim, however, is to demonstrate the importance of ordinary fields to epistemics and to consider whether ordinary practices fall easily (or at all) within the focus and range of convenience of Toulmin's scheme. I am less interested in his aims than in the utility of his program to serve my aims. However, his aims are not irrelevant, since the broad epistemic agenda emerging here might itself be construed as an objection to the narrowness of Toulmin's. It may be that in objecting to Toulmin's blurring of ordinary discourse I shall straightforwardly be objecting to his broad program. Moreover, there are places in *Uses* (Toulmin, 1958) where Toulmin seems to be pursuing an ordinary discourse program and to lose distinctions between notions of ordinary speech and disciplinary working logics. This blurring occurs often enough to permit the inference that he seeks an analytic scheme sufficiently broad to deal with the arguments of ordinary and disciplinary folk alike. Thus the differences between Toulmin's program and my own may prove to be sharp indeed. We can probably bracket this ambiguity without disaster and proceed with a not-too-feisty comparison of two agendas. The full development necessary to a full-dress confrontation is not central to the sorts of comparative arguments I want to make.

3. The claim that Toulmin is working downward is a plausible inference from the topics he has addressed, starting with probability and logic (Toulmin, 1950, 1953a) and ordinary language analysis (Toulmin and Baier, 1952; Toulmin, 1957a, 1957b, 1958, 1964, 1969a), and centering upon a continuing concern with the philosophy of science (Toulmin, 1953b, 1959, 1960, 1963, 1967a, 1967b, 1970, 1972, 1977; Toulmin and Goodfield, 1961). His treatments of psychological and sociological topics (Toulmin, 1969a, 1969b, 1971) have been consonant with his broader epistemological focus. Thus, he introduces his *Human Understanding* trilogy (Toulmin, 1972) with the claim that the general problem of human understanding is "to draw an epistemic self-portrait which is both well-founded and trustworthy." The centrality of the sciences to this aim is manifest, given Toulmin's view that they are man's most consistently successful epistemic enterprises.

4. This argument (and the related claims to follow) should not be construed as a general prohibition of textual analyses (see Wenzel, 1981; Cox, 1981). I by no means want to say that textual evidence cannot bear upon field studies or that texts cannot sometimes serve as accurate records of utterance. My claim is the narrower one that texts are not uniformly *dependable as records of utterance;* there are enough cases for which texts are misleading that they should seldom be used as the sole source of information about utterance. Similarly, a field's textual records are a vital part of its history; and field studies quite properly must take account of them. My claim is that a field's artifacts are not the whole story and are in some cases (for instance, in cost-benefit analysis) highly misleading. Thus I agree with Cox's (1981) argument that many vital features of

public policy argument are "publicly inspectable"; and I agree as well with Wenzel's (1981) claim that a central defining feature of argument is that it is *public*. My sole reservation is that while arguments are public, the intentions of speakers are not always as obvious as the records of their utterances; and there are at least some cases in which texts are utterly misleading (witness our paradigm cases). Strictly speaking, then, texts cannot be one's sole source of information; and in some cases, critics will find themselves (loosely speaking) "refuting the text." The issue is not a black-and-white question of using or not using texts (and my arguments here and below are not intended to frame the issue in such a way). The issue turns upon how trustworthy we think texts are *in general* and for which purposes they seem most appropriate as evidence.

Chapter 4

1. For locutionary convenience, I use "criticism" globally. In every case I mean argument and rhetorical criticism. Literary criticism is a different field with different problem foci and purposes; issue fields within literary criticism (for example, Derrida and the deconstructionists versus the New Critics) display the same differences ascribed to other interfield differences. There are also differences among rhetorical and argument critics of sufficient scope to permit the inference that several issue fields exist. These may become important later, but for now I prefer to refer to criticism globally.

2. The skeptical *doctrine* (as opposed to particular skeptical postures) cuts no ice in fields. Every field has its skeptics. But they operate on case-specific arguments, as Rescher (1977a) suggests. Also, asking skeptical questions is not invariably the mark of a skeptic—witness Kant or (in fact) any reflective scientist who questions the breadth and grounds of particular claims.

3. This notion squares with our field account generally and with the usual understandings of what "risk" entails, namely, the speaker's willingness to accommodate to the communal standard (in our terms, agreement to abide by the consequences of the public system) as a necessary condition of social processes (Kaufer, 1979, p. 181; Gregg, 1970; Jacobs and Laufersweiler, 1981).

4. An objection of the following sort might be raised: "I am unimpressed with your intrafield exception to the risk argument. Your own exposition of field theory suggests that interfield arguments are the most interesting cases. Interfield arguments involve the actor's putting himself at risk of standards outside his field. Thus your objection applies only to uninteresting cases." There are two plausible rejoinders to this objection. First, it is not entirely clear that in cases of interfield argument actors sincerely place themselves at risk (that is, their motives may be predatory or imperialistic). Second, it by no means follows that interfield argument legitimizes the *critic's* standards; granting the tenor of the objection, we may nonetheless say that at most the arguer puts himself at risk of the *other field's standards*. This result does not help the critic; it doubles his problems.

5. An objection of the following sort might arise: "You are throwing out the baby with the bath water. Your brief against evaluation seems to rule instrumental or pragmatic criticism out of the critical enterprise. Most rhetorical

critics merely want to employ their special knowledge of persuasion to illuminate particular attempts at social influence and to point out where people make mistakes (where, that is, they could use their own ideas to better rhetorical advantage). The study of rhetorical successes and errors is not quite the simpleminded form of evaluation you are attacking." By way of reply, let me emphasize that nothing in my present argument is intended to rule pragmatic criticism out of the critical enterprise. Criticism is a field (I have argued) capable of making epistemic progress. Rhetorical critics aim to achieve this progress largely respecting their understandings of the processes of social influence. Considerations of the rhetorical means available in particular situations and of the uses and misuses persuaders make of them are thus of central concern to rhetorical critics. I will also grant, consistent with the weltanschauungen assumptions I am defending, that such pragmatic criticism is evaluative, namely, in the sense that observation is never theory free. The study of the effects of assumptions upon precisely this kind of evaluative activity I take to be the core subject matter of rhetorical criticism. Thus, my objections here bear upon pragmatic concerns mainly when they are taken to be the central critical project. If the critic's aim is to say that A should have said X, not Y, my argument is that this will prove innocuous *unless* integrated into a broader project of studying both the critic's and A's assumptions and procedures.

6. Quoted by permission from Wallace Stevens, "The Man with the Blue Guitar," *The Collected Poems of Wallace Stevens* (New York: Knopf, 1954), p. 165.

7. An objection of the following sort might be raised: "At this point of your argument, you have arrived at a position most critics agree with anyway—which proves that you have been attacking a caricature of criticism, the sort of criticism done decades ago. Black (1965) has already critiqued 'etic' criticism. Most critics nowadays (for example) see themselves evaluating speakers by *the standards of the speakers' own fields.*" This objection is deficient on several counts. First, to evaluate a speaker by the standards of the speaker's own field is something no rhetorical critic is qualified to do. One's credentials for evaluation (on field-dependent grounds) are features of one's status within a particular field. To claim, for instance, that an economist's argument is "true," "false," "inadequately supported," and so forth, is to claim implicitly that one has the appropriate economic credentials for rendering such judgments. The thrust of Goodnight's (1981) argument is that no critic can evaluate (say) a nuclear engineer's claims about nuclear power safety because the veridical and judgmental standards appropriate to such claims reside in the field of nuclear engineering, not in the rhetorical principles special to the critic's expertise. Second, such "evaluation from within the field" risks banality. Except for the ravings of madmen, virtually any statement can be vouched for by one or another group. Thus, to evaluate a speaker by the standards of the speaker's field is to proceed (sans expert credentials) to do work that field actors do anyway. Third, this objection confuses the subject matter and aims of criticism with the subject matters and aims of the fields it studies. If the subject matter of criticism is equated with the substantive characteristics of arguments, criticism is indistinguishable from the routine activities of fields. By the present

epistemic view of criticism, one interests oneself in the particulars of fields not as ends in themselves but as extended examples of far broader concerns, namely, the effects of assumptions upon the arguments people have and make. The critic who assumes a pedagogical stance (of instructing a field to do its job better) adopts a pretension he cannot possibly justify unless the field in question provides him with credentials. My argument, then, is that critics speak to students of knowledge in general and only secondarily to field actors.

Finally, one might question the sincerity with which the present objection might be posed. Would a proponent of this objection seriously argue that the critic who studies National Socialism be concerned with helping Mr. Goebbels improve his propaganda effectiveness? Do critics who study demagogues do so with the aim of helping them improve their persuasiveness? If, on the other hand, the critic deals with a field of which he approves, does he not (on the evaluationist's account) become an apologist?

References

Abel, T. 1948. "The Operation Called *Verstehen.*" *Am. J. Sociol.* 54:211–218.

Abelson, R. P. 1959. "Modes of Resolution in Belief Dilemmas." *J. Conflict Resol.* 3:343–352.

———— and Rosenberg, M. J. 1958. "Symbolic Psychologic: A Model of Attitudinal Cognition." *Behavioral Science* 3:1–13.

Adams-Weber, J. 1969. "Cognitive Complexity and Sociality." *Brit. J. Soc. Clin. Psych.* 8:211–216.

————. 1979. *Personal Construct Theory: Concepts and Applications.* New York: Wiley.

———— et al. 1972. "Personal Constructs and the Perception of Individual Differences." *Can. J. Behav. Sci.* 4:218–224.

Anderson, B. 1974. "What Is Social Phenomenology? An Attempt at a Review Essay." *Summation* 4:91–106.

Anderson, J. P. 1977. "Practical Reasoning in Action." In *Existential Sociology,* ed. J. D. Douglas and J. M. Johnson. New York: Cambridge University Press.

Anderson, R. L., and Mortensen, C. D. 1967. "Logic and Marketplace Argumentation." *Quart. J. Sp.* 53:143–151.

Appelgate, J. L. 1981. "Person and Position Centered Communication in a Day Care Center." In *Studies in Symbolic Interaction,* vol. 3, ed. N. K. Denzin. Greenwich: JAI Press.

———— and Delia, J. G. 1980. "Person-Centered Speech, Psychological Development, and the Contexts of Language Usage." In *The Social and Psychological Contexts of Language,* ed. R. St. Clair and H. Giles. Hillsdale: Erlbaum.

Argyle, M. 1964. *The Psychology of Interpersonal Behavior.* Harmondsworth: Penguin.

————. 1970. *Social Interaction.* London: Methuen.

————, ed. 1973. *Social Encounters.* Harmondsworth: Penguin.

———— and Dean, J. 1965. "Eye Contact, Distance, and Affiliation." *Sociometry.* 28:289–304.

Arnold, C. C. 1974. *Criticism of Oral Rhetoric.* Columbus: Merrill.

Asch, S. E. 1957. "A Psychological Critique of Relativism." In *Philosophic Problems,* ed. M. Mandelbaum, F. W. Gramlich, and A. R. Anderson. New York: Macmillan.

Atherton, M., and Schwartz, R. 1974. "Linguistic Innateness and Its Evidence." *J. Phil.* 71:155–168.

Attwell, P. 1974. "Ethnomethodology Since Garfinkle." *Theory and Society* 1:179–210.

Ayer, A. J. 1936. *Language, Truth, and Logic*. New York: Dover.

———. 1940. *Foundations of Empirical Knowledge*. London: Macmillan.

———. 1956. *The Problem of Knowledge*. Baltimore: Penguin.

———, ed. 1959. *Logical Positivism*. New York: Free Press.

Bach, K., and Harnish, R. M. 1979. *Linguistic Communication and Speech Acts*. Cambridge: MIT Press.

Ball, D. W. 1967. "An Abortion Clinic Ethnography." *Social Problems*. 14:293–301.

———. 1972. "The Definition of Situation: Some Theoretical and Methodological Consequences of Taking W. I. Thomas Seriously." *J. Theory Soc. Behav.* 2:61–82.

Balthrop, V. W. 1980. "Argument as Linguistic Opportunity: A Search for Form and Function." In *Proceedings of the Summer Conference on Argumentation*, ed. J. Rhodes and S. Newell. Annandale: Speech Communication Association.

———. 1982. "Critical Approaches to the Analysis and Evaluation of Argument." In *Advances in Argumentation Theory and Research*, ed. J. R. Cox and C. A. Willard. Carbondale: Southern Illinois University Press.

Bannister, D. 1962. "Personal Construct Theory: A Summary and Experimental Paradigm." *Acta Psych.* 20:104–120.

———. 1966. "A New Theory of Personality." In *New Horizons in Psychology*, ed. B. M. Foss. Harmondsworth: Penguin.

———, ed. 1970. *Perspectives in Personal Construct Theory*. New York: Academic Press.

——— and Agnew, J. 1976. "The Child's Construing Self." In *Nebraska Symposium on Motivation*, vol. 24, ed. J. K. Cole and A. W. Landfield. Lincoln: University of Nebraska Press.

——— and Bott, M. 1973. "Evaluating the Person." In *New Approaches to Psychological Measurement*, ed. P. Klein. London: Wiley.

——— and Fransella, F. 1971. *Inquiring Man: The Theory of Personal Constructs*. Harmondsworth: Penguin.

——— and Mair, J. M. M. 1968. *The Evaluation of Personal Constructs*. London: Academic Press.

Bar-Hillel, Y. 1964. "Indexical Expressions." *Mind* 63:359–379.

———. 1970. *Aspects of Language*. Jerusalem: Magnes Press.

Barrett, W. 1962. *Irrational Man*. Garden City: Doubleday.

Bartley, W. W. 1962. *The Retreat to Commitment*. New York: Knopf.

———. 1964. "Rationality versus the Theory of Rationality." In *The Critical Approach*, ed. M. Bunge. New York: Free Press.

———. 1968. "Theories of Demarcation between Science and Metaphysics." In *Problems in the Philosophy of Science*, ed. I. Lakatos and A. Musgrave. Amsterdam: North Holland.

Bates, E. 1976. *Language and Context: The Acquisition of Pragmatics*. New York: Academic Press.

Bauman, R., and Sherzer, J., eds. 1974. *Explorations in the Ethnography of Speaking.* New York: Cambridge University Press.

Bauman, Z. 1973. "On the Philosophical Status of Ethnomethodology." *Sociol. Rev.* 21:5–23.

Becker, H. S. 1963. *Outsiders.* New York: Free Press.

———. 1970. *Sociological Work.* Chicago: Aldine.

Beldoch, M. 1964. "Sensitivity to Expression of Emotional Meaning in Three Modes of Communication." In *The Communication of Emotional Meaning,* ed. J. R. Davitz et al. New York: McGraw-Hill.

Bennett, J. 1964. *Rationality.* London: Routledge and Kegan Paul.

Berger, P. L., and Kellner, H. 1970. "Marriage and the Construction of Reality." In *Recent Sociology, No. 2: Patterns of Communicative Behavior,* ed. H. P. Dreitzel. New York: Macmillan.

Bergson, H. 1950. *Time and Free Will.* 6th ed. London: Allen and Unwin.

Bernstein, B. 1958. "Some Sociological Determinants of Perception," *Brit. J. Sociol.* 9:159–174.

———. 1964a. "Elaborated and Restricted Codes: Their Social Origins and Some Consequences." In "The Ethnography of Communication," ed. J. J. Gumperz and D. Hymes. *American Anthropologist.* 2:55–69.

———. 1964b. "Aspects of Language in the Genesis of the Social Process." In *Language in Culture and Society,* ed. D. Hymes. New York: Harper and Row.

Bershady, H. 1973. *Ideology and Social Knowledge.* Oxford: Blackwell.

Bieri, J., et al. 1966. *Clinical and Social Judgment.* New York: Wiley.

Bierstedt, R. 1949. "A Critique of Empiricism in Sociology." *Am. Sociol. Rev.* 14:584–592.

Birdwhistle, R. 1968. "Kinesics." *International Encyclopedia of the Social Sciences* 8:379–380.

———. 1970. *Kinesics and Context.* Philadelphia: University of Pennsylvania Press.

Bitzer, L. F. 1978. "Rhetoric and Public Knowledge." In *Rhetoric, Philosophy, and Literature,* ed. D. M. Burkes. West Lafayette: Purdue University Press.

Black, E. 1965. *Rhetorical Criticism: A Study in Method.* New York: Macmillan.

Black, M. 1970. *Margins of Precision.* Ithaca: Cornell University Press.

Blanshard, B. 1962. *Reason and Analysis.* London: Allen and Unwin.

Bloom, L. 1970. *Language Development.* Cambridge, Mass.: MIT Press.

Bloor, D. 1976. *Knowledge and Social Imagery.* London: Routledge and Kegan Paul.

Blum, A. F. 1970. "Theorizing." In *Understanding Everyday Life,* ed. J. D. Douglas. Chicago: Aldine.

Blum, A., and McHugh, P. 1971. "The Social Ascription of Motives." *Am. Sociol. Rev.* 38:98–109.

Blum, J. P., and Gumperz, J. J. 1972. "Some Social Determinants of Verbal Behavior." In *Directions in Sociolinguistics: The Ethnography of Communication,* ed. J. J. Gumperz and D. Hymes. New York: Holt, Rinehart and Winston.

Blumer, H. 1969. *Symbolic Interactionism: Perspective and Method.* Englewood Cliffs: Prentice-Hall.

Bock, K. 1956. *The Acceptance of Histories*. Berkeley: University of California Press.

Bohr, N. 1913. "On the Constitution of Atoms and Molecules." *Philosophical Magazine*, 26:1–25, 476–502, 857–875.

———. 1958. *Atomic Physics and Human Knowledge*. New York: Wiley.

———. 1963. *Essays, 1958–1962, on Atomic Physics and Human Knowledge*. New York: Random House.

Booth, W. C. 1979. *Critical Understanding*. Chicago: University of Chicago Press.

Bourke, V. J. 1966. *Ethics in Crisis*. Milwaukee: Bruce.

Brockriede, W. 1972. "Arguers as Lovers." *Philosophy and Rhetoric* 5:1–11.

———. 1974. "Rhetorical Criticism as Argument." *Quart. J. Sp.* 60:164–174.

———. 1975. "Where Is Argument?" *J. Am. Forensic Assoc.* 11:179–182.

———. 1977. "Characteristics of Arguments and Arguing." *J. Am. Forensic Assoc.* 13:129–132.

———. 1981. "Arguing about Human Understanding." Paper presented at the meeting of the Eastern Communication Association.

Brown, R. H. 1977. *A Poetic for Sociology: Toward a Logic of Discovery for the Human Sciences*. New York: Cambridge University Press.

Bruyn, S. T. 1966. *The Human Perspective in Sociology*. Englewood Cliffs: Prentice-Hall.

Burke, K. 1952. *A Rhetoric of Motives*. Englewood Cliffs: Prentice-Hall.

Burleson, B. R. 1979a. "On the Analysis and Criticism of Arguments: Some Theoretical and Methodological Considerations." *J. Am. Forensic Assoc.* 15:137–147.

———. 1979b. "On the Foundations of Rationality: Toulmin, Habermas, and the *A Priori* of Reason." *J. Am. Forensic Assoc.* 16:112–127.

———. 1979c. "The Justification of Message Strategies: A Developmental Analysis of Interpersonal Reasoning." Paper presented at the meeting of the Speech Communication Association.

———. 1980a. "The Place of Non-Discursive Symbolism, Formal Characterizations, and Hermeneutics in Argument Analysis and Criticism." *J. Am. Forensic Assoc.* 16:222–231.

———. 1980b. "Argument and Constructivism: The Cognitive Developmental Component." Paper presented at the meeting of the Speech Communication Association.

———. 1981. "A Cognitive Developmental Perspective on Social Reasoning Processes." *Western J. Sp. Comm.* 45:133–147.

——— and Kline, S. L. 1979. "Habermas' Theory of Communication: A Critical Explication." *Quart. J. Sp.* 65:412–428.

Butterfield, H. 1965. *The Whig Interpretation of History*. New York: Norton.

Cambell, J. A. 1981. "Historical Reason: Field as Consciousness." In *Dimensions of Argument: Proceedings of the Second Summer Conference on Argumentation*, ed. G. Ziegelmueller and J. Rhodes. Annandale: Speech Communication Association.

Cassirer, E. 1944. *An Essay on Man*. New Haven: Yale University Press.

———. 1946. *Language and Myth*. New York: Harper and Row.

———. 1950. *The Problem of Knowledge.* New Haven: Yale University Press.

———. 1957. *The Philosophy of Symbolic Forms.* Vol. 3. *The Phenomenology of Knowledge.* New Haven: Yale University Press.

———. 1961. *The Logic of the Humanities.* New Haven: Yale University Press.

Chandler, M. J. 1977. "Social Cognition: A Selective Review of Current Research." In *Knowledge and Development,* vol. 1, *Advances in Theory and Research,* ed. W. F. Overton and J. McCarthy. New York: Plenum Press.

Chapman, L. J., and Chapman, J. P. 1959. "Atmosphere Effect Re-examined." *J. Ex. Psychol.* 58:220–266.

Child, A. 1941. "The Problem of Imputation in the Sociology of Knowledge." *Ethics* 51:200–219.

———. 1947. "The Problem of Truth in the Sociology of Knowledge." *Ethics* 58:18–34.

Chisholm, R. 1957. *Perceiving.* Ithaca: Cornell University Press.

——— and Swartz, R., eds. 1974. *Empirical Knowledge.* Englewood Cliffs: Prentice-Hall.

Chomsky, N. 1965. *Aspects of the Theory of Syntax.* Cambridge, Mass.: MIT Press.

———. 1968. *Language and Mind.* New York: Harcourt.

Cicourel, A. V. 1964. *Method and Measurement in Sociology.* New York: Free Press.

———. 1970. "Basic and Normative Rules in the Negotiation of Status and Role." In *Recent Sociology, No. 2: Patterns of Communicative Behavior,* ed. H. P. Dreitzel. New York: Macmillan.

———. 1974. *Cognitive Sociology.* New York: Free Press.

Clark, H. H. 1973. "The Language-as-Fixed-Effect Fallacy: A Critique of Language Statistics in Psychological Research." *J. Verbal Learning and Verbal Behavior* 12:335–359.

———. 1979. "Responding to Indirect Speech Acts." *Cog. Psych.* 11:430–477.

Clark, R. A. 1979. "The Impact of Self Interest and Desire for Liking on a Selection of Communication Strategies." *Comm. Mono.* 46:257–273.

——— and Delia, J. G. 1976. "The Development of Functional Persuasive Skills in Childhood and Early Adolescence." *Child Devel.* 47:1008–1014.

———. 1977. "Cognitive Complexity, Social Perspective Taking, and Functional Persuasive Skills in Second- to Ninth-Grade Children." *Human Comm. Res.* 3:128–134.

Cohen, L. J. 1962. *The Diversity of Meaning.* London: Methuen.

Cooley, C. H. 1902. *Human Nature and the Social Order.* New York: Scribner's.

Coulter, J. 1971. "Decontextualized Meanings: Current Approaches to *Verstehende* Investigations." *Soc. Rev.* 19:301–323.

———. 1979. *The Social Construction of Mind: Studies in Ethnomethodology and Linguistic Philosophy.* London: Macmillan.

Coulthard, M. 1977. *An Introduction to Discourse Analysis.* New York: Longman.

Cox, J. R. 1980. "Argument and the Definition of the Situation." Paper presented at the meeting of the Speech Communication Association.

———. 1981. "Investigating Policy Argument as a Field." In *Dimensions of*

Argument: Proceedings of the Second Summer Conference on Argumentation, ed. G. Ziegelmueller and J. Rhodes. Annandale: Speech Communication Association.

——— and Willard, C. A., eds. 1982. *Advances in Argumentation Theory and Research.* Carbondale: Southern Illinois University Press.

Crockett, W. H. 1965. "Cognitive Complexity and Impression Formation." In *Progress in Experimental Personality Research,* vol. 2, ed. B. A. Maher. New York: Academic Press.

Curry, G. 1980. "The Role of Normative Assumptions in Historical Explanations." *Philosophy of Science* 47:465–473.

Damon, W. 1977. *The Social World of the Child.* San Francisco: Jossey-Bass.

Danto, A. C. 1968. *An Analytical Theory of Knowledge.* Cambridge: Cambridge University Press.

Davis, K. 1948. *Human Society.* New York: Macmillan.

Davis, K. C. 1971. *Discretionary Justice.* Urbana: University of Illinois Press.

Davis, M. 1965. *The Undecidable.* New York: Raven.

Davis, W. A. 1978. *The Act of Interpretation.* Chicago: University of Chicago Press.

Davitz, J., and Davitz, L. 1959. "The Communication of Feelings by Content-Free Speech." *J. Comm.* 9:6–13.

Deese, J. 1973. "Cognitive Structure and Affect in Language." In *Communication and Affect,* ed. P. Krames and T. Alloway. London: Academic Press.

Delia, J. G. 1972. "Dialects and the Effects of Stereotypes on Interpersonal Attraction and Cognitive Processes in Impression Formation." *Quart. J. Sp.* 58:285–297.

———. 1974. "Attitude toward the Disclosure of Self-Attributions and the Complexity of Interpersonal Constructs." *Sp. Mono.* 41:119–126.

———. 1975. "Communication Research and the Variable Analytic Tradition." Paper presented at the meeting of the Speech Communication Association.

———. 1976a. "A Constructivist Analysis of the Concept of Credibility." *Quart. J. Sp.* 62:361–375.

———. 1976b. "Change of Meaning Processes in Impression Formation." *Comm. Mono.* 43:142–157.

———. 1977a. "Alternative Perspectives for the Study of Human Communication." *Comm. Quart.* 25:46–52.

———. 1977b. "Constructivism and the Study of Human Communication." *Quart. J. Sp.* 63:66–83.

———. 1978. "Research and Methodological Commitments of a Constructivist." Paper presented at the meeting of the Speech Communication Association.

——— and Clark, R. A. 1975. "A Constructivist Approach to the Development of Rhetorical Competence." Paper presented at the meeting of the Speech Communication Association.

———. 1977. "Cognitive Complexity, Social Perception, and the Development of Listener-Adapted Communication in Six-, Eight-, and Twelve-Year-Old Boys." *Comm. Mono.* 44:326–345.

—— et al. 1975. "The Dependency of Interpersonal Evaluations on Context-Relevant Beliefs about the Other." *Sp. Mono.* 42:10–19.

—— and Grossberg, L. 1977. "Interpretation and Evidence." *Western J. Sp.* 41:32–42.

—— and O'Keefe, B. J. 1979. "Constructivism: The Development of Communication in Children." In *Children Communicating*, ed. E. Wartella. Beverly Hills: Sage.

——, O'Keefe, B. J., and O'Keefe, D. J. 1982. "The Constructivist Approach to Human Communication." In *Comparative Theories of Human Communication*, ed. F. E. X. Dance. New York: Harper and Row.

Denzin, N. K. 1970. *The Research Act.* Chicago: Aldine.

Dewey, J. 1929. *The Quest of Certainty.* New York: Putnam.

——. 1938. *Logic: The Theory of Inquiry.* New York: Holt.

——. 1958. *Art as Experience.* New York: Capricorn.

—— and Bentley, A. F. 1949. *Knowing and the Known.* Boston: Beacon.

Dilthey, W. 1913–1967. *Gesammelte Schriften.* 14 vols. Göttingen: Vanden-Hoeck and Ruprecht.

——. 1962. *Pattern and Meaning in History.* Trans. and ed. H. P. Rickman. New York: Harper and Row.

Douglas, J. D. 1970a. *Understanding Everyday Life.* Chicago: Aldine.

——. 1970b. *The Relevance of Sociology.* New York: Appleton.

——. 1971. *The American Social Order.* New York: Free Press.

——, ed. 1972. *Research on Deviance.* New York: Random House.

——. 1977a. "Existential Sociology." In *Existential Sociology*, ed. J. D. Douglas and J. M. Johnson. New York: Cambridge University Press.

——. 1977b. "Appendix: The Origins of Existential Sociology." In *Existential Sociology*, ed. J. D. Douglas and J. M. Johnson. New York: Cambridge University Press.

—— and Johnson, J. M. eds. 1977. *Existential Sociology.* New York: Cambridge University Press.

Drietzel, H. P. ed. 1970. *Recent Sociology, No. 2: Patterns of Communicative Behavior.* New York: Macmillan.

Duck, S. W. 1972. "Friendship, Similarity, and the Reptest." *Psych. Reps.* 31:231–234.

——. 1973a. "Similarity and Perceived Similarity of Personal Constructs as Influences on Friendship Choices." *Brit. J. Soc. Clin. Psych.* 12:1–6.

——. 1973b. *Personal Relationships and Personal Constructs.* London: Wiley.

——, ed. 1977. *Theory and Practice in Interpersonal Attraction.* London: Academic Press.

Dufrenne, M. 1946. "Existentialisme et sociologie." *Cahiers internationaux de sociologie.* 1:161–170.

——. 1953. *La personalité de base: Un concept sociologique.* Paris: Presses Universitaires de France.

——. 1960. "The Role of Man in the Social Sciences." *Philosophy Today* 4:36–44.

Dyson, A. E. 1965. *The Crazy Fabric: Essays in Irony.* New York: St. Martin's.

Edie, J. 1967. "Comments on Maurice Natanson's Paper, 'Man as Actor.' " In *Phenomenology of Will and Action*, ed. E. W. Straus and R. M. Griffith. Pittsburgh: Duquesne University Press.

Ekman, P. 1964. "Body Position, Facial Expression, and Verbal Behavior during Interviews," *J. Ab. Soc. Psych.* 68:295–301.

—— and Freisen, W. V. 1973. "Nonverbal Leakage and Clues to Deception." In *Social Encounters*, ed. M. Argyle. Harmondsworth: Penguin.

Eliot, T. S. 1960. *The Sacred Wood: Essays on Poetry and Criticism.* New York: Barnes and Noble.

Emerson, J. P. 1970a. "Behavior in Private Places: Sustaining Definitions of Reality in Gynecological Examinations." In *Recent Sociology, No. 2: Patterns of Communicative Behavior*, ed. H. P. Dreitzel. New York: Macmillan.

——. 1970b. "Nothing Unusual Is Happening." In *Human Nature and Collective Behavior*, ed. T. Shibutani. Englewood Cliffs: Prentice-Hall.

Emmet, D. 1966. *Rules, Roles, and Relations.* Boston: Beacon.

—— and Macintyre, A., eds. 1970. *Sociological Theory and Philosophical Analysis.* London: Macmillan.

Ervin-Tripp, S. 1976. "Is Sybil There? The Structure of American English Directives." *Language in Society* 5:25–66.

—— and Mitchell-Kernan, C. 1977. *Child Discourse.* New York: Academic Press.

Exline, R. V., Gray, D., and Schuette, D. 1965. "Visual Behavior in a Dyad as Affected by Interview Content and Sex of Respondent." *J. Pers. Soc. Psych.* 1:201–209.

Exline, R. V., and Winters, L. C. 1965. "Affective Relations and Mutual Glances in Dyads." In *Affect, Cognition, and Personality*, ed. S. Thompson and C. Izard. New York: Springer.

Fancher, J. 1966. "Explicit Personality Theories and Accuracy in Person Perception." *J. Pers.* 34:252–261.

Farber, M. 1940. "The Idea of Presuppositionless Philosophy." In *Philosophical Essays in Honor of Edmund Husserl*, ed. M. Farber. Cambridge, Mass.: Harvard University Press.

Farrell, K. 1981. "Field Theory and Public Argument Criticism." Paper presented at the Speech Communication Association Doctoral Honors Seminar, Bowling Green, Ohio.

Farrell, T. B. 1976. "Knowledge, Consensus, and Rhetorical Theory." *Quart. J. Sp.* 62:1–14.

——. 1977. "Validity and Rationality: The Rhetorical Constituents of Argumentative Form." *J. Am. Forensic Assoc.* 13:142–149.

——. 1979. "Habermas on Argumentation Theory: Some Emerging Topics." *J. Am. Forensic Assoc.* 16:77–82.

Feinberg, G. 1972. "Philosophical Implications of Contemporary Particle Physics." In *Paradigms and Paradoxes: The Philosophical Challenge of the Quantum Domain*, ed. R. G. Colodny. Pittsburgh: University of Pittsburgh Press.

Ferguson, T. 1973. "The Political Economy of Knowledge and the Changing Politics of Philosophy of Science." *Telos* 15:125–137.

Festinger, L. 1954. "A Theory of Social Comparison Processes." *Hum. Rel.* 7:117–140.

Feyerabend, P. K. 1962. "Explanation, Reduction, and Empiricism." *Minnesota Studies in the Philosophy of Science*, vol. 3, ed. H. Feigl and G. Maxwell. Minneapolis: University of Minnesota Press.

———. 1965a. "Problems in Empiricism." In *Beyond the Edge of Certainty*, ed. R. Colodny. Englewood Cliffs: Prentice-Hall.

———. 1965b. "Reply to Criticism." In *Boston Studies in the Philosophy of Science*, vol. 2, ed. R. S. Cohen and M. W. Wartofsky. New York: Humanities Press.

———. 1969. "Linguistic Arguments and Scientific Method." *Telos* 3:43–63.

———. 1970a. "Against Method: Outline of an Anarchistic Method of Knowledge." In *Minnesota Studies in the Philosophy of Science*, vol. 4, ed. M. Radner and S. Winokur. Minneapolis: University of Minnesota Press.

———. 1970b. "Consolations for the Specialist." In *Criticism and the Growth of Knowledge*, ed. I. Lakatos and A. Musgrave. Cambridge: Cambridge University Press.

Fine, A. 1972. "Some Conceptual Problems of Quantum Theory." In *Paradigms and Paradoxes: The Philosophical Challenge of the Quantum Domain*, ed. R. G. Colodny. Pittsburgh: University of Pittsburgh Press.

Filmer, P., et al. 1973. *New Directions in Sociological Theory*. Cambridge, Mass.: MIT Press.

Filstead, W. J., ed. 1970. *Qualitative Methodology*. Chicago: Markham.

Fisher, W. R. 1978. "Toward a Logic of Good Reasons." *Quart. J. Sp.* 64:376–384.

———. 1980. "Rationality and the Logic of Good Reasons." *Philosophy and Rhetoric* 13:122–125.

———. 1981. "Good Reasons: Fields and Genre." In *Dimensions of Argument: Proceedings of the Second Summer Conference on Argumentation*, ed. G. Ziegelmueller and J. Rhodes. Annandale: Speech Communication Association.

Flavell, J. H., et al. 1968. *The Development of Role-Taking and Communication Skills in Children*. New York: Wiley.

Fodor, J. A. 1968. *Psychological Explanation*. New York: Random House.

———. 1979. *The Language of Thought*. Cambridge, Mass.: Harvard University Press.

Foucalt, M. 1970. *The Order of Things*. New York: Random House.

———. 1972. *The Archaeology of Knowledge*. New York: Harper and Row.

Fransella, F. 1972. *Personal Change and Reconstruction*. London: Academic Press.

———. 1977. "The Self and the Stereotype." In *New Perspectives in Personal Construct Theory*, ed. D. Bannister. London: Academic Press.

——— and Bannister, D. 1977. *A Manual for Repertory Grid Techniques*. London: Academic Press.

Friedrichs, R. W. 1970. *A Sociology of Sociology*. New York: Free Press.

Gadamer, H.-G. 1975. *Truth and Method*. Trans. G. Barden and J. Cumming. New York: Seabury.

———. 1976. *Philosophical Hermeneutics*. Trans. D. E. Linge. Berkeley: University of California Press.

———. 1980. *Dialogue and Dialectic*. Trans. P. C. Smith. New Haven: Yale University Press.

Gamson, W. A. 1974. "Ethnomethodology." In *Concepts of Social Life*, ed. W. A. Gamson and A. Modigliani. Boston: Little, Brown.

Garfinkle, H. 1964. "Studies in the Routine Grounds of Everyday Activities." *Soc. Prob.* 11:220–250.

———. 1967. *Studies in Ethnomethodology*. Englewood Cliffs: Prentice-Hall.

——— and Sacks, H. 1970. "On Formal Structures of Practical Actions." In *Theoretical Sociology*, ed. J. C. McKinney and E. A. Tiryakian. New York: Appleton.

Garvey, C. 1977. "Contingent Queries." In *Interaction, Conversation, and the Development of Language*, ed. M. Lewis and L. A. Rosenblum. New York: Wiley.

Gellner, E. 1959. *Words and Things*. Harmondsworth: Penguin.

———. 1964. *Thought and Change*. London: Weidenfeld.

———. 1975. "Ethnomethodology: The Re-Enchantment Industry; or, The California Way of Subjectivity." *Phil. Soc. Sci.* 5:431–450.

Gendlin, E. T. 1962. *The Experiencing and Creation of Meaning*. Glencoe: Free Press.

Geraets, T. F., ed. 1979. *Rationality Today*. Toronto: University of Toronto Press.

Giddens, A. 1974. *Positivism and Sociology*. London: Heinemann.

Gidlow, B. 1972. "Ethnomethodology: A New Name for Old Practices." *Brit. J. Sociol.* 23:395–405.

Glaser, B., and Strauss, A. 1964. "Awareness Contexts and Social Interaction." *Am. Sociol. Rev.* 29:219–237.

———. 1967. *The Discovery of Grounded Theory*. Chicago: Aldine.

Gödel, K. 1962. *On the Formally Undecidable Propositions of "Principia Mathematica" and Related Systems*. London: Oliver and Boyd.

Goffman, E. 1959. *The Presentation of Self in Everyday Life*. Garden City: Doubleday.

———. 1961a. *Encounters*. Indianapolis: Bobbs-Merrill.

———. 1961b. *Asylums*. Garden City: Doubleday.

———. 1963. *Behavior in Public Places*. New York: Free Press.

———. 1964. *Stigma*. Englewood Cliffs: Prentice-Hall.

———. 1967. *Interaction Ritual*. New York: Doubleday.

———. 1969. *Strategic Interaction*. Philadelphia: University of Pennsylvania Press.

———. 1971. *Relations in Public*. New York: Basic Books.

———. 1974. *Frame Analysis*. New York: Harper and Row.

Goldthorpe, J. H. 1973. "A Revolution in Sociology?" *Sociology* 7:449–462.

Goodman, N. 1951. *The Structure of Appearance*. Cambridge, Mass.: Harvard University Press.

———. 1960. "The Way the World Is." *Rev. Metaphysics* 14:48–56.

Goodnight. G. T. 1980. "The Liberal and Conservative Presumptions: On Political Philosophy and the Foundation of Public Argument." In *Proceedings of the*

Summer Conference on Argumentation, ed. J. Rhodes and S. Newell. Annandale: Speech Communication Association.

———. 1981. "Arguments Lost: The Personal, Technical and Public Spheres of Argument." Unpublished manuscript.

Goodwin, P. D., and Wenzel, J. W. 1979. "Proverbs and Practical Reasoning: A Study in Socio-Logic." *Quart. J. Sp.* 65:289–302.

Goody, E. N., ed. 1978. *Questions and Politeness.* Cambridge, Mass.: Harvard University Press.

Gouldner, A. W. 1970. *The Coming Crisis of Western Sociology.* New York: Avon.

———. 1976. *The Dialectic of Ideology and Technology.* New York: Seabury.

Gregg. R. B. 1970. "The Ego-Function of the Rhetoric of Protest." *Phil. Rhet.*

Grice, H. P. 1957. "Meaning." *Phil. Rev.* 66:377–388.

———. 1975. "Logic and Conversation." In *Syntax and Semantics,* vol. 3, *Speech Acts,* eds. P. Cole and J. Morgan. New York: Academic Press.

———. 1978. "Further Notes on Logic and Conversation." In *Syntax and Semantics,* ed. P. Cole. New York: Academic Press.

Gronbeck, B. 1980. "From Argument to Argumentation: Fifteen Years of Identity Crisis." In *Proceedings of the Summer Conference on Argumentation,* ed. J. Rhodes and S. Newell. Annandale: Speech Communication Association.

———. 1981. "Sociocultural Notions of Argument Fields: A Primer." In *Dimensions of Argument: Proceedings of the Second Summer Conference on Argumentation,* ed. G. Ziegelmueller and J. Rhodes. Annandale: Speech Communication Association.

Gross, L. 1960. "An Epistemological View of Sociological Theory." *Am. J. Sociol.* 65:441–448.

Gumperz, J. J. 1962. "Types of Linguistic Communities." *Anthropological Linguistics* 1:28–40.

——— and Hymes, D., eds. 1972. *Directions in Sociolinguistics: The Ethnography of Communication.* New York: Holt, Rinehart and Winston.

Gurvitch, G. 1971. *The Social Frameworks of Knowledge.* Trans. M. Thompson and K. Thompson. Oxford: Blackwell.

Gurwitsch, A. 1964. *The Field of Consciousness.* Pittsburgh: Duquesne University Press.

———. 1966. *Studies in Phenomenology and Psychology.* Evanston: Northwestern University Press.

Gusdorf, G. 1965. *Speaking.* Trans. P. T. Brockelmas. Evanston: Northwestern University Press.

Habermas, J. 1970a. "Toward a Theory of Communicative Competence." In *Recent Sociology, No. 2: Patterns of Communicative Behavior,* ed. H. P. Dreitzel. New York: Macmillan.

———. 1970b. *Toward a Rational Society.* Trans. J. J. Shapiro. Boston: Beacon.

———. 1971. *Knowledge and Human Interests.* Trans. J. J. Shapiro. Boston: Beacon.

———. 1973. *Theory and Practice.* Trans. J. Viertal. Boston: Beacon.

———. 1975. *Legitimation Crises.* Trans. T. McCarthy. Boston: Beacon.

———. 1976. "Some Distinctions in Universal Pragmatics: A Working Paper." *Theory and Society* 3:155–167.

————. 1979. *Communication and the Evolution of Society*. Trans. T. McCarthy. Boston: Beacon.

Haggard, E. A., and Isaacs, K. S. 1966. "Micromomentary Facial Expressions as Indicators of Ego Mechanisms in Psychotherapy." In *Methods of Research in Psychotherapy*, ed. L. A. Gottschalk and A. H. Auerback. New York: Appleton.

Hall, E. T. 1959. *The Silent Language*. Greenwich: Fawcett.

————. 1966. *The Hidden Dimension*. New York: Doubleday.

Hanson, N. R. 1958. *Patterns of Discovery*. Cambridge: Cambridge University Press.

Hardwig, J. 1973. "The Achievement of Moral Rationality." *Phil. Rhet.* 6:171–185.

Hare, R. M. 1975. "Philosophy at Oxford." In *Philosophical Explorations*, ed. P. A. Finch. Morristown: General Learning Press.

Harré, R. 1974. "Some Remarks on 'Rule' as a Scientific Concept." In *Understanding Other Persons*, ed. T. Mischel. Oxford: Blackwell.

————. 1978. "Architechtonic Man." In *Structure, Consciousness, and History*, ed. R. Brown and S. Lyman. Cambridge: Cambridge University Press.

Hegel, G. W. F. 1942. *Philosophy of Right*. Trans. T. Knox. Oxford: Clarendon Press.

Heidegger, M. 1969. *The Essence of Reasons*. Trans. T. Malick. Evanston: Northwestern University Press.

Heider, F. 1958. *The Psychology of Interpersonal Relations*. New York: Wiley.

Heisenberg, W. 1952. *Philosophical Problems of Nuclear Science*. London: Faber and Faber.

————. 1958. "The Representation of Nature in Contemporary Physics." *Daedalus* 87:95–108.

————. 1966. *Physics and Philosophy*. New York: Harper and Row.

————. 1971. *Physics and Beyond*. New York: Harper and Row.

Helmer, O., and Rescher, N. 1958. *On the Epistemology of the Inexact Sciences*. Santa Monica: Rand.

Henle, M. 1962. "On the Relation between Logic and Thinking." *Psych. Rev.* 69:366–378.

Hintikka, J. 1962. *Knowledge and Belief*. Ithaca: Cornell University Press.

Hirsch, E. D. 1967. *Validity in Interpretation*. New Haven: Yale University Press.

Hollis, M. 1970a. "The Limits of Irrationality." In *Rationality*, ed. B. Wilson. Oxford: Blackwell.

————. 1970b. "Reason and Ritual." In *Rationality*, ed. B. Wilson. Oxford: Blackwell.

Hoy, D. C. 1978. *The Critical Circle*. Berkeley: University of California Press.

Hymes, D. 1962. "The Ethnography of Speaking." In *Anthropology and Human Behavior*, ed. T. Gladwin and W. C. Sturtevent. Washington: Anthropological Society of Washington.

————. 1964. "A Perspective for Linguistic Anthropology." In *Horizons of Anthropology*, ed. S. Tax. London: Aldine.

————. 1966. "Two Types of Linguistic Relativity." In *Sociolinguistics*, ed. W. Bright. The Hague: Mouton.

———. 1967. "Models of Interaction of Language and Social Setting." *J. Social Issues* 23:8–28.

———. 1970. "Linguistic Theory and the Functions of Speech." In *Proceedings of International Days of Sociolinguistics*. Rome: Institu Luigi Sturtzo.

———. 1971. "Sociolinguistics and the Ethnography of Speaking." In *Social Anthropology and Linguistics*, ed. E. Ardener. London: Tavistock.

———. 1972. "Models of Interaction of Language and Social Life." In *Directions in Sociolinguistics: The Ethnography of Communication*, ed. J. J. Gumperz and D. Hymes. New York: Holt, Rinehart and Winston.

Ichleiser, G. 1970. *Appearances and Realities*. San Francisco: Jossey-Bass.

Isaacson, G. I., and Landfield, A. W. 1965. "Meaningfulness of Personal and Common Constructs." *J. Indiv. Psych.* 21:160–166.

Iser, W. 1978. *The Act of Reading*. Baltimore: Johns Hopkins University Press.

Jackson, S. A. 1977. "A Constructivist Analysis of the Perception of Political Candidates." Paper presented at the meeting of the Speech Communication Association.

———. 1980. Review of *Thinking: Readings in Cognitive Science. J. Am. Forensic Assoc.* 17:66–72.

——— and Jacobs, S. 1978. "Adjacency Pairs and the Sequential Description of Arguments." Paper presented at the meeting of the Speech Communication Association.

———. 1980. "Structure of Conversational Argument: Pragmatic Bases for the Enthymeme." *Quart. J. Sp.* 66:251–265.

Jacobs, S. 1980. "Recent Advances in Discourse Analysis." *Quart. J. Sp.* 66:450–472.

——— and Jackson, S. A. 1979. "Collaborative Aspects of Argument Production." Paper presented at the meeting of the Speech Communication Association.

———. 1980. "Structure and Strategy in Conversational Influence." Paper presented at the meeting of the Speech Communication Association.

———. 1981. "Argument as a Natural Category: The Routine Grounds for Arguing in Conversation." *Western J. Sp. Comm.* 45:118–132.

———. 1982. "Ordinary Argument and Conversational Analysis." In *Advances in Argumentation Theory and Research*, ed. J. R. Cox and C. A. Willard. Carbondale: Southern Illinois University Press.

Jacobs, S., and Laufersweiler, C. J. 1981. "The Interactional Organization of Witnessing and Heckling: An Ethnographic Study of Rhetorical Discourse." Paper presented at the meeting of the Central States Speech Association.

James, W. 1950. *Principles of Psychology*. 2 vols. New York: Dover.

Jameson, F. 1972. *The Prison House of Language*. Princeton: Princeton University Press.

Jarvie, I. C., and Agassi, J. 1970. "The Problem of the Rationality of Magic." In *Rationality*, ed. B. Wilson. Oxford: Blackwell.

Johnson, J. M. 1972. "The Practical Use of Rules." In *Theoretical Perspectives on Deviance*, ed. R. A. Scott and J. D. Douglas. New York: Basic Books.

———. 1975. *Doing Field Research*. New York: Free Press.

Johnstone, H. W. 1982. "Bilaterality in Argument." In *Advances in Argumentation Theory and Research*, ed. J. R. Cox and C. A. Willard. Carbondale: Southern Illinois University Press.

Junker, B. H. 1960. *Field Work*. Chicago: University of Chicago Press.

Kaufer, D. S. 1979. "Point of View in Rhetorical Situations: Classical and Romantic Contrasts and Contemporary Implications." *Quart. J. Sp.* 65:171–186.

Kelley, H. H. 1971. "Causal Schemata and the Attribution Process." In *Attribution: Perceiving the Causes of Behavior*, ed. E. E. Jones et al. Morristown: General Learning Press.

Kelly, G. A. 1955. *A Theory of Personality*. New York: Norton.

———. 1961. "The Abstraction of Human Processes." In *Proceedings of the Fourteenth International Congress of Applied Psychologists*. Copenhagen: Munksgaard.

———. 1965. "The Strategy of Psychological Research." *Bull. Brit. Psych. Soc.* 18:1–15.

———. 1969. *Clinical Psychology and Personality*, ed. B. Maher. New York: Wiley.

———. 1977. "The Psychology of the Unknown." In *New Perspectives in Personal Construct Theory*, ed. D. Bannister. London: Academic Press.

Kelvin, R. P. 1970. *The Bases of Social Behavior*. London: Holt.

Kendon, A. 1967. "Some Functions of Gaze Direction in Social Interaction." *Acta Psych.* 26:22–63.

Kline, S. L. 1979. "Toward a Contemporary Linguistic Interpretation of the Concept of Stasis." *J. Am. Forensic Assoc.* 16:95–103.

Kluckhohn, F. 1940. "The Participant-Observer Technique in Small Communities." *Am. J. Sociol.* 46:331–343.

Klumpp, J. F. 1981. "A Dramatistic Approach to Fields." In *Dimensions of Argument: Proceedings of the Second Summer Conference on Argumentation*, ed. G. Ziegelmueller and J. Rhodes. Annandale: Speech Communication Association.

Kneupper, C. W. 1978. "On Arguments and Diagrams." *J. Am. Forensic Assoc.* 14:181–186.

———. 1979. "Paradigms and Problems: Alternative Constructivist/Interactionist Implications for Argumentation Theory." *J. Am. Forensic Assoc.* 15:220–227.

Kohlberg, L. 1969. "Stage and Sequence: The Cognitive Developmental Approach to Socialization." In *Handbook of Socialization Theory and Research*, ed. D. A. Goslin. Chicago: Rand McNally.

———. 1971. "From Is to Ought: How to Commit the Naturalistic Fallacy and Get Away with It." In *Cognitive Development and Epistemology*, ed. T. Mischel. New York: Academic Press.

Kolb, W. L. 1972. "A Critical Evaluation of Mead's 'I' and 'Me' Concepts." In *Symbolic Interaction*, 2d ed., ed. J. G. Manis and B. N. Meltzer. Boston: Allyn and Bacon.

Krutch, J. W. 1954. *The Measure of Man*. New York: Grosset and Dunlap.

Kuhn, T. S. 1970a. *The Structure of Scientific Revolutions*. 2d ed. Chicago: University of Chicago Press.

——. 1970b. "Logic of Discovery or Psychology of Research?" In *Criticism and the Growth of Knowledge,* ed. I. Lakatos and A. Musgrave. Cambridge: Cambridge University Press.

——. 1970c. "Reflections on My Critics." In *Criticism and the Growth of Knowledge,* ed. I. Lakatos and A. Musgrave. Cambridge: Cambridge University Press.

Kyburg, H. E., Jr. 1970. *Probability and Inductive Logic.* New York: Macmillan.

Labov, W. 1968. "The Reflections of Social Processes in Linguistic Structures." In *A Reader in the Sociology of Language,* ed. J. Fishman. The Hague: Mouton.

Ladriere, J. 1970. "Mathematics in a Philosophy of the Sciences." In *Phenomenology and the Natural Sciences,* ed. J. J. Kockelmans and T. J. Kisiel. Evanston: Northwestern University Press.

Lakatos, I. 1968. "Criticism and the Methodology of Scientific Research Programmes." *Proceed. Arist. Soc.* 69:149–186.

——. 1970. "Falsification and the Methodology of Scientific Research Programmes." In *Criticism and the Growth of Knowledge,* ed. I. Lakatos and A. Musgrave. Cambridge: Cambridge University Press.

—— and Musgrave, A., eds. 1970. *Criticism and the Growth of Knowledge.* Cambridge: Cambridge University Press.

Landfield, A. W. 1971. *Personal Construct Systems in Psychotherapy.* Chicago: Rand McNally.

Langer, S. 1942. *Philosophy in a New Key.* Cambridge, Mass.: Harvard University Press.

——. 1957. *Problems of Art.* New York: Scribner's.

——. 1972. *Mind: An Essay on Human Feelings.* 2 vols. Baltimore: Johns Hopkins University Press.

Laudan, L. 1977. *Progress and Its Problems.* Berkeley: University of California Press.

——. 1980. "Views of Progress: Separating the Pilgrims from the Rakes." *Phil. Soc. Sci.* 10:273–286.

Lehrer, K. 1965. "Knowledge, Truth, and Evidence." *Analysis* 25:168–175.

——. 1971. "Why Not Scepticism?" *Phil. Forum* 2:283–298.

——. 1974. *Knowledge.* Oxford: Clarendon Press.

Leiter, K. 1980. *A Primer on Ethnomethodology.* Oxford: Oxford University Press.

Leventhal, H. 1957. "Cognitive Processes and Interpersonal Predictions." *J. Ab. Soc. Psych.* 55:176–180.

Levy, L. H. 1956. "Personal Constructs and Predictive Behavior." *J. Ab. Soc. Psych.* 53:54–58.

Lewis, H. D., ed. 1963. *Clarity Is Not Enough: Essays in Criticism of Linguistic Philosophy.* New York: Humanities Press.

Liska, J., and Cronkhite, G. 1977. "Epilogue for the Apologia: On the Convergent Validation of Epistemologies." *Western J. Sp. Comm.* 41:57–65.

Livesley, W. J., and Bromley, D. B. 1973. *Person Perception in Childhood and Adolescence.* New York: Wiley.

Lobkowicz, N. 1967. *Theory and Practice.* Notre Dame: Notre Dame University Press.

Lofland, J. 1976. *Doing Social Life*. New York: Wiley.

Lukes, S. 1970. "Some Problems about Rationality." In *Rationality*, ed. B. Wilson. Oxford: Blackwell.

MacIver, R. M. 1942. *Social Causation*. Boston: Ginn.

Macksey, R., and Donato, E. 1972. *The Structuralist Controversy*. Baltimore: Johns Hopkins University Press.

Mandelbaum, M. 1938. *The Problem of Historical Knowledge*. New York: Liveright.

———. 1955. *The Phenomenology of Moral Experience*. New York: Free Press.

Manicas, P. T. 1966. "On Toulmin's Contribution to Logic and Argumentation." *J. Am Forensic Assoc*. 3:83–94.

———. 1980. "The Concept of Social Structure." *J. Theory Soc. Behav*. 10:65–82.

Manis, J. G., and Meltzer, B. N., eds. 1967. *Symbolic Interaction*. 2d ed. Boston: Allyn and Bacon.

Manis, M. 1955. "Social Interaction and the Self Concept." *J. Ab. Soc. Psych*. 51:362–370.

Matson, F. W. 1964. *The Broken Image*. New York: Braziller.

Mayo, C., and Crockett, W. H. 1964. "Cognitive Complexity and Primacy-Recency Effects in Impression Formation." *J. Ab. Soc. Psych*. 68:335–338.

McCall, G. J., et al. 1970. *Social Relationships*. Chicago: Aldine.

McCall, M. 1970. "Boundary Rules in Relationships and Encounters." In *Social Relationships*, ed. G. J. McCall et al. Chicago: Aldine.

McEwen, W. P. 1963. *The Problem of Social-Scientific Knowledge*. Ottawa: Bedminister.

McGuire, W. J. 1960. "A Syllogistic Analysis of Cognitive Relations." In *Attitude Organization and Change*, ed. M. J. Rosenberg and C. I. Hovland. New Haven: Yale University Press.

McHugh, P. 1968. *Defining the Situation: The Organization of Meaning in Social Interaction*. New York: Bobbs-Merrill.

McKerrow, R. E. 1973. "Rhetorical Logoi: The Search for a Universal Criterion of Validity." Paper presented at the meeting of the Speech Communication Association.

———. 1977. "Rhetorical Validity: An Analysis of Three Perspectives on Justification." *J. Am. Forensic Assoc*. 13:133–141.

———. 1980a. "Argument Communities: A Quest for Distinctions." In *Proceedings of the Summer Conference on Argumentation*, ed. J. Rhodes and S. Newell. Annandale: Speech Communication Association.

———. 1980b. "On Fields and Rational Enterprises: A Reply to Willard." In *Proceedings of the Summer Conference on Argumentation*, ed. J. Rhodes and S. Newell. Annandale: Speech Communication Association.

———. 1980c. "Reason and Validity: Selected Claims." Paper presented at the meeting of the Speech Communication Association.

———. 1980d. "Validating Arguments: A Phenomenological Perspective." Paper presented at the meeting of the Speech Communication Association.

———. 1982. "Rationality and Reasonableness in a Theory of Argument." In *Advances in Argumentation Theory and Research*, ed. J. R. Cox and C. A. Willard. Carbondale: Southern Illinois Press.

Mehan, H., and Wood, H. 1975. *The Reality of Ethnomethodology.* New York: Wiley.

Mehrabian, A. 1968. "Inference of Attitudes from the Posture, Orientation, and Distance of a Communicator." *J. Consult. Clin. Psych.* 32:296–308.

———. 1969. "Significance of Posture and Position in the Communication of Attitude and Status Relationships." *Psych. Bull.* 71:359–372.

———. 1971. *Silent Messages.* Belmont: Wadsworth.

Meltzer, B. N. 1972. "Mead's Social Psychology." In *Symbolic Interaction,* 2nd ed., ed. J. G. Manis and B. N. Meltzer. Boston: Allyn and Bacon.

———, Crockett, W. H., and Rosencrantz, P. S. 1966. "Cognitive Complexity, Value Congruity, and the Integration of Potentially Incompatible Information in Impressions of Others." *J. Pers. Soc. Psych.* 4:338–343.

———, and Petras, J. W. 1972. "The Chicago and Iowa Schools of Symbolic Interactionism." In *Symbolic Interaction,* 2nd ed., ed. J. G. Manis and B. N. Meltzer. Boston: Allyn and Bacon.

Merleau-Ponty, M. 1973. *The Prose of the World.* Trans. J. O'Neill. Evanston: Northwestern University Press.

Mischel, T., ed. 1971. *Cognitive Development and Epistemology.* New York: Academic Press.

———. 1974. "Motivation, Emotion, and the Conceptual Schemes of Common Sense." In *Psychology and Ethical Development,* ed. R. S. Peters. London: Allen and Unwin.

Mischel, W. 1968. *Personality and Assessment.* New York: Wiley.

Mitamoto, S. F., and Dornbusch, S. M. 1956. "A Test of the Interactionist Hypothesis of Self-Conception." *Am. J. Sociol.* 61:399–403.

Mortensen, C. D., and Anderson, R. L. 1970. "The Limits of Logic." *J. Am. Forensic Assoc.* 7:71–78.

Müller, G. E. 1953. *Dialectic: A Way into and within Philosophy.* New York: Bookman.

———. 1959. "Dialectic: The Logic of Philosophy." *Dialectica* 13:235–361.

Munch, P. 1957. "Empirical Science and Max Weber's *Verstehende* Soziologie." *Am. J. Sociol.* 22:26–32.

Murphy. R. F. 1971. *The Dialectics of Social Life.* New York: Basic Books.

Nagel, E. 1954. Review of *The Philosophy of Science* by S. E. Toulmin. *Mind* 63:403–412.

Natanson, M. 1967. "Man as Actor." In *Phenomonology of Will and Action,* ed. E. W. Strauss and R. M. Griffiths. Pittsburgh: Duquesne University Press.

———. 1970. *The Journeying Self.* Reading: Addison-Wesley.

——— and Johnstone, H. W., Jr., eds. 1965. *Philosophy, Rhetoric, and Argumentation.* University Park: Pennsylvania State University Press.

Nathan, N. M. C. 1980. *Evidence and Assurance.* Cambridge: Cambridge University Press.

Neilsen, K. 1962. "Appealing to Reason." *Inquiry* 5:65–85.

———. 1974. "Principles of Rationality." *Philosophical Papers.* 3:55–89.

Nisbett, R., and Ross, L. 1980. *Human Inference.* Englewood Cliffs: Prentice-Hall.

Nisbett. R., and Wilson, T. D. 1977. "Telling More Than We Can Know: Verbal Reports on Mental Processes." *Psych. Rev.* 84:231–259.

Nofsinger, R. E., Jr. 1976. "On Answering Questions Indirectly." *Hum. Comm. Res.* 2:172–181.

O'Keefe, B. J., and Benoit, P. 1982. "Children's Arguments." In *Advances in Argumentation Theory and Research*, ed. J. R. Cox and C. A. Willard. Carbondale: Southern Illinois University Press.

O'Keefe, B. J., and Delia, J. G. 1978. "Construct Comprehensiveness and Cognitive Complexity." *Percept. Mtr. Skills* 46:548–550.

———. 1979. "Construct Comprehensiveness and Cognitive Complexity as Predictors of the Number and Strategic Adaptation of Arguments and Appeals in a Persuasive Message." *Comm. Mono.* 46:321–340.

———. 1981. "Psychological and Interactional Dimensions of Communicative Development." In *Language and the Paradigms of Social Psychology*, ed. H. Giles, R. St. Clair, and M. Hewstone. Hillsdale: Erlbaum.

——— and O'Keefe, D. J. 1981. "Interaction Analysis and the Analysis of Interactional Organization." In *Studies in Symbolic Interaction*, vol. 3, ed. N. K. Denzin. Greenwich: JAI Press.

O'Keefe, D. J. 1975. "Logical Empiricism and the Study of Human Communication." *Sp. Mono.* 42:169–183.

———. 1978. "Two Concepts of Argument." *J. Am. Forensic Assoc.* 14:121–128.

———. 1980. "Constructivist Approaches to Persuasion: Research Strategies and Methodological Choices." Paper presented at the meeting of the Eastern Speech Association.

———. 1981. "The Relationship of Attitudes and Behavior: A Constructivist Analysis." In *The Message-Attitude-Behavior Relationship*, ed. D. P. Cushman and R. D. McPhee. New York: Academic Press.

———. 1982. "The Concepts of Argument and Arguing." In *Advances in Argumentation Theory and Research*, ed. J. R. Cox and C. A. Willard. Carbondale: Southern Illinois University Press.

——— and Sypher, H. E. 1981. "Cognitive Complexity Measures and the Relationship of Cognitive Complexity to Communication." *Human Comm. Res.* 8:72–92.

O'Neill, J. 1972. *Sociology as a Skin Trade.* New York: Harper and Row.

Osborne, H. 1968. *Aesthetics and Art Theory.* New York: Dutton.

———. 1970. *The Art of Appreciation.* London: Oxford University Press.

Outhwaite, W. 1975. *Understanding Social Life: The Method Called Verstehen.* New York: Holmes and Meier.

Palmer, R. 1969. *Hermeneutics.* Evanston: Northwestern University Press.

Park, P. 1969. *Sociology Tomorrow.* New York: Pegasus.

Parsons, T., and Schils, E. A., eds. 1951. *Toward a General Theory of Action.* Cambridge, Mass.: Harvard University Press.

Pepper, S. 1942. *World Hypothesis.* Berkeley: University of California Press.

Peterson, G. L. 1981. "Historical Self-Understanding in the Social Sciences: The Use of Thomas Kuhn in Psychology." *J. Theory Soc. Behav.* 11:1–30.

Philipsen, G. 1975. "Speaking 'Like a Man' in Teamsterville: Culture Patterns of Role Enactment in an Urban Neighborhood." *Quart. J. Sp.* 61:13–22.

Polanyi, M. 1958. *Personal Knowledge.* Chicago: University of Chicago Press.

——. 1966. *The Tacit Dimension.* Garden City: Doubleday.

—— and Prosch, H. 1975. *Meaning.* Chicago: University of Chicago Press.

Pollner, M. 1970. "On the Foundations of Mundane Reasoning." Ph.D. dissertation, University of California, Los Angeles.

Popper, K. 1963. *Conjectures and Refutations.* London: Routledge.

Psathas, G., ed. 1973. *Phenomenological Sociology.* New York: Wiley.

——, ed. 1979. *Everyday Language.* New York: Wiley.

Quasthoff, U. 1978. "The Uses of Stereotype in Everyday Argument." *J. Pragmatics* 2:1–48.

Rabinow, P., and Sullivan, W. M., eds. 1979. *Interpretive Sociology.* Berkeley: University of California Press.

Radford, J., and Burton, A. 1974. *Thinking.* New York: Wiley.

Rawls, J. 1971. *A Theory of Justice.* Cambridge, Mass.: Harvard University Press.

Reimer, H. 1937. "Socialization in the Prison Community." *Am. Prison Assoc. Proceed.*, pp. 151–155.

Remmling, G. 1973. *Towards the Sociology of Knowledge.* London: Routledge.

Rescher, N. 1958. "A Theory of Evidence." *Phil. Sci.* 25:83–94.

——. 1968. *Studies in Logical Theory.* Oxford: Blackwell.

——. 1970. *Scientific Explanations.* New York: Free Press.

——. 1973. *The Coherence Theory of Truth.* Oxford: Clarendon Press.

——. 1976. *Plausible Reasoning.* Amsterdam: Van Gorcum.

——. 1977a. *Dialectics: A Controversy-Oriented Approach to the Theory of Knowledge.* Albany: State University of New York Press.

——. 1977b. *Methodological Pragmatism.* Oxford: Clarendon Press.

——. 1979. *Cognitive Systematization.* New York: Rowman and Littlefield.

Richards, D. A. 1971. *A Theory of Reasons for Action.* Oxford: Clarendon Press.

Ricoeur, P. 1965a. *Fallible Man.* Trans. C. A. Kelbley. Evanston: Northwestern University Press.

——. 1965b. *History and Truth.* Trans. C. A. Kelbley. Evanston: Northwestern University Press.

——. 1966. *Freedom and Nature.* Trans. E. V. Kohak. Evanston: Northwestern University Press.

Rokeach, M. 1960. *The Open and Closed Mind.* New York: Basic Books.

Rorty, R., ed. 1967. *The Linguistic Turn.* Chicago: University of Chicago Press.

Rosenfield, L. W. 1968. "The Anatomy of Critical Discourse." *Sp. Mono.* 35:50–69.

Ross, R. G. 1951. Introduction to *Ethical Studies,* by F. H. Bradley. Indianapolis: Bobbs-Merrill.

Rowe, D. 1978. *The Experience of Depression.* London: Wiley.

Rowland, R. 1981a. "Toulmin and Fields: From Form to Function." Unpublished manuscript.

——. 1981b. "Argument Fields." In *Dimensions of Argument: Proceedings of the Second Summer Conference on Argumentation,* ed. G. Ziegelmueller and J. Rhodes. Annandale: Speech Communication Association.

Ryan, J. 1974. "Early Language Development: Towards a Communicational

Analysis." In *The Integration of the Child into a Social World,* ed. M. P. M. Richards. Cambridge: Cambridge University Press.

Ryle, G. 1949. *The Concept of Mind.* London: Hutchinson.

———. 1954. *Dilemmas.* Cambridge: Cambridge University Press.

———. 1959. "Philosophical Arguments." In *Logical Positivism,* ed. A. J. Ayer. New York: Free Press.

———. 1966. "Systematically Misleading Expressions." In *Twentieth Century Philosophy: The Analytic Tradition,* ed. M. Weitz. New York: Free Press.

Sacks, H. 1963. "Sociological Description." *Berkeley J. Sociol.* 8:1–16.

———. 1969. "An Initial Investigation of the Usability of Conversational Data for Doing Sociology." In *Studies in Interaction,* ed. D. Sudnow. New York: Free Press.

———. 1972. "On the Analyzability of Stories by Children." In *Directions in Sociolinguistics: The Ethnography of Communication,* ed. J. J. Gumperz and D. Hymes. New York: Holt, Rinehart and Winston.

———, Schegloff, E., and Jefferson, G. 1974. "A Simplest Systematics for the Organization of Turn-Taking in Conversation." *Language* 50:696–735.

Sadock, J. M. 1974. *Toward a Linguistic Theory of Speech Acts.* New York: Academic Press.

Schank, R. C. 1972. "Conceptual Dependency: A Theory of Natural Language Understanding." *Cog. Psych.* 3:553–631.

——— and Abelson, R. P. 1977. "Scripts, Plans, and Knowledge." In *Thinking,* ed. P. N. Johnson-Laird and P. C. Wason. Cambridge: Cambridge University Press.

Scheff, T. J. 1970. "On the Concepts of Identity and Social Relationship." In *Human Nature and Collective Behavior,* ed. T. Shibutani. Englewood Cliffs: Prentice-Hall.

Scheflen, A. E. 1972. *Body Language and Social Order.* Englewood Cliffs: Prentice-Hall.

Schenkein, J., ed. 1978. *Studies in the Organization of Conversational Interaction.* New York: Academic Press.

Schutz, A. 1945. "On Multiple Realities." *Phil. Phen. Res.* 5:533–574.

———. 1953. "Common Sense and Scientific Interpretation of Human Action." *Phil. Phen. Res.* 14:1–37.

———. 1954. "Concept and Theory Formation in the Social Sciences." *J. Phil.* 51:266–267.

———. 1955. "Symbol, Reality, and Society." In *Symbols and Society,* ed. L. Bryson et al. New York: Harper.

———. 1962. *Collected Papers.* Vol. 1. *The Problem of Social Reality.* Ed. M. Natanson. The Hague: Martinus Nijhoff.

———. 1964. *Collected Papers.* Vol. 2. *Studies in Social Theory.* Ed. A. Broderson. The Hague: Martinus Nijhoff.

———. 1966. *Collected Papers.* Vol. 3. *Studies in Phenomenological Philosophy.* Ed. I. Schutz. The Hague: Martinus Nijhoff.

———. 1967. *The Phenomenology of the Social World.* Trans. G. Walsh and F. Lehnert.

———. 1970a. *Reflections on the Problem of Relevance.* ed. R. Zaner. New Haven: Yale University Press.

———. 1970b. *On Phenomenology and Social Relations*. Chicago: University of Chicago Press.

——— and Luckmann, T. 1973. *The Structures of the Life World*. Trans. R. M. Zaner and T. Englehardy, Jr. Evanston: Northwestern University Press.

Schwartz, H., and Jacobs, J. 1979. *Qualitative Sociology: A Method to the Madness*. New York: Free Press.

Schwartz, M. S., and Schwartz, C. G. 1955. "Problems in Participant Observation." *Am. J. Sociol.* 60:344–351.

Searle, J. R. 1969. *Speech Acts*. Cambridge: Cambridge University Press.

———, ed. 1970. *The Philosophy of Language*. London: Oxford University Press.

Sells, S. B. 1936. "The Atmosphere Affect: An Experimental Study of Reasoning." *Arch. Psych.* 29:3–72.

——— and Koob, H. F. 1937. "A Classroom Demonstration of 'Atmosphere Effect' in Reasoning." *J. Ed. Psych.* 28:514–518.

Shimanoff, S. B. 1980. *Communication Rules*. Beverly Hills: Sage.

Shoeman, F. 1974. "A Rational Approach to the Foundations of Ethics." *J. Value Inquiry* 8:241–251.

Shotter, J. 1974. "The Development of Personal Powers." In *The Integration of the Child into a Social World*, ed. M. P. M. Richards. Cambridge: Cambridge University Press.

Simpson, M. E., and Johnson, D. M. 1966. "Atmosphere and Conversion Errors in Syllogistic Reasoning." *J. Exp. Psych.* 72:197–200.

Smith, C. P. 1980. Editor's Introduction to *Dialogue and Dialectic*, by H.-G. Gadamer. New Haven: Yale University Press.

Speier, M. 1973. *How to Observe Face-to-Face Communication*. Pacific Palisades: Goodyear.

Stark, W. 1967. "Sociology of Knowledge." In *The Encyclopedia of Philosophy*, vol. 7, ed. P. Edwards. New York: Macmillan.

Stebbins, R. A. 1967. "A Theory of the Definition of the Situation." *Canadian Rev. Sociol. Anthro.* 4:148–164.

Stich, S. P., and Nisbett, R. W. 1980. "Justification and the Psychology of Human Reasoning." *Phil. Sci.* 47:188–202.

Stone, J. 1964. *Legal System and Lawyers' Reasonings*. Stanford: Stanford University Press.

Strawson, P. F. 1950. "On Referring." *Mind* 59:320–344.

———. 1959. *Individuals*. London: Methuen.

———. 1970. *Meaning and Truth*. Oxford: Oxford University Press.

Suppe, F., ed. 1977. *The Structure of Scientific Theories*. Urbana: University of Illinois Press.

Swain, M., ed. 1970. *Induction, Acceptance, and Rational Belief*. New York: Humanities Press.

Swanson, D. L. 1977a. "A Reflective View of Critical Inquiry." *Comm. Mono.* 44:207–219.

———. 1977b. "The Requirements of Critical Justifications." *Comm. Mono.* 44:306–320.

Swanson, G. 1968. "Review Symposium-Ethnomethodology." *Am. Sociol. Rev.* 33:122–124.

Szasz, T. S. 1961. *The Myth of Mental Illness*. New York: Harper and Row.

———. 1970. *The Manufacture of Madness*. New York: Harper and Row.

Taylor, C. 1964. *The Explanation of Behavior*. New York: Humanities Press.

Taylor, R. 1966. *Action and Purpose*. Englewood Cliffs: Prentice-Hall.

Thomas, W. I., and Znaniecki, F. 1958. *The Polish Peasant in Europe and America*. New York: Dover.

Toulmin, S. E. 1950. "Probability." *Proceed. Arist. Soc.* supp. 24:27–42.

———. 1953a. "What Kind of Discipline Is Logic?" In *Actes du XIème Congrès International de Philosophie*, vol. 5. Amsterdam: North Holland.

———. 1953b. *The Philosophy of Science*. London: Hutchinson.

———. 1957a. "Logical Positivism and After; or, Back to Aristotle." *Universities Quart.* 11:335–347.

———. 1957b. "Mr. Gellner's Spurious Fox." *Universities Quart.* 11:365–367.

———. 1958. *The Uses of Argument*. Cambridge: Cambridge University Press.

———. 1959. "Criticism in the History of Science: Newton on Absolute Space, Time, and Motion." *Phil. Rev.* 68:1–29.

———. 1960. "Concept Formation in Philosophy and Psychology." In *Dimensions of Mind*, ed. S. Hook. New York: New York University Press.

———. 1963. *Foresight and Understanding*. New York: Harper and Row.

———. 1964. *An Examination of the Place of Reason in Ethics*. Cambridge: Cambridge University Press.

———. 1967a. "Conceptual Revolutions in Science." In *Boston Studies in the Philosophy of Science*, vol. 3, ed. R. S. Cohen and M. W. Wartofsky. Dordrecht: Reidel.

———. 1967b. "The Evolutionary Development of Natural Science." *Am. Sci.* 55:456–471.

———. 1969a. "Concepts and the Explanation of Human Behavior." In *Human Action*, ed. T. Mischel. New York: Academic Press.

———. 1969b. "Reasons and Causes." In *Explanation in the Behavioral Sciences*, ed. M. Berger and C. Cioff. London: Cambridge University Press.

———. 1970. "Does the Distinction between Normal and Revolutionary Science Hold Water?" In *Criticism and the Growth of Knowledge*, ed. I. Lakatos and A. Musgrave. Cambridge: Cambridge University Press.

———. 1971. "The Concept of 'Stages' in Psychological Development." In *Cognitive Development and Epistemology*, ed. T. Mischel. New York: Academic Press.

———. 1972. *Human Understanding*. Vol. 1. *The Collective Use and Evolution of Concepts*. Princeton: Princeton University Press.

———. 1976. *Knowing and Acting*. New York: Macmillan.

———. 1977. "The Structure of Scientific Theories." In *The Structure of Scientific Theories*, ed. F. Suppe. Urbana: University of Illinois Press.

——— and Baier, K. 1952. "On Describing." *Mind* 61:13–38.

——— and Goodfield, J. 1961. *The Fabric of the Heavens*. New York: Harper and Row.

———, Rieke, R., and Janik, A. 1979. *An Introduction to Reasoning*. New York: Macmillan.

Trigg, R. 1973. *Reason and Commitment*. Cambridge: Cambridge University Press.

Turner, R. 1974. *Ethnomethodology*. Harmondsworth: Penguin.

Tyler, S. A. 1978. *The Said and the Unsaid*. New York: Academic Press.

Urmson, J. O. 1956. *Philosophical Analysis*. Oxford: Clarendon Press.

Valins, S., and Nesbitt, R. 1971. "Attribution Processes in the Development and Treatment of Mental Disorders." In *Attribution*, ed. E. E. Jones. Morristown: General Learning Press.

Vannoy, J. S. 1965. "Generality of Cognitive Complexity-Simplicity on a Personality Construct." *J. Pers. Soc. Psych.* 2:385–396.

Veatch, H. B. 1962. *Rational Man*. Bloomington: Indiana University Press.

Videback, R. 1960. "Self Conception and the Reactions of Others." *Sociometry* 23:351–359.

Waller, W. 1970. "The Definition of the Situation." In *Social Psychology through Symbolic Interaction*, ed. G. P. Stone and H. Farberman. Waltham: Ginn/Xerox.

———— and Hill, R. 1951. *The Family*. Hinsdale: Dryden.

Wander, P., and Jenkins, S. 1972. "Rhetoric, Society, and the Critical Response." *Quart. J. Sp.* 58:441–450.

Wason, P. C., and Johnson-Laird, P. N. 1972. *Psychology of Reasoning*. Cambridge, Mass.: Harvard University Press.

Watson, J. P. 1970. "A Repertory Grid Method for Studying Groups." *Brit. J. Psychtry.* 117:309–318.

Wax, M. L. 1967. "On Misunderstanding *Verstehen*: A Reply to Abel." *Sociol. Soc. Res.* 51:323–333.

Weaver, R. 1958. *The Ethics of Rhetoric*. Chicago: Regnery.

Webb, E., et al. 1972. *Unobtrusive Measures*. Chicago: Rand McNally.

Weber, M. 1947. *The Theory of Social and Economic Organization*. Trans. A. M. Henderson and T. Parsons. New York: Free Press.

————. 1949. *The Methodology of the Social Sciences*. Trans. E. Shils and H. A. Finch. New York: Free Press.

————. 1962. *Basic Concepts in Sociology*. Trans. H. P. Secher. New York: Philosophical Library.

Weimer, W. B. 1979. *Notes on the Methodology of Scientific Research*. Hillsdale: Erlbaum.

Weitz, M., ed. 1966. *Twentieth Century Philosophy*. New York: Free Press.

Wenzel, J. W. 1977. "Toward a Rationale for Value-Centered Argument." *J. Am. Forensic Assoc.* 13:150–158.

————. 1979a. "Jurgen Habermas and the Dialectical Perspective on Argumentation." *J. Am. Forensic Assoc.* 16:83–94.

————. 1979b. "Three Senses of Argument." Paper presented at the meeting of the Speech Communication Association.

————. 1980. "Perspectives on Argument." In *Proceedings of the Summer Conference on Argumentation*, ed. J. Rhodes and S. Newell. Annandale: Speech Communication Association.

————. 1981. "Fields, Forums, and Contexts of Argument." Paper presented at the meeting of the Speech Communication Association.

Werner, H. 1957. *Comparative Psychology of Mental Development*. New York: International Universities Press.

—— and Kaplan, B. 1963. *Symbol Formation*. New York: Wiley.

Whyte, W. F. 1955. *Street Corner Society*. Chicago: University of Chicago Press.

Wilcox, J. W. 1972. *A Method for Measuring Decision Assumptions*. Cambridge, Mass.: MIT Press.

Wilkins, M. C. 1928. "The Effect of Changed Material on the Ability to Do Formal Syllogistic Reasoning." *Archiv. Psych.* 16:1–83.

Willard, C. A. 1976. "On the Utility of Descriptive Diagrams for the Analysis and Criticism of Arguments." *Comm. Mono.* 64:308–319.

——. 1978a. "A Reformulation of the Concept of Argument: The Constructivist/Interactionist Foundations of a Sociology of Argument." *J. Am. Forensic Assoc.* 14:121–140.

——. 1978b. "Argument as Nondiscursive Symbolism." *J. Am. Forensic Assoc.* 14:187–193.

——. 1978c. "*The Logic of Choice* by Gidon Gottlieb." *J. Am. Forensic Assoc.* 15:124–132.

——. 1978d. "Contributions of Argumentation to Accounts of Moral Judgment." Paper presented at the meeting of the Speech Communication Association.

——. 1979a. "The Epistemic Functions of Argument, 1: Reasoning and Decision-Making from a Constructivist/Interactionist Point of View." *J. Am. Forensic Assoc.* 15:169–191.

——. 1979b. "Argument as Epistemic, 2: A Constructivist/Interactionist View of Reasons and Reasoning." *J. Am. Forensic Assoc.* 15:211–219.

——. 1979c. "Propositional Argument Is to Argument What Talking about Passion Is to Passion." *J. Am. Forensic Assoc.* 16:21–28.

——. 1979d. "Solomon's The Passions." *J. Am. Forensic Assoc.* 16:71–76.

——. 1980a. "Some Questions about Toulmin's View of Argument Fields." In *Proceedings of the Summer Conference on Argumentation*, ed. J. Rhodes and S. Newell. Annandale: Speech Communication Association.

——. 1980b. "Würtzburg Revisited: Some Reasons Why the Deduction-Induction Squabble Is Irrelevant to Argumentation." In *Proceedings of the Summer Conference on Argumentation*, ed. J. Rhodes and S. Newell. Annandale: Speech Communication Association.

——. 1980c. "Some Speculations on Evidence." In *Proceedings of the Summer Conference on Argumentation*, ed. J. Rhodes and S. Newell. Annandale: Speech Communication Association.

——. 1980d. "A Theory of Argumentation." Unpublished manuscript.

——. 1980e. "The Better Part of Valor: Some Reasons Why Arguments Flare Up and Simmer Down." Paper presented at the meeting of the Speech Communication Association.

——. 1981a. "Argument Fields and Theories of Logical Types." *J. Am. Forensic Assoc.* 17:129–145.

——. 1981b. "The Status of the Nondiscursiveness Thesis." *J. Am. Forensic Assoc.* 17:190–214.

——. 1981c. "Field Theory: A Cartesian Meditation." In *Dimensions of Argument: Proceedings of the Second Summer Conference on Argumentation*, ed.

G. Ziegelmueller and J. Rhodes. Annandale: Speech Communication Association.

———. 1981d. *"Legal System and Lawyers' Reasonings* by Julius Stone." *J. Am. Forensic Assoc.* 17:163–181.

———. 1981e. "A Successor View to 'Rhetoric as Epistemic.' " Unpublished manuscript.

———. 1981f. "Argument Fields and the Public Sphere." Paper presented at the meeting of the Speech Communication Association.

———. 1982. "Argument Fields." In *Advances in Argumentation Theory and Research,* ed. J. R. Cox and C. A. Willard. Carbondale: Southern Illinois University Press.

Wilson, B., ed. 1970. *Rationality.* Oxford: Blackwell.

Wimsatt, W. K., Jr. 1963. "Explication as Criticism." In *Aesthetics and the Philosophy of Criticism,* ed. M. Levich. New York: Random House.

Winch, P. 1958. *The Idea of a Social Science.* New York: Humanities Press.

Wisdom, J. 1931–1933. "Logical Constructions." *Mind* 40:188–216, 460–475; 41:441–464; 42:43–66, 186–202.

———. 1965. *Paradox and Discovery.* Oxford: Blackwell.

Wittgenstein, L. 1953. *Philosophical Investigations.* Trans. G. E. M. Anscomb. Oxford: Blackwell.

———. 1961. *The Tractatus Logico-Philosophicus.* Trans. D. F. Pears and B. F. McGuinness. London: Routledge.

Woodworth, R. S., and Sells, S. B. 1935. "An Atmosphere Effect in Formal Syllogistic Reasoning." *J. Exp. Psych.* 18:451–460.

Woozley, A. D. 1949. *Theory of Knowledge.* London: Hutchinson.

Wyer, R. S., and Carlston, D. E. 1979. *Social Cognition, Inference, and Attribution.* Hillsdale: Erlbaum.

Yol Jung, H. 1972. "The Political Relevance of Existential Phenomenology." In *Existential Phenomenology and Political Theory,* ed. H. Yol Jung. Chicago: Regnery.

Zaner, R. M., and Ihde, D. 1973. *Phenomenology and Existentialism.* New York: Putnam.

Zarefsky, D. 1980. "Product, Process, or Point of View?" In *Proceedings of the Summer Conference on Argumentation,* ed. J. Rhodes and S. Newell. Annandale: Speech Communication Association.

———. 1981. "Persistent Questions in the Theory of Argument Fields." Paper presented at the meeting of the Speech Communication Association.

Ziman, J. 1978. *Reliable Knowledge.* Cambridge: Cambridge University Press.

Zimmerman, D. H., and Pollner, M. 1970. "The Everyday World as Phenomenon." In *Understanding Everyday Life,* ed. J. D. Douglas. Chicago: Aldine.

Znaniecki, F. W. 1934. *The Method of Sociology.* New York: Rinehart.

———. 1940. *The Social Role of the Man of Knowledge.* New York: Columbia University Press.

———. 1952. *Cultural Sciences.* Urbana: University of Illinois Press.

———. 1955. *Social Relations and Social Roles.* San Francisco: Chandler.

Index